Renault Clio Diesel Owners Workshop Manual

A K Legg LAE MIMI

Models covered
All Renault Clio Diesel models, including
special/limited editions,
1870 cc Diesel engine
Does not cover petrol engine models

ABCDE
FGHIJ
KLMNO
PQRST

Haynes
THE BOOK
®

Haynes Publishing
Sparkford Nr Yeovil
Somerset BA22 7JJ England

Haynes North America, Inc
861 Lawrence Drive
Newbury Park
California 91320 USA

Acknowledgements

Thanks are due to Champion Spark Plug, who supplied replacement component information, to Holt Lloyd Limited who supplied the illustrations showing bodywork repair, and to Duckhams Oils, who provided lubrication data. Certain other illustrations are the copyright of Renault (UK) Limited, and are used with their permission. Thanks are also due to Kings of Taunton Ltd, who provided technical assistance, Sykes-Pickavant Limited, who provided some of the workshop tools, and to all those people at Sparkford and Newbury Park who helped in the production of this manual.

© Haynes Publishing 1995

A book in the **Haynes Owners Workshop Manual Series**

Printed by J. H. Haynes & Co. Ltd., Sparkford, Nr Yeovil, Somerset BA22 7JJ, England

ISBN 1 85960 031 X

British Library Cataloguing in Publication Data
A catalogue record for this book is available from the British Library.

We take great pride in the accuracy of information given in this manual, but vehicle manufacturers make alterations and design changes during the production run of a particular vehicle of which they do not inform us. No liability can be accepted by the authors or publishers for loss, damage or injury caused by any errors in, or omissions from, the information given.

95-296

Contents

Renault Clio Diesel

About this manual

Its aim

The aim of this manual is to help you get the best value from your vehicle. It can do so in several ways. It can help you decide what work must be done (even should you choose to get it done by a garage), provide information on routine maintenance and servicing, and give a logical course of action and diagnosis when random faults occur. However, it is hoped that you will use the manual by tackling the work yourself. On simpler jobs it may even be quicker than booking the car into a garage and going there twice, to leave and collect it. Perhaps most important, a lot of money can be saved by avoiding the costs a garage must charge to cover its labour and overheads.

The manual has drawings and descriptions to show the function of the various components so that their layout can be understood. Then the tasks are described and photographed in a clear step-by-step sequence.

Its arrangement

The manual is divided into Chapters, each covering a logical sub-division of the vehicle. The Chapters are each divided into Sections, numbered with single figures, eg 5; and the Sections are divided into numbered paragraphs.

It is freely illustrated, especially in those parts where there is a detailed sequence of operations to be carried out. The reference numbers used in illustration captions pinpoint the pertinent Section and the paragraph within that Section. That is, illustration 3.2 means that the illustration refers to Section 3, and paragraph 2 within that Section.

There is an alphabetical index at the back of the manual as well as a contents list at the front. Each Chapter is also preceded by its own individual contents list.

References to the "left" or "right" of the vehicle are in the sense of a person in the driver's seat facing forward.

Unless otherwise stated, nuts and bolts are removed by turning anti-clockwise, and tightened by turning clockwise.

Vehicle manufacturers continually make changes to specifications and recommendations, and these, when notified, are incorporated into our manuals at the earliest opportunity.

We take great pride in the accuracy of information given in this manual, but vehicle manufacturers make alterations and design changes during the production run of a particular vehicle of which they do not inform us. No liability can be accepted by the authors or publishers for loss, damage or injury caused by any errors in, or omissions from, the information given.

Project vehicles

The main project vehicle used in the preparation of this manual, and appearing in many of the photographic sequences was a 1.9 Renault Clio Diesel Hatchback.

Introduction to the Renault Clio Diesel

The Renault Clio was first introduced in France in May 1990, and to the UK in March 1991, to replace the popular Renault 5 range of cars. This manual covers models fitted with Diesel engines, but other models in the range are available with Petrol engines.

Only one Diesel engine is available - the 1870 cc single overhead camshaft (ohc) type. It is of a well-proven design and, provided regular maintenance is carried out, is unlikely to give trouble.

The Clio Diesel is available in 3- and 5-door Hatchback style, with a wide range of fittings and interior trim depending on the model specification.

Fully-independent front suspension is fitted, with the components attached to a subframe assembly, and the rear suspension is semi-independent, with trailing arms and torsion bars.

A five-speed manual gearbox is fitted to the Clio Diesel.

A wide range of standard and optional equipment is available within the Clio range to suit most tastes.

The Clio is conventional in design, and the DIY mechanic should find most servicing work straightforward.

General dimensions and weights

Note: *All figures are approximate, and may vary according to model. Refer to manufacturer's data for exact figures.*

Dimensions

Overall length	3709 to 3716 mm
Overall width (excluding door mirrors)	1616 to 1641 mm
Overall height (unladen)	1365 to 1395 mm
Wheelbase	2472 mm
Front track	1358 to 1372 mm
Rear track	1324 to 1351 mm
Turning circle (between walls)	10.6 metres

Weights

Note: *Exact weights depend on model.*

Kerb weight:	
3-door Hatchback	905 kg
5-door Hatchback	915 kg
Maximum gross vehicle weight:	
3-door Hatchback	1345 kg
5-door Hatchback	1355 kg
Maximum roof rack load	70 kg
Maximum towing weight:	
Braked trailer	800 kg
Unbraked trailer:	
3-door Hatchback	450 kg
5-door Hatchback	455 kg

Note: *Consult a dealer for latest recommendations.*

Jacking, towing and wheel changing

Jacking

The jack supplied with the vehicle tool kit should only be used for changing the roadwheels - see *"Wheel changing""* later in this Section. When carrying out any other kind of work, raise the vehicle using a hydraulic jack, and always supplement the jack with axle stands positioned under the vehicle jacking points.

When using a hydraulic jack or axle stands, always position the jack head or axle stand head under one of the relevant jacking points (note that the jacking points for use with a hydraulic jack are different to those for use with the vehicle jack and axle stands). **Do not** jack the vehicle under the sump or any of the steering or suspension components. The jacking points and axle stand positions are shown in the accompanying illustrations.

When raising the front of the car, apply the handbrake and chock the rear wheels. Use a suitable wooden or metal bar positioned under the front subframe as shown **(see illustration)**. Position the jack head under the centre of the bar.

When raising the rear of the car, chock the front wheels and engage 1st gear. Position the jack head under one of the reinforced rear jacking points provided for use with the car jack **(see illustration)**.

When raising the side of the car, chock the wheels remaining on the ground, apply the handbrake and select a gear, as described previously.

Position a suitable bar under the sill beneath the front door. The bar should have a suitable groove to accommodate the flange on the sill. Ensure that the sill flange is securely engaged with the groove in the bar, then position the jack head under the centre of the bar **(see illustration)**.

Axle stands should be positioned under the reinforced jacking

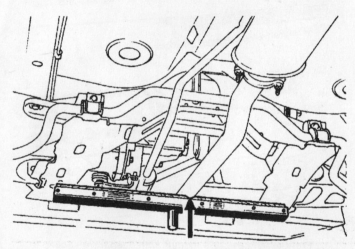
Renault tool positioned under front subframe to raise front of car with trolley jack. Note notch (arrowed) to clear exhaust pipe

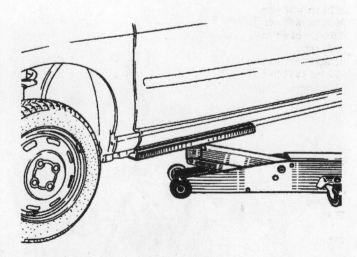
Renault tool positioned under sill to raise side of car with trolley jack

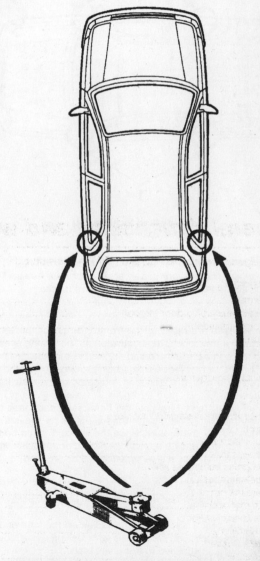
Rear jacking points for use with trolley jack

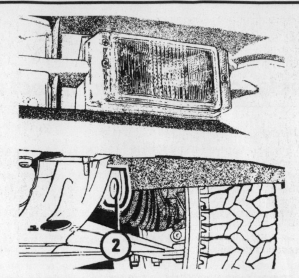

Front towing eye (2) - models with standard front spoiler

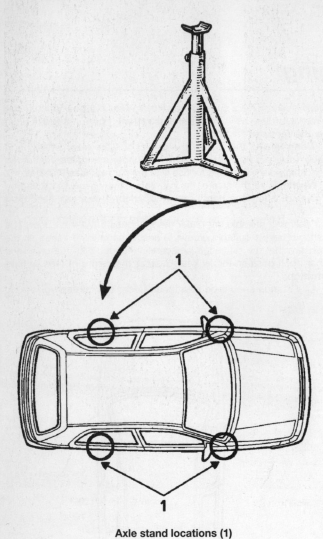

Axle stand locations (1)

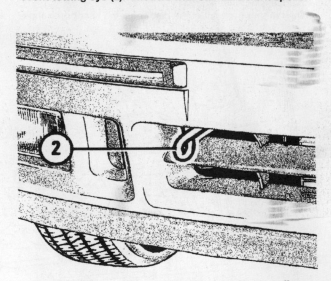

Front towing eye (2) - models with deep front spoiler

points provided for use with the car jack **(see illustration)**.

Warning: *Never work under, around, or near a raised vehicle, unless it is adequately supported in at least two places.*

Towing

Towing eyes are fitted to the front and rear of the vehicle for attachment of a tow rope **(see illustrations)**. The towing eyes can be accessed through slots in the bumpers. Always turn the ignition key to position "M" ("3") when the vehicle is being towed, so that the steering lock is released and the direction indicator and brake lights are operational.

Before being towed, release the handbrake and place the gear lever in neutral. Note that greater than usual pedal pressure will be required to operate the brakes, since the vacuum servo unit is only operational with the engine running. Similarly, on models with power steering, greater than usual steering effort will be required.

Wheel changing

To change a wheel, first remove the wheel brace, spare wheel and jack.

The wheel brace is located in a bracket on the left-hand side of the luggage compartment. On models with locking wheel covers, the key for the covers is attached to the wheel brace.

The spare wheel is located in a cradle under the rear of the car. To remove the spare wheel, unclip the wheel brace from its location on

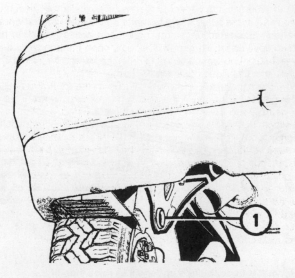

Rear towing eye (1)

Loosening the spare wheel cradle
securing bolt using the wheel brace

Lowering the spare wheel cradle (safety
catch released) . . .

. . . and lifting out the spare wheel

Removing the car jack

Using the key to remove a locking type
wheel cover

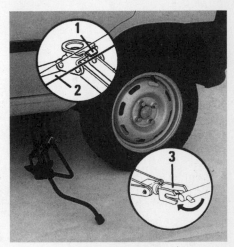

Using the car jack

1   Lug on jack head
2   Jacking point
3   Fork in jack for wheel brace

the left-hand side of the luggage compartment, and use the end of the wheel brace to loosen the spare wheel cradle securing bolt, located in the luggage compartment floor. Support the spare wheel cradle, then pull back the safety catch under the rear bumper, and lower the cradle to the ground. Lift the spare wheel from the cradle (see illustrations).

The jack is located under the right-hand access hatch in the windscreen cowl panel. To remove the jack, open the bonnet and lift the access hatch. Loosen the securing nut, then release the clamp and lift the jack from its location (see illustration).

Apply the handbrake, and place chocks at the front and rear of the wheel diagonally opposite the one to be changed. Select first or reverse gear. Make sure that the vehicle is located on firm level ground. Where applicable, remove the wheel covers (see illustration).

Slightly loosen the wheel bolts with the brace provided. Locate the jack head in the jacking point nearest to the wheel to be changed. Note that the lug on the jack head must engage with the cut-out in the jacking point. Engage the end of the wheel brace with the jack, and turn the wheel brace to raise the car (see illustration).

For additional safety, it is worthwhile sliding the spare wheel under the side of the car, close to the jack, while the car is raised. When the spare wheel is required, put the punctured wheel under the car in its place. This will reduce the risk of personal injury (and of

damage to the car), should the car slip off the jack.

When the wheel is clear of the ground, remove the bolts and lift off the wheel. Check that the threads and the wheel-to-hub mating surfaces are clean and undamaged, and that the inside of the spare wheel is clean. The threads may be cleaned with a brass wire brush if rusty. Apply a thin smear of copper-based anti-seize compound to the threads and roadwheel-to-hub mating surfaces, to prevent the formation of corrosion. *Obviously, you are not likely to be able to do anything about this at the roadside, but it is worthwhile attending to it as soon as possible once the car is running again, or changing a wheel may be even more difficult next time!*

Fit the spare wheel, and tighten the bolts moderately by hand. If you put the punctured wheel under the car, remove it now and lower the car to the ground. Tighten the bolts fully using the wheel brace, working in progressive stages and in a diagonal sequence - if a torque wrench is available, tighten the bolts to the specified setting (see Chapter 1 Specifications). Refit the wheel cover where applicable.

Remove the chocks, then stow the jack and punctured wheel. To stow the wheel, place it in the cradle, then lift the cradle sharply upwards until the safety catch engages, and tighten the cradle securing bolt with the wheel brace. Finally, stow the wheel brace in the left-hand side of the luggage compartment.

Buying spare parts and vehicle identification numbers

Buying spare parts

Spare parts are available from many sources, including maker's appointed garages, accessory shops, and motor factors. To be sure of obtaining the correct parts, it will sometimes be necessary to quote the vehicle identification number. If possible, it can also be useful to take the old parts along for positive identification. Items such as starter motors and alternators may be available under a service exchange scheme - any parts returned should always be clean.

Our advice regarding spare part sources is as follows.

Officially-appointed garages

This is the best source of parts which are peculiar to your car, and are not otherwise generally available (eg badges, interior trim, certain body panels, etc). It is also the only place at which you should buy parts if the vehicle is still under warranty.

Accessory shops

These are very good places to buy materials and components needed for the maintenance of your car (oil, air and fuel filters, spark plugs, light bulbs, drivebelts, oils and greases, brake pads, touch-up paint, etc). Components of this nature sold by a reputable shop are of the same standard as those used by the car manufacturer.

Besides components, these shops also sell tools and general accessories, usually have convenient opening hours, charge lower prices, and can often be found not far from home. Some accessory shops have parts counters where the components needed for almost any repair job can be purchased or ordered.

Motor factors

Good factors will stock all the more important components which wear out comparatively quickly and can sometimes supply individual components needed for the overhaul of a larger assembly (eg brake seals and hydraulic parts, bearing shells, pistons, valves, alternator brushes). They may also handle work such as cylinder block reboring, crankshaft regrinding and balancing, etc.

VIN plate location

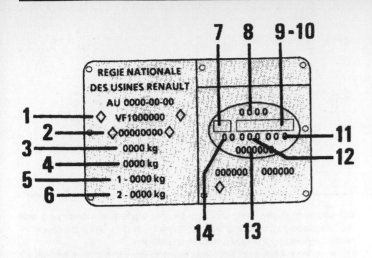

Engine number location (arrowed)

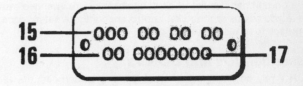

Engine plate codes

15 Engine type
16 Engine type suffix
17 Engine number

VIN plate details

1	Vehicle type	8	Vehicle type
2	Chassis number	9	Equipment number
3	Gross vehicle weight	10	Options
4	Gross train weight	11	Vehicle equipment level
5	Maximum permitted total weight on front axle	12	Original paint reference
6	Maximum permitted total weight on rear axle	13	Fabrication number
7	Vehicle special features	14	Upholstery/trim code number

Tyre and exhaust specialists

These outlets may be independent or members of a local or national chain. They frequently offer competitive prices when compared with a main dealer or local garage, but it will pay to obtain several quotes before making a decision. When researching prices, also ask what 'extras' may be added - for instance, fitting a new valve and balancing the wheel are both commonly charged on top of the price of a new tyre.

Other sources

Beware of parts or materials obtained from market stalls, car boot sales or similar outlets. Such items are not invariably sub-standard, but there is little chance of compensation if they do prove unsatisfactory. In the case of safety-critical components such as brake pads there is the risk not only of financial loss but also of an accident causing injury or death.

Second-hand components or assemblies obtained from a car breaker can be a good buy in some circumstances, but this sort of purchase is best made by the experienced DIY mechanic.

Vehicle identification numbers

Modifications are a continuing and unpublicised process in vehicle manufacture, quite apart from major model changes. Spare parts manuals and lists are compiled upon a numerical basis, the individual vehicle identification numbers being essential to correct identification of the component concerned.

When ordering spare parts, always give as much information as possible. Quote the car model, year of manufacture, body and engine numbers as appropriate.

The *Vehicle Identification Number (VIN) plate* is riveted to the top of the body front panel, and can be viewed once the bonnet is open. The plate carries the VIN, chassis number, vehicle weight information and various other information, depending on territory **(see illustrations)**.

The *chassis number* is given on the VIN plate.

The *engine number* is stamped on a plate riveted to the front flywheel end of the engine cylinder block **(see illustrations)**.

Safety first!

However enthusiastic you may be about getting on with the job in hand, do take the time to ensure that your safety is not put at risk. A moment's lack of attention can result in an accident, as can failure to observe certain elementary precautions. There will always be new ways of having accidents, and the following points do not pretend to be a comprehensive list of all dangers; they are intended rather to make you aware of the risks, and to encourage a safety-conscious approach to all work you carry out on your vehicle.

Essential DOs and DON'Ts

DON'T rely on a single jack when working underneath the vehicle. Always use reliable additional means of support, such as axle stands, securely placed under a structural part of the vehicle that you know will not give way.

DON'T attempt to loosen or tighten high-torque nuts (eg wheel hub nuts) while the vehicle is on a jack; it may be pulled off.

DON'T start the engine without first ascertaining that the transmission is in neutral (or "Park" where applicable) and the handbrake applied.

DON'T suddenly remove the filler cap from a hot cooling system - cover it with a cloth, and release the pressure gradually first, or you may get scalded by escaping coolant.

DON'T attempt to drain oil, automatic transmission fluid, or coolant until you are sure it has cooled sufficiently to avoid scalding you.

DON'T grasp any part of the engine, exhaust or catalytic converter without first ascertaining that it is sufficiently cool to avoid burning you.

DON'T allow brake fluid or antifreeze to contact vehicle paintwork.

DON'T siphon toxic liquids such as fuel, brake fluid or antifreeze by mouth, or allow them to remain on your skin.

DON'T inhale dust - it may be injurious to health (see *Asbestos* below).

DON'T allow any spilt oil or grease to remain on the floor - wipe it up straight away, before someone slips on it.

DON'T use ill-fitting spanners or other tools which may slip and cause injury.

DON'T attempt to lift a heavy component which may be beyond your capability - get assistance.

DON'T rush to finish a job, or take unverified short cuts.

DON'T allow children or animals in or around an unattended vehicle.

DON'T park vehicles with catalytic converters over combustible materials such as dry grass, oily rags, etc if the engine has recently been run. As catalytic converters reach extremely high temperatures, any such materials in close proximity may ignite.

DON'T run vehicles equipped with catalytic converters without the exhaust system heat shields fitted.

DO wear eye protection when using power tools such as an electric drill, sander, bench grinder etc, and when working under the vehicle.

DO use a barrier cream on your hands prior to undertaking dirty jobs - it will protect your skin from infection, as well as making the dirt easier to remove afterwards; but make sure your hands aren't left slippery. Note that long-term contact with used engine oil can be a health hazard.

DO keep loose clothing (cuffs, tie etc) and long hair well out of the way of moving mechanical parts.

DO remove rings, wristwatch etc, before working on the vehicle - especially the electrical system.

DO ensure that any lifting tackle or jacking equipment used has a safe working load rating adequate for the job, and is used precisely as recommended by the equipment manufacturer.

DO keep your work area tidy - it is only too easy to fall over articles left lying around.

DO get someone to check periodically that all is well when working alone on the vehicle.

DO carry out work in a logical sequence, and check that everything is correctly assembled and tightened afterwards.

DO remember that your vehicle's safety affects that of yourself and others. If in doubt on any point, get specialist advice.

IF, in spite of following these precautions, you are unfortunate enough to injure yourself, seek medical attention as soon as possible.

Asbestos

Certain friction, insulating, sealing, and other products - such as brake linings, brake bands, clutch linings, gaskets, etc - contain asbestos. *Extreme care must be taken to avoid inhalation of dust from such products, since it is hazardous to health.* If in doubt, assume that they *do* contain asbestos.

Fire

Remember at all times that fuel is highly flammable. Never smoke, or have any kind of naked flame around, when working on the vehicle. But the risk does not end there - a spark caused by an electrical short-circuit, by two metal surfaces contacting each other, by careless use of tools, or even by static electricity built up in your body under certain conditions, can ignite fuel vapour, which in a confined space is highly explosive.

Whenever possible, disconnect the battery earth terminal before working on any part of the fuel or electrical system, and never risk spilling fuel on to a hot engine or exhaust. Catalytic converters run at extremely high temperatures, and consequently can be an additional fire hazard. Observe the precautions outlined elsewhere in this section.

It is recommended that a fire extinguisher of a type suitable for fuel and electrical fires is kept handy in the garage or workplace at all times. Never try to extinguish a fuel or electrical fire with water.

Note: *Any reference to a "torch" appearing in this manual should always be taken to mean a hand-held battery-operated electric lamp or flashlight. It does NOT mean a welding/gas torch or blowlamp.*

Hydrofluoric acid

Hydrofluoric acid is extremely corrosive. It is formed when certain types of synthetic rubber, which may be found in O-rings, oil seals, brake hydraulic system seals, fuel hoses etc, are exposed to temperatures above 400°C. The obvious circumstance in which this could happen on a vehicle is in the case of a fire. The rubber does not burn but changes into a charred or sticky substance which contains the acid. *Once formed, the acid remains dangerous for years. If it gets onto the skin it may be necessary to amputate the limb concerned.*

When dealing with a vehicle which has suffered a fire, or with components salvaged from such a vehicle, always wear protective gloves and discard them carefully after use. Bear this in mind if obtaining components from a car breaker.

Fumes

Certain fumes are highly toxic, and can quickly cause unconsciousness and even death if inhaled to any extent, especially if inhalation takes place through a lighted cigarette or pipe. Fuel vapour comes into this category, as do the vapours from certain solvents such as trichloroethylene. Any draining or pouring of such volatile fluids should be done in a well-ventilated area.

When using cleaning fluids and solvents, read the instructions carefully. Never use materials from unmarked containers - they may give off poisonous vapours.

Never run the engine of a motor vehicle in an enclosed space such as a garage. Exhaust fumes contain carbon monoxide, which is extremely poisonous; if you need to run the engine, always do so in the open air, or at least have the rear of the vehicle outside the workplace. Although Diesel engines have greatly reduced carbon monoxide emissions, the above precautions should still be observed.

If you are fortunate enough to have the use of an inspection pit, never drain or pour fuel, and never run the engine, while the vehicle is standing over it; the fumes, being heavier than air, will concentrate in the pit, with possibly lethal results.

The battery

Batteries which are sealed for life require special precautions, which are normally outlined on a label attached to the battery. Such precautions are primarily related to situations involving battery charging and jump starting from another vehicle.

With a conventional battery, never cause a spark, or allow a naked light, in close proximity to it. It will normally be giving off a certain amount of hydrogen gas, which is highly explosive.

Whenever possible, disconnect the battery earth terminal before working on the fuel or electrical systems.

If possible, loosen the battery filler plugs or battery cover when charging the battery from an external source. Do not charge at an excessive rate, or the battery may burst. Special care should be taken with the use of high-charge-rate boost chargers to prevent the battery from overheating.

Take care when topping-up and when carrying the battery. The acid electrolyte, even when diluted, is very corrosive, and should not be allowed to contact clothing, eyes or skin.

Always wear eye protection when cleaning the battery, to prevent the caustic deposits from entering your eyes.

The vehicle electrical system

Take care when making alterations or repairs to the vehicle wiring. Electrical faults are the commonest cause of vehicle fires. Make sure that any accessories are wired correctly, using an appropriately-rated fuse and wire of adequate current-carrying capacity. When possible, avoid the use of "piggy-back" or self-splicing connectors to power additional electrical equipment from existing feeds; make up a new feed with its own fuse instead.

When considering the current which a new circuit will have to handle, do not overlook the switch, especially when planning to use an existing switch to control additional components - for instance, if spotlights are to be fed via the main lighting switch. For preference, a relay should be used to switch heavy currents. If in doubt, consult an auto electrical specialist.

Any wire which passes through a body panel or bulkhead must be protected from chafing with a grommet or similar device. A wire which is allowed to chafe bare against the bodywork will cause a short-circuit and possibly a fire.

Mains electricity and electrical equipment

When using an electric power tool, inspection light, diagnostic equipment etc, which works from the mains, always ensure that the appliance is correctly connected to its plug, and that, where necessary, it is properly earthed. Do not use such appliances in damp conditions and, again, beware of creating a spark or applying excessive heat in the vicinity of fuel or fuel vapour. Also ensure that the appliances meet the relevant national safety standards.

Diesel fuel

Diesel injection pumps supply fuel at very high pressure. Extreme care must be taken when working on the fuel injectors and fuel pipes. It is advisable to place an absorbent cloth around the union before slackening a fuel pipe. *Never expose the hands, face or any other part of the body to injector spray: the high working pressure can penetrate the skin, with potentially fatal results.* Injector test rigs produce similarly high pressures and must be treated with the same respect.

Diesel fuel is more irritating to the skin than petrol. It is also harmful to the eyes. Besides the use of a barrier cream to protect the hands, consider using lightweight disposable gloves when fuel spillage is inevitable. Change out of fuel-soaked clothing as soon as possible.

Spilt diesel fuel does not evaporate like petrol. Clear up spillages promptly to avoid accidents caused by slippery patches on the workshop floor. Note also that diesel attacks tarmac surfaces: if working at the roadside or in a drive, put down newspaper or a plastic sheet if fuel spillage is expected.

Jacking and vehicle support

The jack provided with the vehicle is designed primarily for emergency wheel changing, and its use for servicing and overhaul work on the vehicle is best avoided. Instead, a more substantial workshop jack (trolley jack or similar) should be used. Whichever type is employed, it is essential that additional safety support is provided by means of axle stands designed for this purpose. Never use makeshift means such as wooden blocks or piles of house bricks, as these can easily topple or, in the case of bricks, disintegrate under the weight of the vehicle. Further information on the correct positioning of the jack and axle stands is provided in the *"Jacking, towing and wheel changing"* section.

If removal of the wheels is not required, the use of drive-on ramps is recommended. Caution should be exercised to ensure that they are correctly aligned with the wheels, and that the vehicle is not driven too far along them, so that it promptly falls off the other ends, or tips the ramps.

General repair procedures

Whenever servicing, repair or overhaul work is carried out on the vehicle or its components, it is necessary to observe the following procedures and instructions. This will assist in carrying out the operation efficiently, and to a professional standard of workmanship.

Joint mating faces and gaskets

When separating components at their mating faces, never insert screwdrivers or similar implements into the joint between the faces in order to prise them apart. This can cause severe damage, which results in oil leaks, coolant leaks, etc upon reassembly. Separation is usually achieved by tapping along the joint with a soft-faced hammer in order to break the seal. However, note that this method may not be suitable where dowels are used for component location.

Where a gasket is used between the mating faces of two components, ensure that it is renewed on reassembly, and fit it dry, unless otherwise stated in the repair procedure. Make sure that the mating faces are clean and dry, with all traces of old gasket removed. When cleaning a joint face, use a tool which is not likely to score or damage the face, and remove any burrs or nicks with an oilstone or fine file.

Make sure that tapped holes are cleaned with a pipe cleaner, and keep them free of jointing compound, if this is being used, unless specifically instructed otherwise.

Ensure that all orifices, channels or pipes are clear, and blow through them, preferably using compressed air. *Wear eye protection when using compressed air!*

Oil seals

Oil seals can be removed by levering them out with a wide flat-bladed screwdriver or similar implement. Alternatively, a number of self-tapping screws may be screwed into the seal, and these used as a purchase for pliers or some similar device in order to pull the seal free.

Whenever an oil seal is removed from its working location, either individually or as part of an assembly, it should be renewed.

The very fine sealing lip of the seal is easily damaged, and will not seal if the surface it contacts is not completely clean and free from scratches, nicks or grooves. If the original sealing surface of the component cannot be restored, and the manufacturer has not made provision for slight relocation of the seal relative to the sealing surface, the component should be renewed.

Protect the lips of the seal from any surface which may damage them in the course of fitting. Use tape or a conical sleeve where possible. Lubricate the seal lips with oil before fitting and, on dual-lipped seals, fill the space between the lips with grease.

Unless otherwise stated, oil seals must be fitted with their sealing lips toward the lubricant to be sealed.

Use a tubular drift or block of wood of the appropriate size to install the seal and, if the seal housing is shouldered, drive the seal down to the shoulder. If the seal housing is unshouldered, the seal should be fitted with its face flush with the housing top face (unless otherwise instructed).

Screw threads and fastenings

Seized nuts, bolts and screws are quite a common occurrence where corrosion has set in, and the use of penetrating oil or releasing fluid will often overcome this problem if the offending item is soaked for a while before attempting to release it. The use of an impact driver may also provide a means of releasing such stubborn fastening devices, when used in conjunction with the appropriate screwdriver bit or socket. If none of these methods works, it may be necessary to resort to the careful application of heat, or the use of a hacksaw or nut splitter device.

Studs are usually removed by locking two nuts together on the threaded part, and then using a spanner on the lower nut to unscrew the stud. Studs or bolts which have broken off below the surface of the component in which they are mounted can sometimes be removed using a proprietary stud extractor (sometimes called "easy-outs"). Always ensure that a blind tapped hole is completely free from oil, grease, water or other fluid before installing the bolt or stud. Failure to do this could cause the housing to crack, due to the hydraulic action of the bolt or stud as it is screwed in.

When tightening a castellated nut to accept a split pin, tighten the nut to the specified torque, where applicable, and then tighten further to the next split pin hole. Never slacken the nut to align the split pin hole, unless stated in the repair procedure.

When checking or retightening a nut or bolt to a specified torque setting, slacken the nut or bolt by a quarter of a turn, and then retighten to the specified setting. However, this should not be attempted where angular tightening has been used.

For some screw fastenings, notably cylinder head bolts or nuts, torque wrench settings are no longer specified for the latter stages of tightening, "angular tightening" being called up instead. Typically, a fairly low torque wrench setting will be applied to the bolts/nuts in the correct sequence, followed by one or more stages of tightening through specified angles.

Locknuts, locktabs and washers

Any fastening which will rotate against a component or housing in the course of tightening should always have a washer between it and the relevant component or housing.

Spring or split washers should always be renewed when they are used to lock a critical component such as a big-end bearing retaining bolt or nut. Locktabs which are folded over to retain a nut or bolt should always be renewed.

Self-locking nuts can be re-used in non-critical areas, providing resistance can be felt when the locking portion passes over the bolt or stud thread. However, it should be noted that self-locking nuts tend to lose their effectiveness after long periods of use, and in such cases should be renewed as a matter of course.

Split pins must always be replaced with new ones of the correct size for the hole.

When thread-locking compound is found on the threads of a fastener which is to be re-used, it should be cleaned off with a wire brush and solvent, and fresh compound applied on reassembly.

Special tools

Some repair procedures in this manual entail the use of special tools such as a press, two- or three-legged pullers, spring compressors etc. Wherever possible, suitable readily-available alternatives to the manufacturer's special tools are described, and are shown in use. In some instances, where no alternative is possible, it has been necessary to resort to the use of a manufacturer's tool, and this has been done for reasons of safety, as well as the efficient completion of the repair operation. Unless you are highly skilled and have a thorough understanding of the procedures described, never attempt to bypass the use of any special tool when the procedure described specifies its use. Not only is there a very great risk of personal injury, but expensive damage could be caused to the components involved.

Environmental considerations

When disposing of used engine oil, brake fluid, antifreeze etc, give due consideration to any detrimental environmental effects. Do not, for instance, pour any of the above liquids down drains into the general sewage system, or onto the ground to soak away. Many local council refuse tips provide a facility for waste oil disposal, as do some garages. If none of these facilities are available, consult your local Environmental Health Department for further advice.

With the universal tightening-up of legislation regarding the emission of environmentally-harmful substances from motor vehicles, most current vehicles have tamperproof devices fitted to the main adjustment points of the fuel system. These devices are primarily designed to prevent unqualified persons from adjusting the fuel/air mixture with the chance of a consequent increase in toxic emissions. If such devices are encountered during servicing or overhaul, they should, wherever possible, be renewed or refitted in accordance with the vehicle manufacturer's requirements or current legislation. Owners taking their vehicles abroad should note that some countries have strict legislation relating to vehicles driven without these tamperproofing measures in place!

Tools and working facilities

Introduction

A selection of good tools is a fundamental requirement for anyone contemplating the maintenance and repair of a motor vehicle. For the owner who does not possess any, their purchase will prove a considerable expense, offsetting some of the savings made by doing-it-yourself. However, provided that the tools purchased meet the relevant national safety standards and are of good quality, they will last for many years and prove an extremely worthwhile investment.

To help the average owner to decide which tools are needed to carry out the various tasks detailed in this manual, we have compiled three lists of tools under the following headings: *Maintenance and minor repair*, *Repair and overhaul*, and *Special*. Newcomers to practical mechanics should start off with the *Maintenance and minor repair* tool kit, and confine themselves to the simpler jobs around the vehicle. Then, as confidence and experience grow, more difficult tasks can be undertaken, with extra tools being purchased as, and when, they are needed. In this way, a *Maintenance and minor repair* tool kit can be built up into a *Repair and overhaul* tool kit over a considerable period of time, without any major cash outlays. The experienced do-it-yourselfer will have a tool kit good enough for most repair and overhaul procedures, and will add tools from the *Special* category when it is felt that the expense is justified by the amount of use to which these tools will be put.

Maintenance and minor repair tool kit

The tools given in this list should be considered as a minimum requirement if routine maintenance, servicing and minor repair operations are to be undertaken. We recommend the purchase of combination spanners (ring one end, open-ended the other); although more expensive than open-ended ones, they do give the advantages of both types of spanner.

Combination spanners:
Metric - 8, 9, 10, 11, 12, 13, 14, 15, 17, 19, 21, 22 & 26 mm
Adjustable spanner - 35 mm jaw (approx)
Engine sump drain plug key
Set of feeler gauges
Brake bleed nipple spanner
Screwdrivers:
  Flat-bladed - approx 100 mm long x 6 mm dia
  Cross-bladed - approx 100 mm long x 6 mm dia
Combination pliers
Hacksaw (junior)
Tyre pump
Tyre pressure gauge
Oil can
Oil filter removal tool
Fine emery cloth
Wire brush (small)
Funnel (medium size)

Repair and overhaul tool kit

These tools are virtually essential for anyone undertaking any major repairs to a motor vehicle, and are additional to those given in the *Maintenance and minor repair* list. Included in this list is a comprehensive set of sockets. Although these are expensive, they will be found invaluable as they are so versatile - particularly if various drives are included in the set. We recommend the 12.5 mm square-drive type, as this can be used with most proprietary torque wrenches. If you cannot afford a socket set, even bought piecemeal, then inexpensive tubular box spanners are a useful alternative.

The tools in this list will occasionally need to be supplemented by tools from the *Special* list.
Sockets (or box spanners) to cover range in previous list
Reversible ratchet drive (for use with sockets) **(see illustration)**
Extension piece, 250 mm (for use with sockets)
Universal joint (for use with sockets)
Torque wrench (for use with sockets)
Self-locking grips
Ball pein hammer
Soft-faced mallet (plastic/aluminium or rubber)
Screwdrivers:
  Flat-bladed - long & sturdy, short (chubby), and narrow (electrician's) types
  Cross-bladed - Long & sturdy, and short (chubby) types
Pliers:
  Long-nosed
  Side cutters (electrician's)
  Circlip (internal and external)
Cold chisel - 25 mm
Scriber
Scraper
Centre-punch
Pin punch
Hacksaw
Brake hose clamp
Brake bleeding kit
Selection of twist drills
Steel rule/straight-edge
Allen keys (inc. splined/Torx type) **(see illustrations)**
Selection of files
Wire brush
Axle stands
Jack (strong trolley or hydraulic type)
Light with extension lead

Special tools

The tools in this list are those which are not used regularly, are expensive to buy, or which need to be used in accordance with their manufacturers' instructions. Unless relatively difficult mechanical jobs are undertaken frequently, it will not be economic to buy many of these tools. Where this is the case, you could consider clubbing together with friends (or joining a motorists' club) to make a joint purchase, or borrowing the tools against a deposit from a local garage or tool hire specialist. It is worth noting that many of the larger DIY superstores now carry a large range of special tools for hire at modest rates.

The following list contains only those tools and instruments freely available to the public, and not those special tools produced by the vehicle manufacturer specifically for its dealer network. You will find occasional references to these manufacturer's special tools in the text of this manual. Generally, an alternative method of doing the job without the vehicle manufacturer's special tool is given. However,

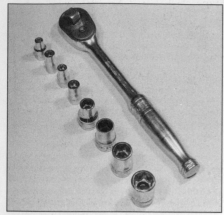
Sockets and reversible ratchet drive

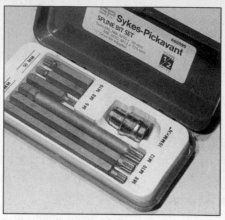
Spline bit set

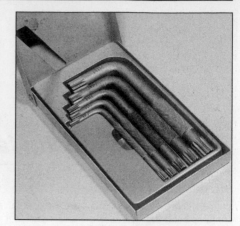
Spline key set

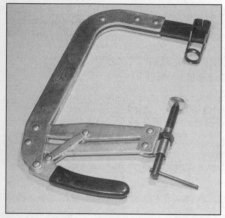
Valve spring compressor

Piston ring compressor

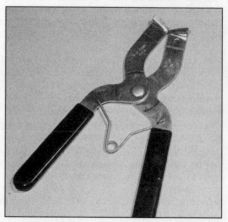
Piston ring removal/installation tool

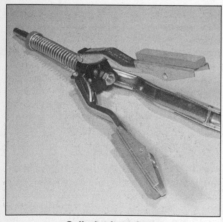
Cylinder bore hone

Three-legged hub and bearing puller

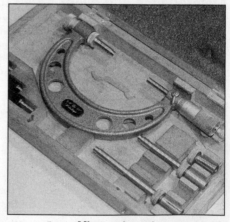
Micrometer set

sometimes there is no alternative to using them. Where this is the case and the relevant tool cannot be bought or borrowed, you will have to entrust the work to a franchised garage.

- *Valve spring compressor* **(see illustration)**
- *Valve grinding tool*
- *Piston ring compressor* **(see illustration)**
- *Piston ring removal/installation tool* **(see illustration)**
- *Cylinder bore hone* **(see illustration)**
- *Balljoint separator*
- *Coil spring compressors*
- *Two-/three-legged hub and bearing puller* **(see illustration)**
- *Impact screwdriver*

- *Micrometer and/or vernier calipers* **(see illustrations)**
- *Dial gauge/dial test indicator* **(see illustration)**
- *Universal electrical multi-meter*
- *Cylinder compression gauge* **(see illustration)**
- *Hand-operated vacuum pump and gauge* **(see illustration)**
- *Clutch plate alignment set* **(see illustration)**
- *Brake shoe steady spring cup removal tool* **(see illustration)**
- *Bush and bearing removal/installation set* **(see illustration)**
- *Stud extractors* **(see illustration)**
- *Tap and die set* **(see illustration)**
- *Lifting tackle*
- *Trolley jack*

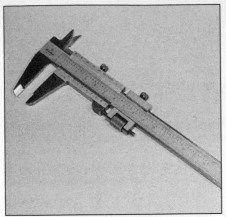

Vernier calipers

Dial test indicator and magnetic stand

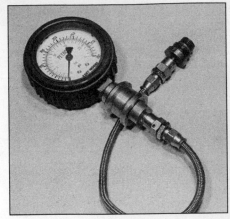

Compression testing gauge

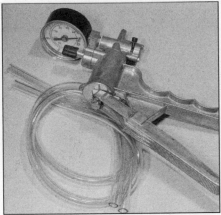

Vacuum pump and gauge

Clutch plate alignment set

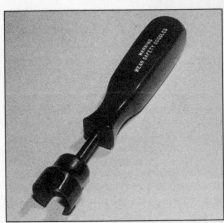

Brake shoe steady spring cup removal tool

Bush and bearing removal/installation set

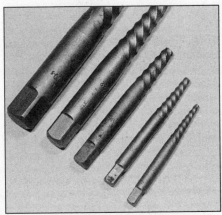

Stud extractor set

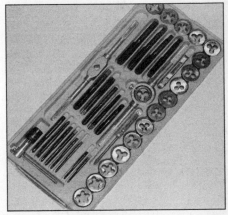

Tap and die set

Buying tools

For practically all tools, a tool factor is the best source, since he will have a very comprehensive range compared with the average garage or accessory shop. Having said that, accessory shops often offer excellent quality tools at discount prices, so it pays to shop around.

Remember, you don't have to buy the most expensive items on the shelf, but it is always advisable to steer clear of the very cheap tools. There are plenty of good tools around at reasonable prices, but always aim to purchase items which meet the relevant national safety standards. If in doubt, ask the proprietor or manager of the shop for advice before making a purchase.

Care and maintenance of tools

Having purchased a reasonable tool kit, it is necessary to keep the tools in a clean and serviceable condition. After use, always wipe off any dirt, grease and metal particles using a clean, dry cloth, before putting the tools away. Never leave them lying around after they have been used. A simple tool rack on the garage or workshop wall, for items such as screwdrivers and pliers, is a good idea. Store all normal spanners and sockets in a metal box. Any measuring instruments, gauges, meters, etc, must be carefully stored, somewhere they cannot be damaged or become rusty.

Take a little care when tools are used. Hammer heads inevitably become marked, and screwdrivers lose the keen edge on their blades from time to time. A little timely attention with emery cloth or a file will soon restore items like this to a good serviceable finish.

Working facilities

Not to be forgotten when discussing tools is the workshop itself. If anything more than routine maintenance is to be carried out, some form of suitable working area becomes essential.

It is appreciated that many an owner-mechanic is forced by circumstances to remove an engine or similar item without the benefit of a garage or workshop. Having done this, however, any repairs should always be done under the cover of a roof.

Wherever possible, any dismantling should be done on a clean, flat workbench or table at a suitable working height.

Any workbench needs a vice; one with a jaw opening of 100 mm is suitable for most jobs. As mentioned previously, some clean dry storage space is also required for tools, as well as for any lubricants, cleaning fluids, touch-up paints and so on, which become necessary.

Another item which may be required, and which has a much more general usage, is an electric drill with a chuck capacity of at least 8 mm. This, together with a good range of twist drills, is virtually essential for fitting accessories.

Last, but not least, always keep a supply of old newspapers and clean, lint-free rags available, and try to keep any working area as clean as possible.

Booster battery (jump) starting

When jump starting a vehicle using a booster battery, observe the following precautions:

a) *Before connecting the booster battery, make sure that the ignition is switched off.*

b) *Ensure that all electrical equipment (lights, heater, wipers etc) is switched off.*

c) *Make sure that the booster battery is the same voltage as the discharged one in the vehicle.*

d) *If the battery is being jump-started from the battery in another vehicle, the two vehicles MUST NOT TOUCH each other.*

e) *Make sure that the transmission is in Neutral.*

Connect one jump lead between the positive (+) terminals of the two batteries. Connect the other jump lead first to the negative (-) terminal of the booster battery, and then to a good earthing point on the vehicle to be started, such as a bolt or bracket on the engine block, at least 45 cm from the battery if possible **(see illustration)**. Make sure that the jump leads will not come into contact with the fan, drivebelts or other moving parts of the engine.

Start the engine using the booster battery, then with the engine running at idle speed, switch on the heater blower motor (to maximum speed) and heated rear window to reduce voltage peaks when the jump leads are disconnected. (Do not switch on the headlights in place of the rear window heater - a high peak could blow the bulbs.) Disconnect the jump leads in the reverse order of connection.

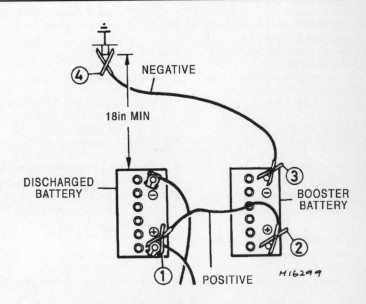

Jump start lead connections for negative-earth vehicles - connect leads in order shown

Radio/cassette unit anti-theft system precaution

The radio/cassette unit fitted as standard equipment by Renault may be equipped with a built-in security code to deter thieves. If the power source to the unit is cut, the anti-theft system will activate. Even if the power source is immediately reconnected, the radio/cassette unit will not function until the correct security code has been entered. Therefore, if you do not know the correct security code for the radio/cassette unit **do not** disconnect the battery negative terminal of the battery or remove the radio/cassette unit from the vehicle.

To enter the correct security code, follow the instructions provided with the radio/cassette player handbook.

If an incorrect code is entered, the unit will become locked, and cannot be operated.

If this happens or if the security code is lost or forgotten, seek the advice of your Renault dealer. On presentation of proof of ownership, a Renault dealer will be able to unlock the unit and provide you with a new security code.

Conversion factors

Length (distance)

Inches (in)	X 25.4	= Millimetres (mm)	X 0.0394	= Inches (in)	
Feet (ft)	X 0.305	= Metres (m)	X 3.281	= Feet (ft)	
Miles	X 1.609	= Kilometres (km)	X 0.621	= Miles	

Volume (capacity)

Cubic inches (cu in; in^3)	X 16.387	= Cubic centimetres (cc; cm^3)	X 0.061	= Cubic inches (cu in; in^3)
Imperial pints (Imp pt)	X 0.568	= Litres (l)	X 1.76	= Imperial pints (Imp pt)
Imperial quarts (Imp qt)	X 1.137	= Litres (l)	X 0.88	= Imperial quarts (Imp qt)
Imperial quarts (Imp qt)	X 1.201	= US quarts (US qt)	X 0.833	= Imperial quarts (Imp qt)
US quarts (US qt)	X 0.946	= Litres (l)	X 1.057	= US quarts (US qt)
Imperial gallons (Imp gal)	X 4.546	= Litres (l)	X 0.22	= Imperial gallons (Imp gal)
Imperial gallons (Imp gal)	X 1.201	= US gallons (US gal)	X 0.833	= Imperial gallons (Imp gal)
US gallons (US gal)	X 3.785	= Litres (l)	X 0.264	= US gallons (US gal)

Mass (weight)

Ounces (oz)	X 28.35	= Grams (g)	X 0.035	= Ounces (oz)
Pounds (lb)	X 0.454	= Kilograms (kg)	X 2.205	= Pounds (lb)

Force

Ounces-force (ozf; oz)	X 0.278	= Newtons (N)	X 3.6	= Ounces-force (ozf; oz)
Pounds-force (lbf; lb)	X 4.448	= Newtons (N)	X 0.225	= Pounds-force (lbf; lb)
Newtons (N)	X 0.1	= Kilograms-force (kgf; kg)	X 9.81	= Newtons (N)

Pressure

Pounds-force per square inch (psi; lbf/in^2; lb/in^2)	X 0.070	= Kilograms-force per square centimetre (kgf/cm^2; kg/cm^2)	X 14.223	= Pounds-force per square inch (psi; lbf/in^2; lb/in^2)
Pounds-force per square inch (psi; lbf/in^2; lb/in^2)	X 0.068	= Atmospheres (atm)	X 14.696	= Pounds-force per square inch (psi; lbf/in^2; lb/in^2)
Pounds-force per square inch (psi; lbf/in^2; lb/in^2)	X 0.069	= Bars	X 14.5	= Pounds-force per square inch (psi; lbf/in^2; lb/in^2)
Pounds-force per square inch (psi; lbf/in^2; lb/in^2)	X 6.895	= Kilopascals (kPa)	X 0.145	= Pounds-force per square inch (psi; lbf/in^2; lb/in^2)
Kilopascals (kPa)	X 0.01	= Kilograms-force per square centimetre (kgf/cm^2; kg/cm^2)	X 98.1	= Kilopascals (kPa)
Millibar (mbar)	X 100	= Pascals (Pa)	X 0.01	= Millibar (mbar)
Millibar (mbar)	X 0.0145	= Pounds-force per square inch (psi; lbf/in^2; lb/in^2)	X 68.947	= Millibar (mbar)
Millibar (mbar)	X 0.75	= Millimetres of mercury (mmHg)	X 1.333	= Millibar (mbar)
Millibar (mbar)	X 0.401	= Inches of water (inH$_2$O)	X 2.491	= Millibar (mbar)
Millimetres of mercury (mmHg)	X 0.535	= Inches of water (inH$_2$O)	X 1.868	= Millimetres of mercury (mmHg)
Inches of water (inH$_2$O)	X 0.036	= Pounds-force per square inch (psi; lbf/in^2; lb/in^2)	X 27.68	= Inches of water (inH$_2$O)

Torque (moment of force)

Pounds-force inches (lbf in; lb in)	X 1.152	= Kilograms-force centimetre (kgf cm; kg cm)	X 0.868	= Pounds-force inches (lbf in; lb in)
Pounds-force inches (lbf in; lb in)	X 0.113	= Newton metres (Nm)	X 8.85	= Pounds-force inches (lbf in; lb in)
Pounds-force inches (lbf in; lb in)	X 0.083	= Pounds-force feet (lbf ft; lb ft)	X 12	= Pounds-force inches (lbf in; lb in)
Pounds-force feet (lbf ft; lb ft)	X 0.138	= Kilograms-force metres (kgf m; kg m)	X 7.233	= Pounds-force feet (lbf ft; lb ft)
Pounds-force feet (lbf ft; lb ft)	X 1.356	= Newton metres (Nm)	X 0.738	= Pounds-force feet (lbf ft; lb ft)
Newton metres (Nm)	X 0.102	= Kilograms-force metres (kgf m; kg m)	X 9.804	= Newton metres (Nm)

Power

Horsepower (hp)	X 745.7	= Watts (W)	X 0.0013	= Horsepower (hp)

Velocity (speed)

Miles per hour (miles/hr; mph)	X 1.609	= Kilometres per hour (km/hr; kph)	X 0.621	= Miles per hour (miles/hr; mph)

Fuel consumption*

Miles per gallon, Imperial (mpg)	X 0.354	= Kilometres per litre (km/l)	X 2.825	= Miles per gallon, Imperial (mpg)
Miles per gallon, US (mpg)	X 0.425	= Kilometres per litre (km/l)	X 2.352	= Miles per gallon, US (mpg)

Temperature

Degrees Fahrenheit = (°C x 1.8) + 32   Degrees Celsius (Degrees Centigrade; °C) = (°F - 32) x 0.56

It is common practice to convert from miles per gallon (mpg) to litres/100 kilometres (l/100km), where mpg (Imperial) x l/100 km = 282 and mpg (US) x l/100 km = 235

Fault diagnosis

Contents

Introduction

The vehicle owner who does his or her own maintenance according to the recommended service schedules should not have to use this section of the manual very often. Modern component reliability is such that, provided those items subject to wear or deterioration are inspected or renewed at the specified intervals, sudden failure is comparatively rare. Faults do not usually just happen as a result of sudden failure, but develop over a period of time. Major mechanical failures in particular are usually preceded by characteristic symptoms over hundreds or even thousands of miles. Those components which do occasionally fail without warning are often small and easily carried in the vehicle.

With any fault finding, the first step is to decide where to begin investigations. Sometimes this is obvious, but on other occasions a little detective work will be necessary. The owner who makes half a dozen haphazard adjustments or replacements may be successful in curing a fault (or its symptoms), but will be none the wiser if the fault recurs and ultimately may have spent more time and money than was necessary. A calm and logical approach will be found to be more satisfactory in the long run. Always take into account any warning signs or abnormalities that may have been noticed in the period preceding the fault - power loss, high or low gauge readings, unusual smells, etc - and remember that failure of components such as fuses or relays may only be pointers to some underlying fault.

The pages which follow provide an easy reference guide to the more common problems which may occur during the operation of the vehicle. These problems and their possible causes are grouped under headings denoting various components or systems, such as Engine, Cooling system, etc. The Chapter and/or Section which deals with the problem is also shown in brackets. Whatever the fault, certain basic principles apply. These are as follows:

Verify the fault. This is simply a matter of being sure that you know what the symptoms are before starting work. This is particularly important if you are investigating a fault for someone else who may not have described it very accurately.

Don't overlook the obvious. For example, if the vehicle won't start, is there fuel in the tank? (Don't take anyone else's word on this particular point, and don't trust the fuel gauge either!) If an electrical fault is indicated, look for loose or broken wires before digging out the test gear.

Cure the disease, not the symptom. Substituting a flat battery with a fully charged one will get you off the hard shoulder, but if the underlying cause is not attended to, the new battery will go the same way.

Don't take anything for granted. Particularly, don't forget that a "new" component may itself be defective (especially if it's been rattling around in the boot for months), and don't leave components out of a fault diagnosis sequence just because they are new or recently fitted. When you do finally diagnose a difficult fault, you'll probably realise that all the evidence was there from the start.

---

1   Engine

Engine fails to rotate when attempting to start

- Battery terminal connections loose or corroded (Chapter 1).
- Battery discharged or faulty (Chapter 5).
- Broken, loose or disconnected wiring in the starting circuit (Chapter 5).
- Defective starter solenoid or switch (Chapter 5).
- Defective starter motor (Chapter 5).
- Starter pinion or flywheel ring gear teeth loose or broken (Chapter 5 and Chapter 2A).
- Engine earth strap broken or disconnected (Chapter 5).

Starter motor turns engine slowly

- Partially discharged battery (recharge, use jump leads, or push start) (Chapter 5).

- Battery terminals loose or corroded (Chapter 1).
- Battery earth to body defective (Chapter 5).
- Engine earth strap loose (Chapter 5).
- Starter motor (or solenoid) wiring loose (Chapter 5).
- Starter motor internal fault (Chapter 5).

Starter motor spins without turning engine

- Starter motor reduction gears stripped (Chapter 5).
- Starter motor mounting bolts loose (Chapter 5).

Starter motor noisy or excessively rough in engagement

- Starter pinion or flywheel ring gear teeth loose or broken (Chapter 5 and Chapter 2A).
- Starter motor mounting bolts loose or missing (Chapter 5).
- Starter motor internal components worn or damaged (Chapter 5).

Engine rotates but will not start

- Fuel tank empty.
- Battery discharged (engine rotates slowly) (Chapter 5).
- Battery terminal connections loose or corroded (Chapter 1).
- Air in fuel (Chapter 4).
- Wax formed in fuel (in very cold weather).
- Faulty stop solenoid (Chapter 4).
- Low cylinder compressions (Chapter 2A).
- Fuel system or preheating system fault (Chapters 4 and 5).
- Major mechanical failure (eg camshaft drive) (Chapter 2A).

Engine fires but will not run

- Preheating system fault (Chapter 5).
- Air in fuel (Chapter 4).
- Wax formed in fuel (in very cold weather).
- Other fuel system fault (Chapter 4).

Engine difficult to start when cold

- Battery discharged (Chapter 5).
- Battery terminal connections loose or corroded (Chapter 1).
- Air in fuel (Chapter 4).
- Air filter element dirty or clogged (Chapter 1).
- Wax formed in fuel (in very cold weather).
- Preheating system fault (Chapter 5).
- Other fuel system fault (Chapter 4).
- Low cylinder compressions (Chapter 2A).

Engine difficult to start when hot

- Battery discharged (Chapter 5).
- Battery terminal connections loose or corroded (Chapter 1).
- Air filter element dirty or clogged (Chapter 1).
- Air in fuel (Chapter 4).
- Low cylinder compressions (Chapter 2A).

Engine idles erratically

- Incorrectly adjusted idle speed (Chapter 1).
- Air filter element clogged (Chapter 1).
- Incorrectly adjusted valve clearances (Chapter 2A).
- Uneven or low cylinder compressions (Chapter 2A).
- Camshaft lobes worn (Chapter 2A).
- Timing belt incorrectly tensioned (Chapter 2A).
- Incorrect fuel injection pump timing (Chapter 4).

Engine misfires at idle speed

- Air in fuel (Chapter 4).
- Wax formed in fuel (in very cold weather).
- Other fuel system fault (Chapter 4).
- Incorrectly adjusted valve clearances (Chapter 2A).
- Uneven or low cylinder compressions (Chapter 2A).
- Disconnected, leaking or perished crankcase ventilation hoses (Chapters 1 and 4).
- Incorrect fuel injection pump timing (Chapter 4).

Engine misfires throughout the driving speed range

- Fuel filter choked (Chapter 1).
- Fuel tank vent blocked or fuel pipes restricted (Chapter 4).
- Uneven or low cylinder compressions (Chapter 2A).
- Incorrect fuel injection pump timing (Chapter 4).

Engine stalls

- Incorrectly adjusted idle speed (Chapter 1).
- Fuel filter choked (Chapter 1).
- Fuel tank vent blocked or fuel pipes restricted (Chapter 4).

Engine lacks power

- Air in fuel (Chapter 4).
- Incorrect fuel injection pump timing (Chapter 4).
- Timing belt incorrectly fitted or tensioned (Chapter 2A).
- Fuel filter choked (Chapter 1).
- Uneven or low cylinder compressions (Chapter 2A).
- Brakes binding (Chapters 1 and 9).
- Clutch slipping (Chapter 6).

Oil pressure warning light illuminated with engine running

- Low oil level or incorrect grade (Chapter 1).
- Faulty oil pressure switch (Chapter 5).
- Worn engine bearings and/or oil pump (Chapters 2A and 2B).
- High engine operating temperature (Chapter 3).
- Oil pressure relief valve defective (Chapter 2A).
- Oil pick-up strainer clogged (Chapter 2A).

Note: *Low oil pressure in a high-mileage engine at tickover is not necessarily a cause for concern. Sudden pressure loss at speed is far more significant. In any event, check the gauge or warning light sender before condemning the engine.*

Engine runs-on after switching off

- Faulty stop solenoid (Chapter 4).

Engine noises

Note: *To inexperienced ears, the diesel engine can sound alarming even when there is nothing wrong with it, so it may be prudent to have an unusual noise expertly diagnosed before making renewals or repairs.*

Whistling or wheezing noises

- Leaking manifold gasket (Chapter 4).
- Leaking vacuum hose (Chapters 1 and 4).
- Blowing cylinder head gasket (Chapter 2A).

Tapping or rattling noises

- Incorrect valve clearances (Chapter 2A).
- Worn valve gear or camshaft (Chapter 2A).
- Broken piston ring (ticking noise) (Chapter 2B).
- Ancillary component fault (water pump, alternator etc) (Chapters 3 and 5).

Knocking or thumping noises

- Air in fuel (Chapter 4).
- Worn drivebelt (Chapter 1 and Chapter 2A).
- Fuel injector(s) leaking or sticking (Chapter 4).
- Worn big-end bearings (regular heavy knocking, perhaps less under load) (Chapter 2B).
- Worn main bearings (rumbling and knocking, perhaps worsening under load) (Chapter 2B).
- Piston slap (most noticeable when cold) (Chapter 2B).
- Ancillary component fault (alternator, water pump etc) (Chapters 3 and 5).

2 Cooling system

Overheating

- Insufficient coolant in system (Chapter 1).
- Thermostat faulty (Chapter 3).
- Radiator core blocked or grille restricted (Chapter 3).
- Electric cooling fan or thermoswitch faulty (Chapter 3).
- Pressure cap faulty (Chapter 3).
- Timing belt worn, or incorrectly adjusted (Chapter 2A).
- Inaccurate temperature gauge sender unit (Chapter 3).
- Air lock in cooling system (Chapter 1).

Overcooling

- Thermostat faulty (Chapter 3).
- Inaccurate temperature gauge sender unit (Chapter 3).

External coolant leakage

- Deteriorated or damaged hoses or hose clips (Chapter 1).
- Radiator core or heater matrix leaking (Chapter 3).
- Pressure cap faulty (Chapter 3).
- Water pump seal leaking (Chapter 3).
- Boiling due to overheating (Chapter 3).
- Core plug leaking (Chapter 2B).

Internal coolant leakage

- Leaking cylinder head gasket (Chapter 2A).
- Cracked cylinder head or cylinder bore (Chapters 2A and 2B).

Corrosion

- Infrequent draining and flushing (Chapter 1).
- Incorrect antifreeze mixture or inappropriate type (Chapter 1).

3 Fuel and exhaust system

Excessive fuel consumption

- Air filter element dirty or clogged (Chapter 1).
- Preheating system fault (Chapter 5).
- Incorrect idle speed (Chapter 1).
- Incorrect fuel injection pump timing (Chapter 4).
- Brakes binding (Chapter 9).
- Tyres underinflated (Chapter 1).

Fuel leakage and/or fuel odour

- Damaged or corroded fuel tank, pipes or connections (Chapters 1 and 4).

Excessive noise or fumes from exhaust system

- Leaking exhaust system or manifold joints (Chapter 4).
- Leaking, corroded or damaged silencers or pipe (Chapter 4).
- Broken mountings causing body or suspension contact (Chapter 4).

4 Clutch

Pedal travels to floor - no pressure or very little resistance

- Broken clutch cable (Chapter 6).
- Incorrect clutch adjustment (Chapter 6).
- Broken clutch release bearing or fork (Chapter 6).
- Broken diaphragm spring in clutch pressure plate (Chapter 6).

Clutch fails to disengage (unable to select gears)

- Incorrect clutch adjustment (Chapter 6).
- Friction plate sticking on gearbox input shaft splines (Chapter 6).
- Friction plate sticking to flywheel or pressure plate (Chapter 6).
- Faulty pressure plate assembly (Chapter 6).
- Clutch release mechanism worn or incorrectly assembled (Chapter 6).

Clutch slips (engine speed increases with no increase in vehicle speed)

- Incorrect clutch adjustment (Chapter 6).
- Friction plate linings excessively worn (Chapter 6).
- Friction plate linings contaminated with oil or grease (Chapter 6).
- Faulty pressure plate or weak diaphragm spring (Chapter 6).

Judder as clutch is engaged

- Friction plate linings contaminated with oil or grease (Chapter 6).
- Friction plate linings excessively worn (Chapter 6).
- Clutch cable sticking or frayed (Chapter 6).
- Faulty or distorted pressure plate or diaphragm spring (Chapter 6).
- Worn or loose engine or gearbox mountings (Chapter 2A).
- Friction plate hub or gearbox input shaft splines worn (Chapter 6).

Noise when depressing or releasing clutch pedal

- Worn clutch release bearing (Chapter 6).
- Worn or dry clutch pedal bushes (Chapter 6).
- Faulty pressure plate assembly (Chapter 6).
- Pressure plate diaphragm spring broken (Chapter 6).
- Broken friction plate cushioning springs (Chapter 6).

5   Manual gearbox

Noisy in neutral with engine running

- Input shaft bearings worn (noise apparent with clutch pedal released but not when depressed) (Chapter 7).*
- Clutch release bearing worn (noise apparent with clutch pedal depressed, possibly less when released) (Chapter 6).

Noisy in one particular gear

- Worn, damaged or chipped gear teeth (Chapter 7).*

Difficulty engaging gears

- Clutch fault (Chapter 6).
- Worn or damaged gear linkage (Chapter 7).
- Incorrectly adjusted gear linkage (Chapter 7).
- Worn synchroniser units (Chapter 7).*

Jumps out of gear

- Worn or damaged gear linkage (Chapter 7).
- Incorrectly adjusted gear linkage (Chapter 7).
- Worn synchroniser units (Chapter 7).*
- Worn selector forks (Chapter 7).*

Vibration

- Lack of oil (Chapter 1).
- Worn bearings (Chapter 7).*

Lubricant leaks

- Leaking oil seal (Chapter 7).
- Leaking housing joint (Chapter 7).*

Although the corrective action necessary to remedy the symptoms described is beyond the scope of the home mechanic, the above information should be helpful in isolating the cause of the condition so that the owner can communicate clearly with a professional mechanic.

6   Driveshafts

Clicking or knocking noise on turns (at slow speed on full lock)

- Lack of constant velocity joint lubricant (Chapter 8).
- Worn outer constant velocity joint (Chapter 8).

Vibration when accelerating or decelerating

- Worn inner constant velocity joint (Chapter 8).
- Bent or distorted driveshaft (Chapter 8).

7   Braking system

Note: *Before assuming that a brake problem exists, make sure that the tyres are in good condition and correctly inflated, the front wheel alignment is correct and the vehicle is not loaded with weight in an unequal manner.*

Vehicle pulls to one side under braking

- Worn, defective, damaged or contaminated front or rear brake pads/shoes on one side (Chapter 9).
- Seized or partially seized front or rear brake caliper/wheel cylinder piston (Chapter 9).
- A mixture of brake pad/shoe lining materials fitted between sides (Chapter 9).
- Brake caliper mounting bolts loose (Chapter 9).
- Rear brake backplate mounting bolts loose (Chapter 9).
- Worn or damaged steering or suspension components (Chapter 10).

Noise (grinding or high-pitched squeal) when brakes applied

- Brake pad or shoe friction lining material worn down to metal backing (Chapter 9).
- Excessive corrosion of brake disc or drum. (May be apparent after the vehicle has been standing for some time (Chapter 9).

Excessive brake pedal travel

- Inoperative rear brake self-adjust mechanism (Chapter 9).
- Faulty master cylinder (Chapter 9).
- Air in hydraulic system (Chapter 9).
- Faulty vacuum servo unit (Chapter 9).
- Faulty brake vacuum pump (Chapter 9).

Brake pedal feels spongy when depressed

- Air in hydraulic system (Chapter 9).
- Deteriorated flexible rubber brake hoses (Chapter 9).
- Master cylinder mountings loose (Chapter 9).
- Faulty master cylinder (Chapter 9).

Excessive brake pedal effort required to stop vehicle

- Faulty vacuum servo unit (Chapter 9).
- Disconnected, damaged or insecure brake servo vacuum hose (Chapters 1 and 9).
- Faulty brake vacuum pump (Chapter 9).
- Primary or secondary hydraulic circuit failure (Chapter 9).
- Seized brake caliper or wheel cylinder piston(s) (Chapter 9).
- Brake pads or brake shoes incorrectly fitted (Chapter 9).

- Incorrect grade of brake pads or brake shoes fitted (Chapter 9).
- Brake pads or brake shoe linings contaminated (Chapter 9).

Judder felt through brake pedal or steering wheel when braking

- Excessive run-out or distortion of front discs or rear drums (Chapter 9).
- Brake pad or brake shoe linings worn (Chapter 9).
- Brake caliper or rear brake backplate mounting bolts loose (Chapter 9).
- Wear in suspension or steering components or mountings (Chapter 10).

Brakes binding

- Seized brake caliper or wheel cylinder piston(s) (Chapter 9).
- Incorrectly adjusted handbrake mechanism or linkage (Chapter 9).
- Faulty master cylinder (Chapter 9).

Rear wheels locking under normal braking

- Rear brake shoe linings contaminated (Chapter 9).
- Faulty brake pressure regulator (Chapter 9).

8   Suspension and steering

Note: *Before diagnosing suspension or steering faults, be sure that the trouble is not due to incorrect tyre pressures, mixtures of tyre types or binding brakes.*

Vehicle pulls to one side

- Defective tyre (Chapter 1).
- Excessive wear in suspension or steering components (Chapter 10).
- Incorrect front wheel alignment (Chapter 10).
- Accident damage to steering or suspension components (Chapter 10).

Wheel wobble and vibration

- Front roadwheels out of balance (vibration felt mainly through the steering wheel) (Chapter 10).
- Rear roadwheels out of balance (vibration felt throughout the vehicle) (Chapter 10).
- Roadwheels damaged or distorted (Chapter 1).
- Faulty or damaged tyre (Chapter 1).
- Worn steering or suspension joints, bushes or components (Chapter 10).
- Wheel bolts loose (Chapter 1).

Excessive pitching and/or rolling around corners or during braking

- Defective shock absorbers (Chapter 10).
- Broken or weak coil spring and/or suspension component (Chapter 10).
- Worn or damaged anti-roll bar or mountings (Chapter 10).

Wandering or general instability

- Incorrect front wheel alignment (Chapter 10).
- Worn steering or suspension joints, bushes or components (Chapter 10).
- Roadwheels out of balance (Chapter 10).
- Faulty or damaged tyre (Chapter 1).
- Wheel bolts loose (Chapter 1).
- Defective shock absorbers (Chapter 10).

Excessively stiff steering

- Lack of steering gear lubricant (Chapter 10).
- Seized track-rod end balljoint or suspension balljoint (Chapter 10).

- Faulty electric power steering pump (Chapter 10).
- Incorrect front wheel alignment (Chapter 10).
- Steering rack or column bent or damaged (Chapter 10).

Excessive play in steering

- Worn steering column universal joint(s) or intermediate coupling (Chapter 10).
- Worn steering track-rod end balljoints (Chapter 10).
- Worn rack and pinion steering gear (Chapter 10).
- Worn steering or suspension joints, bushes or components (Chapter 10).

Lack of power assistance

- Faulty electric power steering pump (Chapter 10).
- Incorrect power steering fluid level (Chapter 1).
- Restriction in power steering fluid hoses (Chapter 1).
- Faulty rack and pinion steering gear (Chapter 10).

Tyre wear excessive

Tyres worn on inside or outside edges

- Tyres underinflated (wear on both edges) (Chapter 1).
- Incorrect camber or castor angles (wear on one edge only) (Chapter 10).
- Worn steering or suspension joints, bushes or components (Chapter 10).
- Excessively hard cornering.
- Accident damage.

Tyre treads exhibit feathered edges

- Incorrect toe setting (Chapter 10).

Tyres worn in centre of tread

- Tyres overinflated (Chapter 1).

Tyres worn on inside and outside edges

- Tyres underinflated (Chapter 1).

Tyres worn unevenly

- Tyres out of balance (Chapter 1).
- Excessive wheel or tyre run-out (Chapter 1).
- Worn shock absorbers (Chapter 10).
- Faulty tyre (Chapter 1).

9   Electrical system

Note: *For problems associated with the starting system, refer to the faults listed under "Engine" earlier in this Section.*

Battery will not hold a charge for more than a few days

- Battery defective internally (Chapter 5).
- Battery electrolyte level low - where applicable (Chapter 1).
- Battery terminal connections loose or corroded (Chapter 1).
- Alternator drivebelt worn or incorrectly adjusted (Chapter 1).
- Alternator not charging at correct output (Chapter 5).
- Alternator or voltage regulator faulty (Chapter 5).
- Short-circuit causing continual battery drain (Chapter 5).

Ignition warning light remains illuminated with engine running

- Alternator drivebelt broken, worn, or incorrectly adjusted (Chapter 1).
- Alternator brushes worn, sticking, or dirty (Chapter 5).
- Alternator brush springs weak or broken (Chapter 5).
- Internal fault in alternator or voltage regulator (Chapter 5).
- Broken, disconnected, or loose wiring in charging circuit (Chapter 5).

Ignition warning light fails to come on
- Warning light bulb blown (Chapter 12).
- Broken, disconnected, or loose wiring in warning light circuit (Chapter 12).
- Alternator faulty (Chapter 5).

Lights inoperative
- Bulb blown (Chapter 12).
- Corrosion of bulb or bulbholder contacts (Chapter 12).
- Blown fuse (Chapter 12).
- Faulty relay (Chapter 12).
- Broken, loose, or disconnected wiring (Chapter 12).
- Faulty switch (Chapter 12).

Instrument readings inaccurate or erratic

Instrument readings increase with engine speed
- Faulty voltage regulator (Chapter 12).

Fuel or temperature gauge give no reading
- Faulty gauge sender unit (Chapters 3 or 4).
- Wiring open-circuit (Chapter 5).
- Faulty gauge (Chapter 12).

Fuel or temperature gauges give continuous maximum reading
- Faulty gauge sender unit (Chapters 3 or 4).
- Wiring short-circuit (Chapter 5).
- Faulty gauge (Chapter 12).

Horn inoperative or unsatisfactory in operation

Horn operates all the time
- Horn push either earthed or stuck down (Chapter 12).
- Horn cable to horn push earthed (Chapter 12).

Horn fails to operate
- Blown fuse (Chapter 12).
- Cable or cable connections loose, broken or disconnected (Chapter 12).
- Faulty horn (Chapter 12).

Horn emits intermittent or unsatisfactory sound
- Cable connections loose (Chapter 12).
- Horn mountings loose (Chapter 12).
- Faulty horn (Chapter 12).

Windscreen/tailgate wipers inoperative or unsatisfactory in operation

Wipers fail to operate or operate very slowly
- Wiper blades stuck to screen or linkage seized or binding (Chapters 1 and 12).
- Blown fuse (Chapter 12).
- Cable or cable connections loose, broken or disconnected (Chapter 12).
- Faulty relay (Chapter 12).
- Faulty wiper motor (Chapter 12).

Wiper blades sweep over too large or too small an area of the glass
- Wiper arms incorrectly positioned on spindles (Chapter 12).
- Excessive wear of wiper linkage (Chapter 12).
- Wiper motor or linkage mountings loose or insecure (Chapter 12).

Wiper blades fail to clean the glass effectively
- Wiper blade rubbers worn or perished (Chapter 1).
- Wiper arm tension springs broken or arm pivots seized (Chapter 12).
- Insufficient windscreen washer additive to adequately remove road film (Chapter 1).

Windscreen/tailgate washers inoperative or unsatisfactory in operation

One or more washer jets inoperative
- Blocked washer jet (Chapter 12).
- Disconnected, kinked or restricted fluid hose (Chapter 12).
- Insufficient fluid in washer reservoir (Chapter 1).

Washer pump fails to operate
- Broken or disconnected wiring or connections (Chapter 12).
- Blown fuse (Chapter 12).
- Faulty washer switch (Chapter 12).
- Faulty washer pump (Chapter 12).

Washer pump runs for some time before fluid is emitted from jets
- Faulty one-way valve in fluid supply hose (Chapter 12).

Electric windows inoperative or unsatisfactory in operation

Window glass will only move in one direction
- Faulty switch (Chapter 11).

Window glass slow to move
- Regulator seized or damaged, or in need of lubrication (Chapter 11).
- Door internal components or trim fouling regulator (Chapter 11).
- Faulty motor (Chapter 11).

Window glass fails to move
- Blown fuse (Chapter 12).
- Faulty relay (Chapter 12).
- Broken or disconnected wiring or connections (Chapter 12).
- Faulty motor (Chapter 11).

Central locking system inoperative or unsatisfactory in operation

Complete system failure
- Blown fuse (Chapter 12).
- Faulty relay (Chapter 12).
- Broken or disconnected wiring or connections (Chapter 12).

Latch locks but will not unlock, or unlocks but will not lock
- Faulty switch (Chapter 12).
- Broken or disconnected latch operating rods or levers (Chapter 11).
- Faulty relay (Chapter 12).

One solenoid/motor fails to operate
- Broken or disconnected wiring or connections (Chapter 12).
- Faulty solenoid/motor (Chapter 11).
- Broken, binding or disconnected latch operating rods or levers (Chapter 11).
- Fault in door latch (Chapter 11).

MOT test checks

Introduction

Motor vehicle testing has been compulsory in Great Britain since 1960 when the Motor Vehicle (Tests) Regulations were first introduced. At that time testing was only applicable to vehicles ten years old or older, and the test itself only covered lighting equipment, braking systems and steering gear. Current vehicle testing is far more extensive and, in the case of private vehicles, is now an annual inspection commencing three years after the date of first registration. Test standards are becoming increasingly stringent; for details of changes consult the latest edition of the MOT Inspection Manual (available from HMSO or bookshops).

This section is intended as a guide to getting your vehicle through the MOT test. It lists all the relevant testable items, how to check them yourself, and what is likely to cause the vehicle to fail. Obviously it will not be possible to examine the vehicle to the same standard as the professional MOT tester who will be highly experienced in this work and will have all the necessary equipment available. However, working through the following checks will provide a good indication as to the condition of the vehicle and will enable you to identify any problem areas before submitting the vehicle for the test. Where a component is found to need repair or renewal, reference should be made to the appropriate Chapter in the manual where further information will be found.

The following checks have been sub-divided into four categories as follows.

a) Checks carried out from the driver's seat.
b) Checks carried out with the vehicle on the ground.
c) Checks carried out with the vehicle raised and with the wheels free to rotate.
d) Exhaust emission checks.

In most cases the help of an assistant will be necessary to carry out these checks thoroughly.

Checks carried out from the driver's seat

Handbrake

Test the operation of the handbrake by pulling on the lever until the handbrake is in the normal fully-applied position. Ensure that the travel of the lever (the number of clicks of the ratchet) is not excessive before full resistance of the braking mechanism is felt. If so this would indicate incorrect adjustment of the rear brakes or incorrectly adjusted handbrake cables.

With the handbrake fully applied, tap the lever sideways and make sure that it does not release which would indicate wear in the ratchet and pawl. Release the handbrake and move the lever from side to side to check for excessive wear in the pivot bearing. Check the security of the lever mountings and make sure that there is no corrosion of any part of the body structure within 30 cm of the lever mounting. If the lever mountings cannot be readily seen from inside the vehicle, carry out this check later when working underneath.

Footbrake

Check that the brake pedal is sound without visible defects such as excessive wear of the pivot bushes or broken or damaged pedal pad. Check also for signs of fluid leaks on the pedal, floor or carpets which would indicate failed seals in the brake master cylinder.

Depress the brake pedal slowly at first, then rapidly until sustained pressure can be held. Maintain this pressure and check that the pedal does not creep down to the floor which would again indicate problems with the master cylinder. Release the pedal, wait a few seconds then depress it once until firm resistance is felt. Check that this resistance occurs near the top of the pedal travel. If the pedal travels nearly to the floor before firm resistance is felt, this would indicate incorrect brake adjustment resulting in "insufficient reserve travel" of the footbrake. If firm resistance cannot be felt, ie the pedal feels spongy, this would indicate that air is present in the hydraulic system which will necessitate complete bleeding of the system.

Check that the servo unit is operating correctly by depressing the brake pedal several times to exhaust the vacuum. Keep the pedal depressed and start the engine. As soon as the engine starts, the brake pedal resistance will be felt to alter. If this is not the case, there may be a leak from the brake servo vacuum hose, or the servo unit itself may be faulty.

Steering wheel and column

Examine the steering wheel for fractures or looseness of the hub, spokes or rim. Move the steering wheel from side to side and then up and down, in relation to the steering column. Check that the steering wheel is not loose on the column, indicating wear in the column splines or a loose steering wheel retaining nut. Continue moving the steering wheel as before, but also turn it slightly from left to right. Check that there is no abnormal movement of the steering wheel, indicating excessive wear in the column upper support bearing, universal joint(s) or flexible coupling.

Check the security of the seat belt mountings

Windscreen and mirrors

The windscreen must be free of cracks or other damage which will seriously interfere with the driver's field of view, or which will prevent the windscreen wipers from operating properly. Small stone chips are acceptable. Any stickers, dangling toys or similar items must also be clear of the field of view.

Rear view mirrors must be secure, intact and capable of being adjusted. The nearside (passenger side) door mirror is not included in the test unless the interior mirror cannot be used - for instance, in the case of a van with blacked-out rear windows.

Seat belts and seats

Note: *The following checks are applicable to all seat belts, front and rear. Front seat belts must be of a type that will restrain the upper part of the body; lap belts are not acceptable. Various combinations of seat belt types are acceptable at the rear.*

Carefully examine the seat belt webbing for cuts or any signs of serious fraying or deterioration. If the seat belt is of the retractable type, pull the belt all the way out and examine the full extent of the webbing.

Fasten and unfasten the belt ensuring that the locking mechanism holds securely and releases properly when intended. If the belt is of the retractable type, check also that the retracting mechanism operates correctly when the belt is released.

Check the security of all seat belt mountings and attachments which are accessible, without removing any trim or other components, from inside the vehicle **(see illustration)**. Any serious corrosion, fracture or distortion of the body structure within 30 cm of any mounting point will cause the vehicle to fail. Certain anchorages will not be accessible or even visible from inside the vehicle; in this instance further checks should be carried out later, when working underneath. If any part of the seat belt mechanism is attached to the front seat, then the seat mountings are treated as anchorages and must also comply as above.

The front seats themselves must be securely attached so that they cannot move unexpectedly and the backrests must lock in the upright position.

Doors

Both front doors must be able to be opened and closed from outside and inside, and must latch securely when closed. In the case of a pick-up, the tailgate must be securely attached and capable of being securely fastened.

Electrical equipment

Switch on the ignition and operate the horn. The horn must operate and produce a clear sound audible to other road users. Note that a gong, siren or two-tone horn fitted as an alternative to the manufacturer's original equipment is not acceptable.

Check the operation of the windscreen washers and wipers. The washers must operate with adequate flow and pressure and with the jets adjusted so that the liquid strikes the windscreen near the top of the glass.

Operate the windscreen wipers in conjunction with the washers and check that the blades cover their designed sweep of the windscreen without smearing. The blades must effectively clean the glass so that the driver has an adequate view of the road ahead and to the front nearside and offside of the vehicle. If the screen smears or does not clean adequately, it is advisable to renew the wiper blades before the MOT test.

Depress the footbrake with the ignition switched on and have your assistant check that both rear stop lights operate, and are extinguished when the footbrake is released. If one stop light fails to operate it is likely that a bulb has blown or there is a poor electrical contact at, or near, the bulbholder. If both stop lights fail to operate, check for a blown fuse, faulty stop light switch or possibly two blown bulbs. If the lights stay on when the brake pedal is released, it is possible that the switch is at fault.

Checks carried out with the vehicle on the ground

Vehicle identification

Front and rear number plates must be in good condition, securely fitted and easily read. Letters and numbers must be correctly spaced, with the gap between the group of numbers and the group of letters at least double the gap between adjacent numbers and letters.

The vehicle identification number on the plate under the bonnet must be legible. It will be checked during the test as part of the measures taken to prevent the fraudulent acquisition of certificates.

Electrical equipment

Switch on the side lights and check that both front and rear side lights and the number plate lights are illuminated and that the lenses and reflectors are secure and undamaged. This is particularly important at the rear where a cracked or damaged lens would allow a white light to show to the rear, which is unacceptable. Note in addition that any lens that is excessively dirty, either inside or out, such that the light intensity is reduced, could also constitute a fail.

Switch on the headlamps and check that both dipped beam and main beam units are operating correctly and at the same light intensity. If either headlamp shows signs of dimness, this is usually attributable to a poor earth connection or severely corroded internal reflector. Inspect the headlamp lenses for cracks or stone damage. Any damage to the headlamp lens will normally constitute a fail, but this is very much down to the tester's discretion. Bear in mind that with all light units they must operate correctly when first switched on. It is not acceptable to tap a light unit to make it operate.

The headlamps must not only be aligned so as not to dazzle other road users when switched to dipped beam, but also so as to provide adequate illumination of the road. This can only be accurately checked using optical beam setting equipment so if you have any doubts about the headlamp alignment, it is advisable to have this professionally checked and if necessary reset, before the MOT test.

With the ignition switched on, operate the direction indicators and check that they show amber lights to the front and to the rear, that they flash at the rate of between one and two flashes per second and that the "tell-tale" on the instrument panel also functions. Operation of the side lights and stop lights must not affect the indicators - if it does, the cause is usually a bad earth at the rear light cluster. Similarly check the operation of the hazard warning lights, which must work with the ignition on and off. Examine the lenses for cracks or damage as described previously.

Check the operation of the rear foglight(s). The test only concerns itself with the statutorily required foglight, which is the one on the offside. The light must be secure and emit a steady red light. The warning light on the instrument panel or in the switch must also work.

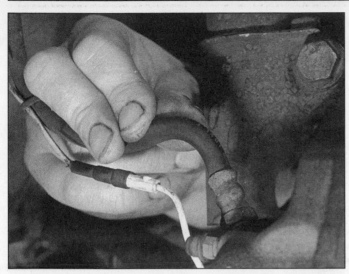

Check the flexible brake hoses for cracks or deterioration

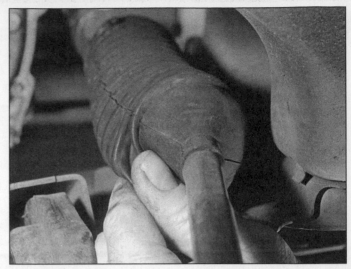

Examine the steering rack rubber gaiters for condition and security

Footbrake

From within the engine compartment examine the brake pipes for signs of leaks, corrosion, insecurity, chafing or other damage and check the master cylinder and servo unit for leaks, security of their mountings or excessive corrosion in the vicinity of the mountings. The master cylinder reservoir must be secure; if it is of the translucent type, the fluid level must be between the upper and lower level markings.

Turn the steering as necessary so that the right-hand front brake flexible hose can be examined. Inspect the hose carefully for any sign of cracks or deterioration of the rubber. This will be most noticeable if the hose is bent in half and is particularly common where the rubber portion enters the metal end fitting **(see illustration)**. Turn the steering onto full left then full right lock and ensure that the hose does not contact the wheel, tyre, or any part of the steering or suspension mechanism. While your assistant depresses the brake pedal firmly, check the hose for any bulges or fluid leaks under pressure. Now repeat these checks on the left-hand front hose. Should any damage or deterioration be noticed, renew the hose.

Steering mechanism and suspension

Have your assistant turn the steering wheel from side to side slightly, up to the point where the steering gear just begins to transmit this movement to the roadwheels. Check for excessive free play between the steering wheel and the steering gear which would indicate wear in the steering column joints, wear or insecurity of the steering column to steering gear coupling, or insecurity, incorrect adjustment, or wear in the steering gear itself. Generally speaking, free play greater than 1.3 cm for vehicles with rack and pinion type steering or 7.6 cm for vehicles with steering box mechanisms should be considered excessive.

Have your assistant turn the steering wheel more vigorously in each direction up to the point where the roadwheels just begin to turn. As this is done, carry out a complete examination of all the steering joints, linkages, fittings and attachments. Any component that shows signs of wear, damage, distortion, or insecurity should be renewed or attended to accordingly. On vehicles equipped with power steering also check that the power steering pump is secure, that the pump drivebelt is in satisfactory condition and correctly adjusted, that there are no fluid leaks or damaged hoses, and that the system operates correctly. Additional checks can be carried out later with the vehicle raised when there will be greater working clearance underneath.

Check that the vehicle is standing level and at approximately the correct ride height. Ensure that there is sufficient clearance between the suspension components and the bump stops to allow full suspension travel over bumps.

Shock absorbers

Depress each corner of the vehicle in turn and then release it. If the shock absorbers are in good condition the corner of the vehicle will rise and then settle in its normal position. If there is no noticeable damping effect from the shock absorber, and the vehicle continues to rise and fall, then the shock absorber is defective and the vehicle will fail. A shock absorber which has seized will also cause the vehicle to fail.

Exhaust system

Start the engine and with your assistant holding a rag over the tailpipe, check the entire system for leaks which will appear as a rhythmic fluffing or hissing sound at the source of the leak. Check the effectiveness of the silencer by ensuring that the noise produced is of a level to be expected from a vehicle of similar type. Providing that the system is structurally sound, it is acceptable to cure a leak using a proprietary exhaust system repair kit or similar method.

Checks carried out with the vehicle raised and with the wheels free to rotate

Jack up the front and rear of the vehicle and securely support it on axle stands positioned at suitable load bearing points under the vehicle structure. Position the stands clear of the suspension assemblies and ensure that the wheels are clear of the ground and that the steering can be turned onto full right and left lock.

Steering mechanism

Examine the steering rack rubber gaiters for signs of splits, lubricant leakage or insecurity of the retaining clips **(see illustration)**. If power steering is fitted, check for signs of deterioration, damage, chafing or leakage of the fluid hoses, pipes or connections. Also check for excessive stiffness or binding of the steering, a missing split pin or locking device or any severe corrosion of the body structure within 30 cm of any steering component attachment point.

Have your assistant turn the steering onto full left then full right lock. Check that the steering turns smoothly without undue tightness or roughness and that no part of the steering mechanism, including a wheel or tyre, fouls any brake flexible or rigid hose or pipe, or any part of the body structure.

On vehicles with four-wheel steering, similar considerations apply to the rear wheel steering linkages. However, it is permissible for a rear wheel steering system to be inoperative, provided that the rear wheels are secured in the straight-ahead position and that the front wheel steering system is operating effectively.

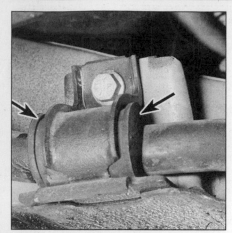

Check all rubber suspension mounting bushes (arrowed) for damage or deterioration

Shake the roadwheel vigorously to check for excess play in the wheel bearings and suspension components

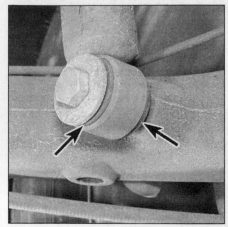

Check the condition of the shock absorber mountings and bushes (arrowed)

Front and rear suspension and wheel bearings

Starting at the front right-hand side of the vehicle, grasp the roadwheel at the 3 o'clock and 9 o'clock positions and shake it vigorously. Check for any free play at the wheel bearings, suspension ball joints, or suspension mountings, pivots and attachments. Check also for any serious deterioration of the rubber or metal casing of any mounting bushes, or any distortion, deformation or severe corrosion of any components **(see illustration)**. Look for missing split pins, tab washers or other locking devices on any mounting or attachment, or any severe corrosion of the vehicle structure within 30 cm of any suspension component attachment point.

If any excess free play is suspected at a component pivot point, this can be confirmed by using a large screwdriver or similar tool and levering between the mounting and the component attachment. This will confirm whether the wear is in the pivot bush, its retaining bolt or in the mounting itself (the bolt holes can often become elongated).

Now grasp the wheel at the 12 o'clock and 6 o'clock positions, shake it vigorously and repeat the previous inspection **(see illustration)**. Rotate the wheel and check for roughness or tightness of the front wheel bearing such that imminent failure of the bearing is indicated.

Carry out all the above checks at the other front wheel and then at both rear wheels.

Roadsprings and shock absorbers

On vehicles with strut type suspension units, examine the strut assembly for signs of serious fluid leakage, corrosion or severe pitting of the piston rod or damage to the casing. Check also for security of the mounting points **(see illustration)**.

If coil springs are fitted check that the spring ends locate correctly in their spring seats, that there is no severe corrosion of the spring and that it is not cracked, broken or in any way damaged.

If the vehicle is fitted with leaf springs, check that all leaves are intact, that the axle is securely attached to each spring and that there is no wear or deterioration of the spring eye mountings, bushes, and shackles.

The same general checks apply to vehicles fitted with other suspension types, such as torsion bars, hydraulic displacer units etc. In all cases ensure that all mountings and attachments are secure, that there are no signs of excessive wear, corrosion, cracking, deformation or damage to any component or bush, and that there are no fluid leaks or damaged hoses or pipes (hydraulic types).

Inspect the shock absorbers for signs of serious fluid leakage. (Slight seepage of fluid is normal for some types of shock absorber and is not a reason for failing.) Check for excessive wear of the mounting bushes or attachments or damage to the body of the unit.

Driveshafts

With the steering turned onto full lock, rotate each front wheel in turn and inspect the constant velocity joint gaiters for splits or damage **(see illustration)**. Also check the gaiter is securely attached to its respective housings by clips or other methods of retention.

Continue turning the wheel and check that each driveshaft is straight with no sign of damage.

Braking system

If possible, without dismantling, check for wear of the brake pads and the condition of the discs. Ensure that the friction lining material has not worn excessively and that the discs are not fractured, pitted, scored or worn excessively.

Carefully examine all the rigid brake pipes underneath the vehicle and the flexible hoses at the rear. Look for signs of excessive corrosion, chafing or insecurity of the pipes and for signs of bulging under pressure, chafing, splits or deterioration of the flexible hoses.

Look for signs of hydraulic fluid leaks at the brake calipers or on the brake backplates indicating failed hydraulic seals in the components concerned.

Slowly spin each wheel while your assistant depresses the footbrake then releases it. Ensure that each brake is operating and that the wheel is free to rotate when the pedal is released. It is not possible to test brake efficiency without special equipment, but (traffic and local conditions permitting) a road test can be carried out to check that the vehicle pulls up in a straight line.

Examine the handbrake mechanism and check for signs of frayed or broken cables, excessive corrosion or wear or insecurity of the linkage. Have your assistant operate the handbrake while you check that the mechanism works on each relevant wheel and releases fully without binding **(see illustration)**.

Fuel and exhaust systems

Inspect the fuel tank, fuel pipes, hoses and unions (including the unions at the pump, filter and carburettor). All components must be secure and free from leaks. The fuel filler cap must also be secure and of an appropriate type.

Examine the exhaust system over its entire length checking for any damaged, broken or missing mountings, security of the pipe retaining clamps and condition of the system with regard to rust and corrosion **(see illustration)**.

Wheels and tyres

Carefully examine each tyre in turn on both the inner and outer walls and over the whole of the tread area and check for signs of cuts, tears, lumps, bulges, separation of the tread and exposure of the ply or cord due to wear or other damage. Check also that the tyre bead is correctly seated on the wheel rim and that the tyre valve is sound and

Inspect the constant velocity joint gaiters for splits or damage

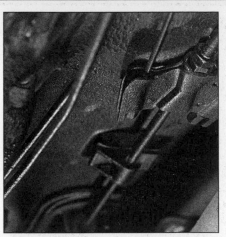

Check the handbrake mechanism for signs of frayed or broken cables or insecurity of the linkage

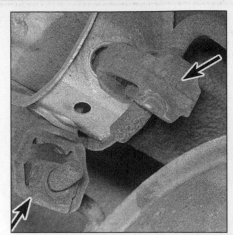

Check the condition of the exhaust system paying particular attention to the mountings (arrowed)

properly seated. Spin the wheel and check that it is not excessively distorted or damaged particularly at the bead rim.

Check that the tyres are of the correct size for the vehicle and that they are of the same size and type on each axle. (Having a "space saver" spare tyre in use is not acceptable.) The tyres should also be inflated to the specified pressures.

Using a suitable gauge check the tyre tread depth. The current legal requirement states that the tread pattern must be visible over the whole tread area and must be of a minimum depth of 1.6 mm over at least three-quarters of the tread width. It is acceptable for some wear of the inside or outside edges of the tyre to be apparent but this wear must be in one even circumferential band and the tread must be visible. Any excessive wear of this nature may indicate incorrect front wheel alignment which should be checked before the tyre becomes excessively worn. See the appropriate Chapters for further information on tyre wear patterns and front wheel alignment.

Body corrosion

Check the condition of the entire vehicle structure for signs of corrosion in any load bearing areas. For the purpose of the MOT test all chassis box sections, side sills, crossmembers, pillars, suspension, steering, braking system and seat belt mountings and anchorages should all be considered as load bearing areas. As a general guide, any corrosion which has seriously reduced the metal thickness of a load bearing area to weaken it, is likely to cause the vehicle to fail. Should corrosion of this nature be encountered, professional repairs are likely to be needed.

Body damage or corrosion which causes sharp or otherwise dangerous edges to be exposed will also cause the vehicle to fail.

Exhaust emission checks

Have the engine at normal operating temperature and make sure

that the preliminary conditions for checking idle speed (injection system in good order, air filter element clean, etc) have been met.

Before any measurements are carried out, raise the engine speed to around 2500 rpm and hold it at this speed for 10 seconds. Allow the engine speed to return to idle and watch for smoke emissions from the exhaust tailpipe. If the idle speed is obviously much too high, or if dense blue or black smoke comes from the tailpipe for more than 5 seconds, the vehicle will fail. As a rule of thumb, blue smoke signifies oil being burnt (worn valve stem oil seals, valve guides, piston rings or bores) while black smoke signifies unburnt fuel (dirty air cleaner element, injection timing incorrect, injector(s) leaking or sticking, or other fuel injection system fault).

The only emission check currently specified for Diesel engines is for smoke. (CO and HC emission checks as carried out on petrol engines are not significant for Diesels.)

Smoke testing

In principle, the testing station should measure exhaust smoke using suitable testing equipment. At the time of writing, the free acceleration smoke test introduced at the beginning of 1993 had been abandoned. The test involves accelerating the engine several times to its maximum unloaded speed; a number of vehicles suffered serious damage during the test because of timing belt failure.

For the time being the old situation has been restored, in that the MOT tester decides by visual inspection and by experience (the "calibrated eyeball") whether smoke emission is excessive. Some more precise test will probably be introduced in due course. Consult an MOT testing station for details of the latest regulations.

Note: *If the free acceleration smoke test is reintroduced, it is of the utmost importance that the engine timing belt be in good condition before the test is carried out.*

Notes

Chapter 1
Routine maintenance and servicing

Contents

Specifications

Engine

Oil filter .... Champion F121

Antifreeze mixtures:

	Antifreeze	Water
Antifreeze mixture (ethylene glycol antifreeze):		
Protection to -23°C	35%	65%
Protection to -40°C	50%	50%

Fuel system

Idle speed	825 ± 25 rpm
Fast idle speed:	
Roto-Diesel/Lucas injection pump..	Not adjustable (factory set)
Bosch injection pump	1000 ± 50 rpm
Anti-stall speed:	
Roto-Diesel/Lucas injection pump (with 5 mm shim - see text)	1600 ± 100 rpm
Bosch injection pump:	
F8Q 714 and 730 models (with 4 mm shim - see text)...............	1300 ± 50 rpm
F8Q 732 models (with 1 mm shim - see text).............................	Idle speed should raise by 10 to 20 rpm
Air filter..	Champion V429
Fuel filter:	
Roto-Diesel/Lucas	Champion L131 or L137
Bosch	Champion L136
Glow plugs..	Champion CH155

Brakes

Minimum front brake disc pad thickness (including backplate)..............	6.0 mm
Minimum rear brake shoe lining thickness (including shoe)...................	2.5 mm

Suspension and steering

	Front	Rear
Tyre pressures (tyres cold)	2.4 bars	2.4 bars

Note: *Recommended tyre pressures are marked on a label attached to the driver's door edge or frame. Pressures apply only to original equipment tyres, and may vary if any other make or type of tyre is fitted; check with the tyre manufacturer or supplier for correct pressures if necessary.*

Electrical system

Alternator drivebelt tension...	See Section 10 of this Chapter
Wiper blades:	
Front	Champion X-4503
Rear	Champion X-4103

Torque wrench settings

	Nm	lbf ft
Engine sump drain plug..	15	11
Roadwheel bolts	90	67

Lubricants, fluids and capacities

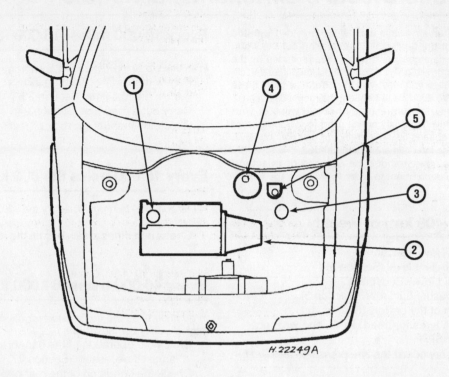

H 22249A

Lubricants and fluids

Component or system	Lubricant type/specification	Duckhams recommendation
1 Engine	Multigrade engine oil, viscosity SAE 10W/30 to 15W/40, to CCMC-PD2, API SG CD, or better	Duckhams Diesel, QS, QXR or Hypergrade Plus
2 Manual gearbox	Tranself TRX 80W	-
3 Power steering fluid reservoir	Elf Renaultmatic D2, Dexron type ATF	Duckhams Uni-Matic
4 Cooling system	Ethylene-glycol based antifreeze	Duckhams Universal Antifreeze and Summer Coolant
5 Brake fluid reservoir	Hydraulic fluid to DOT 3 or 4 or SAE J1703F	Duckhams Universal Brake and Clutch Fluid
Fuel	Commercial diesel fuel for road vehicles (DERV)	-

Capacities

Engine oil:
At oil change .... 5.0 litres
At oil and filter change .... 5.5 litres
Difference between "MAX" and "MIN" dipstick marks .... 2.0 litres
Cooling system .... 6.6 litres
Manual gearbox .... 3.4 litres
Fuel tank .... 43.0 litres

1 Renault Clio Diesel maintenance schedule

The maintenance intervals in this manual are provided with the assumption that you, not the dealer, will be carrying out the work. These are the minimum maintenance intervals recommended by the manufacturer for vehicles driven daily. If you wish to keep your vehicle in peak condition at all times, you may wish to perform some of these procedures more often. We encourage frequent maintenance because it enhances the efficiency, performance and resale value of your vehicle. If the vehicle is driven in dusty areas, used to tow a trailer, or driven frequently at slow speeds (idling in traffic) or on short journeys, more frequent maintenance intervals are recommended.

When the vehicle is new, it should be serviced by a factory-authorised dealer service department in order to preserve the factory warranty.

Every 250 miles (400 km) or weekly

Check the engine oil level (Section 3)
Check the engine coolant level (Section 3)
Check the brake fluid level (Section 3)
Check the screen washer fluid level (Section 3)
Check the condition of the battery (Section 4)
Visually examine the tyres for tread depth, and wear or damage (Section 5)
Check and if necessary adjust the tyre pressures (Section 5)

Every 5000 miles (8000 km)

In addition to all the items listed previously, carry out the following:
Renew the engine oil (Section 6)
Renew the engine oil filter (Section 6)
Drain any water from the fuel filter (Section 7)
Check the power steering fluid level, where applicable (Section 8)
Check all underbonnet components and hoses for fluid leaks (Section 9)
Check the condition of the auxiliary drivebelt, and renew if necessary (Section 10)
Check the operation of the clutch mechanism (Section 11)
Check the operation of the horn, all lights, all instrument and warning lights, the wipers and washers (Section 12)
Check the operation of the heating system (Section 13)
Check the headlight beam alignment (Section 14)
Check the condition of the wiper blades (Section 15)
Check the condition of the front brake pads and renew if necessary (Section 16)
Check the suspension and steering components for condition and security (Section 17)
Check the condition of the driveshafts (Section 18)
Check the bodywork and underframe for damage and corrosion (Section 19)
Check all door mechanisms, central locking, and seat belts (Section 20)
Check the condition of the exhaust system components (Section 21)

Every 10 000 miles (16 000 km)

In addition to all the items listed previously, carry out the following:
Renew the air filter (Section 22)
Renew the fuel filter (Section 23)
Carry out a road test (Section 24)
Check the manual gearbox oil level (Section 25)

Every 15 000 miles (24 000 km)

In addition to all the items listed for the 5000 mile interval, carry out the following:
Check and if necessary adjust the idle speed (Section 26)

Every 40 000 miles (64 000 km)

In addition to all the items listed for the 5000 mile and 10 000 mile intervals, carry out the following:
Check the operation of the handbrake mechanism, and adjust if necessary (Section 27)
Check the condition of the rear brake shoes and renew if necessary (Section 28)
Renew the brake fluid (Section 29)
Check the front wheel alignment, and adjust if necessary (Section 30)

Every 70 000 miles (112 000 km)

In addition to all the items listed previously, carry out the following:
Renew the timing belt (Chapter 2A)

Every 2 years

In addition to all the items listed previously, carry out the following:
Renew the coolant (Section 32)

Note: *Renault do not specify renewal intervals for the antifreeze mixture, as the mixture used to fill the system when the vehicle is new is designed to last the lifetime of the vehicle. However, it is strongly recommended that the coolant is renewed at the intervals specified in the "Maintenance schedule", as a precaution against possible engine corrosion problems. This is particularly advisable if the coolant has been renewed previously, using an antifreeze other than that specified by Renault. With many antifreeze types, the corrosion inhibitors become progressively less effective with age. It is up to the individual owner whither or not to follow this advice.*

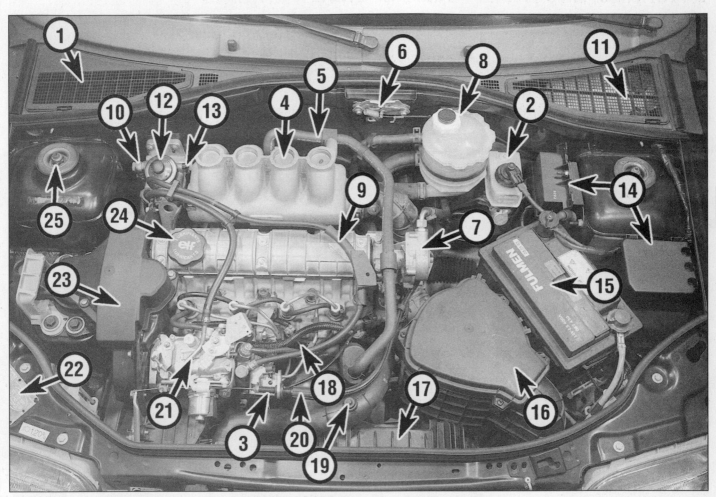

Typical underbonnet view of Renault Clio Diesel

1 Jack location
2 Brake fluid reservoir
3 Accelerator cable
4 Inlet manifold
5 Crankcase ventilation hose
6 Bonnet lock assembly
7 Brake vacuum pump
8 Coolant expansion tank
9 Fuel filter outlet hose
10 Fuel filter inlet union
11 Washer fluid reservoir location
12 Fuel system priming plunger
13 Fuel filter bleed screw

14 Relay box
15 Battery
16 Air cleaner assembly
17 Radiator cowl
18 Engine oil level dipstick
19 Bleed screw on the radiator top hose
20 Oil filter
21 Fuel injection pump
22 VIN plate
23 Right-hand engine mounting cover
24 Engine oil filler cap
25 Suspension strut top mounting

1

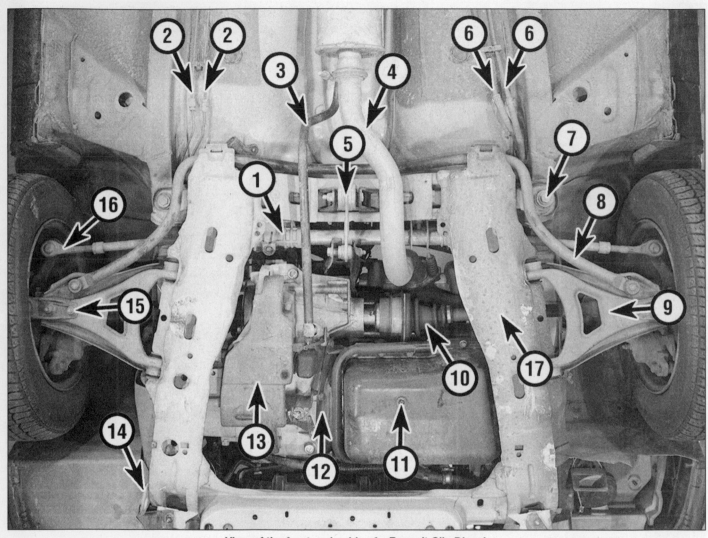

View of the front underside of a Renault Clio Diesel

1   Steering gear
2   Hydraulic brake pipes
3   Gearchange link rod
4   Exhaust downpipe
5   Rear engine mounting link
6   Fuel pipes
7   Subframe mounting bolt
8   Anti-roll bar
9   Front suspension lower arm

10   Right-hand driveshaft
11   Engine oil drain plug
12   Flywheel cover plate/engine-to-gearbox bracing bracket
13   Gearbox bottom cover
14   Front towing eye
15   Front lower arm balljoint
16   Steering track rod end
17   Subframe

View of the rear underside

1   Fuel filler pipe
2   Fuel tank
3   Brake pipes
4   Handbrake cables
5   Exhaust rear silencer
6   Rear axle support bracket

7   Rear axle
8   Shock absorber
9   Spare wheel
10 Trailing arm
11 Anti-roll bar

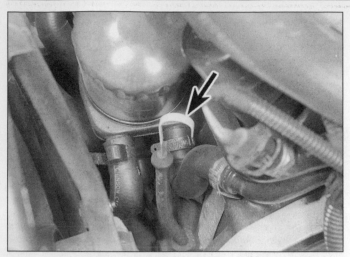

3.1 Engine oil level dipstick (arrowed)

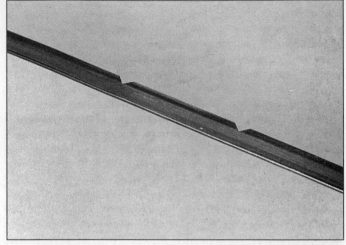

3.3a Engine oil level dipstick "MIN" and "MAX" level notches

2   Introduction

General information

This Chapter is designed to help the home mechanic maintain his/her vehicle for safety, economy, long life and peak performance.

The Chapter contains a master maintenance schedule, followed by Sections dealing specifically with each task on the schedule. Visual checks, adjustments, component renewal and other helpful items are included. Refer to the accompanying illustrations of the engine compartment and the underside of the vehicle for the locations of the various components.

Servicing of your vehicle in accordance with the mileage/time maintenance schedule and the following Sections will provide a planned maintenance program, which should result in a long and reliable service life. This is a comprehensive plan, so maintaining some items but not others at the specified service intervals will not produce the same results.

As you service your vehicle, you will discover that many of the procedures can - and should - be grouped together because of the particular procedure being performed, or because of the close proximity of two otherwise unrelated components to one another. For example, if the vehicle is raised for any reason, the exhaust can be inspected at the same time as the suspension and steering components.

The first step in this maintenance program is to prepare yourself before the actual work begins. Read through all the Sections relevant to the work to be carried out, then make a list and gather together all the parts and tools required. If a problem is encountered, seek advice from a parts specialist, or a dealer service department.

Intensive maintenance

If, from the time the vehicle is new, the routine maintenance schedule is followed closely and frequent checks are made of fluid levels and high wear items, as suggested throughout this manual, the engine will be kept in relatively good running condition and the need for additional work will be minimised.

It is possible that there will be times when the engine is running poorly due to the lack of regular maintenance. This is even more likely if a used vehicle, which has not received regular and frequent maintenance checks, is purchased. In such cases, additional work may need to be carried out, outside of the regular maintenance intervals.

If engine wear is suspected, a compression or leakdown test (Chapter 2A) will provide valuable information regarding the overall performance of the main internal components. Such a test can be used as a basis to decide on the extent of the work to be carried out. If for example a compression or leakdown test indicates serious internal

engine wear, conventional maintenance as described in this Chapter will not greatly improve the performance of the engine, and may prove a waste of time and money, unless extensive overhaul work (Chapter 2B) is carried out first.

The following series of operations are those most often required to improve the performance of a generally poor-running engine.

Clean, inspect and test the battery (Section 4)
Check the levels of all the engine related fluids (Section 3)
Check the condition and tension of the alternator (auxiliary) drivebelt (Section 10)
Check the fuel filter - drain off any water and renew the filter if necessary (Sections 7 and 23)
Check the condition of the air filter, and renew if necessary (Section 22)
Check the condition of all hoses and check for fluid leaks (Section 9)
Check and if necessary adjust the idle speed (Section 26)

3   Fluid level checks (every 250 miles/400 km or weekly)

Engine oil

1   The engine oil level is checked with a dipstick that extends through a tube and into the sump at the bottom of the engine. The dipstick is located towards the front of the engine **(see illustration)**. On models equipped with an oil level gauge, the check can be made by switching on the ignition - the upper and lower limits on the gauge correspond to the upper and lower marks on the dipstick.

2   The oil level should be checked with the vehicle standing on level ground and before it is driven, or at least 5 minutes after the engine has been switched off. If the oil is checked immediately after driving the vehicle, some of the oil will remain in the upper engine components and oil galleries, resulting in an inaccurate reading on the dipstick.

3   Withdraw the dipstick from the tube and wipe all the oil from the end with a clean rag or paper towel. Insert the clean dipstick back into the tube as far as it will go, then withdraw it once more. Check that the oil level is between the upper ("MAX") and lower ("MIN") marks/notches on the dipstick. If the level is towards the lower ("MIN") mark/notch, unscrew the oil filler cap on the valve cover and add fresh oil until the level is on the upper ("MAX") mark/notch **(see illustrations)**. Note that the difference between the minimum and maximum marks/notches on the dipstick corresponds to 2 litres.

4   Always maintain the level between the two dipstick marks/notches. If the level is allowed to fall below the lower mark/notch, oil starvation may result which could lead to severe engine damage. If the engine is overfilled by adding too much oil, this may result in oil leaks or oil seal failures.

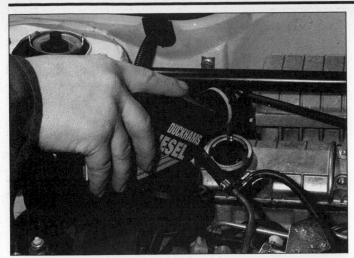

3.3b Oil is added through the filler on the valve cover

5   An oil can spout or funnel may help to reduce spillage when adding oil to the engine. Always use the correct grade and type of oil as shown in *"Lubricants, fluids and capacities"*.

Coolant

Warning: *DO NOT attempt to remove the expansion tank pressure cap when the engine is hot, as there is a very great risk of scalding. Do not allow antifreeze to come in contact with your skin, or with the painted surfaces of the vehicle. Rinse off spills immediately with plenty of water. Never leave antifreeze lying around in an open container, or in a puddle on the floor. Children and pets are attracted by its sweet smell, but antifreeze can be fatal if ingested.*

6   All vehicles covered by this manual are equipped with a pressurised cooling system. An expansion tank is located on the bulkhead in the engine compartment towards the left-hand side. The expansion tank has a continual flow of coolant passing through it in order to purge air from the cooling system.

7   The coolant level in the expansion tank should be checked regularly. The level in the tank varies with the temperature of the engine. When the engine is cold, the coolant level should be up to the maximum ("MAX") level mark on the side of the tank. When the engine is hot, the level will be slightly above the mark.

8   If topping up is necessary, wait until the engine is cold, then slowly unscrew the pressure cap on the expansion tank. Allow any remaining pressure to escape then fully unscrew the cap.

9   Add a mixture of water and antifreeze (see Section 32) through the expansion tank filler neck until the coolant is up to the maximum ("MAX")

level mark **(see illustration)**. Refit and tighten the pressure cap.

10   With a sealed type cooling system, the addition of coolant should only be necessary at very infrequent intervals. If frequent topping up is required, it is likely there is a leak in the system. Check the radiator, all hoses and joint faces for any sign of staining or actual wetness, and rectify as necessary. If no leaks can be found, it is advisable to have the pressure cap and the entire system pressure tested by a dealer or suitably equipped garage as this will often show up a small leak not previously visible.

Brake fluid

Warning: *Hydraulic fluid is poisonous; wash off immediately and thoroughly in the case of skin contact, and seek immediate medical advice if any fluid is swallowed or gets into the eyes. Certain types of hydraulic fluid are inflammable, and may ignite when allowed into contact with hot components; when servicing any hydraulic system, it is safest to assume that the fluid is inflammable, and to take precautions against the risk of fire as though it is petrol that is being handled. Hydraulic fluid is also an effective paint stripper, and will attack plastics; if any is spilt, it should be washed off immediately using copious quantities of fresh water. Finally, it is hygroscopic (it absorbs moisture from the air) - old fluid may be contaminated and unfit for further use. When topping-up or renewing the fluid, always use the recommended type (see "Lubricants, fluids and capacities"), and ensure that it comes from a freshly-opened, previously-sealed container.*

11   The brake master cylinder and fluid reservoir assembly is mounted on the front of the vacuum servo unit in the engine compartment. The "MAX" and "MIN" level marks are indicated on the side of the reservoir, and the fluid level should be maintained between these marks at all times **(see illustration)**. Note that on some models the "MIN" mark is formed by the ridge on the reservoir body.

12   The fluid level in the master cylinder reservoir will drop **slowly** as the brake shoes and/or pads (as applicable) wear down during normal operation. Provided the level stays above the "MIN" mark, there is no need to top-up to compensate for this fall. If the reservoir requires repeated topping-up to maintain the proper level, or if a sudden fall in level occurs, this is an indication of an hydraulic leak somewhere in the system, which should be investigated immediately.

13   If topping-up is necessary, wipe the area around the filler cap with a clean rag, and disconnect the wiring connector from the fluid level switch. Unscrew the cap and remove it from the reservoir, taking care not to damage the sender unit - also take care not to allow brake fluid to drip onto the vehicle paintwork. When adding fluid, pour it carefully into the reservoir to avoid spilling it on surrounding painted surfaces **(see illustration)**. Be sure to use only the specified brake hydraulic fluid, since mixing different types of fluid can cause damage to the system. See *"Lubricants, fluids and capacities"* at the beginning of this Chapter. **Warning:** *Brake hydraulic fluid can harm your eyes and damage painted surfaces, so use extreme caution when handling and*

1

3.9 Use antifreeze, or a mixture of antifreeze and water, for topping-up the cooling system

3.11 Check that the brake fluid in the master cylinder reservoir is between the MAX and MIN level marks (arrows)

3.13 Topping up the brake fluid reservoir

3.17 Topping up the windscreen washer fluid reservoir

5.3 Checking the tyre tread depth with an indicator gauge

pouring it. Do not use fluid that has been standing open for some time, as it absorbs moisture from the air. Excess moisture can cause a dangerous loss of braking effectiveness.

14   When adding fluid, it is a good idea to inspect the reservoir for contamination. The system should be drained and refilled if deposits, dirt particles or contamination are seen in the fluid.

15   After filling the reservoir to the proper level, make sure that the cap is refitted securely, to avoid leaks and the entry of foreign matter, and reconnect the fluid level wiring connector.

Washer fluid

16   The washer fluid reservoir is located under the left-hand access hatch in the windscreen cowl panel. For access to the reservoir, open the bonnet and lift the hatch.

17   Check, and if necessary top-up, the washer fluid level in the reservoir **(see illustration)**.

18   **Never** use engine antifreeze in the washer fluid, as it can damage the car paintwork.

4   Battery check (every 250 miles/400 km or weekly)

Warning: *Before carrying out any work on the vehicle battery, read through the precautions given in Safety first! at the beginning of this manual.*

1   The battery is located at the front left-hand corner of the engine compartment.

2   The exterior of the battery should be inspected for damage such as a cracked case or cover.

3   Check the tightness of the battery cable clamp nuts to ensure good electrical connections, and check the entire length of each cable for cracks and frayed conductors.

4   If corrosion (visible as white, fluffy deposits) is evident, remove the cables from the battery terminals, clean them with a small wire brush, then refit them. Corrosion can be kept to a minimum by applying a thin layer of petroleum jelly to the clamps and terminals after they have been reconnected.

5   Make sure that the battery tray is in good condition, and that the retaining clamp is tight.

6   Corrosion on the tray, retaining clamp and the battery itself can be removed with a solution of water and baking soda. Thoroughly rinse all cleaned areas with plain water. Dry the battery and its surroundings with rags or tissues, which should then be discarded.

7   Any metal parts damaged by corrosion should be covered with a zinc-based primer, then painted.

8   Most models are fitted with a "maintenance-free" battery which does not require topping-up. If this is the case, the battery will be sealed, and it will not be possible to remove the cell covers.

9   On models fitted with a low-maintenance or a conventional battery, the electrolyte level should be checked periodically as follows.

10   Pull out the cell covers from the top of the battery.

11   Check that the level of electrolyte is approximately 15 mm above the tops of the cell plates.

12   If necessary top-up the level, using only distilled or demineralised water.

13   Refit the cell covers.

14   Further information on the battery, charging and jump-starting can be found in Chapter 5 and in the preliminary Sections of this manual.

5   Tyre and wheel checks (every 250 miles/400 km or weekly)

1   Periodically remove the wheels, and clean any dirt or mud from the inside and outside surfaces. Examine the wheel rims for signs of rusting, corrosion or other damage. Light alloy wheels are easily damaged by "kerbing" whilst parking, and similarly steel wheels may become dented or buckled. Renewal of the wheel is very often the only course of remedial action possible.

2   To check that the roadwheel bolts are securely fastened, remove the wheel cover (where fitted), then slacken each bolt in turn through one-quarter of a turn and tighten it to the specified torque wrench setting. Refit the trim, where applicable.

3   The tyres originally fitted are equipped with tread wear indicators which will appear flush with the surface of the tread, thus producing the effect of a continuous band of rubber across the width of the tyre, when the tread depth is reduced to approximately 1.6 mm. **At this point, the tyre must be renewed immediately**. Tread wear can be monitored with an inexpensive device known as a tread depth indicator gauge **(see illustration)**.

4   Note any abnormal tread wear **(see illustration)**. Tread pattern irregularities such as feathering, flat spots and more wear on one side than the other are indications of front wheel alignment and/or balance problems. If any of these conditions are noted, they should be rectified as soon as possible.

5   General tyre wear is influenced to a large degree by driving style - harsh braking and acceleration or fast cornering will all produce more rapid tyre wear. Interchanging of tyres may result in more even wear, but it is worth bearing in mind that if this is completely effective, the added expense is incurred of replacing a complete set of tyres simulta-neously, which may prove financially-restrictive for many owners.

6   Front tyres may wear unevenly as a result of wheel misalignment. The front wheels should always be correctly aligned according to the settings specified. Refer to Chapter 10 for further information.

Condition	Probable cause	Corrective action	Condition	Probable cause	Corrective action
Shoulder wear	• Underinflation (wear on both sides) • Incorrect wheel camber (wear on one side) • Hard cornering	• Check and adjust pressure • Repair or renew suspension parts • Reduce speed	**Feathered edge** **Toe wear**	• Incorrect toe setting	• Adjust front wheel alignment
Centre wear	• Overinflation	• Measure and adjust pressure	**Uneven wear**	• Incorrect camber or castor • Malfunctioning suspension • Unbalanced wheel • Out-of-round brake disc/drum	• Repair or renew suspension parts • Repair or renew suspension parts • Balance tyres • Machine or renew disc/drum

5.4 Tyre wear patterns and causes

1

7   Regularly check the tyres for damage in the form of cuts or bulges, especially in the sidewalls. Remove any nails or stones embedded in the tread before they penetrate the tyre to cause deflation. If removal of a nail does reveal that the tyre has been punctured, refit the nail so that its point of penetration is marked, then immediately change the wheel and have the tyre repaired by a tyre dealer. **Do not** drive on a tyre in such a condition. If in any doubt as to the possible consequences of any damage found, consult your local tyre dealer for advice.

8   Ensure that tyre pressures are checked regularly and maintained correctly **(see illustration)**. Checking should be carried out with the tyres cold, and **not** immediately after the car has been in use. If the pressures are checked with the tyres hot, an apparently-high reading will be obtained, owing to heat expansion. **Under no circumstances** should an attempt be made to reduce the pressures to the quoted cold reading in this instance, or effective under-inflation will result.

9   Under-inflation will cause overheating of the tyre owing to excessive flexing of the casing, and the tread will not sit correctly on the road surface. This will cause a consequent loss of adhesion and excessive wear, not to mention the danger of sudden tyre failure due to heat build-up.

10   Over-inflation will cause rapid wear of the centre part of the tyre tread, coupled with reduced adhesion, harsher ride, and the danger of shock damage occurring in the tyre casing.

11   The balance of each wheel and tyre assembly should be maintained to avoid excessive wear, not only to the tyres but also to the steering and suspension components. Wheel imbalance is normally indicated by vibration through the car's bodyshell, although in many cases it is particularly noticeable through the steering wheel at certain speeds. Conversely, it should be noted that wear or damage in suspension or steering components may cause excessive tyre wear. Out-of-round or out-of-true tyres, damaged wheels and wheel bearing wear also fall into this category. Balancing will not usually cure vibration caused by such wear.

12   Wheel balancing may be carried out with the wheel either on or off the car. If balanced on the car, ensure that the wheel-to-hub relationship is marked in some way prior to subsequent wheel removal

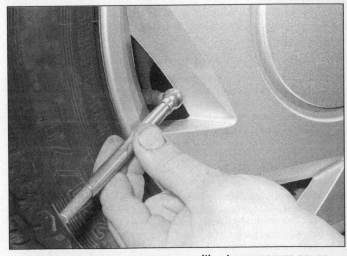

5.8 Checking the tyre pressures with a tyre pressure gauge

so that it may be refitted in its original position.

13   Legal restrictions apply to many aspects of tyre fitting and usage, and in the UK this information is contained in the Motor Vehicle Construction and Use Regulations. It is suggested that a copy of these regulations is obtained from your local police if in doubt as to current legal requirements with regard to tyre type and condition, minimum tread depth, etc.

6   Engine oil and filter renewal (every 5000 miles/8000 km)

1   Frequent oil and filter changes are the most important preventative maintenance procedures that can be undertaken by the DIY owner. As engine oil ages, it becomes diluted and contaminated, which leads to premature engine wear.

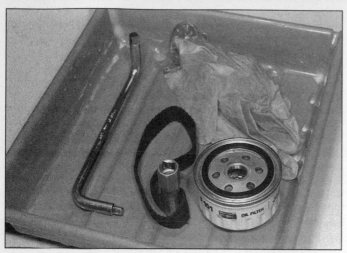

6.2 Tools and materials necessary for engine oil change and filter renewal

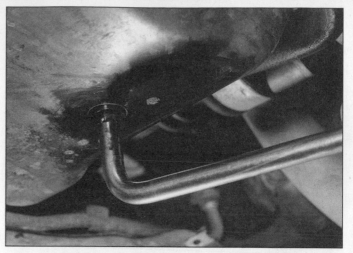

6.3 Using the special drain plug key to unscrew the sump drain plug

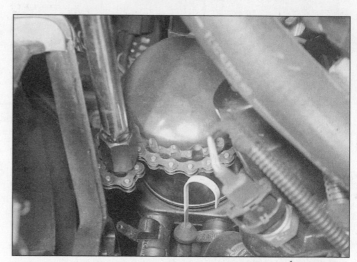

6.7 Slackening the oil filter with a removal tool

2   Before starting this procedure, gather together all the necessary tools and materials **(see illustration)**. Also make sure that you have plenty of clean rags and newspapers handy to mop up any spills. Ideally, the engine oil should be warm, as it will drain better and more built-up sludge will be removed with it. Take care, however, not to touch the exhaust or any other hot parts of the engine when working under the vehicle. To avoid any possibility of scalding, and to protect yourself from possible skin irritants and other harmful contaminants in used engine oils, it is advisable to wear rubber gloves when carrying out this work. Access to the underside of the vehicle will be greatly improved if it can be raised on a lift, driven onto ramps or jacked up and supported on axle stands. Whichever method is chosen, make sure that the car remains as level as possible, to enable the oil to drain fully.

3   Remove the oil filler cap from the valve cover, then position a suitable container beneath the sump. Clean the drain plug and the area around it, then slacken it half a turn using a special drain plug key (8mm square) **(see illustration)**. If possible, try to keep the plug pressed into the sump while unscrewing it by hand the last couple of turns. As the plug releases from the threads, move it away sharply so the stream of oil issuing from the sump runs into the container, not up your sleeve!

4   Allow some time for the old oil to drain, noting that it may be necessary to reposition the container as the oil flow slows to a trickle.

5   After all the oil has drained, wipe off the drain plug with a clean rag and renew its sealing washer. Clean the area around the drain plug opening, then refit and tighten the plug to the specified torque setting.

6   Move the container into position under the oil filter, located on the front of the cylinder block.

7   Using an oil filter removal tool, slacken the filter initially **(see illustration)**. Loosely wrap some rags around the oil filter, then unscrew it and immediately position it with its open end uppermost to prevent further spillage of oil. Remove the oil filter from the engine compartment and empty the oil into the container.

8   Use a clean rag to remove all oil, dirt and sludge from the filter sealing area on the engine. Check the old filter to make sure that the rubber sealing ring hasn't stuck to the engine. If it has, carefully remove it.

9   Apply a light coating of clean oil to the sealing ring on the new filter, then screw it into position on the engine **(see illustration)**. Tighten the filter firmly by hand only - do not use any tools. Wipe clean the exterior of the oil filter.

10   Remove the old oil and all tools from under the car, then (if applicable) lower the car to the ground.

11   Fill the engine with the specified quantity and grade of oil, as described earlier in this Section. Pour the oil in slowly, otherwise it may overflow from the top of the valve cover. Check that the oil level is up to the maximum mark on the dipstick, then refit and tighten the oil filler cap.

12   Note that when the engine is first started, there will be a delay of a few seconds before the oil pressure warning light goes out while the new filter fills with oil. Do not race the engine while the warning light is on.

13   Run the engine for a few minutes, and check that there are no leaks around the oil filter seal and the sump drain plug.

14   Switch off the engine and wait a few minutes for the oil to settle in the sump once more. With the new oil circulated and the filter now completely full, recheck the level on the dipstick and add more oil if necessary.

15   Dispose of the used engine oil safely with reference to *"General repair procedures"* in the preliminary Sections of this manual.

7   Fuel filter water draining (every 5000 miles/8000 km)

1   A water drain plug is provided at the base of the fuel filter housing. Better access to the base of the filter may be gained by raising the front of the vehicle and supporting it on axle stands, then reaching up from beneath the vehicle.

2   Place a suitable container beneath the plug. To make draining easier, a suitable length of tubing can be attached to the outlet on the plug to direct the fuel flow.

6.9 Screw the new filter into position by hand

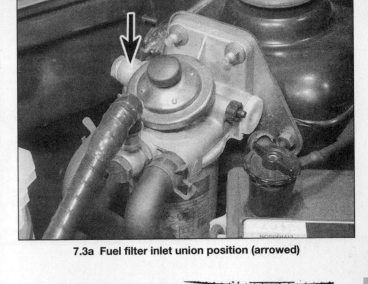

7.3a Fuel filter inlet union position (arrowed)

1

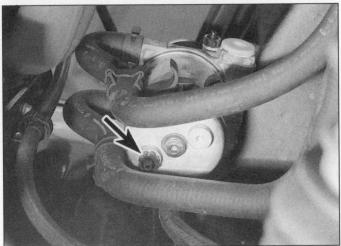

7.3b Showing the fuel filter drain plug (arrowed)

3   Slacken the fuel inlet union on the filter head, then open the drain plug by turning it anti-clockwise (see illustrations).
4   Allow the entire contents of the filter (or filters) to drain into the container, then tighten the fuel inlet union and drain plug.
5   Dispose of the drained fuel safely.
6   Prime and bleed the fuel system as described in Chapter 4.
7   As applicable, lower the vehicle to the ground.

8   Power steering fluid level check (every 5000 miles/ 8000 km)

1   The power steering fluid reservoir is located behind the battery on the left-hand side of the engine compartment (see illustration).
2   For the check, the front wheels should be pointing straight-ahead and the engine should be stopped and cold. The car should be positioned on level ground.
3   The marking on the side of the reservoir indicates the "MIN" and "MAX" levels.
4   Before removing the filler cap use a clean rag to wipe the cap and the surrounding area to prevent any foreign matter from entering the reservoir. Unscrew and remove the filler cap.
5   Top up if necessary with the specified grade of automatic transmission fluid. Be careful not to introduce dirt into the system, and do not overfill. Frequent topping up indicates a leak which should be investigated.

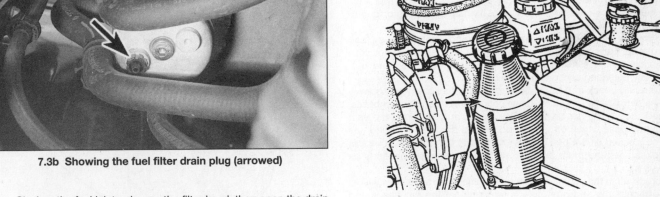

8.1 Typical location of power steering fluid reservoir (arrowed)

9   Hose and fluid leak check (every 5000 miles/8000 km)

1   Visually inspect the engine joint faces, gaskets and seals for any signs of water or oil leaks. Pay particular attention to the areas around the valve cover, cylinder head, oil filter and sump joint faces. Bear in mind that over a period of time some very slight seepage from these areas is to be expected but what you are really looking for is any indication of a serious leak. Should a leak be found, renew the offending gasket or oil seal by referring to the appropriate Chapter(s) in this manual.
2   Also check the security and condition of all the engine related pipes and hoses. Ensure that all cable ties or securing clips are in place and in good condition. Clips which are broken or missing can lead to chafing of the hoses pipes or wiring which could cause more serious problems in the future.
3   Carefully check the radiator and heater hoses along their entire length. Renew any hose which is cracked, swollen or deteriorated. Cracks will show up better if the hose is squeezed. Pay close attention to the hose clips that secure the hoses to the cooling system components. Hose clips can pinch and puncture hoses, resulting in cooling system leaks. If wire type hose clips are used, it may be a good idea to replace them with screw-type clips.

9.5 Pay particular attention to the condition of the rubber hose (arrowed) which joins the fuel filler neck to the fuel tank

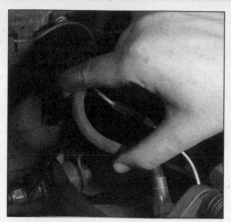

9.6 Checking the condition of a flexible brake hose

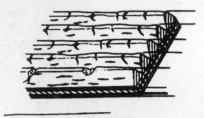

10.5 Checking for drivebelt wear - multi-ribbed type shown

4   Inspect all the cooling system components (hoses, joint faces etc.) for leaks. A leak in the cooling system will usually show up as white or rust coloured deposits on the area adjoining the leak. Where any problems of this nature are found on system components, renew the component or gasket with reference to Chapter 3.

5   With the vehicle raised, inspect the fuel tank and filler neck for punctures, cracks and other damage. The connection between the filler neck and tank is especially critical. Sometimes a rubber filler neck or connecting hose will leak due to loose retaining clamps or deteriorated rubber **(see illustration)**.

6   Similarly, inspect all brake hoses and metal pipes **(see illustration)**. If any damage or deterioration is discovered, do not drive the vehicle until the necessary repair work has been carried out. Renew any damaged sections of hose or pipe.

7   Carefully check all rubber hoses and metal fuel lines leading away from the petrol tank. Check for loose connections, deteriorated hoses, crimped lines and other damage. Pay particular attention to the vent pipes and hoses which often loop up around the filler neck and can become blocked or crimped. Follow the lines to the front of the vehicle carefully inspecting them all the way. Renew damaged sections as necessary.

8   From within the engine compartment, check the security of all fuel hose attachments and pipe unions, and inspect the fuel hoses and vacuum hoses for kinks, chafing and deterioration.

9   Where applicable, check the condition of the power steering fluid hoses and pipes.

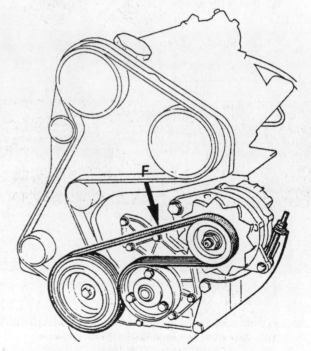

10.6 Auxiliary drivebelt tension checking point (F)

Deflection under a force of 30 N = 2.5 to 3.5 mm cold, or 3.5 to 4.5 mm hot

10   Auxiliary drivebelt checking and renewal (every 5000 miles/8000 km)

Checking

1   The auxiliary drivebelt is located on the front right-hand side of the engine.

2   Due to their function and material makeup, drivebelts are prone to failure after a period of time and should therefore be inspected, and if necessary adjusted periodically.

3   Since the drivebelt is located very close to the right-hand side of the engine compartment, it is possible to gain better access by raising the front of the vehicle and removing the right-hand wheel.

4   Remove the splash shield from inside the wheelarch.

5   With the engine switched off, inspect the full length of the drivebelt for cracks and separation of the belt plies **(see illustration)**. It will be necessary to turn the crankshaft (using a socket or spanner on the crankshaft pulley bolt) in order to move the belt from the pulleys so that the full length of the belt can be inspected thoroughly. Twist the belt between the pulleys so that both sides can be viewed. Also check

for fraying, and glazing which gives the belt a shiny appearance. Check the pulleys for nicks, cracks, distortion and corrosion.

Tensioning

6   The tension of the belt is checked by pushing midway between the pulleys at the point indicated **(see illustration)**. Renault technicians use a special spring-tensioned tool which applies a force of 30 N to the belt and then measures the deflection. An alternative arrangement can be made by using a straight-edge, steel rule and spring balance. Hold the straight-edge across the two pulleys, then position the steel rule on the belt, apply the force with the spring balance, and measure the deflection.

7   If adjustment is necessary, loosen the alternator pivot bolt first, then loosen the locknut and adjustment bolt (as applicable). Alternatively, on models equipped with a separate belt tensioner/adjuster mechanism, loosen the tensioner bolt(s) and move or turn the tensioner (as applicable) to set the tension in the belt.

8   To apply tension to the belt, on models without a separate belt

the cable is routed correctly, with no sharp turns.
2   Inspect the ends of the clutch inner cable, both at the gearbox end and inside the vehicle, for signs of wear and fraying.

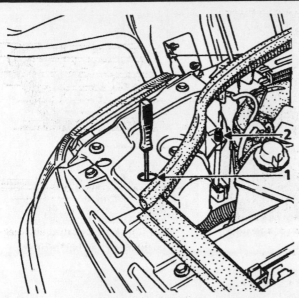

14.1 Headlight beam adjustment screws

1   *Vertical adjustment screw*
2   *Horizontal adjustment screw*

15.3 Releasing the securing catch to remove a windscreen wiper blade

tensioner/adjuster mechanism, insert a lever between the pulley end of the alternator (as applicable), and move the relevant component to tension the belt. Tighten the adjustment bolt and the pivot bolt.
9   To apply tension to the belt, on models with a separate belt tensioner/adjuster mechanism, turn or reposition the tensioner (as applicable) to achieve the correct belt tension. Where applicable, tighten the tensioner locknut on completion.
10   Run the engine for about 5 minutes, then recheck the tension.

Removal and refitting

11   To remove a belt, slacken the belt tension fully as described previously. Slip the belt off the pulleys, then fit the new belt ensuring that it is routed correctly.
12   With the belt in position, adjust the tension as previously described.

11 Clutch mechanism check (every 5000 miles/8000 km)

1   Check that the clutch pedal moves smoothly and easily through its full travel, and that the clutch itself functions correctly, with no trace of slip or drag. If the movement is uneven or stiff in places, check that

12 Electrical system check (every 5000 miles/8000 km)

1   Check the operation of all the electrical equipment, ie lights, direction indicators, horn, fuel gauge, coolant temperature gauge, warning lights, engine oil level indicator (where fitted) etc. Refer to the appropriate Sections of Chapters 5 and 12 for details if any of the circuits are found to be inoperative.
2   Note that stop light switch adjustment is described in Chapter 9.
3   Visually check all accessible wiring connectors, harnesses and retaining clips for security and for signs of chafing or damage. Rectify any faults found.

13 Heating system check (every 5000 miles/8000 km)

Check that the heating system operates correctly. See Chapter 3. Operate all of the control knobs and check that ventilation and heating air direction is functioning correctly. Make sure that the heater blower operates correctly.

14 Headlight beam alignment check (every 5000 miles/ 8000 km)

1   Accurate adjustment of the headlight beam is only possible using optical beam setting equipment, and this work should therefore be carried out by a Renault dealer or service station with the necessary facilities. For reference, the location of the beam adjusting screws are as shown **(see illustration)**.
2   On all models it is possible to adjust the headlight beam to compensate for the load being carried. An adjustment knob is located on the rear of each headlight on some models, whereas on other models a four-position knob is located on the facia panel inside the car (which operates an electric motor to adjust the headlights). In the latter case, position 0 should be selected for an unladen vehicle, and position 4 should be selected for maximum load. On models with electrically-adjustable headlights, a screw is provided for manual adjustment on the rear of the motor.

15 Wiper blade check (every 5000 miles/8000 km)

1   The wiper blades should be renewed if their cleaning action has deteriorated, or if they are cracked, or if they no longer clean the glass effectively.
2   Lift the wiper arm away from the glass. Note that the tailgate wiper arm can only be lifted a limited distance.
3   To remove a windscreen wiper arm, depress the catch, then turn the blade through 90° and withdraw the blade from the end of the arm **(see illustration)**.
4   To remove a tailgate wiper blade, lift the catch, then push the blade from the arm.
5   Insert the new blade into the arm, making sure that it locates securely.

16 Front brake disc pad check (every 5000 miles/8000 km)

Warning: *The dust created by wear of the pads may contain asbestos, which is a health hazard. Never blow it out with compressed air and don't inhale any of it. An approved filtering mask should be worn when working on the brakes. DO NOT use petroleum based solvents to clean brake parts. Use brake cleaner or methylated spirit only.*
1   Firmly apply the handbrake, then jack up the front of the vehicle and support it securely on axle stands. Remove the front roadwheels.

1

16.2 Brake pad thickness viewing aperture on the caliper

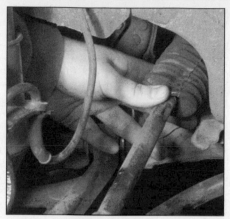

17.2 Checking the condition of a steering gear rubber gaiter

17.4 Checking for wear in the front suspension and hub bearings

2   For a quick check, the thickness of friction material remaining on each brake pad can be measured through the aperture in the caliper body **(see illustration)**. If any pad's friction material is worn to the specified thickness or less, all four pads must be renewed as a set. (Pad wear warning contacts are fitted to the inboard pads, but this should not be used as an excuse for omitting a visual check.)

3   For a comprehensive check, the brake pads should be removed and cleaned. This will allow the operation of the caliper to be checked, and the brake disc itself to be fully examined for condition on both sides. Refer to Chapter 9 for further information.

17 Suspension and steering check (every 5000 miles/ 8000 km)

Front suspension and steering check

1   Raise the front of the car and support it securely on axle stands.

2   Visually inspect the balljoint dust covers and the steering gear rubber gaiters for splits, chafing or deterioration **(see illustration)**. Any wear of these components will cause loss of lubricant, together with dirt and water entry, resulting in rapid deterioration of the balljoints or steering gear.

3   On cars with power steering, check the fluid hoses for chafing or deterioration, and the pipe and hose unions for fluid leakage. Also check for signs of fluid leakage under pressure from the steering gear rubber gaiters, which would indicate failed fluid seals within the steering gear.

4   Grasp the roadwheel at the 12 o'clock and 6 o'clock positions, and try to rock it **(see illustration)**. Very slight free play may be felt, but if the movement is appreciable, further investigation is necessary to determine the source. Continue rocking the wheel while an assistant depresses the brake pedal. If the movement is now eliminated or significantly reduced, it is likely that the hub bearings are at fault. If the free play is still evident with the brake pedal depressed, then there is wear in the suspension joints or mountings.

5   Now grasp the roadwheel at the 9 o'clock and 3 o'clock positions, and try to rock it as before. Any movement felt now may again be caused by wear in the hub bearings, or in the track rod balljoints. If a balljoint is worn, the visual movement will be obvious. If the inner joint is suspect, it can be felt by placing a hand over the steering gear rubber gaiter and gripping the track rod. If the wheel is now rocked, movement will be felt at the inner joint if wear has taken place.

6   Using a large screwdriver or flat bar, check for wear in the suspension mounting bushes by levering between the relevant suspension component and its attachment point. Some movement is to be expected, as the mountings are made of rubber, but excessive wear should be obvious. Also check the condition of any visible rubber bushes, looking for splits, cracks or contamination of the rubber.

7   With the car standing on its wheels, have an assistant turn the steering wheel back and forth about an eighth of a turn each way.

18.1 Checking the condition of a driveshaft outer constant velocity (CV) joint rubber gaiter

There should be very little, if any, lost movement between the steering wheel and the roadwheels. If this is not the case, closely observe the joints and mountings previously described, but in addition check for wear of the steering column universal joint and the steering gear itself.

Rear suspension check

8   Chock the front wheels, then jack up the rear of the car and support it securely on axle stands.

9   Working as described previously for the front suspension, check the rear hub bearings, the suspension bushes and the shock absorber mountings for wear.

18 Driveshaft check (every 5000 miles/8000 km)

1   With the car raised and securely supported on axle stands, turn the steering onto full-lock, then slowly rotate the roadwheel. Inspect the condition of the outer constant velocity (CV) joint rubber gaiters while squeezing the gaiters to open out the folds **(see illustration)**. Check for signs of cracking, splits or deterioration of the rubber, which may allow the grease to escape and lead to the entry of water and grit into the joint. Also check the security and condition of the retaining clips/fasteners. Repeat these checks on the inner CV joints. If any damage or deterioration is found, the gaiters should be renewed as described in Chapter 8.

2   At the same time, check the general condition of the CV joints themselves by first holding the driveshaft and attempting to rotate the roadwheel. Repeat this check by holding the inner joint and attempting to rotate the driveshaft. Any appreciable movement indicates wear in the joints, in the driveshaft splines, or a loose driveshaft nut.

22.1 Remove the air cleaner cover

22.2 Removing the air cleaner element

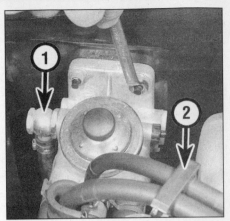

23.3a Removing the fuel filter mounting nuts. Note the fuel inlet union (1) and hose retaining clip (2)

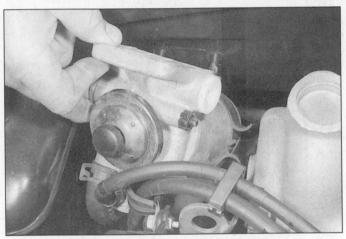

23.3b Remove the fuel filter assembly

19 Bodywork and underframe check (every 5000 miles/8000 km)

1   With the car raised and supported on axle stands or over an inspection pit, thoroughly inspect the underbody and wheelarches for signs of damage and corrosion. In particular examine the bottom of the side sills and concealed areas where mud can collect. Where corrosion and rust is evident, press firmly on the panel by hand and check for possible repairs. If the panel is not seriously corroded, clean away the rust and apply a new coating of underseal. Refer to Chapter 11 for more details of body repairs.
2   Check all external body panels for damage and rectify where necessary.

20 Door mechanism, central locking and seat belt check (every 5000 miles/8000 km)

1   Check that all doors operate correctly and close securely. Operate the central locking system and check that all doors lock.
2   Check all seat belts for condition and security

21 Exhaust system check (every 5000 miles/8000 km)

1   With the engine cold (at least an hour after the vehicle has been driven), check the complete exhaust system from the engine to the end of the tailpipe. Ideally the inspection should be carried out with the vehicle on a hoist to permit unrestricted access, but if a hoist is not available raise and support the vehicle safely on axle stands.
2   Check the exhaust pipes and connections for evidence of leaks, severe corrosion and damage. Make sure that all brackets and mountings are in good condition and tight. Leakage at any of the joints or in other parts of the system will usually show up as a black sooty stain in the vicinity of the leak.
3   Rattles and other noises can often be traced to the exhaust system, especially the brackets and mountings. Try to move the pipes and silencers. If the components can come into contact with the body or suspension parts, secure the system with new mountings or if possible, separate the joints and twist the pipes as necessary to provide additional clearance.
4   Run the engine at idling speed then temporarily place a cloth rag over the rear end of the exhaust pipe and listen for any escape of exhaust gases that would indicate a leak.
5   On completion lower the car to the ground.

22 Air filter renewal (every 10 000 miles/16 000 km)

1   Remove the securing screws from around the edge of the air cleaner cover and remove the cover (see illustration).
2   Lift the filter element from the air cleaner casing (see illustration).
3   Clean the inside of the air cleaner casing and the cover, and fit a new filter element.
4   Refit the cover using a reversal of the removal procedure.

23 Fuel filter renewal (every 10 000 miles/16 000 km)

Note: Certain models are fitted with a dual-element filter assembly. On these models, only the inlet (fuel tank side) filter should be renewed at the normal (10 000 mile/16 000 km) specified interval. The outlet (injection pump) side filter should be renewed at every third inlet filter change.

1   Drain the filter bowl, as described in Section 7 of this Chapter.
2   Position a suitable container on the engine to accept the fuel filter assembly when it is removed.
3   Unscrew the mounting nuts and move the fuel filter assembly away from the bulkhead (see illustrations).
4   Place some cloth rags beneath the inlet union on the side of the fuel filter housing then unscrew the union bolt and disconnect the inlet hose. Recover the sealing washers.
5   Tape over the end fitting of the inlet hose to prevent entry of dust and dirt.
6   Release the outlet hose from the retaining clip.

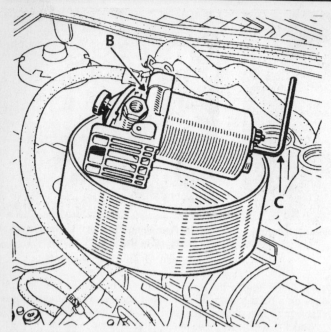

23.7 Fuel filter assembly located in the container on the engine

B *Fuel outlet*	C *Allen key*

7 Release the coolant hoses from the bulkhead and from the clips on the fuel filter chamber, then position the assembly in the container on the engine. The fuel outlet should be uppermost **(see illustration)**.

8 Using an Allen key, unscrew the through-bolt from the bottom of the fuel chamber and withdraw the chamber.

9 Recover the seals noting their locations.

10 Clean out the filter bowl.

11 Fit a new element and new seals (supplied with the filter) to the bowl, making sure that the seals are correctly located.

12 Fit the element and the bowl to the filter head, with the drain plug positioned on the engine side of the bowl. Tighten the through-bolt using the Allen key.

13 Refit the fuel filter assembly making sure that the coolant hoses are correct located. Tighten the mounting nuts.

14 Locate the outlet hose in its retaining clip.

15 Remove the tape, then reconnect the inlet hose together with new sealing washers. Tighten the union bolt.

16 Prime and bleed the fuel system as described in Chapter 4.

24 Road test (every 10 000 miles/16 000 km)

Instruments and electrical equipment

1 Check the operation of all instruments and electrical equipment.

2 Make sure that all instruments read correctly, and switch on all electrical equipment in turn to check that it functions properly.

Steering and suspension

3 Check for any abnormalities in the steering, suspension, handling or road feel

4 Drive the vehicle and check that there are no unusual vibrations or noises.

5 Check that the steering feels positive, with no excessive "sloppiness", or roughness, and check for any suspension noises when cornering and driving over bumps.

Drivetrain

6 Check the performance of the engine, clutch, gearbox and driveshafts.

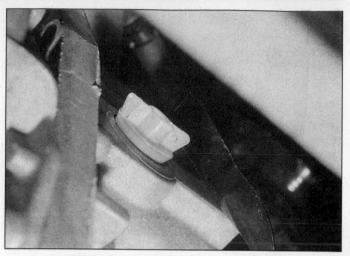

25.2 Filler plug on the front of the gearbox

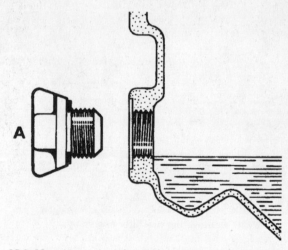

25.3 Manual gearbox filler/level plug - correct oil level shown

7 Listen for any unusual noises from the engine, clutch and gearbox.

8 Make sure that the engine runs smoothly when idling, and that there is no hesitation when accelerating.

9 Check that the clutch action is smooth and progressive, that the drive is taken up smoothly, and that the pedal travel is not excessive. Also listen for any noises when the clutch pedal is depressed.

10 Check that all gears can be engaged smoothly without noise and that the gear lever action is not abnormally vague or "notchy".

11 Listen for a metallic clicking sound from the front of the vehicle as the vehicle is driven slowly in a circle with the steering on full lock. Carry out this check in both directions. If a clicking noise is heard, this indicates wear in a driveshaft joint, in which case renew the joint if necessary.

Check the operation and performance of the braking system

12 Make sure that the vehicle does not pull to one side when braking, and that the wheels do not lock prematurely when braking hard.

13 Check that there is no vibration through the steering when braking.

14 Check that the handbrake operates correctly without excessive movement of the lever, and that it holds the vehicle stationary on a slope.

25.4 Topping up the manual gearbox oil level

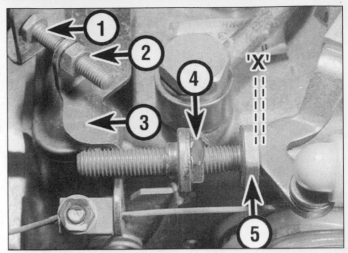

26.4 Idle speed and anti-stall speed adjustment points - Roto-Diesel/Lucas injection pump

1   Idle speed adjustment screw
2   Locknut
3   Fast idle lever
4   Locknut
5   Anti-stall speed adjustment screw
X = Clearance between accelerator lever and anti-stall speed adjustment screw (see Specifications)

26.7 Idle speed adjustment screw (1) and anti-stall speed adjustment screw (2) - Bosch injection pump

15   Test the operation of the brake servo unit as follows. Depress the footbrake four or five times to exhaust the vacuum, then start the engine. As the engine starts there should be a noticeable "give" in the brake pedal as vacuum builds up. Allow the engine to run for at least two minutes and then switch it off. If the brake pedal is now depressed again, it should be possible to detect a hiss from the servo as the pedal is depressed. After about four or five applications, no further hissing should be heard and the pedal should feel considerably harder.

25   Manual gearbox oil level check (every 10 000 miles/16 000 km)

1   Position the car over an inspection pit, on car ramps, or jack it up, but make sure that it is level.
2   Unscrew the filler/level plug from the front-facing side of the gearbox (see illustration).
3   The oil level should be up to the lower edge of the filler hole. Insert a finger to check the level (see illustration).
4   Where necessary top up the level using the correct grade of oil, then refit and tighten the filler plug (see illustration).
5   If the gearbox requires frequent topping up, check it for leakage, especially around the driveshaft oil seals, and repair as necessary.
6   Lower the car to the ground.

26   Idle speed and anti-stall speed checking and adjustment (every 15 000 miles/24 000 km)

1   The usual type of tachometer (rev counter), which works from ignition system pulses, cannot be used on diesel engines. A diagnostic socket is provided for the use of Renault test equipment, but this will not normally be available to the home mechanic. If it is not felt that adjusting the idle speed "by ear" is satisfactory, one of the following alternatives may be used.

a)   Purchase or hire of an appropriate tachometer.
b)   Delegation of the job to a Renault dealer or other specialist.
c)   Timing light (strobe) operated by a petrol engine running at the desired speed. If the timing light is pointed at a mark on the camshaft or injection pump sprocket, the mark will appear stationary when the two engines are running at the same speed (or multiples of that speed). The sprocket will be rotating at half the crankshaft speed but this will not affect the adjustment. (In practice it was found impossible to use this method on the crankshaft pulley due to the acute viewing angle.)

2   Before making adjustments warm up the engine to normal operating temperature. Make sure that the accelerator cable is correctly adjusted (see Chapter 4).

Idle speed checking and adjustment

3   Warm the engine up to normal operating temperature, so that the accelerator lever is resting against the idle stop, check that the engine idles at the specified speed. If necessary adjust as follows.

Roto-Diesel/Lucas injection pump

4   Loosen the locknut on the idle speed adjustment screw. Turn the screw as required and retighten the locknut (see illustration).
5   Check the anti-stall adjustment as described later in this Section.
6   Stop the engine and disconnect the tachometer, where applicable.

Bosch injection pump

7   Loosen the locknut and unscrew the anti-stall adjustment screw until it is clear of the pump accelerator lever (see illustration).

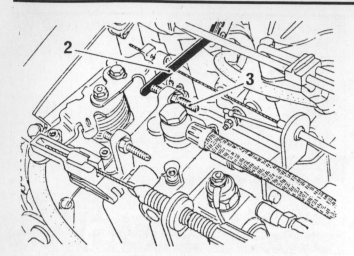

**26.21 Checking the anti-stall speed adjustment -
Bosch injection pump**

2   *Feeler blade*
3   *Anti-stall speed adjustment screw*

8   Loosen the locknut and turn the idle speed adjustment screw as required, then retighten the locknut.
9   Make the anti-stall adjustment as described later in this Section.
10   Stop the engine and disconnect the tachometer, where applicable.

Anti-stall checking and adjustment

11   Make sure that the engine is at normal operating temperature, and idling at the specified speed, as described previously.

Roto-Diesel/Lucas injection pump

12   Insert a shim or feeler blade, of the correct thickness (see Specifications), between the pump accelerator lever and the anti-stall adjustment screw.
13   The engine speed should increase to the specified anti-stall speed (see Specifications).
14   If adjustment is necessary, loosen the locknut, turn the anti-stall adjustment screw as required, then tighten the locknut **(see illustration 26.4)**.
15   Remove the shim or feeler blade and check the idle speed as described previously.
16   Move the pump accelerator lever to increase the engine speed to approximately 3000 rpm, then quickly release the lever. The deceleration period should be approximately 2.5 to 3.5 seconds, and the engine speed should drop to approximately 50 rpm below idle.
17   If the deceleration is too fast and the engine stalls, unscrew the anti-stall adjustment screw 1/4 turn towards the accelerator lever. If the deceleration is too slow, resulting in poor engine braking, turn the screw 1/4 turn away from the lever.
18   Retighten the locknut after making an adjustment, then recheck the idle speed and adjust if necessary as described previously.
19   With the engine idling check the operation of the manual stop control by turning the stop lever clockwise (see Chapter 4, Section 1). The engine must stop instantly.
20   Where applicable, disconnect the tachometer on completion.

Bosch injection pump

21   Insert a shim or feeler blade of the correct thickness (see Specifications) between the pump accelerator lever and the anti-stall adjustment screw **(see illustration)**.
22   The engine speed should be as specified for the anti-stall speed (see Specifications).
23   If adjustment is necessary, loosen the locknut and turn the anti-stall adjustment screw as required. Retighten the locknut.

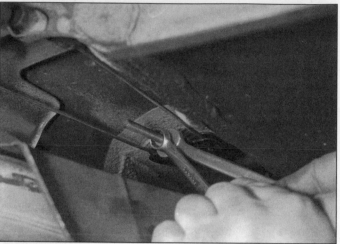

27.3 Slacken the locknut and adjuster nut on the handbrake cable

24   Remove the shim or feeler blade and allow the engine to idle.
25   Move the fast idle lever fully towards the flywheel end of the engine and check that the engine speed increases to the specified fast idle speed. If necessary loosen the locknut and turn the fast idle adjusting screw as required, then retighten the locknut.
26   With the engine idling, check the operation of the manual stop control by turning the stop lever (see Chapter 4, Section 1). The engine must stop instantly.
27   Where applicable, disconnect the tachometer on completion.

27   Handbrake checking and adjustment (every 40 000 miles/64 000 km)

Warning: *The dust created by wear of the brake shoes may contain asbestos, which is a health hazard. Never blow it out with compressed air and don't inhale any of it. An approved filtering mask should be worn when working on the brakes. DO NOT use petroleum based solvents to clean brake parts. Use brake cleaner or methylated spirit only.*

1   The handbrake should be capable of holding the parked vehicle stationary, even on steep slopes, when applied with moderate force. The mechanism should be firm and positive in feel, with no trace of stiffness or sponginess from the cables, and should release immediately the handbrake lever is released. If the mechanism is faulty in any of these respects, it must be checked immediately as follows.
Note: *If the handbrake is not functioning correctly or is incorrectly adjusted, the rear brake self-adjust mechanism will not function. This will lead to the brake pedal travel becoming excessive as the shoe linings wear. Under no circumstances should the handbrake cables be tightened in an attempt to compensate for excessive brake pedal travel.*
2   Chock the front wheels and release the handbrake. Jack up the rear of the vehicle and support it securely on axle stands.
3   Slacken the locknut, then fully slacken the cable adjuster nut **(see illustration)**.
4   Remove both the rear brake drums as described in Chapter 9.
5   Check that the knurled adjuster wheel on the adjuster strut is free to rotate in both directions. If it is seized, the brake shoes and strut must be removed and overhauled as described in Section 13 of Chapter 9.
6   If all is well, back off the adjuster wheel by five or six teeth so that the diameter of the brake shoes is slightly reduced.
7   Check that the handbrake cables slide freely by pulling on their front ends. Also check that the operating levers on the rear brake trailing shoes return to their correct positions, with their stop-pegs in contact with the edge of the trailing shoe web.
8   With the aid of an assistant, tighten the adjuster nut on the handbrake lever operating rod so that the lever on each rear brake

assembly starts to move as the handbrake is moved between the first and second notch (click) of its ratchet mechanism. This is the case when the stop-pegs are still in contact with the shoes when the handbrake is on the first notch of the ratchet, but no longer contact the shoes when the handbrake is on the second notch. Once the adjustment is correct, hold the adjuster nut and securely tighten the locknut.

9   Refit the brake drums as described in Chapter 9, then lower the vehicle to the ground.

10   With the vehicle standing on its wheels, repeatedly depress the footbrake to adjust the shoe-to-drum clearance. Whilst depressing the pedal, have an assistant listen to the rear drums to check that the adjuster strut mechanism is functioning; if this is so, a clicking sound will be heard from the adjuster strut as the pedal is depressed.

28 Rear brake shoe lining check (every 40 000 miles/ 64 000 km)

Warning: *The dust created by wear of the shoes may contain asbestos, which is a health hazard. Never blow it out with compressed air and don't inhale any of it. An approved filtering mask should be worn when working on the brakes. DO NOT use petroleum based solvents to clean brake parts. Use brake cleaner or methylated spirit only.*

1   Remove the rear brake drums with reference to Chapter 9.

2   Check that each brake shoe lining thickness (including the shoe) is not less than the thickness given in the Specifications.

3   If any one lining thickness is less than the minimum amount, renew all of the rear brake shoes, as described in Chapter 9.

29 Brake fluid renewal (every 40 000 miles/64 000 km)

Warning: *Hydraulic fluid is poisonous; wash off immediately and thoroughly in the case of skin contact, and seek immediate medical advice if any fluid is swallowed or gets into the eyes. Certain types of hydraulic fluid are inflammable, and may ignite when allowed into contact with hot components; when servicing any hydraulic system, it is safest to assume that the fluid is inflammable, and to take precautions against the risk of fire as though it is petrol that is being handled. Hydraulic fluid is also an effective paint stripper, and will attack plastics; if any is spilt, it should be washed off immediately using copious quantities of fresh water. Finally, it is hygroscopic (it absorbs moisture from the air) - old fluid may be contaminated and unfit for further use. When topping-up or renewing the fluid, always use the recommended type (see Specifications), and ensure that it comes from a freshly-opened, previously-sealed container.*

1   The procedure is similar to that for the bleeding of the hydraulic system described in Chapter 9. Before starting, remove as much old brake fluid as possible from the reservoir by syphoning, using a clean poultry baster or similar.

2   Working as described in Chapter 9, open the first bleed nipple in the sequence, and pump the brake pedal gently until nearly all the old fluid has been emptied from the master cylinder reservoir. Top-up to the "MAX" level with new fluid, and continue pumping until only the new fluid remains in the reservoir and new fluid can be seen emerging from the bleed nipple. Tighten the nipple and top the reservoir level up to the "MAX" level line.

3   Old hydraulic fluid is invariably much darker in colour than the new, making it easy to distinguish the two.

4   Work through all the remaining nipples in the sequence until new fluid can be seen at all of them. Be careful to keep the master cylinder reservoir topped-up to above the "MIN" level at all times, or air may enter the system and greatly increase the length of the task.

5   When the operation is complete, check that all nipples are securely tightened and that their dust caps are refitted. Wash off all traces of spilt fluid, and recheck the master cylinder reservoir fluid level.

6   Check the operation of the brakes before taking the vehicle on the road.

30 Front wheel alignment check (every 40 000 miles/ 64 000 km)

Refer to the information given in Chapter 10.

31 Timing belt renewal (every 70 000 miles/112 000 km)

The procedure is described in Chapter 2A.

32 Coolant renewal (every 2 years)

Coolant draining

Warning: *Wait until the engine is cold before starting this procedure. Do not allow antifreeze to come in contact with your skin, or with the painted surfaces of the vehicle. Rinse off spills immediately with plenty of water. Never leave antifreeze lying around in an open container, or in a puddle on the floor. Children and pets are attracted by its sweet smell, but antifreeze can be fatal if ingested.*

1   If the engine is cold, unscrew and remove the pressure cap from the expansion tank. If it is not possible to wait until the engine is cold, place a cloth over the pressure cap of the expansion tank and **slowly** unscrew the cap. Wait until all pressure has escaped, then remove the cap.

2   Place a suitable container beneath the bottom hose connection to the radiator.

3   Loosen the clip, then disconnect the bottom hose and allow the coolant to drain into the container. The hose clips fitted as original equipment are released by squeezing the tags together with pliers.

4   Move the container beneath the cylinder block drain plug, located at the rear right-hand side of the cylinder block.

5   Unscrew the plug, and drain the coolant into the container.

6   Flush the system if necessary as described in the following paragraphs, then refit the drain plug and secure the bottom hose. Use a new hose clip if necessary. Refill the system as described later in this Section.

System flushing

7   With time, the cooling system may gradually lose its efficiency if the radiator matrix becomes choked with rust and scale deposits. If this is the case, the system must be flushed as follows. First drain the coolant as already described.

8   Loosen the clip and disconnect the top hose from the radiator. Insert a garden hose in the radiator top hose connection stub, and allow the water to circulate through the radiator until it runs clear from the bottom outlet.

9   To flush the engine and the remainder of the system, remove the thermostat as described in Chapter 3. Insert the garden hose, and allow the water to circulate through the engine until it runs clear from the bottom hose.

10   In severe cases of contamination, the radiator should be reverse-flushed. To do this, first remove it from the vehicle, as described in Chapter 3, invert it and insert a hose in the bottom outlet. Continue flushing until clear water runs from the top hose outlet.

11   If, after a reasonable period, the water still does not run clear, the radiator should be flushed with a good proprietary cleaning system.

12   Regular renewal of the antifreeze mixture as specified should prevent severe contamination of the system. Note that as the radiator is made of aluminium, it is important not to use caustic soda or alkaline compounds to clean it. See Chapter 3 for more details.

Coolant filling

13   Refit the cylinder block drain plug, radiator bottom hose and any other hoses removed if the system has just been flushed.

14   Open the coolant bleed screw(s), located at the top left-hand corner of the radiator and, if fitted, on the top hose. **(see illustrations)**.

32.14a Open the bleed screw (arrowed) on the radiator and . . .

32.14b . . .on the top hose (if fitted) when refilling the cooling system

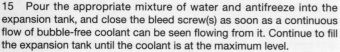

15   Pour the appropriate mixture of water and antifreeze into the expansion tank, and close the bleed screw(s) as soon as a continuous flow of bubble-free coolant can be seen flowing from it. Continue to fill the expansion tank until the coolant is at the maximum level.

16   Start the engine and run it at 1500 rpm (ie a fast idle speed) for approximately 4 minutes. Keep the expansion tank topped-up to the maximum level during this period.

17   Refit the pressure cap to the expansion tank, and run the engine at 1500 rpm for approximately 10 minutes until the electric cooling fan cuts in. During this period, the coolant will circulate around the engine and any remaining air will be purged to the expansion tank.

18   Switch off the engine and allow it to cool, then check the coolant level as described in Section 3 of this Chapter, and top-up if necessary.

Antifreeze mixture

Note: *Refer to the warning at the beginning of this Section. Renault do not specify renewal intervals for the antifreeze mixture, as the mixture used to fill the system when the vehicle is new is designed to last the lifetime of the vehicle. However, it is strongly recommended that the coolant is renewed at the intervals specified in the "Maintenance schedule", as a precaution against possible engine corrosion problems.*

This is particularly advisable if the coolant has been renewed previously, using an antifreeze other than that specified by Renault. With many antifreeze types, the corrosion inhibitors become progressively less effective with age. It is up to the individual owner whither or not to follow this advice.

19   It is advisable to renew the antifreeze mixture at the specified intervals. This is necessary not only to maintain the antifreeze properties, but also to prevent corrosion which would otherwise occur as the corrosion inhibitors become progressively less effective.

20   Always use an ethylene-glycol based antifreeze which is suitable for use in mixed-metal cooling systems. The proportion of antifreeze and levels of protection afforded are indicated in the Specifications.

21   Before adding antifreeze, the cooling system should be completely drained, preferably flushed, and all hoses checked for condition and security.

22   After filling with the correct water/antifreeze mixture, a label should be attached to the radiator or expansion tank stating the type and concentration of antifreeze used and the date installed. Any subsequent topping-up should be made with the same type and concentration of antifreeze.

23   Do not use engine antifreeze in the screen washer system, as it will cause damage to the vehicle paintwork.

Chapter 2 Part A:
In-car engine repair procedures

Contents

Specifications

General

Type	Four-cylinder, in-line, overhead camshaft
Designation	F8Q 714, F8Q 730 and F8Q 732
Capacity	1870 cc
Bore	80.0 mm
Stroke	93.0 mm
Firing order	1-3-4-2 (No 1 cylinder at flywheel end)
Direction of crankshaft rotation	Clockwise viewed from timing belt end
Compression ratio	21.5:1
Maximum power output (typical)	47.0 kW (61 bhp) at 4500 rpm
Maximum torque (typical)	118 Nm (87 lbf ft) at 2250 rpm

Compression pressures (engine warm - approximately 80°C)
Minimum pressure .... 20 bars
Maximum difference between cylinders .... 4 bars

Camshaft
Drive... Toothed belt
Number of bearings 5
Camshaft endfloat .... 0.05 to 0.13 mm

Valve clearances
Inlet .... 0.20 mm
Exhaust .... 0.40 mm

Timing belt
Tension setting using Renault tool Elé. 364.04 (see text)......................... 7.0 to 8.0 mm deflection under a load of 30 N

Lubrication system
System pressure (at 80°C):
    At 1000 rpm... 2.0 bars minimum
    At 3000 rpm... 3.5 bars minimum
Oil pump type .... Two-gear
Oil pump clearances:
    Gear-to-body (minimum)... 0.10 mm
    Gear-to-body (maximum).. 0.24 mm
    Gear endfloat (minimum).. 0.02 mm
    Gear endfloat (maximum)... 0.085 mm

Torque wrench settings

	Nm	lbf ft
Camshaft sprocket	50	37
Camshaft bearing caps:		
8 mm diameter bolts	20	15
6 mm diameter bolts	10	7
Timing belt tensioner roller nut	50	37
Auxiliary shaft sprocket bolt	50	37
Crankshaft pulley bolt	90 to 100	66 to 74
Connecting rod (big-end) cap bolts	45 to 50	33 to 37
Sump bolts	12 to 15	9 to 11
Flywheel bolts*	50 to 55	37 to 41
Valve cover nuts/bolts	12	9
Main bearing caps	60 to 65	44 to 48
Cylinder head bolts (new bolts may be required - see Section 9):		
Engines with hexagon socket-head bolts:		
Stage 1	30	22
Stage 2	70	51
Stage 3	Wait for 3 minutes minimum	
Stage 4	Loosen all the bolts completely	
Stage 5	20	15
Stage 6	Angle-tighten a further 123° ± 2°	
Engines with T55 Torx bolts:		
Stage 1	30	22
Stage 2	Angle-tighten a further 50° ± 4°	
Stage 3	Wait for 3 minutes minimum	
Stage 4	Loosen all the bolts completely	
Stage 5	25	18
Stage 6	Angle-tighten a further 213° ± 7°	
Left-hand engine/gearbox mounting plate-to-body nuts	22	16
Left-hand engine/gearbox mounting bracket-to-body mounting nut	75	55
Lower engine steady bracket nuts	45	33
Right-hand engine mounting plate-to-body nuts	45	33

*Note: Use new bolts.

1   General information

How to use this Chapter

This Part of Chapter 2 is devoted to in-car repair procedures. All procedures concerning engine removal and refitting, and engine block/cylinder head overhaul can be found in Chapter 2B.

Refer to the *"Buying spare parts and vehicle identification numbers"* Section at the beginning of this manual for details of engine code locations.

Most of the operations included in Chapter 2A are based on the assumption that the engine is still installed in the car. Therefore, if this information is being used during a complete engine overhaul, with the engine already removed, many of the steps included here will not apply.

Engine description

The engine is of four-cylinder, in-line, single overhead camshaft type, mounted transversely at the front of the vehicle **(see illustration)**.

The crankshaft is supported in five shell-type main bearings. Thrust washers are fitted to No 2 main bearing to control crankshaft endfloat.

The connecting rods are attached to the crankshaft by horizontally split shell-type big-end bearings and to the pistons by gudgeon pins. The gudgeon pins are fully floating and are retained by circlips. The aluminium alloy pistons are of the slipper type and are fitted with three piston rings, comprising two compression rings and a scraper-type oil control ring.

The single overhead camshaft is mounted directly in the cylinder head, and is driven by the crankshaft via a toothed timing belt.

2A

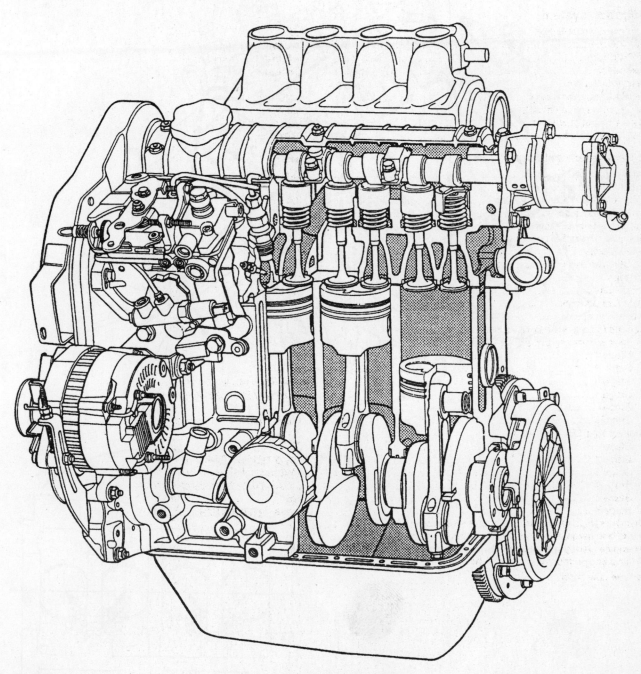

1.4 Cutaway view of the F8Q engine

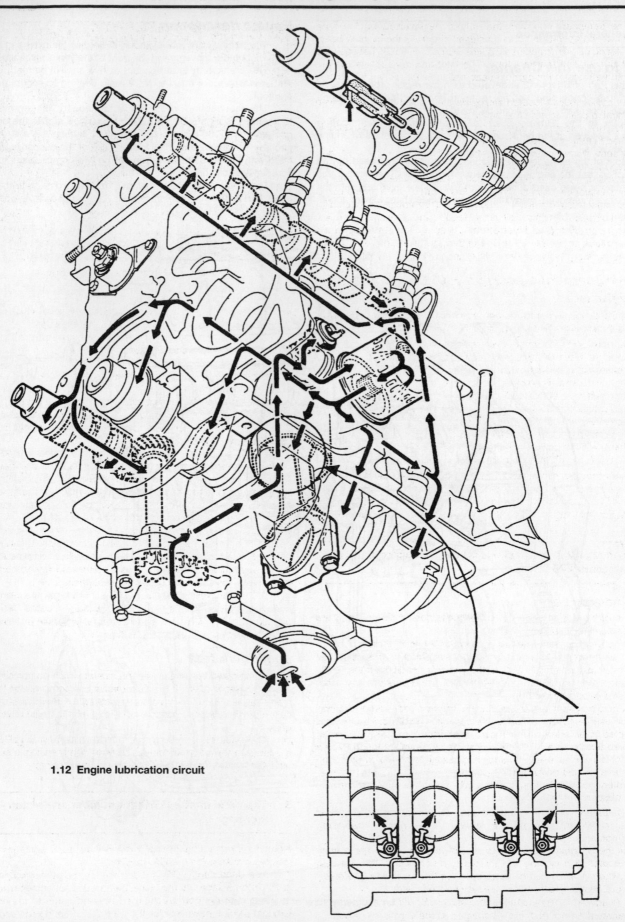

1.12 Engine lubrication circuit

The camshaft operates the valves via inverted bucket-type tappets, which operate in bores machined directly in the cylinder head. Valve clearance adjustment is by shims located externally between the tappet bucket and the cam lobe. The inlet and exhaust valves are mounted vertically in the cylinder head and are each closed by a single valve spring.

An auxiliary shaft located alongside the crankshaft is also driven by the timing belt and actuates the oil pump via a skew gear.

The fuel injection pump is driven by the timing belt, and is described in further detail in Chapter 4.

A semi-closed crankcase ventilation system is employed, and crankcase fumes are drawn from an oil separator on the cylinder block and passed via a hose to the inlet tract (see Chapter 4 for further details).

Engine lubrication is by pressure feed from a gear-type oil pump located beneath the crankshaft. Engine oil is fed through an externally-mounted oil filter to the main oil gallery feeding the crankshaft, auxiliary shaft and camshaft **(see illustration)**. Oil spray jets are fitted to the cylinder block to supply oil to the underside of the pistons. An oil cooler is mounted between the oil filter and the cylinder block.

Repair operations possible with the engine in the vehicle

The following operations can be carried out without having to remove the engine from the vehicle:

a) *Removal and refitting of the cylinder head.*
b) *Removal and refitting of the timing belt and sprockets.*
c) *Renewal of the camshaft oil seals.*
d) *Removal and refitting of the camshaft.*
e) *Removal and refitting of the sump.*
f) *Removal and refitting of the connecting rods and pistons**
g) *Removal and refitting of the oil pump.*
h) *Renewal of the crankshaft oil seals.*
i) *Renewal of the engine mountings.*
j) *Removal and refitting of the flywheel.*

*Although the operation marked with an asterisk can be carried out with the engine in the car after removal of the sump, it is better for the engine to be removed in the interests of cleanliness and improved access. For this reason, the procedure is described in Chapter 2B.

2 Compression and leakdown tests - description and interpretation

Compression test

Note: *A compression tester specifically designed for diesel engines must be used for this test.*

1   When engine performance is down, or if misfiring occurs which cannot be attributed to a fault in the fuel system, a compression test can provide diagnostic clues as to the engine's condition. If the test is performed regularly it can give warning of trouble before any other symptoms become apparent.

2   A compression tester specifically intended for diesel engines must be used, because of the higher pressures involved. The tester is connected to an adaptor which screws into the glow plug or injector hole **(see illustration)**. It is unlikely to be worthwhile buying such a tester for occasional use, but it may be possible to borrow or hire one - if not, have the test performed by a garage.

3   Unless specific instructions to the contrary are supplied with the tester, observe the following points:

a) *The battery must be in a good state of charge, the air filter must be clean and the engine should be at normal operating temperature.*
b) *All the injectors or glow plugs should be removed before starting the test. If removing the injectors, also remove the fire seal washers (which must be renewed when the injectors are refitted - see Chapter 4), otherwise they may be blown out.*
c) *It is advisable to disconnect the stop solenoid on the pump to reduce the amount of fuel discharged as the engine is cranked.*

2.2 Carrying out a compression test

4   There is no need to hold the accelerator pedal down during the test because the diesel engine air inlet is not throttled.

5   The actual compression pressures measured are not so important as the balance between cylinders. Values are given in the Specifications.

6   The cause of poor compression is less easy to establish on a diesel engine than on a petrol one. The effect of introducing oil into the cylinders ("wet" testing) is not conclusive, because there is a risk that the oil will sit in the swirl chamber or in the recess on the piston crown instead of passing to the rings. However, the following can be used as a rough guide to diagnosis.

7   All cylinders should produce very similar pressures; any difference greater than that specified indicates the existence of a fault. Note that the compression should build up quickly in a healthy engine; low compression on the first stroke, followed by gradually increasing pressure on successive strokes, indicates worn piston rings. A low compression reading on the first stroke, which does not build up during successive strokes, indicates leaking valves or a blown head gasket (a cracked head could also be the cause). Deposits on the undersides of the valve heads can also cause low compression.

8   A low reading from two adjacent cylinders is almost certainly due to the head gasket having blown between them.

9   If the compression reading is unusually high, the cylinder head surfaces, valves and pistons are probably coated with carbon deposits. If this is the case, the cylinder head should be removed and decarbonised (see Chapter 2B, Section 7).

Leakdown test

10   A leakdown test measures the rate at which compressed air fed into the cylinder is lost. It is an alternative to a compression test and in many ways it is better, since the escaping air provides easy identification of where pressure loss is occurring (piston rings, valves or head gasket).

11   The equipment needed for leakdown testing is unlikely to be available to the home mechanic. If poor compression is suspected, have the test performed by a suitably equipped garage.

3 Top dead centre (TDC) for number one piston - locating

Note: *An 8 mm diameter rod or drill will be required if it is desired to lock the crankshaft in the TDC position.*

1   Top dead centre (TDC) is the highest point in the cylinder that each piston reaches as the crankshaft turns. Each piston reaches TDC at the end of the compression stroke and again at the end of the exhaust stroke; however, for the purpose of timing the engine, TDC

2A

3.3 View of the crankshaft pulley bolt with the lower
wheel arch cover removed

3.4 Flywheel timing mark aligned with TDC (0°)
mark on bellhousing

refers to the position of No 1 piston at the end of its compression stroke. On all engines in this manual, No 1 piston (and cylinder) is at the flywheel end of the engine.

2   When No 1 piston is at TDC, the timing mark on the camshaft sprocket should be aligned with the pointer on the outer timing belt cover (the sprocket mark can be viewed through the cut-out in the timing belt cover, below the pointer). Additionally, the timing mark on the flywheel should be aligned with the TDC mark on the gearbox bellhousing.

3   To align the timing marks, the crankshaft must be turned. This should be done by using a spanner on the crankshaft pulley bolt. Improved access to the pulley bolt can be obtained by jacking up the front right-hand corner of the vehicle and removing the roadwheel and the lower wheel arch cover (secured by plastic clips) **(see illustration)**. If desired, to enable the engine to be turned more easily, remove the glow plugs (Chapter 5) or the fuel injectors (Chapter 4).

4   Look through the timing aperture in the gearbox bellhousing, and turn the crankshaft until the timing mark on the flywheel is aligned with the TDC (0°) mark on the bellhousing **(see illustration)**.

5   Unscrew the three securing bolts, and remove the plastic cover from the upper right-hand engine mounting bracket **(see illustration)**. Note the locations of any brackets which may be secured by the bolts.

6   Check that the timing mark on the camshaft sprocket is aligned with the pointer on the outer timing belt cover **(see illustration)**. Note that the mark may not align exactly due to the possible movement of the timing belt cover within its bolts holes.

7   It is possible to lock the crankshaft in the TDC position as follows. Remove the air cleaner housing assembly as described in Chapter 4.

8   Remove the plug on the lower front-facing side of the cylinder

3.5 Removing the cover from the engine mounting bracket

block, at the flywheel end, and obtain a metal rod which is a snug fit in the plug hole (8 mm diameter). Turn the crankshaft slightly if necessary to the TDC position, then push the rod through the hole to locate in the slot in the crankshaft web. Make sure that the crankshaft is exactly at TDC for No 1 piston (flywheel end) by aligning the timing mark on the flywheel with the TDC (0°) mark on the gearbox bellhousing as described previously. If the crankshaft is not positioned accurately, it is possible to engage the rod with a balance hole in the crankshaft web

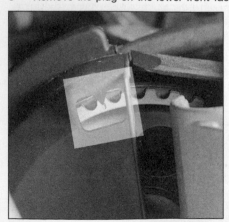

3.6 Camshaft sprocket timing mark
aligned with pointer on timing belt cover

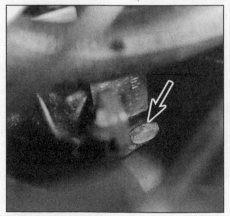

3.8a Remove the plug (arrowed) from the
cylinder block . . .

3.8b . . . and insert a suitable 8 mm
rod (arrowed)

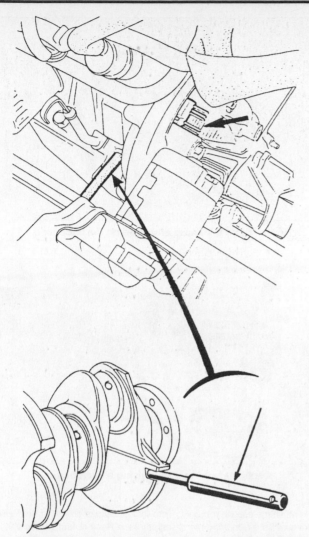

3.8c TDC mark on flywheel viewed through bellhousing aperture, and TDC locking tool engaged with crankshaft (arrowed)

by mistake, instead of the TDC slot. It is a good idea to put a notice on the engine warning that the timing rod is in position **(see illustrations)**.

9   Refit the air cleaner housing assembly with reference to Chapter 4.

---

4   Valve clearances - checking and adjustment

Note: *This operation is not part of the maintenance schedule. It should be undertaken if noise from the valvegear becomes evident, or if loss of performance gives cause to suspect that the clearances may be incorrect. A new valve cover gasket may be required on refitting.*

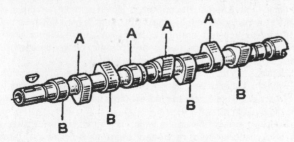

4.6 Cam lobe identification

A   Inlet   B   Exhaust

3.8d Timing rod warning notice on the engine

Checking

1   Where necessary for improved access, unclip any hoses which are routed across the top of the valve cover, and move them to one side out of the way. If fuel lines are disconnected, cover open unions to prevent dirt ingress.

2   Where applicable, unscrew the securing bolts, and remove the upper timing belt/engine mounting cover. Note the locations of any brackets secured by the bolts.

3   Unscrew the nuts from the valve cover, and withdraw the cover from the engine. Recover the gasket.

4   During the following procedure, the crankshaft must be turned, using a spanner on the crankshaft pulley bolt. Improved access to the pulley bolt can be obtained by jacking up the front right-hand corner of the vehicle and removing the roadwheel and the lower wheel arch cover (secured by plastic clips).

5   If desired, to enable the crankshaft to be turned more easily, remove the glow plugs (Chapter 5) or the fuel injectors (Chapter 4).

6   Draw the valve positions on a piece of paper, numbering them 1 to 8 from the flywheel end of the engine. Identify them as inlet or exhaust (ie 1E, 2I, 3E, 4I, 5I, 6E, 7I, 8E) **(see illustration)**.

7   Turn the crankshaft until the valves of No 1 cylinder (flywheel end) are "rocking". The exhaust valve will be closing and the inlet valve will be opening. The piston of No 4 cylinder will be at the top of its compression stroke, with both valves fully closed. The clearances for both valves of No 4 cylinder may be checked at the same time.

8   Insert a feeler blade of the correct thickness (see Specifications) between the cam lobe and the shim on the top of the tappet bucket, and check that it is a firm sliding fit **(see illustration)**. If it is not, use the feeler blades to ascertain the exact clearance, and record this for use

4.8 Measuring a valve clearance

2A

VALVES ROCKING ON CYLINDER	CHECK CLEARANCE ON CYLINDER

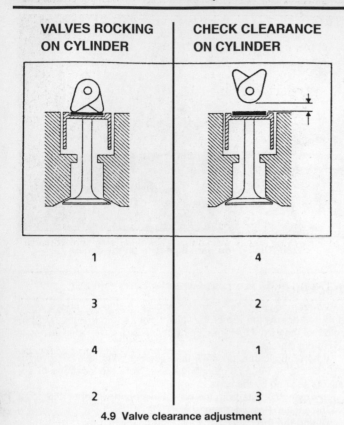

1	4
3	2
4	1
2	3

4.9 Valve clearance adjustment

4.10a Shim thickness engraved on the underside

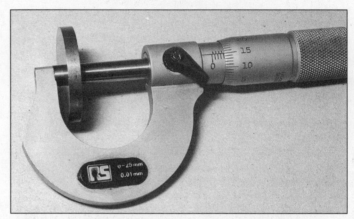

4.10b Measuring a shim using a micrometer

when calculating the new shim thickness required. Note that the inlet and exhaust valve clearances are different (see Specifications).

9   With No 4 cylinder valve clearances checked, turn the engine through half a turn so that No 3 valves are "rocking", then check the valve clearances of No 2 cylinder in the same way. Similarly check the remaining valve clearances in the sequence shown **(see illustration)**.

Adjustment

Note: *A micrometer will be required for this operation.*

10   Where a valve clearance differs from the specified value, then the shim for that valve must be replaced with a thinner or thicker shim accordingly. The shim size is stamped on the bottom face of the shim, but it is prudent to use a micrometer to measure the true thickness of any shim removed, as it may have been reduced by wear **(see illustrations)**.

11   The size of shim required is calculated as follows. If the measured clearance is less than specified, subtract the measured clearance from the specified clearance, and deduct the result from the thickness of the existing shim. For example:

Sample calculation - clearance too small

Clearance measured (A) = 0.15 mm
Desired clearance (B) = 0.20 mm
Difference (B - A) = 0.05 mm
Shim thickness fitted = 3.70 mm
Shim thickness required = 3.70 - 0.05 = 3.65 mm

12   If the measured clearance is greater than specified, subtract the specified clearance from the measured clearance, and add the result to the thickness of the existing shim. For example:

Sample calculation - clearance too big

Clearance measured (A) = 0.50 mm
Desired clearance (B) = 0.40 mm
Difference (A - B) = 0.10 mm
Shim thickness fitted = 3.45 mm
Shim thickness required = 3.45 + 0.10 = 3.55 mm

13   The shims can be removed from their locations on top of the tappet buckets without removing the camshaft if the Renault tool shown can be borrowed, or a suitable alternative fabricated **(see illustration)**.

14   To remove the shim, the tappet bucket has to be pressed down against valve spring pressure just far enough to allow the shim to be slid out. Theoretically, this could be done by levering against the camshaft between the cam lobes with a suitable screwdriver or similar tool to push the bucket down, but this is not recommended by the manufacturers. If this method is to be used, take great care not to damage the camshaft, cylinder head, or tappet bucket **(see illustration)**.

15   An arrangement similar to the Renault tool can be made by bolting a bar to the camshaft bearing studs and levering down against this with a stout screwdriver. The contact pad should be a triangular-shaped metal block with a lip filed along each side to contact the edge of the buckets. Levering down against this will open the valve and allow the shim to be withdrawn.

16   Make sure that the cam lobe peaks are uppermost when depressing a tappet, and rotate the buckets so that the notches are at right-angles to the camshaft centre-line. When refitting the shims, ensure that the size markings face the tappet buckets (ie face downwards).

17   If the Renault tool cannot be borrowed or a suitable alternative improvised, then it will be necessary to remove the camshaft to gain access to the shims, as described in Section 8.

18   Remove the spanner from the crankshaft pulley bolt.

19   Refit the valve cover, using a new gasket where necessary.

20   Where applicable, refit the fuel injectors (as described in Chapter 4), or the glow plugs (Chapter 5).

21   Refit/reconnect any hoses which were moved for access. If fuel lines were disconnected, reconnect them, then prime and bleed the fuel system as described in Chapter 4.

22   Where applicable, refit the upper timing belt/engine mounting cover.

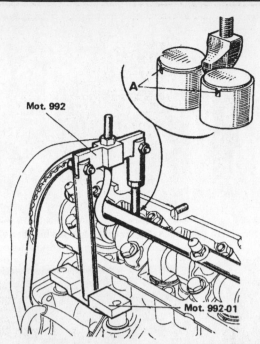

4.14 Removing a shim from a tappet bucket using screwdrivers

4.13 Renault tool for compressing tappet buckets to change shims

A   Notches positioned at right-angles to camshaft centre-line

---

5   Timing belt - removal, inspection and refitting

Caution: *If the timing belt breaks or slips in service, extensive engine damage may result. Renew the belt at the intervals specified in Chapter 1, or earlier if its condition is at all doubtful.*

Note: *A suitable tool will be required to check the timing belt tension on completion of refitting - see text. A suitable puller may be required to remove the crankshaft pulley.*

Removal

1   Disconnect both the battery leads.

2   Remove the bonnet with reference to Chapter 11.

3   Apply the handbrake, then jack up the front right-hand side of the car and support on axle stands. Remove the roadwheel.

4   Remove the plastic cover from within the right-hand wheel arch, to give access to the crankshaft pulley.

5   Unbolt the fuel filter assembly and position it vertically on the engine.

6   Remove the air cleaner housing assembly as described in Chapter 4.

7   Remove the electric cooling fan as described in Chapter 3.

8   Remove the auxiliary drivebelt as described in Chapter 1.

9   Unscrew the crankshaft pulley bolt while holding the crankshaft stationary. To hold the crankshaft, working under the vehicle, remove the flywheel cover plate/engine-to-gearbox bracing bracket. Note the locations of any brackets secured by the bolts. Refit one of the cover plate-to-gearbox bolts to act as a fulcrum, and have an assistant insert a screwdriver or similar tool in the starter ring gear teeth **(see illustrations)**.

5.9a Unscrew the side . . .

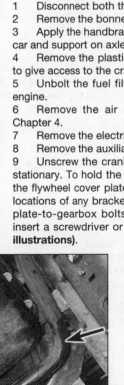

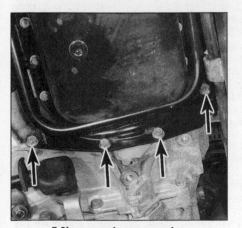

5.9b . . . and rear securing bolts (arrowed) . . .

5.9c . . . and remove the flywheel cover plate/engine-to-gearbox bracing bracket (arrowed)

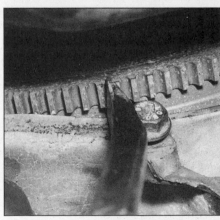

5.9d Insert a lever in the starter ring gear teeth

2A

5.10a Remove the crankshaft
pulley bolt . . .

5.10b . . . and the pulley

5.15 Unscrew the right-hand engine
mounting securing bolts/nuts (arrowed)

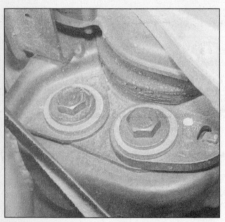

5.16 Engine mounting rubber/movement
limiter mounting bolts

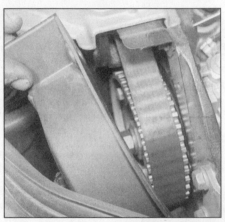

5.17 Removing the timing belt cover from
the fuel injection pump sprocket

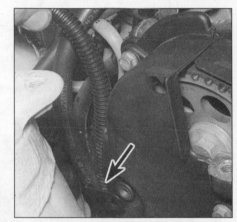

5.18a Note the location of any brackets
(arrowed) secured by the bolts . . .

10   Remove the bolt and the pulley from the front of the crankshaft
(see illustrations). Use a puller if the pulley is tight.

11   Unbolt and remove the lower timing cover.

12   Temporarily refit the crankshaft pulley bolt. Turn the crankshaft to
position No 1 piston at TDC on the compression stroke, and lock the
crankshaft in position, as described in Section 3.

13   The right-hand upper engine mounting bracket must be removed
to enable the timing belt to be removed, therefore the engine must be
supported. The assembly can be supported using a jack and a suitable
block of wood to spread the load under the sump. Alternatively,
connect a hoist and suitable lifting tackle to the engine lifting brackets.

14   Ensure that the engine/gearbox assembly is adequately
supported, then unscrew the nut securing the upper mounting bracket
to the mounting on the body.

15   Unscrew the three bolts securing the upper mounting bracket to
the engine, then withdraw the bracket **(see illustration)**.

16   Unscrew the bolts securing the engine mounting
rubber/movement limiter assembly to the body, and withdraw the
assembly **(see illustration)**.

17   Unscrew the securing bolts, and withdraw the timing belt cover
which covers the fuel injection pump sprocket **(see illustration)**. Due
to the limited working space it may be necessary to raise or lower the
engine in order to reach the bolts.

18   Unscrew the securing bolts, noting the locations of any brackets
secured by the bolts, and remove the timing belt cover which covers
the camshaft sprocket **(see illustrations)**. Again it will be necessary to
raise or lower the engine.

19   With the crankshaft locked in position with No 1 piston at TDC
(see paragraph 12), note the position of the timing mark on the fuel
injection pump sprocket **(see illustrations)**. **Note:** *On models fitted*

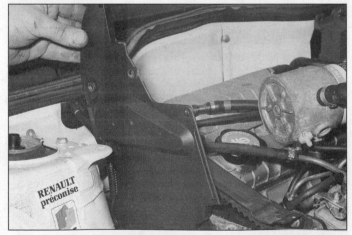

5.18b . . . and remove the timing belt cover from
the camshaft sprocket

*with a two-piece adjustable injection pump sprocket, the sprocket
timing mark may differ from those shown for the one-piece sprocket. If
this is the case, take note of the type of mark found, and its location, for
use when refitting.* Note that on models with a single-piece sprocket,
there are two timing marks on the sprocket. The mark used depends
on whether a Bosch or Roto-Diesel/Lucas injection pump is fitted.

20   If the original belt is to be re-used, check if the belt is marked with
arrows to indicate its running direction, and if necessary mark it **(see
illustration)**. Similarly, make accurate alignment marks on the belt,

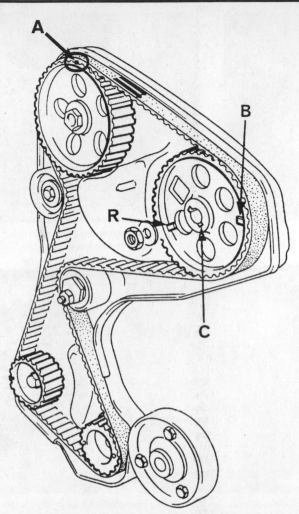

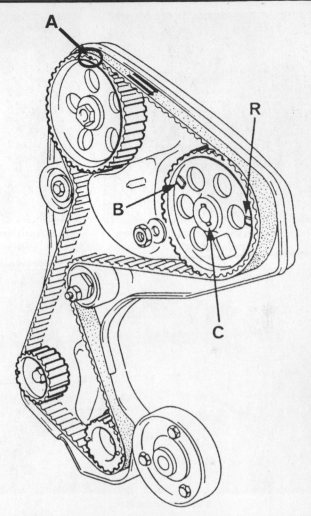

5.19a Camshaft sprocket and fuel injection pump sprocket timing mark positions with No 1 piston at TDC - models with one-piece fuel injection pump sprocket and Bosch injection pump

A   Camshaft sprocket mark (aligned with pointer on outer timing belt cover - cover removed in this view)
B   Injection pump sprocket mark for use with Bosch pump
R   Injection pump sprocket mark for use with Roto-Diesel/Lucas pump
C   Position of injection pump shaft woodruff key

5.19b Camshaft sprocket and fuel injection pump sprocket timing mark positions with No 1 piston at TDC - models with one-piece fuel injection pump sprocket and Roto-Diesel/Lucas injection pump

A   Camshaft sprocket mark (aligned with pointer on outer timing belt cover - cover removed in this view)
B   Injection pump sprocket mark for use with Bosch pump
R   Injection pump sprocket mark for use with Roto-Diesel/Lucas pump
C   Position of injection pump shaft woodruff key

5.19c Fuel injection pump sprocket timing mark location with No 1 piston at TDC - Roto-Diesel/Lucas injection pump

5.20 Running direction arrows on timing belt

2A

5.21 Loosen the timing belt tensioner
adjuster nut

5.27a The running direction arrows on the
belt must point clockwise

5.27b Align the timing marks on the belt
with the crankshaft . . .

5.27c . . . camshaft . . .

5.27d . . . and injection pump sprocket marks (model with
Roto-Diesel/Lucas injection pump shown)

corresponding to the timing marks on the camshaft, fuel injection pump and crankshaft sprockets.

21   Loosen the adjuster nut, and slide the timing belt tensioner back to relieve the tension from the belt **(see illustration)**. Re-tighten the nut.

22   Release the belt from the camshaft sprocket, fuel injection pump sprocket, idler wheel, crankshaft sprocket and auxiliary shaft sprocket, and remove it from the engine.

23   **Do not** turn the camshaft or the crankshaft whilst the timing belt is removed, as there is a risk of piston-to-valve contact. If it is necessary to turn the camshaft for any reason, before doing so, remove the TDC locking tool from the cylinder block, and turn the crankshaft anti-clockwise (viewed from the timing belt end of the engine) by a quarter turn to position all four pistons half way down their bores.

Inspection

24   Clean the sprockets, idler wheel and tensioner and wipe them dry, although do not apply excessive amounts of solvent to the idler and tensioner wheels otherwise the bearing lubricant may be contaminated. Also clean the rear timing belt cover, and the front of the cylinder head and block.

25   Examine the timing belt carefully for any signs of cracking, fraying or general wear, particularly at the roots of the teeth. Renew the belt if there is any sign of deterioration of this nature, or if there is any oil or grease contamination. The belt must, of course, be renewed if it has completed the maximum mileage given in Chapter 1.

Refitting

26   Check that the crankshaft is positioned with No 1 piston at TDC, and locked in position using the tool through the hole in the cylinder

block as described previously. If the pistons have been positioned halfway down their bores (see paragraph 23), temporarily refit the outer timing belt cover which covers the camshaft sprocket, and check that the TDC mark on the camshaft sprocket is aligned with the pointer on the timing belt cover, then turn the crankshaft clockwise (viewed from the timing belt end of the engine) until the TDC locking tool can be refitted.

27   Align the timing marks on the belt with those on the crankshaft, camshaft and fuel injection pump sprockets, ensuring that the running direction arrows on the belt are pointing clockwise (viewed from the timing belt end of the engine). Note that the belt should be marked with lines across its width to act as timing marks **(see illustrations)**. If the original belt is to be refitted, and the timing marks have deteriorated (in which case, it is likely that the belt is in need of renewal in any case), use the alignment marks made on the belt before removal. Fit the timing belt over the crankshaft sprocket first, followed by the idler wheel, fuel injection pump sprocket, camshaft sprocket, tensioner, and auxiliary shaft sprocket.

28   Check that all the timing marks are still aligned.

29   The belt must now be tensioned as follows.

Adjustment using Renault special tool Elé. 346.04

Note: *The tension of the belt must be adjusted with the engine cold. The manufacturers specify the use of a special gauge, Renault tool Elé. 346.04 for checking the timing belt tension. If access to a suitable tool cannot be obtained, it is strongly recommended that the vehicle is taken to a Renault dealer to have the belt tension checked at the earliest opportunity.*

30   Fit the gauge to the engine, as shown **(see illustration)**.

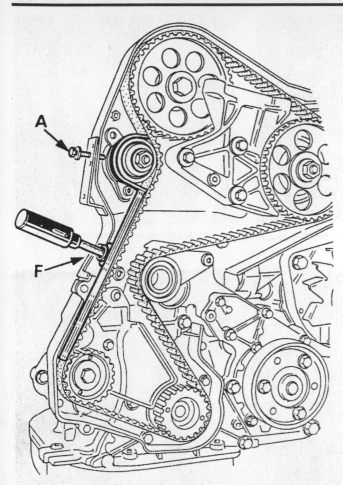

5.30 Renault tool (F) and M6 bolt (A) used to tension timing belt

5.31 M6 bolt (arrowed) fitted to rear timing belt cover

5.52 Twisting the timing belt as an approximate tension check

2A

31   Screw an M6 bolt through the threaded hole in the rear timing belt cover next to the tensioner. Loosen the tensioner nut, and tighten the bolt so that it pushes against the tensioner roller bracket to tension the belt (see illustration).

32   Adjust the bolt pushing against the tensioner roller bracket to give the specified reading on the gauge.

33   With the correct tension applied, re-tighten the tensioner nut to the specified torque. This torque is critical, since if the nut were to come loose considerable engine damage would result. Loosen the bolt fitted to the rear timing belt cover so that it no longer rests on the tensioner roller bracket.

34   Remove the TDC locking tool from the cylinder block, then refit the lower timing cover, crankshaft pulley and securing bolt. Prevent the crankshaft turning using the method described previously, and tighten the bolt to the specified torque. Refit the flywheel cover plate/engine-to-gearbox bracing bracket.

35   Check that the crankshaft is still positioned with No 1 piston at TDC (by temporarily refitting the locking tool to the cylinder block), then remove the TDC locking tool, and turn the crankshaft two complete turns in the normal direction of rotation, returning it to the TDC position again. Re-insert the TDC locking tool in the cylinder block.

36   Temporarily refit the timing belt cover which covers the camshaft sprocket, and check that the camshaft sprocket timing mark still aligns with the pointer on the cover, as noted before removal (see Section 3).

37   Re-check the belt tension as described previously. If the tension is incorrect, the setting and checking procedure must be repeated until the correct tension is achieved.

38   With the belt tensioned correctly, remove the M6 bolt from the rear timing belt cover, and remove the TDC locking tool from the cylinder block, if not already done. Refit the plug to the cylinder block TDC hole.

39   Check the fuel injection pump timing as described in Chapter 4.

40   Refit the upper timing belt covers, ensuring that any brackets secured by the bolts are in position as noted before removal.

41   Refit the engine mounting rubber/movement limiter assembly to the body, and refit the upper mounting bracket to the engine, as described in Section 14.

42   Refit the fuel filter assembly.

43   Refit the auxiliary drivebelt as described in Chapter 1.

44   Refit the electric cooling fan as described in Chapter 3.

45   Refit the air cleaner housing assembly as described in Chapter 4.

46   Withdraw the jack, or the lifting tackle, as applicable, used to support the engine.

47   Refit the wheel arch cover and the roadwheel and tighten the bolts.

48   Lower the vehicle to the ground.

49   Refit the bonnet with reference to Chapter 11.

50   Reconnect the battery leads.

Approximate adjustment

51   Refer to the note at the beginning of paragraph 30 before proceeding.

52   If the special gauge is not available, the timing belt tension can be checked approximately by twisting the belt between the thumb and forefinger, at the centre of the run between the tensioner pulley and the auxiliary shaft pulley. It should be just possible to twist the belt through 90° using moderate pressure (see illustration).

6.2 Removing the crankshaft sprocket

6.8 Removing the auxiliary shaft sprocket

6.13 Unscrewing the fuel injection pump sprocket nut

6.15 Using a puller to release the fuel injection pump sprocket

6.17a Make an alignment mark on the timing belt

6.17b Disengage the sprocket from the timing belt

53 The checking, adjustment and final refitting procedures are as described previously in paragraphs 31 to 50, noting the following.
  a) *Have the belt tension checked by a Renault dealer at the earliest opportunity.*
  b) *If in doubt, err on the tight side when adjusting the tension, as if the belt is too slack, it may jump on the sprockets, which could result in serious engine damage.*

6 Timing belt sprockets, idler roller and tensioner - removal and refitting

Crankshaft sprocket

Note: *A suitable puller may be required for this operation.*

Removal

1 Remove the timing belt as described in Section 5.
2 It should be possible to simply pull the sprocket from the front of the crankshaft, however in some cases a puller may be required **(see illustration)**. It is a simple matter to make up a puller using two bolts, a metal bar and the existing crankshaft pulley bolt. By unscrewing the crankshaft pulley bolt, the sprocket is pulled from the end of the crankshaft.
3 Recover the Woodruff key if it is loose.

Refitting

4 Refitting is a reversal of removal. Note that the sprocket fits with the flange against the end of the cylinder block/rear timing belt cover.
5 Refit the timing belt as described in Section 5.

Auxiliary shaft sprocket

Removal

6 Remove the timing belt as described in Section 5.
7 Hold the sprocket stationary using a suitable gear-holding tool. Alternatively, an old timing belt can be wrapped around the sprocket and held firmly with a pair of grips.
8 Unscrew the securing bolt, then pull the sprocket from the end of the shaft **(see illustration)**. If necessary, use two levers or screwdrivers to free the sprocket (if necessary, a puller can be used as described previously for the crankshaft sprocket).

Refitting

9 Refitting is a reversal of removal. Tighten the sprocket securing bolt to the specified torque.
10 Refit the timing belt as described in Section 5.

Fuel injection pump sprocket

Note: *A suitable puller will be required for this operation.*

Removal

11 Remove the timing belt as described in Section 5.
12 Hold the sprocket stationary using a suitable gear-holding tool. Alternatively, an old timing belt can be wrapped around the sprocket and held firmly with a pair of grips.
13 Unscrew the sprocket securing nut, as far as the end of the pump shaft. Do not remove the nut at this stage **(see illustration)**. **Note:** *On models with a two-piece adjustable sprocket, do not loosen the three sprocket adjuster bolts, as this will alter the injection pump timing.*
14 On models with a single-piece sprocket, note the location of the

6.21 Remove the plastic alternator shield (arrowed)

6.23 Removing the alternator mounting bracket

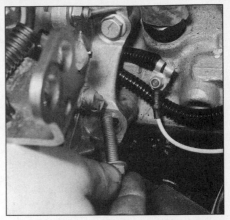

6.25 Removing one of the bolts securing the injection pump rear mounting bracket to the cylinder head

6.27 Remove the bolt (arrowed) securing the rear timing belt cover to the bracket

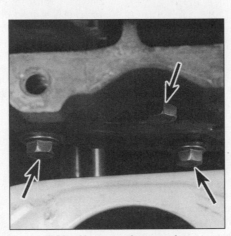

6.28a Unscrew the securing bolts (arrowed) . . .

6.28b . . . and withdraw the mounting bracket complete with the injection pump

2A

Woodruff key in the end of the injection pump shaft. There are two key slots in the sprocket (for use with Bosch and Roto-Diesel/Lucas injection pumps - **(see illustrations 5.19a and 5.19b)**. Mark the relevant key slot in the sprocket to ensure correct refitting.

15   Using a suitable puller, acting on the sprocket nut (not on the end of the pump shaft), release the sprocket from the taper on the pump shaft **(see illustration)**.

16   Remove the puller, then remove the sprocket securing nut, and recover the washer.

17   Make a mark on the timing belt corresponding to the location of the fuel injection pump sprocket timing mark **(see illustrations 5.19a and 5.19b)** to aid alignment when refitting. Disengage the sprocket from the timing belt, remove the sprocket, and recover the Woodruff key from the end of the pump shaft if it is loose **(see illustrations)**.

Refitting

18   Refitting is a reversal of removal, bearing in mind the following points.

a) *On models with a single-piece sprocket, ensure that the Woodruff key is engaged with the correct slot in the sprocket.*

b) *Tighten the sprocket securing nut to the specified torque.*

c) *Refit and tension the timing belt as described in Section 5.*

d) *Before refitting the timing belt cover over the injection pump sprocket, check the injection timing as described in Chapter 4.*

Camshaft sprocket

Note: *This is an involved procedure due to the location of the upper engine mounting/fuel injection pump mounting bracket, which leaves*

insufficient clearance to remove the sprocket from the end of the camshaft. It is suggested that this procedure is read through thoroughly before beginning work.

Removal

19   Disconnect the battery negative lead.

20   Remove the timing belt as described in Section 5.

21   Remove the plastic alternator shield **(see illustration)**.

22   Remove the alternator, with reference to Chapter 5.

23   Unbolt the alternator mounting bracket from the cylinder block **(see illustration)**. Also remove the alternator drivebelt tensioner mounting if not already done.

24   Disconnect all cables, hoses, pipes and wiring from the fuel injection pump, to facilitate removal, with reference to Chapter 4, Section 11.

25   Remove the bolts securing the injection pump rear mounting bracket to the cylinder head **(see illustration)**.

26   Unscrew the nuts and withdraw the bracket from the rear of the injection pump.

27   Remove the bolt securing the rear timing belt cover to the upper engine mounting/fuel injection pump mounting bracket **(see illustration)**.

28   Unscrew the three securing bolts, and remove the upper engine mounting/fuel injection pump mounting bracket, complete with the injection pump from the engine **(see illustrations)**. The assembly is removed by sliding it out towards the front of the vehicle. Note that it may not be possible to fully withdraw the upper two bolts from the bracket (due to limited clearance), in which case slide out the assembly with the bolts in position in their holes.

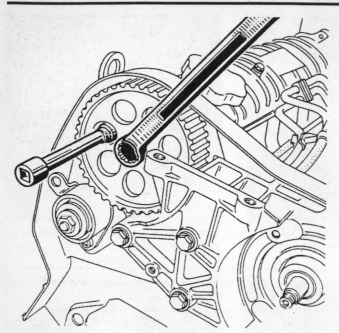

6.30 Using a socket and extension bar to counterhold the camshaft sprocket whilst unscrewing the sprocket bolt

29   If not already done, remove the crankshaft TDC locking tool, and turn the engine a quarter of a turn anti-clockwise (viewed from the timing belt end of the engine) to position the pistons halfway down their bores. This is to avoid any possibility of piston-to-valve contact if the camshaft is inadvertently turned when loosening the sprocket bolt.

30   Unscrew the camshaft sprocket bolt. The sprocket can be held using a suitable socket and extension bar engaged with one of the rear timing belt cover securing bolts as shown **(see illustration)**. Alternatively, use an old timing belt wrapped around the sprocket. Recover the washer.

31   Remove the bolt and washer and the sprocket from the front of the camshaft **(see illustrations)**. A puller may be required, in which case ensure that the legs of the puller act on the holes in the sprocket, **not** on the sprocket teeth.

32   Recover the Woodruff key from the end of the camshaft if it is loose **(see illustration)**.

Refitting

33   Ensure that the Woodruff key is in place in the end of the camshaft, then refit the camshaft sprocket, noting that the projecting hub fits towards the cylinder head.

34   Ensure that the washer is in place, then refit the sprocket bolt, and tighten it to the specified torque, holding the sprocket as during removal.

35   Refit the upper engine mounting/fuel injection pump mounting bracket, complete with the injection pump, and tighten the securing bolts. Where applicable, refit the upper two bolts to the holes in the bracket before the assembly is refitted.

36   Refit the bolt securing the rear timing belt cover to the upper engine mounting/fuel injection pump mounting bracket.

37   Refit the injection pump rear mounting bracket and tighten the securing bolts and nuts.

38   Reconnect all relevant cables, hoses, pipes and wiring to the fuel injection pump with reference to Chapter 4, Section 11.

39   Refit the alternator mounting bracket to the cylinder block, and tighten the securing bolts. Also, where applicable, refit the alternator drivebelt tensioner mounting.

40   Refit the alternator, with reference to Chapter 5.

41   Refit the plastic alternator shield.

42   Temporarily refit the outer timing belt cover which covers the camshaft sprocket, and check that the TDC mark on the camshaft sprocket is aligned with the pointer on the timing belt cover.

43   Turn the crankshaft clockwise (viewed from the timing belt end of the engine) until the crankshaft locking tool can be refitted (to position No 1 piston at TDC).

44   Refit and tension the timing belt, as described in Section 5.

45   Reconnect the battery negative lead.

46   Bleed the fuel system as described in Chapter 4.

Idler roller

Removal

47   Remove the timing belt as described in Section 5.

48   Unscrew the two securing bolts, and withdraw the idler roller assembly, manipulating it out from the rear timing belt covers.

Refitting

49   Refitting is a reversal of removal, but check that the roller turns freely without binding or excessive play.

50   Refit and tension the timing belt as described in Section 5.

Tensioner

Removal

51   Remove the timing belt as described in Section 5.

52   Remove the securing nut and the washer, and the pivot bolt, and withdraw the tensioner assembly from the engine.

Refitting

53   Refitting is a reversal of removal, but check that the roller turns freely without binding or excessive play.

54   Refit and tension the timing belt as described in Section 5.

6.31a Remove the bolt and washer . . .

6.31b . . . and the sprocket

6.32 Recover the Woodruff key from the end of the camshaft if it is loose

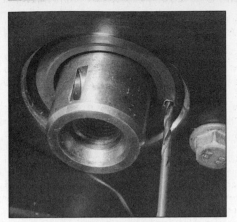
7.3a Drill a small hole . . .

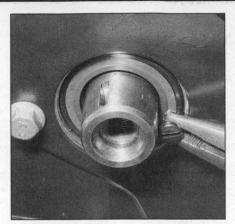
7.3b . . . and use a screw and pliers to pull out the seal

8.2 Withdraw the timing belt tensioner roller

7 Camshaft oil seals - renewal

Front (timing belt) end oil seal

1 Remove the camshaft sprocket as described in Section 6.

2 Remove the Woodruff key from the end of the camshaft, if not already done. Note the fitted depth of the oil seal in the cylinder head.

3 Using a small screwdriver, prise out the oil seal from the cylinder head, taking care not to damage the surface of the camshaft. Alternatively, the oil seal can be removed by drilling a small hole and inserting a self-tapping screw. A pair of grips can then be used to pull out the oil seal, by pulling on the screw **(see illustrations)**. If difficulty is experienced, insert two screws diagonally opposite each other. To ensure correct fitting, note the fitted position of the old oil seal.

4 Wipe clean the oil seal seating in the cylinder head, then dip the new seal in fresh engine oil, and locate it over the camshaft with its closed side facing outwards. Make sure that the oil seal lip is not damaged as it is located on the camshaft.

5 Using a tube of suitable diameter, drive the oil seal squarely into the housing to the previously noted depth. A block of wood cut to pass over the end of the camshaft may be used instead.

6 Refit the camshaft sprocket as described in Section 6.

Rear (flywheel end) oil seal

7 No oil seal is fitted to the flywheel end of the camshaft. The sealing is provided by a gasket between the cylinder head and the brake vacuum pump housing, and on certain models by an O-ring fitted between the vacuum pump and the housing. The gasket and the O-ring, where applicable, can be renewed after unbolting the vacuum pump from the cylinder head (see Chapter 9).

8 Camshaft and tappets - removal, inspection and refitting

Note: A new camshaft front oil seal should be fitted, and a new valve cover gasket may be required on refitting. Suitable sealant will be required for the camshaft bearing caps and the bearing cap bolts.

Removal

1 Remove the camshaft sprocket as described in Section 6.

2 Remove the securing nut and bolt, and withdraw the timing belt tensioner roller from the engine **(see illustration)**.

3 Unscrew and remove the two bolts securing the upper rear timing belt cover to the cylinder head **(see illustration)**.

4 Unscrew the lower bolt(s) securing the upper rear timing belt cover to the cylinder block.

5 Remove the timing belt idler pulley securing bolt which also passes through the rear timing belt cover.

6 Manipulate the rear timing belt cover from the front of the camshaft and, where possible, withdraw the cover from the engine **(see illustration)**.

7 Remove the brake vacuum pump as described in Chapter 9.

8 Where necessary for improved access, unclip any hoses which are routed across the top of the valve cover, and move them to one side out of the way. If fuel lines are disconnected, cover open unions to prevent dirt ingress.

9 Unscrew the nuts from the valve cover, and withdraw the cover from the engine. Recover the gasket.

10 Using a dial gauge, measure the camshaft endfloat, and compare with the value given in the Specifications **(see illustration)**. This will give an indication of the amount of wear present on the thrust surfaces.

2A

8.3 Remove the bolts securing the rear timing belt cover to the cylinder head

8.6 Withdrawing the rear timing belt cover from the engine

8.10 Measuring the camshaft endfloat using a dial gauge

11   If the original camshaft is to be refitted, it is advisable to measure the valve clearances at this stage, as described in Section 4, so that any shims required can be obtained before the camshaft is refitted.

12   Check the camshaft bearing caps for identification marks, and if none are present, make identifying marks so that they can be refitted in their original positions and the same way round. Number the caps from the flywheel end of the engine **(see illustrations)**.

13   Progressively slacken the bearing cap bolts and studs until the valve spring pressure is relieved. Remove the bolts and studs (noting their locations to ensure correct refitting), and the bearing caps themselves **(see illustrations)**. Note that No 1 bearing cap is secured by 2 studs and 2 additional bolts.

14   Lift out the camshaft together with the oil seal **(see illustration)**.

15   Remove the tappets, keeping each with its shim **(see illustration)**. Place them in a compartmented box, or on a sheet of card marked into eight sections, so that they may be refitted to their original locations. Write down the shim thicknesses - they will be needed later if any of the valve clearances are incorrect. The shim size is stamped on the bottom face of the shim, but it is prudent to use a micrometer to measure the true thickness of any shim removed, as it may have been reduced by wear.

Inspection

16   Examine the camshaft bearing surfaces and cam lobes for wear ridges, pitting or scoring. Renew the camshaft if evident.

17   Renew the oil seal at the front end of the camshaft as a matter of course. Lubricate the lips of the new seal before fitting, and store the camshaft so that its weight is not resting on the seal.

18   Examine the camshaft bearing surfaces in the cylinder head and bearing caps. Deep scoring or other damage means that the cylinder head must be renewed.

8.12a Number the camshaft bearing caps from the flywheel end of the engine

19   Inspect the tappet buckets and shims for scoring, pitting and wear ridges. Renew as necessary.

Refitting

20   Ensure that the pistons are positioned half way down their bores, as described for sprocket removal in Section 6.

21   Oil the tappets and fit them to the bores from which they were removed. Fit the correct shim, numbered side downwards, to each tappet.

22   Oil the camshaft bearings. Place the camshaft with its oil seal

8.12b Identification mark on No 3 . . .

8.12c . . . and No 5 camshaft bearing caps

8.13a Removing a bearing cap bolt

8.13b Note that No 1 bearing cap is secured by 2 additional bolts

8.14 Lifting out the camshaft

8.15 Lift out the tappets

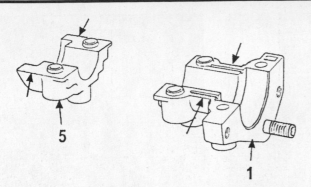

8.23 **Apply sealant to the cylinder head mating faces (arrowed) of camshaft bearing caps Nos 1 and 5**

onto the cylinder head. The oil seal must be positioned so that it is flush with the cylinder head face.

23   Apply sealant (CAF 4/60 THIXO, or a suitable equivalent) to the cylinder head mating faces of the rear and front camshaft bearing caps (Nos 1 and 5) **(see illustration)**.

24   Refit the camshaft bearing caps to their original locations, ensuring that the front oil seal is correctly located in the bearing cap.

25   Apply sealant to the threads of the bearing cap bolts and studs **(see illustration)**. Fit the bolts and studs, and tighten them progressively to the specified torque.

8.25 **Apply sealant to the threads of the bearing cap bolts and studs**

9.5a **Unscrewing the fuel supply pipe banjo union**

26   If a new camshaft has been fitted, measure the endfloat using a dial gauge, and check that it is within the specified limits.

27   Refit the brake vacuum pump with reference to Chapter 9.

28   Refit the rear timing belt cover, then refit and tighten the securing bolts.

29   Refit and tighten the bolt securing the timing belt idler pulley assembly.

30   Refit the timing belt tensioner roller, ensuring that the peg on the cylinder block engages with the hole in the tensioner roller bracket.

31   Refit the camshaft sprocket as described in Section 6, ignoring the reference to bleeding the fuel system at this stage.

32   Check the valve clearances as described in Section 4, and take any corrective action necessary.

33   Refit the valve cover, using a new gasket if necessary, and tighten the securing nuts.

34   Refit/reconnect any hoses which were moved for access.

35   Reconnect the battery negative lead.

36   Bleed the fuel system as described in Chapter 4.

9   Cylinder head - removal, inspection and refitting

Note: *A new cylinder head gasket must be fitted, and a new valve cover gasket and new cylinder head bolts may be required on refitting - see text.*

Removal

1   The following procedure describes removal and refitting of the cylinder head complete with manifolds and the fuel injection pump.

2   Disconnect the battery negative lead.

3   Drain the cooling system with reference to Chapter 1. Also drain the cylinder block by unscrewing the drain plug located on the right-hand rear face of the engine. Refit the plug after draining.

4   Disconnect the accelerator cable from the fuel injection pump, and move the cable clear of the engine, noting its routing, with reference to Chapter 4 if necessary.

5   Undo the banjo union and disconnect the fuel supply pipe from the injection pump. Recover the sealing washers from the banjo union. Cover the open end of the pipe, and plug the opening in the injection pump to keep dirt out (the banjo bolt can be refitted to the pump and covered) **(see illustrations)**.

6   Remove the securing clip, and disconnect the main fuel return hose from the pipe on the fuel injection pump. Cover the open ends of the pipe and the hose to prevent dirt ingress.

7   Release the fuel inlet and return hoses from their supports on the cylinder head and move them to one side.

8   Disconnect the breather hose from the crankcase oil separator, and disconnect the corresponding hose ends from the manifold.

9   Disconnect the coolant hose from the thermostat housing.

2A

9.5b **Cover the open end of the pipe and the opening in the injection pump**

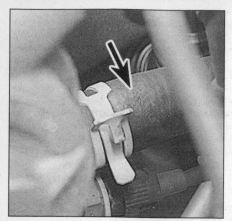

9.11 Coolant hose located on the left-hand rear of the cylinder head

9.13 Disconnecting the brake vacuum pump hose

9.25 Slackening a cylinder head bolt

10   Disconnect the air trunking running from the air cleaner to the inlet manifold, and remove the trunking (note that where applicable, the breather hoses which connect to the trunking will also have to be disconnected).

11   Disconnect the coolant hose from the left-hand rear of the cylinder head, and move the hose clear **(see illustration)**.

12   Disconnect the engine earth lead from the rear engine lifting bracket assembly.

13   Disconnect the vacuum hose from the brake vacuum pump **(see illustration)**.

14   Disconnect all relevant wiring from the fuel injection pump. Note that on certain pumps, this can be achieved by simply disconnecting the wiring connectors at the brackets on the pump. On some pumps it will be necessary to disconnect the wiring from the individual components (some connections may be protected by rubber covers). Label all connections to aid correct refitting.

15   Disconnect the electrical feed wires from the relevant glow plugs.

16   Disconnect the wiring plug from the temperature gauge/warning light sender unit, located at the left-hand front or rear of the cylinder head.

17   Disconnect all relevant pipes and hoses from the manifolds with reference to the relevant Section(s) of Chapter 4. Label all pipes and hoses to aid correct refitting.

18   Where applicable, unbolt any hose brackets from the manifolds and surrounding area, and move the hoses to one side.

19   Remove the timing belt as described in Section 5.

20   Remove the bolt(s) securing the upper rear timing belt cover to the cylinder block.

21   Unbolt the alternator tensioner bracket from the cylinder head.

22   Remove the timing belt idler pulley securing bolt which also passes through the rear timing belt cover.

23   Either disconnect the exhaust downpipe from the exhaust manifold or remove the exhaust front section complete (Chapter 4).

24   If not already done, remove the TDC locking tool from the cylinder block, and turn the crankshaft anti-clockwise (viewed from the timing belt end of the engine) by a quarter turn to position all four pistons half way down their bores.

25   Progressively slacken the cylinder head bolts in the reverse sequence to that shown in illustration 9.46 **(see illustration)**. When the tension has been relieved, remove all the bolts.

26   The cylinder head assembly complete with ancillaries is heavy, and it is advisable to attach a hoist and suitable lifting tackle to the lifting brackets on the cylinder head in order to lift it from the engine.

27   Lift the cylinder head (complete with manifolds, injection pump, and upper rear timing belt cover) upwards and off the cylinder block **(see illustration)**. If it is stuck, tap it upwards using a hammer and block of wood (taking care not to damage the fuel injection pump). **Do not** try to turn the cylinder head (it is located by two dowels), nor attempt to prise it free using a screwdriver inserted between the block

9.27 Lifting the cylinder head assembly from the engine

and head faces.

28   If desired, the manifolds and injection pump can be removed from the cylinder head with reference to the relevant Sections of Chapter 4.

Inspection

29   The mating faces of the cylinder head and block must be perfectly clean before refitting the head. Use a scraper to remove all traces of gasket and carbon, and also clean the tops of the pistons. Take particular care with the aluminium cylinder head, as the soft metal is damaged easily. Also, make sure that debris is not allowed to enter the oil and water channels - this is particularly important for the oil circuit, as carbon could block the oil supply to the camshaft or crankshaft bearings. Using adhesive tape and paper, seal the water, oil and bolt holes in the cylinder block. To prevent carbon entering the gap between the pistons and bores, smear a little grease in the gap. After cleaning the piston, rotate the crankshaft so that the piston moves down the bore, then wipe out the grease and carbon with a cloth rag. Clean the piston crowns in the same way.

30   Check the block and head for nicks, deep scratches and other damage. If slight, they may be removed carefully with a file. Machining of the cylinder head or cylinder block is not recommended by the manufacturers.

31   If warpage of the cylinder head is suspected, use a straight-edge to check it for distortion. Refer to Chapter 2B if necessary.

32   Clean out the bolt holes in the block using a pipe cleaner, or a rag and screwdriver. Make sure that all oil is removed, otherwise there is a possibility of the block being cracked by hydraulic pressure when the bolts are tightened.

9.35 Measuring piston protrusion using a dial test indicator

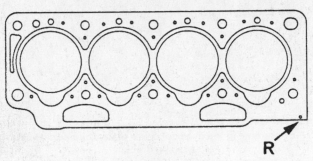

9.37a Location (R) of cylinder head gasket thickness identification hole(s)

33   Examine the bolt threads and the threads in the cylinder block for damage. If necessary, use the correct-size tap to chase out the threads in the block, and use a die to clean the threads on the bolts.

Gasket selection

34   Turn the crankshaft to bring piston Nos 1 and 4 to just below the TDC position (just below the top face of the cylinder block). Position a dial test indicator (DTI) on the cylinder block and zero it on the block face. Transfer the probe to the centre of No 1 piston, then slowly turn the crankshaft back and forth past TDC, noting the highest reading

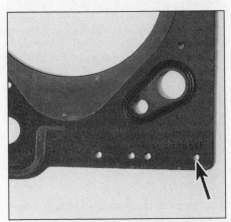

9.37b Cylinder head gasket thickness identification hole (arrowed) - "1 hole" type shown (ignore remaining holes - see text)

produced on the indicator. Record this reading.

35   Repeat this measurement procedure on No 4 piston, then turn the crankshaft half a turn (180º) and repeat the procedure on Nos 2 and 3 pistons **(see illustration)**. Ensure that all measurements are taken along the longitudinal centreline of the crankshaft (this will eliminate errors due to piston slant).

36   If a dial test indicator is not available, piston protrusion may be measured using a straight-edge and feeler blades or vernier calipers. However, these methods are inevitably less accurate and cannot therefore be recommended.

37   Ascertain the greatest piston protrusion measurement and use this to determine the correct cylinder head gasket from the following table.

Piston protrusion	Gasket identification
Less than 0.868 mm	*2 holes*
0.868 to 1.000 mm	*1 hole*
More than 1.000 mm	*3 holes*

The identification holes are located at the front corner of the gasket, at the flywheel end **(see illustrations)**. **Note:** *The gasket thickness identification holes are located in an area 25 mm from the flywheel end of the gasket. Do not take into account any other holes outside this area.*

Cylinder head bolt examination

38   On models fitted with T55 Torx cylinder head bolts, the manufacturers recommend that the bolts are measured to determine whether renewal is necessary, however some owners may wish to renew the bolts as a matter of course. The manufacturers do not specify checking or renewal for the hexagon socket-head-type bolts.

39   Where applicable, measure the length of each bolt from the base of the head (without a washer fitted) to the end of the shank **(see illustration)**.

40   If the length of any bolt exceeds 120.5 mm, all ten bolts **must** be renewed.

Refitting

41   Where applicable, refit the manifolds and fuel injection pump to the cylinder head, with reference to the relevant Sections of Chapter 4.

42   Turn the crankshaft clockwise (viewed from the timing belt end) until Nos 1 and 4 pistons pass bottom dead centre (BDC) and begin to rise, then position them halfway up their bores. Nos 2 and 3 pistons will also be at their mid-way positions, but descending their bores. Do not turn the crankshaft again until the timing belt is to be refitted (this is to prevent the possibility of piston-to-valve contact).

43   Ensure that the cylinder head locating dowels are fitted to the cylinder block, then fit the correct gasket the right way round on the cylinder block with the identification mark(s) at the front corner of the engine at the flywheel end **(see illustration)**.

2A

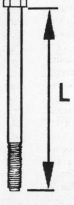

9.39 Measure the length (L) of the cylinder head bolts, to determine whether renewal is required

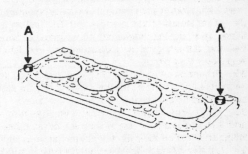

9.43 Cylinder head locating dowel locations (A)

44   Lower the cylinder head onto the block. Ensure that the upper rear timing belt cover engages correctly with the lower rear timing belt cover on the cylinder block. Where applicable, disconnect the lifting tackle and hoist. Ensure that the swirl chambers do not drop out of their locations in the cylinder head as it is lowered into position.

45   Lubricate the cylinder head bolt threads, and the undersides of the bolt heads with a little engine oil, then insert them, together with their washers. Screw the bolts into their threads as far as possible by hand.

46   Tighten the bolts in the order shown, and in the stages given in the Specifications - ie, tighten all bolts in sequence to the Stage 1 torque, then tighten all bolts in sequence to the Stage 2 torque, and so on **(see illustration)**. **Warning:** *On models with Torx type cylinder head bolts, the final tightening stages involve very high forces. Ensure that the tools used are in good condition. If the engine has been removed from the vehicle, it is recommended that tightening to the Stage 6 torque wrench setting is carried out with the engine refitted to the vehicle (it may be necessary to remove the right-hand upper engine mounting bracket for access to one of the bolts with the engine in the vehicle).*

47   Refit the exhaust front section or connect the downpipe with reference to Chapter 4.

48   Refit the timing belt idler pulley securing bolt.

49   Refit the alternator tensioner bracket and tighten the bolts.

50   Refit the bolts securing the upper rear timing belt cover to the cylinder block.

51   Refit the timing belt as described in Section 5.

52   Refit any hose brackets to the manifolds, as noted before removal.

53   Reconnect all relevant pipes and hoses to the manifolds as noted before removal.

54   Reconnect the wiring plug to the temperature gauge/warning light sender unit.

55   Reconnect the feed wires to the relevant glow plugs.

56   Reconnect all wiring to the fuel injection pump.

57   Reconnect the vacuum hose to the brake vacuum pump.

58   Reconnect the engine earth lead to the rear engine lifting bracket.

59   Reconnect the coolant hose to the cylinder head.

60   Reconnect the air trunking between the air cleaner and inlet manifold. Ensure that any breather hoses are correctly reconnected.

61   Reconnect the coolant hose to the thermostat housing.

62   Reconnect the crankcase oil separator breather hose.

63   Refit the hose bracket to the fuel injection pump mounting bracket.

64   Reconnect the fuel inlet and return hoses to their supports on the cylinder head.

65   Reconnect the main fuel return hose to the pipe on the fuel injection pump and secure it in its clip.

66   Reconnect the fuel supply pipe to the injection pump together with new sealing washers, and tighten the banjo union.

67   Reconnect the accelerator cable with reference to Chapter 4.

68   Refill and bleed the cooling system as described in Chapter 1.

69   Reconnect the battery negative lead.

70   Prime and bleed the fuel system as described in Chapter 4.

10   Sump - removal and refitting

Note: *A new sump gasket or suitable sealant (as applicable) must be used on refitting.*

Removal

1   Disconnect both battery leads.

2   Apply the handbrake, then jack up the front of the vehicle and support it securely on axle stands. Remove the right-hand roadwheel and wheel arch cover.

3   Drain the engine oil as described in Chapter 1, then refit and tighten the drain plug.

4   Remove the bonnet as described in Chapter 11. This is necessary

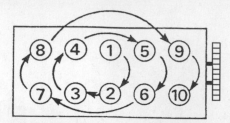

9.46 Cylinder head bolt tightening sequence

10.7 Removing the flywheel cover plate/engine-to-gearbox bracing bracket

in order to attach an engine hoist for lifting the engine.

5   Remove the air cleaner assembly with reference to Chapter 4.

6   Working beneath the car, loosen (but do no remove) the rear engine mounting link's rearmost bolt. Unscrew and remove the front bolt, and swivel the link downwards.

7   Unscrew the bolts securing the flywheel cover/engine-to-gearbox bracing bracket to the gearbox bellhousing and engine block, and lower it from the sump **(see illustration)**. A Torx key may be required to unscrew the bolts.

8   Unscrew and remove the bolts securing the sump to the cylinder block, but leave two bolts finger-tight at this stage. Note that the bolts on the right-hand side of the sump are most easily reached working under the wheel arch.

9   Mark the position of the right-hand mounting stud in relation to the upper bracket, then unscrew the nut. Attach a hoist to the engine lifting eyes, and raise the engine as far as possible without straining the left-hand mounting and exhaust downpipe.

10   Remove the two remaining bolts, then break the joint by striking the sump with the palm of the hand. Lower the sump over the oil pump, and withdraw it.

Refitting

11   Clean all traces of gasket or sealing compound from the mating faces of the sump and cylinder block.

12   Apply a bead of CAF 4/60 THIXO sealant (or equivalent) to the sump mating faces.

13   It is important that the sump is positioned correctly the first time and not moved around after the sealant has touched the cylinder block. Temporary long bolts or dowel rods may be used to help achieve this.

14   To prevent oil dripping from the oil pump and crankcase, wipe these areas clean before refitting the sump.

15   Lift the sump into position, then insert the bolts and tighten them progressively to the specified torque.

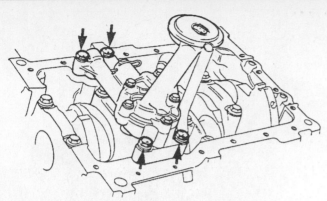

11.2a Oil pump securing bolts (arrowed)

11.2b Removing the oil pump

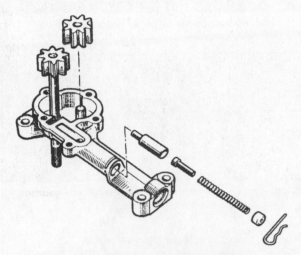

11.4 Oil pump components

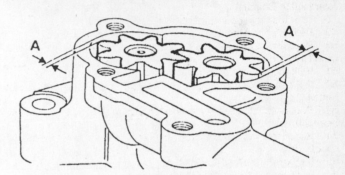

11.7a Oil pump gear-to-body measurement points (A)

16   Lower the engine onto the right-hand mounting stud, and refit the nut. Make sure that the nut is in the same position as when removed, then tighten it to the specified torque.
17   Refit the flywheel cover plate/engine-to-gearbox bracing bracket and tighten the securing bolts.
18   Refit the rear engine mounting link.
19   Refit the air cleaner with reference to Chapter 4.
20   Refit the bonnet with reference to Chapter 11.
21   Refit the wheel arch cover and the right-hand roadwheel, and lower the car to the ground.
22   Fill the engine with fresh oil with reference to Chapter 1.
23   Reconnect the battery leads.

11 Oil pump - removal, inspection and refitting

Removal

1   Remove the sump as described in Section 10.
2   Unscrew the four retaining bolts, and withdraw the pump from the cylinder block and drivegear **(see illustrations)**.

Inspection

3   Unscrew the retaining bolts and lift off the pump cover.
4   Withdraw the idler gear and the drivegear/shaft. Mark the idler gear before removal so that it can be refitted in its original position **(see illustration)**.
5   Extract the retaining clip, and remove the oil pressure relief valve spring retainer, spring, and plunger.

6   Clean the components, and carefully examine the gears, pump body and relief valve plunger for any signs of scoring or wear. Renew the complete pump assembly if excessive wear is evident (no spare parts are available).
7   If the components appear serviceable, measure the clearance between the pump body and the gears using feeler blades. Also measure the gear endfloat, and check the flatness of the end cover **(see illustrations)**. If the clearances exceed the specified tolerances, the pump must be renewed. There should be no perceivable distortion of the end cover.

11.7b Measuring the oil pump-to-body clearance

2A

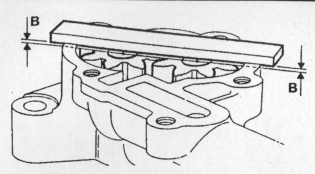

11.7c Oil pump gear endfloat measurement points (B)

11.7d Measuring the oil pump gear endfloat

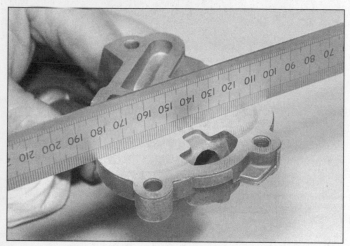

11.7e Checking the flatness of the oil pump cover

11.8a Tightening the oil pump cover bolts

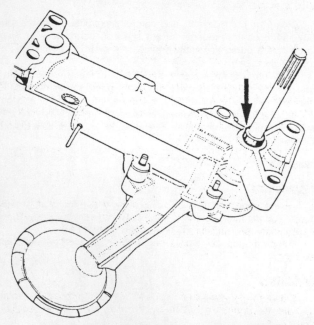

11.8b Dowel location (arrowed) in oil pump body

11.10 Tightening the oil pump securing bolts

8   If the pump is satisfactory, reassemble the components in the reverse order of removal. Fill the pump with oil, then refit the cover and tighten the bolts securely. (A new pump should also be primed with oil.) Check that the locating dowel is in position where the driveshaft enters the oil pump body (see illustrations).

Refitting

9   Wipe clean the mating faces of the oil pump and cylinder block.
10   Lift the oil pump into position, engaging the driveshaft with the drivegear. Insert and fully tighten the retaining bolts (see illustration).
11   Refit the sump as described in Section 10.

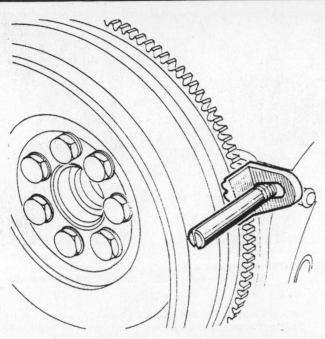

13.4 Tool bolted to cylinder block to hold flywheel stationary

13.10a Fit new flywheel bolts . . .

13.10b . . . and tighten them to the specified torque. Note bar (arrowed) used to hold flywheel stationary

12 Crankshaft oil seals - renewal

Front (timing belt) oil seal

1   Remove the crankshaft sprocket, as described in Section 6.
2   Prise out the old oil seal using a small screwdriver, taking care not to damage the surface of the crankshaft. Alternatively, the oil seal can be removed by drilling two small holes diagonally opposite each other and inserting self-tapping screws in them. A pair of grips can then be used to pull out the oil seal, by pulling on each side in turn.
3   Inspect the seal rubbing surface on the crankshaft. If it is grooved or rough in the area where the old seal was fitted, the new seal should be fitted slightly less deeply, so that it rubs on an unworn part of the crankshaft surface.
4   Wipe clean the oil seal seating, then dip the new seal in fresh engine oil, and locate it over the crankshaft with its closed side facing outwards. Make sure that the oil seal lip is not damaged as it is located on the crankshaft.

5   Using a tube of suitable diameter, drive the oil seal squarely into the housing until flush. A block of wood cut to pass over the end of the crankshaft may be used instead.
6   Refit the crankshaft sprocket as described in Section 6.

Rear (flywheel end) oil seal

7   Remove the flywheel as described in Section 13.
8   Renew the oil seal as described in paragraphs 2 to 5 inclusive.
9   Refit the flywheel with reference to Section 13.

13 Flywheel - removal, inspection and refitting

Note: *New flywheel bolts must be used on refitting.*

Removal

1   Remove the gearbox as described in Chapter 7.
2   Remove the clutch as described in Chapter 6.
3   Mark the flywheel in relation to the crankshaft to aid refitting.
4   The flywheel must now be held stationary while the securing bolts are loosened. To do this, locate a long bolt in one of the engine-to-gearbox mounting bolt holes and insert a wide-bladed screwdriver or length of bent metal bar in the starter ring gear or use a suitable locking tool as shown **(see illustration)**.
5   Unscrew the securing bolts and withdraw the flywheel from the crankshaft.

Inspection

6   Examine the flywheel for scoring of the clutch face and for wear or chipping of the ring gear teeth. If the clutch face is scored, the flywheel may be machined until flat, but renewal is preferable.
7   If the ring gear teeth are worn or damaged, the flywheel must be renewed.

Refitting

8   Clean the flywheel and crankshaft faces, then coat the locating face on the crankshaft with Loctite Autoform, or an equivalent compound.
9   Locate the flywheel on the crankshaft making sure that the previously made marks are aligned. The securing bolt holes are offset, so the flywheel cannot be fitted incorrectly.
10   Fit the new securing bolts, then tighten them in a diagonal sequence to the specified torque. Hold the flywheel stationary as during removal **(see illustrations)**.
11   Refit the clutch as described in Chapter 6.
12   Refit the gearbox with reference to Chapter 7.

2A

14.7 Withdrawing the right-hand upper mounting bracket

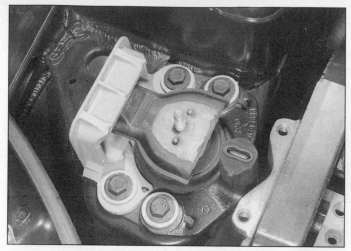

14.8 Withdrawing the right-hand engine mounting plate/movement limiting rubber assembly

14 Engine mountings - renewal

Note: *The engine mountings are positioned with a jig at the Renault factory, and it is important to mark the exact position of each mounting before removing it, to ensure correct alignment of the engine/gearbox.*

Inspection

1   Apply the handbrake, then jack up the front of the car and support it on axle stands.
2   Visually inspect the rubber pads on the engine/transmission mountings for signs of cracking and deterioration. Careful use of a lever will help to determine the condition of the rubber pads. If there is excessive movement in the mounting, or if the rubber has deteriorated, the mounting should be renewed.

Renewal

Right-hand mounting

3   Unscrew the screw and remove the plastic cover from the top of the mounting.
4   Mark the position of the mounting, using a scriber or dab of paint on the washer beneath the central nut, and around the lower mounting bracket.

5   Unscrew the nut and remove the washer.
6   Support the weight of the engine, using a hoist on the right-hand lifting eye, or a trolley jack and block of wood beneath the sump.
7   Unbolt the upper mounting bracket from the timing cover bracket on the end of the cylinder head **(see illustration)**.
8   Unbolt the lower mounting bracket and movement limiter from the body **(see illustration)**.
9   Fit the new components using a reversal of the removal procedure, but leave the mounting nuts and bolts loose. Finally, carry out the mounting adjustment procedure described later in this Section.

Gearbox mounting

10   Remove the battery as described in Chapter 5.
11   Take the weight of the transmission, using a trolley jack and block of wood, or by using a hoist on the left-hand engine lifting eye.
12   Mark the position of the mounting using a scriber or dab of paint.
13   Unscrew the central nut and the two nuts securing the mounting pad to the upper bracket **(see illustration)**.
14   Unbolt the upper mounting bracket from the body, and remove the mounting pad **(see illustrations)**.
15   If necessary, unbolt the lower bracket from the gearbox.
16   Refitting is a reversal of the removal procedure, but leave the mounting nuts and bolts loose. Finally, carry out the mounting adjustment procedure described later in this Section.

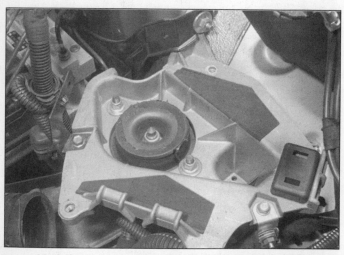

14.13 Gearbox mounting showing central nut and pad mounting nuts

14.14a Removing the rear bolt from the gearbox upper mounting bracket

14.14b Gearbox upper mounting bracket front bolt (arrowed)

14.14c Gearbox upper mounting bracket lower bolt (arrowed)

Rear mounting/lower link

17 Working beneath the car, unscrew the bolts securing the rear mounting link to the brackets on the subframe and cylinder block. Withdraw the link from under the car.

18 If necessary, unbolt and remove the brackets.

19 Refitting is a reversal of the removal procedure, but leave the mounting bolts loose. Finally, carry out the mounting adjustment procedure described later in this Section.

Adjustment

20 If just one mounting is being renewed, fit the new mounting in the same position as the old one, and check that the dimensions are correct. If more than one mounting has been renewed, take the weight of the engine/gearbox assembly on a hoist, loosen all of the mounting bolts and carry out the following procedure.

Gearbox mounting

21 Refer to the accompanying illustration (see illustration). Pre-tighten the turret nut (I) and lower mounting bolt (II) to 3 Nm. Tighten the two upper mounting bolts (III) to 20 Nm, then tighten the nut (I) and bolt (II) to the same torque.

22 With the gearbox mounting pad and lower bracket and the right-hand mounting lower bracket in place, check that the mounting bolts are loose.

23 Remove the right-hand front roadwheel, then remove the inner wheel arch plastic panel for access to the crankshaft pulley. Refer to the accompanying illustration (see illustration) and check that there is a minimum clearance of 37.0 mm (models without power steering) or 31.0 mm (models with power steering) between the inner edge of the crankshaft pulley and the edge of the body next to the strengthening rod.

24 Maintaining this clearance, centre the left-hand mounting pad in the longitudinal direction in the middle of the upper bracket/battery tray gaps. Tighten the mounting nuts and bolts.

2A

14.21 Gearbox mounting components and adjustment.
For I, II and III see text

1 Upper bracket/battery mounting
2 Rubber mounting pad
3 Gearbox mounting (lower) bracket

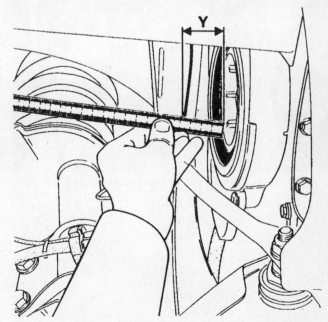

14.23 Checking the clearance (Y) between the crankshaft pulley and the edge of the body

Right-hand mounting

25   Unbolt the upper bracket if it has already been fitted, then measure the dimension between the outer edge of the lower bracket and the centre of the mounting stud **(see illustration)**.

26   Refit the upper bracket, and tighten the bolts securing it to the specified torque.

27   With the lower mounting bracket and movement limiter bolts loose, lower the hoist supporting the engine/transmission, and allow it to rest on its mountings. Measure again between the outer edge of the movement limiter case and the centre of the mounting stud. If necessary, adjust the mounting so that the dimension (Y) is the same as recorded previously in paragraph 25. Tighten the two lower bracket bolts to the specified torque.

28   With the remaining bolts loose, centre the limiter within the hole in the upper bracket so that the clearance is the same on both sides. Tighten the limiter mounting bolts to the specified torque.

29   Working under the car, refit the rear mounting link and tighten the bolts to the specified torque.

30   Recheck dimension Y on the right-hand mounting, and adjust if necessary.

15 Engine oil cooler - removal and refitting

Removal

1   Drain the cooling system as described in Chapter 1.

2   Remove the oil filter with reference to Chapter 1.

3   Loosen the clips, and disconnect the coolant hoses from the oil cooler.

4   Unscrew the oil filter mounting stud, which also secures the oil cooler to the adaptor on the front of the cylinder block, and withdraw the oil cooler from the engine. Recover the sealing ring **(see illustrations)**.

5   If necessary the adaptor may be removed by unscrewing the hollow bolt. Recover the O-ring and sealing washer.

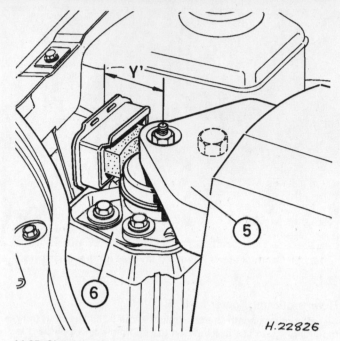

H.22826

14.25 Checking the clearance between the outer edge of the lower bracket and the centre of its stud. For "Y" see text

| 5 | Upper bracket | 6 | Lower bracket |

Refitting

6   Refitting is a reversal of removal, but use a new sealing ring, O-ring and sealing washer.

15.4a Remove the oil filter mounting stud . . .

15.4b . . . then withdraw the oil cooler and recover the sealing ring

Chapter 2 Part B: Engine removal and general engine overhaul procedures

Contents

Specifications

Lubrication system
Minimum oil pressure at 80°C:
    At 1000 rpm .... 2 bars
    At 3000 rpm .... 3.5 bars

Cylinder block
Material .... Cast iron
Cylinder bore diameter:
    Class A or 1 .... 80.000 to 80.015 mm
    Class B or 2 .... 80.015 to 80.030 mm

Auxiliary shaft
Endfloat .... 0.07 to 0.15 mm

Crankshaft

Number of main bearings	5
Main bearing journal diameter:	
Standard......	54.795 ± 0.01 mm
Undersize	54.545 ± 0.01 mm
Main bearing running clearance	0.020 to 0.058 mm
Crankpin (big-end) journal diameter:	
Standard......	48.00 mm
Undersize	47.75 mm +0.02 mm - 0.00 mm
Big-end bearing running clearance	0.014 to 0.053 mm
Big-end cap side play	0.220 to 0.400 mm
Crankshaft endfloat	0.070 to 0.230 mm
Thrust washer thicknesses	2.30, 2.35, 2.40 and 2.45 mm

Pistons and piston rings

Piston ring end gaps......	Rings supplied pre-set
Piston ring thickness:	
Top compression ring	2.0 mm
Second compression ring	2.0 mm
Oil control ring......	3.0 mm
Piston clearance in bore	0.015 to 0.030 mm (suggested values)

Connecting rods

Big-end cap side play......	0.220 to 0.400 mm

Cylinder head

Material	Aluminium
Height	159.50 ± 0.20 mm
Maximum acceptable gasket face distortion	0.05 mm
Swirl chamber protrusion	0.01 to 0.04 mm

	Inlet	Exhaust
Valve depth below cylinder head gasket face	0.85 ± 0.09 mm	0.97 ± 0.09 mm
Valve seat angle......	120°	90°
Valve seat width......	1.8 mm	
Valve guide bore	8.0 mm	
Valve guide outer diameter:		
Standard......	13.00 mm	
Oversize......	13.30 mm	

Valves

Head diameter:	
Inlet:	
Conventional valve seat	36.1 mm
Stellite valve seat*	36.35 mm
Exhaust......	31.5 mm
Stem diameter	8.0 mm
Valve spring free length	43.41 mm

Stellite valve seats are used with steel inlet valves

Torque wrench settings

Refer to Chapter 2 Part A Specifications.

1 General information

Included in this part of Chapter 2 are the engine removal and general overhaul procedures for the cylinder head, cylinder block/crankcase and internal engine components (see illustrations).

The information ranges from advice concerning preparation for an overhaul and the purchase of replacement parts, to detailed step-by-step procedures covering removal, inspection, renovation and refitting of internal engine parts.

The following Sections have been compiled based on the assumption that the engine has been removed from the vehicle. For information concerning in-vehicle engine repair, as well as the removal and refitting of the external components necessary for the overhaul, refer to Chapter 2A, and to Section 5 of this Part.

2 Engine overhaul - general information

It is not always easy to determine when, or if, an engine should be completely overhauled, as a number of factors must be considered.

High mileage is not necessarily an indication that an overhaul is needed, while low mileage does not preclude the need for an overhaul. Frequency of servicing is probably the most important consideration. An engine which has had regular and frequent oil and filter changes, as well as other required maintenance, will most likely give many thousands of miles of reliable service. Conversely, a neglected engine may require an overhaul very early in its life.

Excessive oil consumption is an indication that piston rings, valve seals and/or valve guides are in need of attention. Make sure that oil leaks are not responsible before deciding that the rings and/or guides

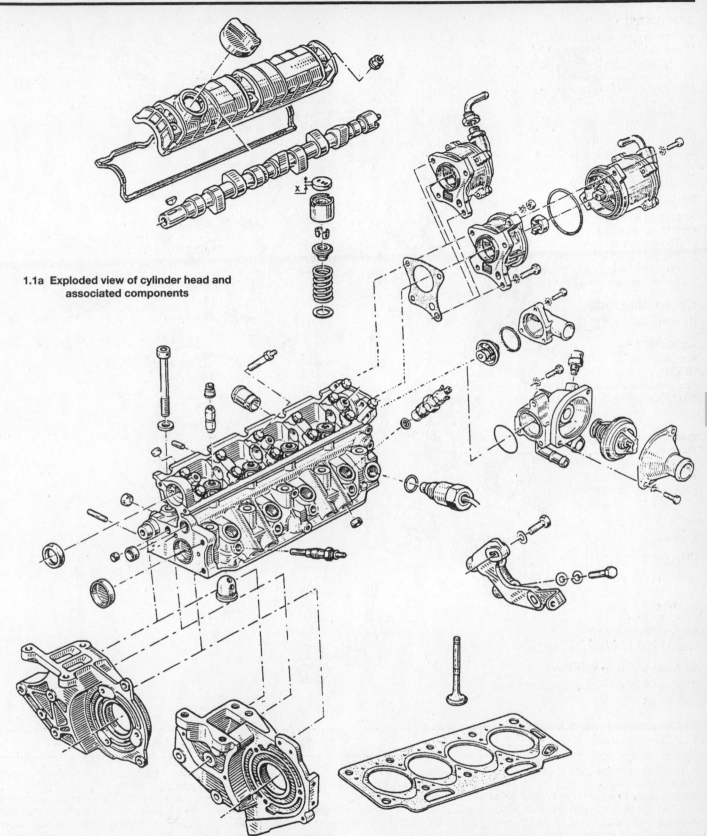

1.1a Exploded view of cylinder head and associated components

are bad. Perform a cylinder compression or leakdown check to determine the extent of the work required (see Chapter 2A, Section 2).

Check the oil pressure with a gauge fitted in place of the oil pressure sender, and compare it with the Specifications. If it is extremely low, the main and big-end bearings and/or the oil pump are probably worn out.

Loss of power, rough running, knocking or metallic engine noises, excessive valve gear noise and high fuel consumption may also point to the need for an overhaul, especially if they are all present at the same time. If a complete tune-up does not remedy the situation, major mechanical work is the only solution.

An engine overhaul involves restoring the internal parts to the

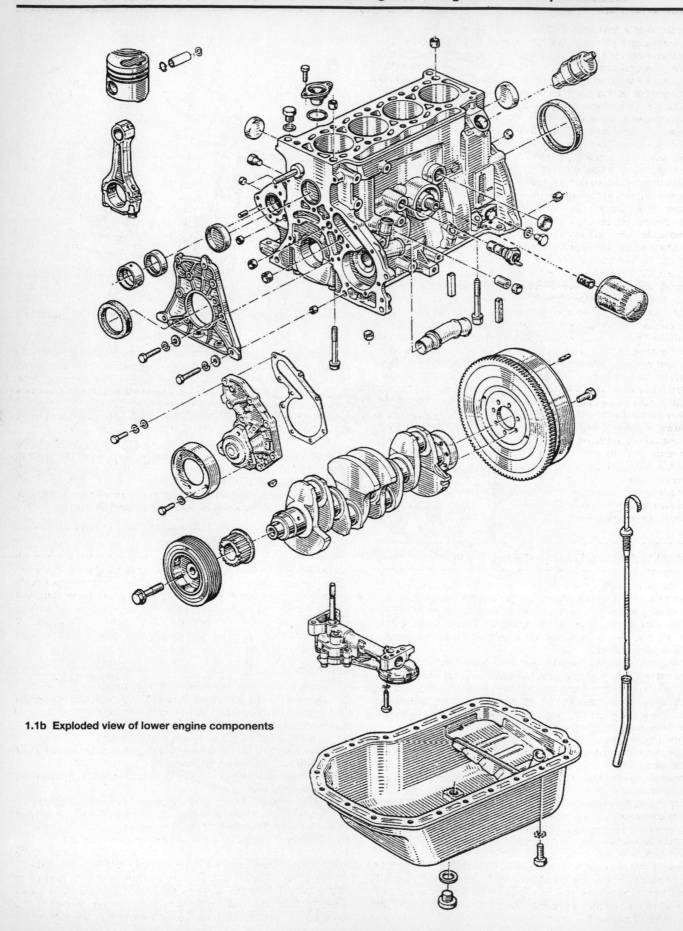

1.1b Exploded view of lower engine components

specifications of a new engine. During an overhaul, the pistons and rings are replaced and the cylinder bores are reconditioned. New main bearings and connecting rod bearings are generally fitted, and if necessary, the crankshaft may be reground to restore the journals. The valves are also serviced as well, since they are usually in less than perfect condition at this point. While the engine is being overhauled, other components, such as the starter and alternator, can be overhauled as well. The end result should be a like-new engine that will give many trouble-free miles. **Note:** *Critical cooling system components such as the hoses, thermostat and water pump MUST be renewed when an engine is overhauled. The radiator should be checked carefully to ensure that it is not clogged or leaking. Also it is a good idea to renew the oil pump whenever the engine is overhauled.*

Before beginning the engine overhaul, read through the entire procedure to familiarize yourself with the scope and requirements of the job. Overhauling an engine is not difficult if you follow all of the instructions carefully, have the necessary tools and equipment and pay close attention to all specifications; however, it can be time consuming. Plan on the vehicle being tied up for a minimum of two weeks, especially if parts must be taken to an engineering works for repair or reconditioning. Check on the availability of parts and make sure that any necessary special tools and equipment are obtained in advance. Most work can be done with typical hand tools, although a number of precision measuring tools are required for inspecting parts to determine if they must be renewed. Often the engineering works will handle the inspection of parts and offer advice concerning reconditioning and renewal. **Note:** *Always wait until the engine has been completely disassembled and all components, especially the engine block have been inspected before deciding what service and repair operations must be performed by an engineering works. Since the condition of the block will be the major factor to consider when determining whether to overhaul the original engine or buy a reconditioned unit, do not purchase parts or have overhaul work done on other components until the block has been thoroughly inspected. As a general rule, time is the primary cost of an overhaul, so it does not pay to fit worn or substandard parts.*

As a final note, to ensure maximum life and minimum trouble from a reconditioned engine, everything must be assembled with care in a spotlessly clean environment.

3 Engine removal - methods and precautions

If you have decided that an engine must be removed for overhaul or major repair work, several preliminary steps should be taken.

Locating a suitable place to work is extremely important. Adequate work space, along with storage space for the vehicle, will be needed. If a garage is not available, at the very least a flat, level, clean work surface is required.

Cleaning the engine compartment and engine before beginning the removal procedure will help keep tools clean and organized.

An engine hoist or A-frame will also be necessary. Make sure the equipment is rated in excess of the combined weight of the engine and gearbox. Safety is of primary importance, considering the potential hazards involved in lifting the engine out of the vehicle.

If the engine is being removed by a novice, an assistant should be available. Advice and aid from someone more experienced would also be helpful. There are many instances when one person cannot simultaneously perform all of the operations required when lifting the engine out of the vehicle.

Plan the operation ahead of time. Arrange for, or obtain, all of the tools and equipment you will need, prior to beginning the job. Some of the equipment necessary to perform engine removal and installation safely and with relative ease are (in addition to an engine hoist) a heavy duty floor jack, complete sets of spanners and sockets as described at the front of this manual, wooden blocks and plenty of rags and cleaning solvent for mopping up spilled oil, coolant and fuel. If the hoist must be hired, make sure that you arrange for it in advance, and perform all of the operations possible without it beforehand. This will save you money and time.

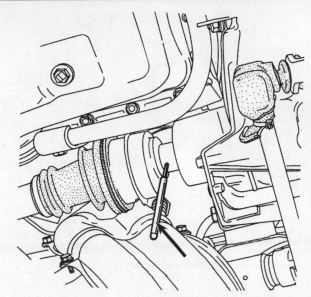

4.9 Using a pin punch (arrowed) to drive out the driveshaft roll pin

Plan for the vehicle to be out of use for quite a while. An engineering works will be required to perform some of the work which the do-it-yourselfer cannot accomplish without special equipment. These places often have a busy schedule, so it would be a good idea to consult them before removing the engine in order to accurately estimate the amount of time required to rebuild or repair components that may need work.

Always be extremely careful when removing and refitting the engine. Serious injury can result from careless actions. Plan ahead, take your time and you will find that a job of this nature, although major, can be accomplished successfully.

The engine is most easily removed complete with the gearbox by lifting the assembly upwards from the engine compartment.

4 Engine - removal and refitting

Note: *All engine types are removed upwards from the engine compartment together with the manual gearbox, and then separated on the bench. Downwards removal together with the engine subframe is possible, but this method is not described, as it requires the use of a special cradle and trolley. An engine hoist and suitable lifting tackle will be required for this operation. New roll pins and sealant will be required when reconnecting the right-hand driveshaft.*

Removal

1   Remove the battery with reference to Chapter 5.
2   Remove the radiator with reference to Chapter 3. Also disconnect the top hose from the thermostat housing, and the bottom hose from the cylinder block inlet elbow.
3   Drain the gearbox oil with reference to Chapter 7.
4   If necessary, drain the engine oil with reference to Chapter 1. On completion refit and tighten the drain plug.
5   Remove the bonnet with reference to Chapter 11. If necessary remove the front bumper.
6   Remove the air cleaner assembly with reference to Chapter 4.
7   Apply the handbrake, then jack up the front of the car and support it on axle stands. Remove both front roadwheels.
8   Disconnect the clutch cable with reference to Chapter 6.
9   Working beneath the car, drive out the double roll pin securing the right-hand driveshaft to the differential sun gear shaft **(see illustration)**.
10   Unscrew the upper bolt securing the right-hand front suspension strut to the stub axle carrier. (Note that the nut is on the brake caliper side). Slacken the lower bolt, then pull out the driveshaft and disengage it from the sun gear. Tie the driveshaft to one side, taking

2B

4.27 Gearbox earth strap securing bolt (arrowed)

4.36 Lift the engine/gearbox assembly from the engine compartment

care not to strain the flexible hydraulic brake hose.

11   Unscrew the two mounting bolts securing the left-hand brake caliper to the stub axle carrier. Tie the caliper to the coil spring, taking care not to strain the hose.

12   Unscrew the nut from the left-hand track rod end, and disconnect it from the stub axle carrier steering arm using a balljoint separator tool.

13   Unscrew the bolts securing the left-hand driveshaft inner rubber boot to the gearbox.

14   Unscrew and remove the pinch-bolt securing the front left lower balljoint to the bottom of the stub axle carrier.

15   Support the weight of the stub axle carrier and driveshaft on a trolley jack, then unscrew the two bolts and separate the stub axle carrier from the bottom of the suspension strut.

16   Withdraw the left-hand driveshaft and stub axle carrier from the gearbox. Make sure that the tripod components remain in position on the inner end of the driveshaft, otherwise they may fall into the gearbox. There may be some loss of oil from the gearbox, so position a small container on the floor to catch it.

17   Disconnect the coolant and fuel hoses from the fuel filter assembly (be prepared for fuel spillage). Cover the open ends of the fuel unions to prevent dirt ingress.

18   Remove the two securing bolts, and withdraw the fuel filter assembly.

19   Disconnect the wiring from the preheating control unit on the engine compartment bulkhead, labelling the connections to ensure correct refitting. Remove the securing nut, and withdraw the unit.

20   Support the weight of the engine/gearbox assembly beneath the gearbox on a trolley jack and piece of wood.

21   Unbolt and remove the battery tray/gearbox mounting from the gearbox and body.

22   Disconnect all relevant coolant, heater, vacuum and breather hoses from the engine, labelling each hose to avoid confusion when refitting.

23   Disconnect the fuel return hose from the pipe on the fuel injection pump, and where applicable, withdraw it from the brackets and clips on the engine, noting its routing. Cover the open ends of the pipe and hose to prevent dirt ingress.

24   Disconnect all relevant wiring from the sensors, switches and actuators on the engine, labelling all wires to aid refitting.

25   Disconnect the accelerator cable from the fuel injection pump, with reference to Chapter 4 if necessary.

26   Disconnect the speedometer cable with reference to Chapter 12.

27   Disconnect the engine earth strap from the rear engine lifting bracket, and disconnect the gearbox earthing strap from the end of the gearbox **(see illustration)**.

28   Cut the plastic tie and pull back the rubber boot, then disconnect the gearchange rod from the lever on the gearbox by unscrewing the nut and removing the bolt. Recover the bush from inside the lever. Do

4.40 Note the location of any wiring brackets (arrowed) secured by the engine-to-gearbox nuts and bolts

not separate the gearchange rod at the clamp, otherwise it will be necessary to adjust the gear lever position on refitting. Tie the gearchange rod to one side.

29   Remove the exhaust downpipe with reference to Chapter 4.

30   On models fitted with power-assisted steering, it may be necessary to remove the electric pump from its position on the side of the engine compartment with reference to Chapter 10. Leave the hoses attached, and position the pump to one side.

31   Make a final check to ensure that all relevant hoses and wires have been disconnected, and removed from any brackets or clips to facilitate engine removal.

32   Disconnect the engine rear mounting/lower link, referring if necessary to Part A of this Chapter.

33   Remove the remaining part of the gearbox mounting.

34   Connect a hoist to the engine lifting eyes, and take the weight of the engine/gearbox.

35   Disconnect the engine right-hand mounting, referring if necessary to Part A of this Chapter.

36   With the help of an assistant, slowly lift the engine/gearbox assembly from the engine compartment, taking care not to damage any components on the surrounding panels **(see illustration)**. When high enough, lift it over the front body panel and lower the unit to the ground.

37   To separate the gearbox from the engine, proceed as follows.

38   Support the engine and gearbox on blocks of wood.

4.41 Separate the gearbox from the engine

4.63 Secure the driveshaft to the differential using a
new double roll pin (arrowed)

39   Remove the securing bolts, and remove the flywheel cover plate/engine-to-gearbox bracing bracket.
40   Unscrew and remove the engine-to-gearbox nuts and bolts from around the gearbox and from the starter motor. There is no need to remove the starter motor. Note the locations of any brackets which may be secured by the bolts and nuts **(see illustration)**.
41   Ensure that the engine and gearbox are adequately supported, then carefully withdraw the gearbox from the engine, ensuring that the weight of the gearbox is not allowed to hang on the input shaft while it is engaged with the clutch friction disc **(see illustration)**.

Refitting

42   Where applicable, reconnect the engine to the gearbox, noting the following points.

 a) *Ensure that the clutch disc has been centralised as described in Chapter 6.*
 b) *Apply a little high melting point grease to the splines of the gearbox input shaft. Do not apply too much grease, as it may contaminate the clutch.*
 c) *Ensure that the weight of the gearbox is not allowed to hang on the input shaft as it is engaged with the clutch disc.*
 d) *Make sure that any brackets noted before removal are in place on the engine-to-gearbox bolts, and tighten the bolts/nuts.*

43   Refit the flywheel cover plate/engine-to-gearbox bracing bracket, and tighten the securing bolts.
44   Suspend the engine/gearbox assembly from a hoist, as during removal, and lower the assembly into position in the engine compartment.
45   Refit and reconnect the left-hand engine/gearbox/ mounting and battery tray, the right-hand engine mounting, and the rear mounting/lower link as described in Chapter 2A. Note the adjustment procedure for positioning the engine/gearbox assembly in the engine compartment.
46   Remove the hoist and lifting tackle.
47   Where applicable, refit the power steering pump as described in Chapter 10.
48   Refit the exhaust downpipe with reference to Chapter 4.
49   Reconnect the gear linkage to the gearbox as described in Chapter 7.
50   Reconnect the engine and gearbox earthing straps.
51   Reconnect the speedometer cable with reference to Chapter 12.
52   Reconnect the accelerator cable with reference to Chapter 4.
53   Reconnect all relevant wiring to the sensors, switches and actuators on the engine.
54   Reconnect the fuel return hose to the pipe on the fuel injection pump.

55   Reconnect all coolant, heater, vacuum and breather hoses to the engine.
56   Refit the preheating system control unit, and reconnect the wiring.
57   Refit the fuel filter assembly, then reconnect the coolant and fuel hoses.
58   Reconnect the left-hand driveshaft to the gearbox.
59   Reconnect the stub axle carrier to the suspension strut and lower arm, with reference to Chapter 10. Note that the stub axle carrier-to-strut nuts must be positioned on the rear side of the strut.
60   Refit and tighten the bolts securing the left-hand driveshaft rubber gaiter retaining plate to the gearbox.
61   Reconnect the steering track rod end to the stub axle carrier, and tighten the nut to the specified torque (see Chapter 10).
62   Refit the left-hand brake caliper and tighten the bolts with reference to Chapter 9.
63   Reconnect the right-hand driveshaft to the differential, and secure using a new double roll pin **(see illustration)**.
64   Reconnect the clutch cable as described in Chapter 6.
65   Refit the upper nut and bolt securing the right-hand stub axle carrier to the suspension strut (note that the nut must be positioned on the rear side of the strut), and tighten both fixings to the specified torque (see Chapter 10).
66   Refit the air cleaner assembly with reference to Chapter 4.
67   Refit the bonnet and where applicable the front bumper with reference to Chapter 11.
68   Refit the radiator with reference to Chapter 3, then reconnect the bottom hose to the cylinder block inlet elbow and the top hose to the thermostat housing.
69   Refit the roadwheels and lower the vehicle to the ground.
70   Fit a new oil filter, and fill the engine with oil as described in Chapter 1.
71   Refill the cooling system as described in Chapter 1.
72   Fill the gearbox with oil, and top up if necessary, as described in Chapter 1.
73   Prime and bleed the fuel system as described in Chapter 4.

5   Engine overhaul - dismantling sequence

1   It is much easier to disassemble and work on the engine if it is mounted on a portable engine stand. These stands can often be hired from a tool hire shop. Before the engine is mounted on a stand, the flywheel should be removed from the engine, so that the engine stand bolts can be tightened into the end of the cylinder block.
2   If a stand is not available, it is possible to disassemble the engine with it blocked up on a sturdy workbench or on the floor. Be extra-careful not to tip or drop the engine when working without a stand.

2B

3   If you are going to obtain a reconditioned engine, all the external components must come off first, in order to be transferred to the replacement engine (just as they will if you are doing a complete engine overhaul yourself). Check with the engine supplier for details. Normally these components include.

a) *Alternator mounting bracket.*
b) *Fuel injection pump (and mounting bracket), fuel injectors and glow plugs (see Chapter 4).*
c) *Thermostat and cover.*
d) *Inlet and exhaust manifolds.*
e) *Oil cooler.*
f) *Engine lifting brackets, hose brackets and wiring brackets.*
g) *Oil pressure warning light switch and oil level sensor (where applicable) (see Chapter 5).*
h) *Coolant temperature sensors (see Chapters 3 and 5).*
i) *Wiring harnesses and brackets.*
j) *Coolant pipes and hoses.*
k) *Oil filler tube and dipstick.*
l) *Clutch (Chapter 6).*

Note: *When removing the external components from the engine, pay close attention to details that may be helpful or important during refitting. Note the fitted position of gaskets, seals, spacers, pins, washers, bolts and other small items.*

4   If you are obtaining a "short" motor (which, when available, consists of the engine cylinder block, crankshaft, pistons and connecting rods all assembled), then the cylinder head, flywheel, sump, oil pump, and timing belt (where applicable) will have to be removed also.

5   If you are planning a complete overhaul, the engine can be disassembled and the internal components removed in the following order

a) *Inlet and exhaust manifolds.*
b) *Timing belt and sprockets.*
c) *Cylinder head.*
d) *Flywheel.*
e) *Sump.*
f) *Oil pump.*
g) *Pistons.*
h) *Crankshaft.*

6   Before beginning the disassembly and overhaul procedures, make sure that you have all of the correct tools necessary. Refer to the introductory pages at the beginning of this manual for further information.

6   Cylinder head - dismantling

Note: *New and reconditioned cylinder heads are available from the manufacturers or from engine overhaul specialists. Due to the fact that some specialist tools are required for the dismantling and inspection procedures, and new components may not be readily available, it may be more practical and economical for the home mechanic to purchase a reconditioned head rather than to dismantle, inspect and recondition the original head. A valve spring compressor tool will be required for this operation.*

1   With the cylinder head removed as described in Chapter 2A, clean away all external dirt, then remove the following components, if not already done.

a) *Manifolds (Chapter 4).*
b) *Fuel injection pump and mounting bracket (Chapter 4).*
c) *Thermostat (Chapter 3).*
d) *Brake vacuum pump (Chapter 9).*
e) *Fuel injectors (Chapter 4).*
f) *Glow plugs (Chapter 5).*
g) *Camshaft (Chapter 2A).*

2   Withdraw the bucket tappets, together with their respective shims, keeping them all identified for location. Place them on a sheet of cardboard numbered 1 to 8, with No 1 at the flywheel end. It is a good idea to write the shim thickness size on the card alongside each

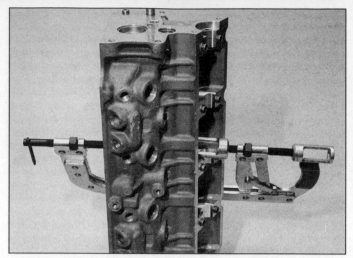

6.3 Using a valve spring compressor tool to remove a valve

bucket, in case the shims are accidentally knocked off their buckets and mixed up. The size is etched on the shim bottom face.

3   To remove a valve, fit a valve spring compressor tool. Ensure that the arms of the compressor tool are securely positioned on the head of the valve and the spring cap. The valves are deeply recessed, so the end of the compressor may need to be extended with a tube or box section with a "window" for access **(see illustration)**.

4   Compress the valve spring to relieve the pressure of the spring cap acting on the split collets. If the spring cap sticks to the valve stem, support the compressor tool and give the end a light tap with a soft-faced mallet to help free the spring cap.

5   Extract the two split collets, then slowly release the compressor tool.

6   Remove the spring cap, spring, and the spring seat, then withdraw the valve.

7   Remove the valve stem oil seal, using pliers if necessary, as the seals must be renewed on refitting **(see illustration)**.

8   Repeat the procedure for the remaining valves, keeping all components in strict order so that they can be refitted in their original positions, unless all the components are to be renewed. If the components are to be kept and used again, place each valve assembly in a labelled polythene bag or a similar small container **(see illustrations)**. Note that as with cylinder numbering, the valves are normally numbered from the flywheel end of the engine.

6.7 Removing a valve stem oil seal using pliers

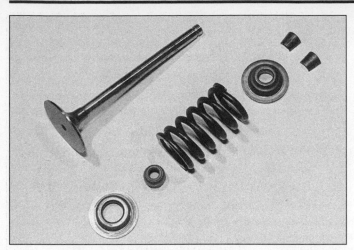

6.8a Valve components

9   If desired, any remaining brackets can be unbolted from the cylinder head, noting their locations before removal.
10   Dismantling of the cylinder head is now complete.

7   Cylinder head and valve components - cleaning, inspection and renovation

1   Thorough cleaning of the cylinder head and valve components, followed by a detailed inspection, will enable a decision to be made on whether further work is necessary before reassembling the components.

Cleaning

2   Scrape away all traces of old gasket material and sealing compound from the cylinder head surfaces. Take care not to damage the cylinder head surfaces.
3   Scrape away the carbon from the surfaces of the cylinder head surrounding the valves, then wash the cylinder head thoroughly with paraffin or a suitable solvent.
4   Scrape off any heavy carbon deposits that may have formed on the valves, then use a power-operated wire brush to remove deposits from the valve heads and stems.
5   For complete cleaning, ideally the core plugs should be removed. Drill a small hole in the plugs, then insert a self-tapping screw and pull out the plugs using a pair of grips or a slide hammer. Additionally, the swirl chambers should be removed from their locations if they are loose (if this is done, mark the swirl chambers so that they can be refitted in their original locations **(see illustration)**.
6   If the head is extremely dirty, it should be steam cleaned.
7   If the head has been steam cleaned, clean all oil holes and oil galleries one more time on completion. Flush all internal passages with warm water until the water runs clear, dry the head thoroughly and wipe all machined surfaces with a light oil. If you have access to compressed air, use it to speed the drying process and to blow out all the oil holes and galleries. **Warning:** *Wear eye protection when using compressed air!*
8   If the head is relatively clean, an adequate cleaning job can be achieved with hot soapy water and a stiff brush. Take plenty of time and do a thorough job. Regardless of the cleaning method used, be sure to clean all oil holes and galleries very thoroughly, dry the head completely and coat all machined surfaces with light oil.
9   The threaded holes in the cylinder head must be clean to ensure accurate torque readings when tightening fixings during reassembly. Run the correct size tap (which can be determined from the size of the relevant bolt which fits in the hole) into each of the holes to remove rust, corrosion, thread sealant or other contamination, and to restore damaged threads. If possible, use compressed air to clear the holes of debris produced by this operation. Do not forget to clean the threads of all bolts and nuts as well.
10   After coating the mating surfaces of the new core plugs with suitable sealant, fit them to the cylinder head. Make sure that they are driven in straight and seated correctly, or leakage could result. Special tools are available for this purpose, but a large socket, with an outside diameter which will just fit into the core plug will work just as well.

Inspection

Note: *Be sure to perform all the following inspection procedures before concluding that the services of a machine shop or engine overhaul specialist are required. Make a list of all items that require attention.*

Cylinder head
Note: *A dial test indicator will be required for this operation.*
11   Inspect the head very carefully for cracks, evidence of coolant leakage and other damage. If cracks are found, a new cylinder head should be obtained.
12   Use a straight-edge and feeler blade to check that the cylinder head gasket surface is not distorted **(see illustration)**. Check the head surface both diagonally, and along its edge. Do not position the straight-edge over the swirl chambers, as these may be proud of the cylinder head face. If the specified distortion limit is exceeded, machining of the gasket face is not recommended by the manufacturers, so the only course of action is to renew the cylinder head.
13   Check that the overall height of the cylinder head is as specified, which will indicate if the head has been machined in a mistaken attempt to compensate for surface distortion **(see illustration)**.

2B

6.8b Store the valve components in a labelled polythene bag

7.5 Removing a swirl chamber

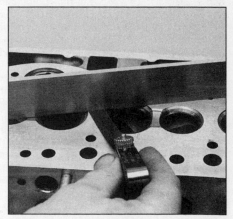

7.12 Checking the cylinder head gasket face for distortion

7.13 Check the overall height of the cylinder head

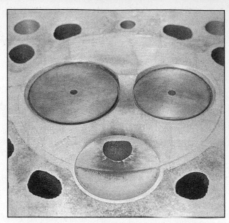

7.14 This swirl chamber shows the initial stages of cracking and burning

7.15 Measuring swirl chamber protrusion using a dial gauge

14 Inspect the valve seats and swirl chambers for burning or cracks **(see illustration)**. Both can be renewed but the work should be entrusted to a specialist.

15 Using a dial test indicator check that the swirl chamber protrusion is within the limits given in the Specifications. Zero the dial test indicator on the gasket surface of the cylinder head, then measure the protrusion of the swirl chamber **(see illustration)**.

16 Examine the valve seats in the cylinder head. If the seats are severely pitted, cracked or burned, then they will need to be recut or renewed by an engine overhaul specialist. If only slight pitting is evident, this can be removed by grinding the valve heads and seats together with coarse then fine grinding paste as described later in this Section. Note that the valve seats can only be recut to a limited depth, to avoid decreasing the compression ratio. Using a dial test indicator, check that the valve depth below the cylinder head gasket surface is within the limits given in the Specifications **(see illustration)**.

17 Check for play (side-to-side movement) of the valves in the valve guides. Excessive play in the guide may be caused by wear in either component. Measure the valve stem with a micrometer, or try the fit of a new valve, if available, to establish whether it is the valve or the guide which is worn. If the valve guides are worn, they can be renewed, but this work is best carried out by a Renault dealer or an engine overhaul specialist.

18 Check the tappet bores in the cylinder head for wear. If excessive wear is evident, the cylinder head must be renewed.

19 Examine the camshaft bearing surfaces in the cylinder head and bearing caps. Wear here can only be corrected by renewing the head. Also examine the camshaft as described in Chapter 2A.

20 Inspect the studs for the manifolds and camshaft bearing caps. Renew them if necessary by using a proprietary stud extractor, or lock two nuts together on the exposed threads. Studs which have come out by mistake should be cleaned up and refitted using thread locking fluid.

Valves

Note: *A micrometer will be required for this operation.*

21 Examine the head of each valve for pitting, burning, cracks and general wear, and check the valve stem for scoring and wear ridges. Rotate the valve and check for any obvious indication that it is bent. Look for pitting and excessive wear on the end of each valve stem. If the valve appears satisfactory at this stage, measure the valve stem diameter at several points using a micrometer **(see illustration)**. Any significant difference in the readings obtained indicates wear of the valve stem. Should any of these conditions be apparent, the valve(s) must be renewed.

22 If the valves are in satisfactory condition, they should be ground (lapped) onto their respective seats to ensure a smooth gas-tight seal.

23 Valve grinding is carried out as follows. Place the cylinder head upside down on a bench, with a block of wood at each end to give clearance for the valve stems.

24 Smear a trace of coarse carborundum paste on the seat face in the cylinder head, and press a suction grinding tool onto the relevant valve head. With a semi-rotary action, grind the valve head to its seat, lifting the valve occasionally to redistribute the grinding paste **(see illustration)**. When a dull, matt, even surface is produced on the faces of both the valve seat and the valve, wipe off the paste and repeat the process with fine carborundum paste. A light spring placed under the valve head will greatly ease this operation. When a smooth unbroken ring of light grey matt finish is produced on both the valve and seat faces, the grinding operation is complete. Carefully clean away every trace of grinding paste, taking great care to leave none in the ports or in the valve guides. Clean the valves and valve seats with a paraffin-soaked rag, then with a clean rag, and finally, if an air line is available, blow the valves, valve guides and cylinder head ports clean. **Warning:** *Wear eye protection when using compressed air!*

Valve springs

25 Check that all the valve springs are intact. If any one is broken, all should be renewed.

26 Check the free length of the springs against the figure given in the Specifications, then stand each spring on a flat surface and check it for squareness **(see illustration)**. If a spring is found to be too short, or damaged in any way, renew all the springs as a set. Springs suffer from fatigue, and it is a good idea to renew them even if they look serviceable.

7.16 Measuring the valve depth

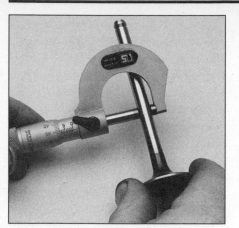

7.21 Measuring a valve stem using a micrometer

7.24 Grinding a valve to its seat - lift the valve to redistribute the paste

7.26 Checking a valve spring free length

Tappets

27   Examine the surfaces of the bucket tappets for wear or scoring. If excessive wear is evident, the tappet should be renewed.

Valve stem oil seals

28   All valve stem oil seals should be renewed as a matter of course.

8   Cylinder head - reassembly

Note: *A valve spring compressor will be required for this operation. New valve stem oil seals should be fitted on reassembly.*
1   If the swirl chambers have been removed, refit them to their original locations. With all the components cleaned, starting at one end of the cylinder head, fit the valve components as follows **(see illustration)**. If the original components are being refitted, all components must be refitted in their original positions.
2   Lubricate the valve stem oil seal with clean engine oil, then fit the oil seal by pushing it into position in the cylinder head using a suitable socket **(see illustration)**. Ensure that the seal is fully engaged with the cylinder head.
3   Insert the appropriate valve into its guide (if new valves are being fitted, insert each valve into the location to which it has been ground), ensuring that the valve stem is well lubricated with clean engine oil **(see illustration)**. Take care not to damage the valve stem oil seal as the valve is fitted.
4   Fit the spring seat **(see illustration)**.

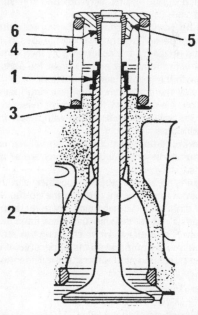

8.1 Fit the valve components in the order shown

1 *Valve stem oil seal*	4 *Spring*
2 *Valve*	5 *Spring cap*
3 *Spring seat*	6 *Split collets*

8.2 Fitting a valve stem oil seal

8.3 Inserting a valve into its guide

8.4 Fit the spring seat . . .

8.5a . . . spring . . .

8.5b . . . and cap

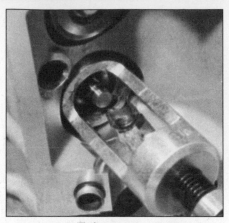

8.7 Fitting a split collet

5   Fit the valve spring (either way up) and the spring cap **(see illustrations)**.

6   Fit the spring compressor tool, and compress the valve spring until the spring cap passes beyond the collet groove in the valve stem.

7   Apply a little grease to the collet groove, then fit the split collets into the groove, with the narrow ends nearest the spring. The grease should hold them in the groove **(see illustration)**.

8   Slowly release the compressor tool, ensuring that the collets are not dislodged from the groove. When the compressor is fully released, give the top of the valve assembly a tap with a soft-faced mallet to settle the components.

9   Repeat the procedure for the remaining valves, ensuring that if the original components are being used, they are all refitted in their original positions.

10   Oil and insert the bucket tappets, together with their respective shims, making sure that they are fitted in the correct locations, and with the size markings downwards (where applicable) **(see illustration)**. Make a note of the shim thickness fitted at each position, if not already done, for reference when checking the valve clearances.

11   Refit the following components, as applicable (if desired, these components can be refitted after refitting the cylinder head):

a) *Camshaft (Chapter 2A).*
b) *Glow plugs (Chapter 5).*
c) *Fuel injectors (Chapter 4).*
d) *Brake vacuum pump (Chapter 9).*
e) *Thermostat (Chapter 3).*
f) *Fuel injection pump and mounting bracket (Chapter 4).*
g) *Manifolds (Chapter 4).*

12   Ensure that any brackets removed during dismantling are refitted in their correct positions.

9   Auxiliary shaft - removal and refitting

Note: *A new auxiliary shaft oil seal, housing gasket (or suitable sealant, as applicable), and oil pump drivegear cover plate O-ring will be required on refitting.*

Removal

1   With the engine removed from the vehicle, proceed as follows.

2   Remove the timing belt as described in Chapter 2A.

8.10 Oil and insert the bucket tappets

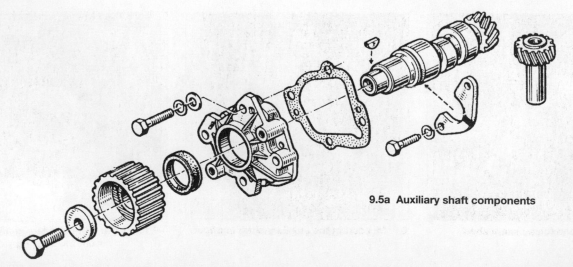

9.5a Auxiliary shaft components

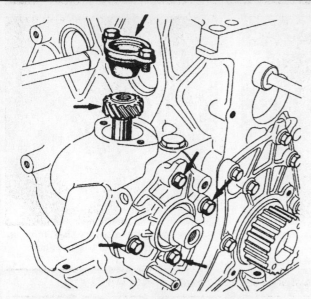

9.5b Auxiliary shaft housing retaining bolt locations, oil pump driveshaft and cover plate

3   Remove the auxiliary shaft sprocket with reference to Chapter 2A, Section 6.
4   Unbolt the timing belt rear lower cover from the cylinder block, and remove it. If necessary remove the timing belt tensioner.

5   Unscrew the four bolts and withdraw the auxiliary shaft housing **(see illustrations)**, then remove the gasket (if fitted). Note that the housing locates on two dowels.
6   Unscrew the two bolts and withdraw the oil pump drivegear cover plate/breather noting the location of the O-ring. Withdraw the drivegear from its location. Use a screwdriver or similar tool to hook the drivegear out if necessary **(see illustrations)**.
7   Unscrew the two bolts and washers, and lift out the auxiliary shaft thrustplate and the auxiliary shaft **(see illustrations)**.

Inspection

8   Examine the auxiliary shaft and oil pump driveshaft for pitting, scoring or wear ridges on the bearing journals, and for chipping or wear of the gear teeth. Renew as necessary. Check the auxiliary shaft bearings in the cylinder block for wear and, if worn, have these renewed by your Renault dealer or suitably-equipped engineering works. Wipe them clean if they are still serviceable.
9   Temporarily fit the thrustplate to its position on the auxiliary shaft, and use a feeler gauge to check that the endfloat is as given in the Specifications **(see illustration)**. If it is greater than the upper tolerance, a new thrustplate should be obtained, but first check the thrust surfaces on the shaft to ascertain if wear has occurred here.

Refitting

10   Clean off all traces of the old gasket or sealant from the auxiliary shaft housing, and prise out the oil seal with a screwdriver. Install the new oil seal using a block of wood, or a suitable socket, and tap it in until it is flush with the outer face of the housing. The open side of the seal must be towards the engine **(see illustrations)**.
11   Liberally lubricate the auxiliary shaft, and slide it into its bearings.

2B

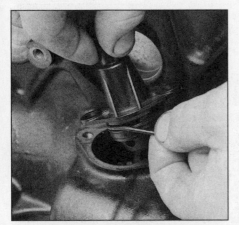

9.6a Removing the oil pump drivegear cover plate/breather and O-ring

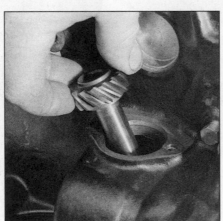

9.6b Removing the oil pump drivegear

9.7a Removing the auxiliary shaft thrust plate . . .

9.7b . . . and the auxiliary shaft

9.9 Measuring the auxiliary shaft endfloat

9.10a Prising the auxiliary shaft oil seal from the housing

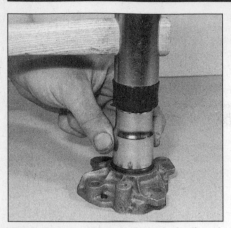

9.10b Fitting a new auxiliary shaft oil seal

9.13 Auxiliary shaft gasket positioned over the dowels

9.14 Refitting the auxiliary shaft housing. Note tape around front of shaft

12 Place the thrustplate in position with its curved edge away from the crankshaft, and refit the two retaining bolts, tightening them securely.

13 Place a new housing gasket in position over the dowels of the cylinder block (see illustration). If a gasket was not used previously, apply a bead of CAF 4/60 THIXO sealant (or alternative) to the housing mating face.

14 Wind a length of tape around the end of the auxiliary shaft to prevent damage to the oil seal as the housing is refitted. Liberally lubricate the oil seal lips, and then locate the housing in place, engaging it with the dowels (see illustration). Refit and tighten the housing retaining bolts progressively in a diagonal sequence. Remove the tape from the end of the shaft.

15 Lubricate the oil pump drivegear, and lower the gear into its location. Ensure that the splines on the drivegear engage with the oil pump.

16 Inspect the O-ring seal on the oil pump drivegear cover plate/breather, and renew it if necessary. Fit the cover plate/breather and secure with the two retaining bolts.

17 Refit the rear lower timing belt cover to the cylinder block, and tighten the bolts. If removed refit the timing belt tensioner.

18 Refit the auxiliary shaft sprocket with reference to Chapter 2A, Section 6.

19 Refit and tension the timing belt as described in Chapter 2A.

10 Piston/connecting rod assemblies - removal

1 Before proceeding, the following components must be removed as described in Chapter 2A.
   a) Cylinder head.
   b) Sump.
   c) Oil pump.

2 Rotate the crankshaft so that No 1 big-end cap (nearest the flywheel end of the engine) is at the lowest point of its travel. If the big-end cap and rod are not already numbered, mark them with a centre-punch (see illustration). Mark both cap and rod to identify the cylinder they operate in, noting that No 1 is nearest the flywheel end of the engine.

3 Before removing the big-end cap, use a feeler blade to check the amount of side play between the cap and the crankshaft webs (see illustration).

4 Unscrew and remove the big-end bearing cap bolts. Withdraw the cap, complete with bearing shell, from the connecting rod (see illustration). Strike the cap with a wooden or copper mallet if it is stuck. Tape the bearing shell to the cap if it is to be re-used.

5 If only the bearing shells are being attended to, push the connecting rod up and off the crankpin, and remove the upper bearing shell. Again, tape the bearing shell to the rod if it is to be re-used.

10.2 Identification marks on No 4 big-end cap

10.3 Checking the side play between a big-end cap and the crankshaft web

6 If desired, push the connecting rod up, and remove the piston and rod assembly from the bore. Note that if there is a pronounced wear ridge at the top of the bore, there is a risk of damaging the piston as the rings foul the ridge. However, it is reasonable to assume that a

10.4 Removing a big-end bearing cap

11.4 Checking the crankshaft endfloat using a dial gauge

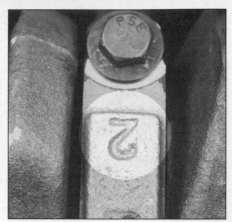
11.6 Identification marking on No 2 main bearing cap

11.9 Lifting the crankshaft from the crankcase

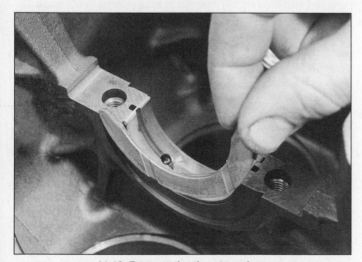
11.10 Remove the thrust washers

2B

11 Crankshaft - removal

1 Before proceeding, the following components must be removed.
 a) *Timing belt, sprockets and tensioner, and upper rear timing belt cover (Chapter 2A).*
 b) *Flywheel (Chapter 2A).*
 c) *Piston/connecting rod assemblies (Section 10).*
2 Unscrew the securing bolts, and remove the lower rear timing belt cover.
3 Unscrew the securing bolts, and remove the crankshaft front oil seal housing, along with the oil seal. Note that the housing is fitted using sealant.
4 Before the crankshaft is removed, check the endfloat using a dial gauge in contact with the end of the crankshaft (see illustration). Push the crankshaft fully one way, and then zero the gauge. Push the crankshaft fully the other way, and check the endfloat. The result can be compared with the specified amount, and will give an indication as to whether new thrustwashers are required.
5 If a dial gauge is not available, feeler blades can be used. First push the crankshaft fully towards the flywheel end of the engine, then slip the feeler blade between the web of No 1 crankpin and the thrust washer of No 2 main bearing (located in the crankcase).
6 Identification numbers should already be cast onto the base of each main bearing cap on the auxiliary shaft side of the engine. If not, number the caps and crankcase using a centre-punch, as was done for the connecting rods and caps (see illustration). Again note that No 1 cylinder is at the flywheel end of the engine.
7 Unscrew and remove the main bearing cap securing bolts, noting their locations, as two different types and lengths of bolts are used, and they are not interchangeable. In most cases, hexagonal head bolts are used to secure all except No 1 (flywheel end), which is secured by Allen bolts.
8 Withdraw the caps, complete with bearing shells. Tap the caps with a wooden or copper mallet if they are stuck. Note that the sides of No 1 bearing cap are sealed to the cylinder block using silicon sealant or butyl seals. Tape the shells to their relevant caps if they are to be re-used.
9 Carefully lift the crankshaft from the crankcase (see illustration).
10 Remove the thrustwashers at each side of No 2 main bearing, then remove the bearing shell upper halves from the crankcase (see illustration). Place each shell with its respective bearing cap.
11 Remove the oil seal from the rear of the crankshaft.

12 Cylinder block/crankcase - cleaning and inspection

Cleaning

1 For complete cleaning, the core plugs should be removed. Drill a small hole in them, then insert a self-tapping screw and pull out the

rebore and new pistons will be required in any case if the ridge is so pronounced.
7 Repeat the procedure for the remaining piston/connecting rod assemblies. Ensure that the caps and rods are marked before removal, as described previously, and keep all components in order.

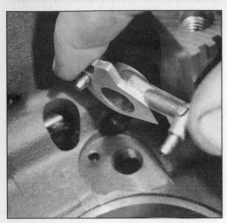

12.1 Removing a piston oil spray jet

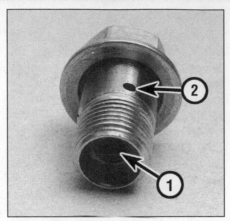

12.9a Check the gauze filters (1) and the oil holes (2) in the oil spray jet securing bolts . . .

12.9b . . . and the oil holes (arrowed) in the jets for blockage

plugs using a pair of grips or a slide-hammer. Also remove all external components, brackets and senders (if not already done), noting their locations. Remove the securing bolts, and withdraw the piston oil spray jets from the bottom of the cylinder block (**see illustration**).

2   Scrape all traces of gasket and sealant from the cylinder block, taking care not to damage the head and sump mating faces.

3   If the block is extremely dirty, it should be steam-cleaned.

4   After the block has been steam-cleaned, clean all oil holes and oil galleries one more time. Flush all internal passages with warm water until the water runs clear, dry the block thoroughly and wipe all machined surfaces with a light rust-preventative oil. If you have access to compressed air, use it to speed up the drying process and to blow out all the oil holes and galleries. **Warning:** *Wear eye protection when using compressed air!*

5   If the block is not very dirty, you can do an adequate cleaning job with hot soapy water and a stiff brush. Take plenty of time, and do a thorough job. Regardless of the cleaning method used, be sure to clean all oil holes and galleries very thoroughly, dry the block completely and coat all machined surfaces with light oil.

6   The threaded holes in the block must be clean to ensure accurate torque wrench readings during reassembly. Run the proper-size tap into each of the holes to remove rust, corrosion, thread sealant or sludge, and to restore damaged threads. If possible, use compressed air to clear the holes of debris produced by this operation, noting the warning given in paragraph 4. Now is a good time to clean the threads on the head bolts and the main bearing cap bolts as well.

7   Refit the main bearing caps, and tighten the bolts finger-tight.

8   After coating the mating surfaces of the new core plugs with sealant, refit them in the cylinder block. Make sure that they are driven in straight and seated properly, or leakage could result. Special tools are available for this purpose, but a large socket, with an outside diameter that will just slip into the core plug, will work just as well.

9   Check the gauze filters and the oil holes in the piston oil spray jet securing bolts, and the oil holes in the jets themselves for blockage (**see illustrations**). Clean if necessary, then refit the jets and tighten the securing bolts. Ensure that the locating pegs on the jets engage with the corresponding holes in the cylinder block.

10   If the engine is not going to be reassembled right away, cover it with a large plastic bag to keep it clean and prevent it rusting.

Inspection

11   Visually check the block for cracks, rust and corrosion. Look for stripped threads in the threaded holes. If there has been any history of internal water leakage, it may be worthwhile having an engine overhaul specialist check the block with special equipment. If defects are found, have the block repaired, if possible, or renewed.

12   Check the cylinder bores for scuffing and scoring. Normally, bore wear will be evident in the form of a wear ridge at the top of the bore. This ridge marks the limit of piston travel.

13   Measure the diameter of each cylinder at the top (just under the ridge area), centre and bottom of the cylinder bore, parallel to the crankshaft axis.

14   Next measure each cylinder's diameter at the same three locations across the crankshaft axis. If the difference between any of the measurements is greater than 0.20 mm, indicating that the cylinder is excessively out-of-round or tapered, then remedial action must be considered.

15   Repeat this procedure for the remaining cylinders.

16   If the cylinder walls are badly scuffed or scored, or if they are excessively out-of-round or tapered, have the cylinder block rebored. New pistons (oversize in the case of a rebore) will also be required.

17   If the cylinders are in reasonably good condition, then it may only be necessary to renew the piston rings.

18   If this is the case, the bores should be honed in order to allow the new rings to bed in correctly and provide the best possible seal. The conventional type of hone has spring-loaded stones, and is used with a power drill. You will also need some paraffin or honing oil and rags. The hone should be moved up and down the cylinder to produce a crosshatch pattern, and plenty of honing oil should be used. Ideally, the crosshatch lines should intersect at approximately a 60° angle. Do not take off more material than is necessary to produce the required finish. If new pistons are being fitted, the piston manufacturers may specify a finish with a different angle, so their instructions should be followed. Do not withdraw the hone from the cylinder while it is still being turned, but stop it first. After honing a cylinder, wipe out all traces of the honing oil. If equipment of this type is not available, or if you are not sure whether you are competent to undertake the task yourself, an engine overhaul specialist will carry out the work at a moderate cost.

19   Where applicable, refit all external components and senders in their correct locations, as noted before removal.

13   Piston/connecting rod assemblies - inspection and reassembly

1   Before the inspection process can begin, the piston/connecting rod assemblies must be cleaned, and the original piston rings removed from the pistons.

2   Carefully expand the old rings over the top of the pistons. The use of two or three old feeler blades will be helpful in preventing the rings dropping into empty grooves (**see illustration**).

3   Scrape away all traces of carbon from the top of the piston. A hand-held wire brush or a piece of fine emery cloth can be used once the majority of the deposits have been scraped away.

4   Remove the carbon from the ring grooves in the piston by cleaning them using an old ring. Break the ring in half to do this. Be very careful to remove only the carbon deposits; do not remove any

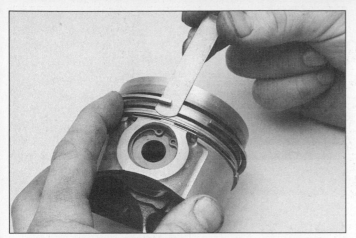

13.2 Removing a piston ring with the aid of a feeler blade

13.11a Measuring a piston diameter using a micrometer

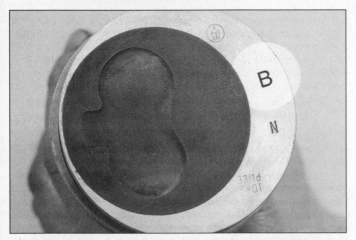

13.11b Piston diameter grade marked on piston crown

13.13 Gudgeon pin retaining circlip (arrowed)

2B

metal, nor nick or scratch the sides of the ring grooves. Protect your fingers - piston rings are sharp.

5   Once the deposits have been removed, clean the piston/connecting rod assembly with paraffin or a suitable solvent, and dry thoroughly. Make sure the oil return holes in the back sides of the ring grooves are clear.

6   If the pistons and cylinder bores are not damaged or worn excessively, and if the cylinder block does not need to be rebored, the original pistons can be re-used. Normal piston wear appears as even vertical wear on the piston thrust surfaces, and slight looseness of the top ring in its groove. New piston rings, however, should always be used when the engine is reassembled.

7   Carefully inspect each piston for cracks around the skirt, at the gudgeon pin bosses, and at the piston ring lands (between the piston ring grooves).

8   Look for scoring and scuffing on the sides of the skirt, holes in the piston crown, and burned areas at the edge of the crown. If the skirt is scored or scuffed, the engine may have been suffering from overheating and/or abnormal combustion, which caused excessively-high operating temperatures. The cooling and lubricating systems should be checked thoroughly. Scorch marks on the sides of the pistons show that blow-by has occurred. A hole in the piston crown, or burned areas at the edge of the piston crown indicates that abnormal combustion (pre-ignition, knocking, or detonation) has been occurring. If any of the above problems exist, the causes must be investigated and corrected, or the damage will occur again. The causes may include incorrect injection pump timing, or a faulty injector.

9   Corrosion of the piston, in the form of small pits, indicates that coolant is leaking into the combustion chamber and/or the crankcase.

Again, the cause must be corrected, or the problem may persist in the rebuilt engine.

10   If new rings are being fitted to old pistons, measure the piston ring-to-groove clearance by placing a new piston ring in each ring groove and measuring the clearance with a feeler blade. Check the clearance at three or four places around each groove. No values are specified, but if the measured clearance is excessive - say greater than 0.10 mm - new pistons will be required. If the new ring is excessively tight, the most likely cause is dirt remaining in the groove.

11   Check the piston-to-bore clearance by measuring the cylinder bore (see Section 12) and the piston diameter. Measure the piston across the skirt, at a 90° angle to the gudgeon pin, approximately half way down the skirt. Subtract the piston diameter from the bore diameter to obtain the clearance. If this is greater than the figures given in the Specifications, the block will have to be rebored and new pistons and rings fitted. The piston diameter grade, which corresponds to the cylinder bore grade, is marked on the piston crown **(see illustrations)**.

12   Check the fit of the gudgeon pin by twisting the piston and connecting rod in opposite directions. Any noticeable play indicates excessive wear, which must be corrected.

13   To separate a piston from its connecting rod, prise out the circlips and push out the gudgeon pin **(see illustration)**. Hand pressure is sufficient to remove the pin. Identify the piston and rod to ensure correct reassembly.

14   The connecting rods themselves should not be in need of renewal unless seizure or some other major mechanical failure has occurred. Check the alignment of the connecting rods visually, and if the rods are not straight, take them to an engine overhaul specialist for a more detailed check.

15 Examine the mating faces of the big-end caps and connecting rods to see if they have ever been filed, in a mistaken attempt to take up bearing wear. This is extremely unlikely, but if evident, the offending connecting rods and caps must be renewed.

16 Where applicable, reassemble the pistons and rods. Make sure that the pistons are fitted the right way round - the oil hole in the connecting rod big-end should face away from the combustion chamber in the piston crown **(see illustration)**. Oil the gudgeon pins before fitting them. When assembled, the piston should pivot freely on the rod.

17 Before refitting the rings to the pistons, check their end gaps by inserting each of them in their cylinder bores. Use the piston to make sure that they are square **(see illustrations)**. No values are specified, but typical gaps would be of the order of 0.50 mm for compression rings, perhaps somewhat greater for the oil control rings. Renault rings are supplied pre-gapped; no attempt should be made to adjust the gaps by filing.

18 Once the ring end gaps have been checked, the rings can be fitted to the pistons.

19 Fit the piston rings using the same technique as for removal. Fit the bottom (oil control) ring first and work up. When fitting the oil control ring, first insert the expander, then fit the ring. Where applicable, ensure that the "TOP" marking on the face of the piston ring faces the piston crown. Arrange the gaps of the middle and upper rings 120° either side of the oil control ring gap **(see illustrations)**.
Note: *Always follow the instructions supplied with the new piston ring sets - different manufacturers may specify different procedures. Do not mix up the top and middle rings, as they have different cross sections.*

14 Crankshaft - inspection

Note: *A micrometer will be required for this operation.*
1 Clean the crankshaft using paraffin or a suitable solvent, and dry it, preferably with compressed air if available. **Warning:** *Wear eye protection when using compressed air!* Be sure to clean the oil holes with a pipe cleaner or similar probe, to ensure that they are not obstructed.
2 Check the main and big-end bearing journals for uneven wear, scoring, pitting and cracking.
3 Big-end bearing wear is accompanied by distinct metallic knocking when the engine is running, particularly noticeable when the engine is pulling from low revs, and some loss of oil pressure.
4 Main bearing wear is accompanied by severe engine vibration and rumble - getting progressively worse as engine revs increase - and again by loss of oil pressure.
5 Check the bearing journal for roughness by running a finger lightly over the bearing surface. Any roughness (which will be accompanied by obvious bearing wear) indicates that the crankshaft requires regrinding.

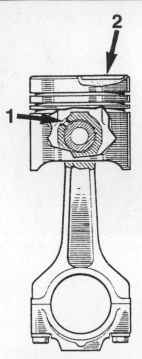

13.16 The oil hole (1) in the connecting rod small-end should face away from the combustion chamber (2) in the piston crown

6 If the crankshaft has been reground, check for burrs around the crankshaft oil holes (the holes are usually chamfered, so burrs should not be a problem unless regrinding has been carried out carelessly). Remove any burrs with a fine file or scraper, and thoroughly clean the oil holes as described previously.
7 Using a micrometer, measure the diameter of the main and big-end bearing journals and compare the results with the Specifications **(see illustration)**. By measuring the diameter at a number of points around each journal's circumference, you will be able to determine whether or not the journal is out-of-round. Take the measurement at each end of the journal, near the webs, to determine if the journal is tapered. If the crankshaft journals are damaged, tapered, out-of-round or worn beyond the limits given in the Specifications, the crankshaft will have to be reground and undersize bearings fitted.
8 Check the oil seal contact surfaces at each end of the crankshaft for wear and damage. If the seal has worn an excessive groove in the surface of the crankshaft, consult an engine overhaul specialist who will be able to advise whether a repair is possible or whether a new crankshaft is necessary.

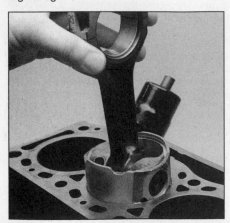

13.17a Use the piston to push the rings into the cylinder bores ...

13.17b ... then measure the ring end gaps

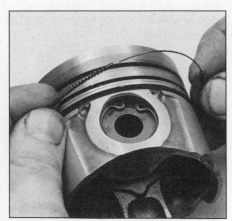

13.19a Fit the oil control ring expander ...

13.19b ... followed by the ring

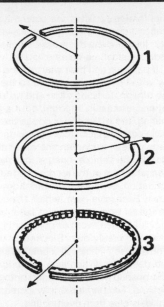

13.19c Position the piston ring end gaps 120° apart as shown

1   Top compression ring
2   Lower compression ring
3   Oil control ring

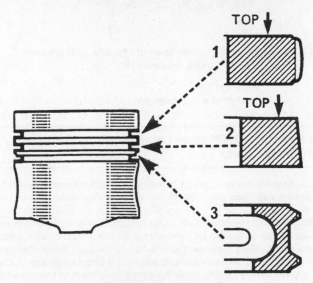

13.19d Piston ring profiles

1   Top compression ring
2   Lower compression ring
3   Oil control ring
Where applicable position the "TOP" markings as shown

14.7 Measuring a main bearing journal diameter using a micrometer

15 Main and big-end bearings - inspection

1   Even though the main and big-end bearings should be renewed during engine overhaul, the old bearings should be retained for close examination, as they may reveal valuable information about the condition of the engine. The bearing shells carry identification marks to denote their size in the form of a code marked on the back of the shell. If the shells are to be renewed, without carrying out any crankshaft regrinding, the old shells should be taken along when obtaining new shells to ensure that the correct shells are obtained.

2   Bearing failure occurs because of lack of lubrication, the presence of dirt or other foreign particles, overloading the engine, or corrosion. If a bearing fails, the cause must be found and eliminated before the engine is reassembled to prevent the failure from happening again **(see illustration)**.

3   To examine the bearing shells, remove them from the cylinder block, the main bearing caps, the connecting rods and the big-end bearing caps, and lay them out on a clean surface in the same order as they were fitted to the engine. This will enable any bearing problems to be matched with the corresponding crankshaft journal.

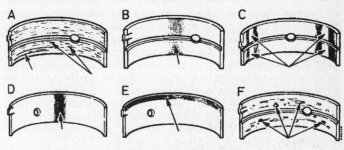

15.2 Typical bearing failures

A   *Scratched by dirt; dirt embedded into bearing material*
B   *Lack of oil; overlay wiped out*
C   *Improper seating; bright (polished) sections*
D   *Tapered journal; overlay gone from entire surface*
E   *Radius ride*
F   *Fatigue failure; craters or pockets*

2B

4   Dirt and other foreign particles can enter the engine in a variety of ways. Contamination may be left in the engine during assembly, or it may pass through filters or the crankcase ventilation system. Normal engine wear produces small particles of metal, which can eventually cause problems. If particles find their way into the lubrication system, it is likely that they will eventually be carried to the bearings. Whatever the source, these foreign particles often end up embedded in the soft bearing material and are easily recognized. Large particles will not embed in the bearing and will score or gouge the bearing and journal. To prevent possible contamination, clean all parts thoroughly and keep everything spotlessly clean during engine assembly. Once the engine has been installed in the vehicle, ensure that regular engine oil and filter changes are carried out at the recommended intervals.

5   Lack of lubrication (or lubrication breakdown) has a number of interrelated causes. Excessive heat (which thins the oil), overloading (which squeezes the oil from the bearing face) and oil leakage (from excessive bearing clearances, worn oil pump or high engine speeds) all contribute to lubrication breakdown. Blocked oil passages, which may be the result of misaligned oil holes in a bearing shell, will also starve a bearing of oil and destroy it. When lack of lubrication is the cause of bearing failure, the bearing material is wiped or extruded from the steel backing of the bearing. Temperatures may increase to the point where the steel backing turns blue from overheating.

6   Driving habits can have a definite effect on bearing life. Full throttle, low speed operation (labouring the engine) puts very high loads on bearings, which tends to squeeze out the oil film. These loads cause the bearings to flex, which produces fine cracks in the bearing face (fatigue failure). Eventually the bearing material will loosen in pieces and tear away from the steel backing. Regular short journeys can lead to corrosion of bearings because insufficient engine heat is produced to drive off the condensed water and corrosive gases which form inside the engine. These products collect in the engine oil, forming acid and sludge. As the oil is carried to the bearings, the acid attacks and corrodes the bearing material.

7   Incorrect bearing installation during engine assembly will also lead to bearing failure. Tight fitting bearings leave insufficient bearing lubrication clearance and will result in oil starvation. Dirt or foreign particles trapped behind a bearing shell results in high spots on the bearing which can lead to failure.

8   If new bearings are to be fitted, the bearing running clearances should be measured before the engine is finally reassembled, to ensure that the correct bearing shells have been obtained (see Sections 17 and 18). If the crankshaft has been reground, the engineering works which carried out the work will advise on the correct size bearing shells to suit the work carried out. If there is any doubt as to which bearing shells should be used, seek advice from a Renault dealer.

16   Engine overhaul - reassembly sequence

1   Before reassembly begins, ensure that all new parts have been obtained, and that all necessary tools are available. Read through the entire procedure to familiarise yourself with the work involved, and to ensure that all items necessary for reassembly of the engine are at hand. In addition to all normal tools and materials, a thread-locking compound will be needed. A tube of RTV sealing compound will also be required for the joint faces that are fitted without gaskets; it is recommended that CAF 4/60 THIXO paste (obtainable from Renault dealers) is used, as it is specially-formulated for this purpose.

2   In order to save time and avoid problems, engine reassembly can be carried out in the following order.

a) *Crankshaft.*
b) *Pistons/connecting rod assemblies.*
c) *Oil pump.*
d) *Sump.*
e) *Flywheel.*
f) *Cylinder head.*
g) *Timing belt and sprockets.*
h) *Engine external components.*

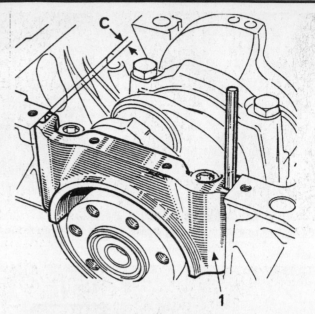

17.1 Measuring No 1 main bearing cap side seal grooves using a dowel rod

1   Bearing cap
C   Seal groove measurement

17   Crankshaft - refitting and main bearing running clearance check

Note: *Butyl seals and/or a sealant kit will be required when refitting No 1 main bearing cap - see text. New crankshaft oil seals should be used on refitting.*

1   Before fitting the crankshaft and main bearings, a decision has to be made on the method to be used to seal the No 1 main bearing cap. The cap has sealing grooves in the sides of the cap, which can be sealed using butyl seals or silicone sealant. If butyl seals are to be used, it is necessary to determine the correct thickness of the seals to obtain from Renault, as follows **(see illustration)**.

a) *Place the bearing cap in position without any seals, and secure it with the two retaining bolts.*
b) *Locate a twist drill, dowel rod or any other suitable implement which will just fit in the side seal groove.*
c) *Now measure the implement - this dimension is the side seal groove size. If the dimension is less than or equal to 5.0 mm, a 5.10 mm thick side seal is needed. If the dimension is more than 5.0 mm, a 6.0 mm thick side seal is required.*
d) *Having determined the side seal size and obtained the necessary seals, proceed as follows.*

Main bearing running clearance check

Note: *Suitable measuring equipment will be required for this check - see text.*

2   Clean the backs of the bearing shells and the bearing recesses in both the cylinder block and main bearing caps. If new shells are being fitted, ensure that all traces of the protective grease are cleaned off using paraffin.

3   Press the bearing shells without oil holes into the caps, ensuring that the tag on the shell engages in the notch in the cap.

4   Press the bearing shells with the oil holes/grooves into the recesses in the cylinder block. Note that if the original main bearing shells are being re-used, these must be refitted to their original locations in the block and caps.

5   Before the crankshaft can be permanently installed, the main bearing running clearance should be checked; this can be done in either of two ways. One method is to fit the main bearing caps to the cylinder

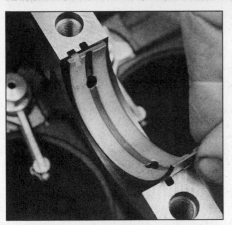

17.6 The upper main bearing shells have oil grooves

17.7 Thread of Plastigage (arrowed) placed on a crankshaft main journal

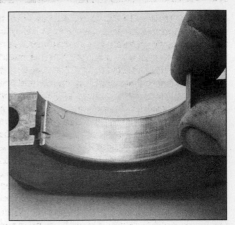

17.8 The lower main bearing shells have no oil grooves

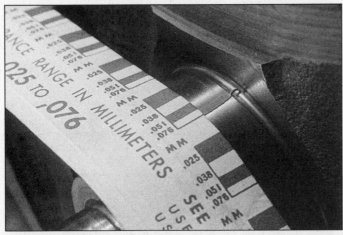

17.11 Measuring the Plastigage width with the special gauge

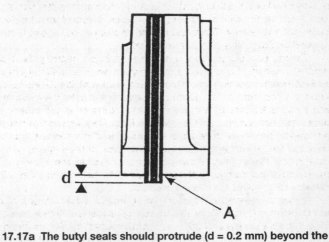

17.17a The butyl seals should protrude (d = 0.2 mm) beyond the lower face (A) of No 1 main bearing cap

2B

block, with the bearing shells in place. With the cap retaining bolts tightened to the specified torque, measure the internal diameter of each assembled pair of bearing shells using a vernier dial indicator or internal micrometer. If the diameter of each corresponding crankshaft journal is measured and then subtracted from the bearing internal diameter, the result will be the main bearing running clearance. The second (and more accurate) method is to use an American product known as "Plastigage". This consists of a fine thread of perfectly-round plastic which is compressed between the bearing cap and the journal. When the cap is removed, the deformation of the plastic thread is measured with a special card gauge supplied with the kit. The running clearance is determined from this gauge. Plastigage is sometimes difficult to obtain in the UK, but enquiries at one of the larger specialist chains of quality motor factors should produce the name of a stockist in your area. The procedure for using Plastigage is as follows.

6   With the upper main bearing shells in place (the upper shells have oil grooves), carefully lay the crankshaft in position (see illustration). Do not use any lubricant; the crankshaft journals and bearing shells must be perfectly clean and dry.

7   Cut several pieces of the appropriate-size Plastigage (they should be slightly shorter than the width of the main bearings), and place one piece on each crankshaft journal axis (see illustration).

8   With the lower bearing shells in position in the caps (the shells have no oil grooves), fit the caps to their numbered or previously-noted locations (see illustration). Take care not to disturb the Plastigage.

9   Starting with the centre main bearing and working outward, tighten the main bearing cap bolts progressively to their specified torque setting. Don't rotate the crankshaft at any time during this operation.

10   Remove the bolts and carefully lift off the main bearing caps,

keeping them in order. Don't disturb the Plastigage or rotate the crankshaft. If any of the bearing caps are difficult to remove, tap them from side-to-side with a soft-faced mallet.

11   Compare the width of the crushed Plastigage on each journal to the scale printed on the Plastigage envelope to obtain the main bearing running clearance (see illustration).

12   If the clearance is not as specified, the bearing shells may be the wrong size (or excessively-worn if the original shells are being re-used). Before deciding that different size shells are needed, make sure that no dirt or oil was trapped between the bearing shells and the caps or block when the clearance was measured. If the Plastigage was wider at one end than at the other, the journal may be tapered.

13   Carefully scrape away all traces of the Plastigage material from the crankshaft and bearing shells, using a fingernail or something similar which is unlikely to score the shells.

Final refitting

14   Carefully lift the crankshaft out of the cylinder block once more.

15   Using a little grease, stick the thrustwashers to each side of No 2 main bearing location in the crankcase. Ensure that the oilway grooves on each thrustwasher face outwards from the bearing location, towards the crankshaft webs.

16   Liberally lubricate each bearing shell in the cylinder block, and lower the crankshaft into position.

17   Lubricate the bearing shells, then fit the bearing caps in their numbered or previously-noted locations. Note the following points (see illustrations).

a) If using butyl seals to seal No 1 main bearing cap (see paragraph 1), fit the seals with their grooves facing outwards. Position the seals so

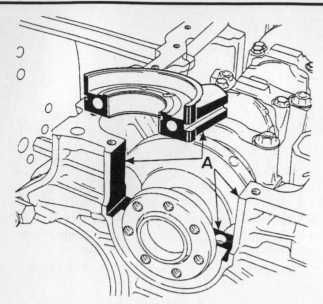

17.17b Clean the cylinder block and bearing cap mating faces (A) when using silicone sealant to seal No 1 main bearing cap ...

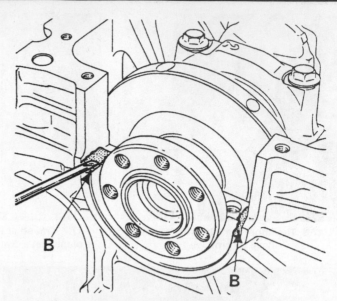

17.17c ... and coat the lower faces of the cylinder block (B) with sealant

17.18a Fitting No 1 main bearing cap bolts

17.18b Tightening a main bearing cap bolt

that approximately 0.2 mm of seal protrudes at the lower face of the cap (the side towards the crankcase). Lubricate the seals with a little oil, and apply a little CAF 4/60 THIXO sealant to the bottom corners of the cap prior to fitting it. When the cap is being fitted, use the bolts as a guide by just starting them in their threads, then pressing the cap firmly into position. When the cap is almost fully home, check that the seals still protrude slightly at the cylinder block mating face.

b) If silicone sealant is to be used to seal No 1 main bearing cap (see paragraph 1), clean all the mating faces of the cylinder block and bearing cap using a degreasing agent, then allow the cleaned areas to dry. Lightly coat the lower faces of the cylinder block with CAF 4/60 THIXO sealant.

18   Fit the main bearing cap bolts, and tighten them progressively to the specified torque **(see illustrations)**.

19   Where butyl seals have been fitted to seal No 1 bearing cap, trim the protruding ends flush with the surface of the cylinder block sump mating face.

20   Where silicone sealant is to be used to seal No 1 main bearing cap, mix the sealant and the hardener as described in the instructions supplied with the kit. Inject the mixture into the bearing cap grooves, allowing the mixture to flow out slightly either side of the grooves, and

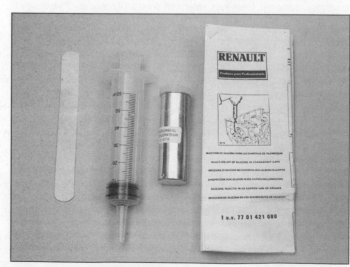

17.20a Renault silicone sealant kit for sealing No 1 main bearing cap

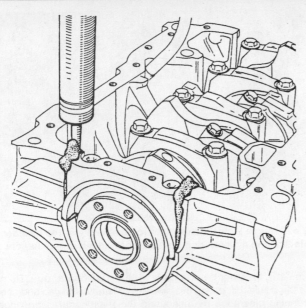

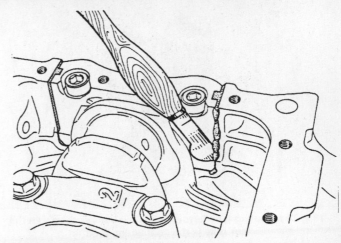

17.20c Cut away the surplus sealant from inside the block . . .

17.20b Injecting sealant into the sealing grooves of No 1 main bearing cap

at the cylinder block sump mating face, to ensure that the grooves are completely filled. Allow the sealant to dry for a few minutes, then cut away surplus sealant from the joint face, both inside and outside the cylinder block, and at the sump mating face **(see illustrations)**.

21   Check that the crankshaft is free to turn. Some stiffness is normal if new components have been fitted, but there must be no jamming or tight spots.

22   Check the crankshaft endfloat with reference to Section 11.

23   Fit a new oil seal to the crankshaft front oil seal housing, with reference to Chapter 2A, Section 12.

24   Smear the cylinder block mating face of the oil seal housing liberally with CAF 4/60 THIXO sealant (or alternative), ensuring that the oilway is not blocked **(see illustration)**.

25   Lubricate the inner lips of the oil seal, then fit the housing over the front of the crankshaft, taking care not to damage the seal. Refit and tighten the housing securing bolts **(see illustrations)**.

26   Fit a new crankshaft rear oil seal, with reference to Chapter 2A.

27   Refit the lower rear timing belt cover.

28   On completion, refit the piston/connecting rod assemblies as described in Section 18, and the flywheel, timing belt, sprockets and tensioner, and the upper rear timing belt cover as described in Chapter 2A.

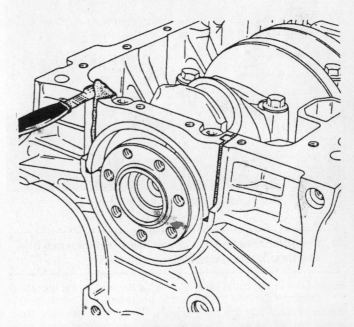

17.20d . . . and from the sump mating face

2B

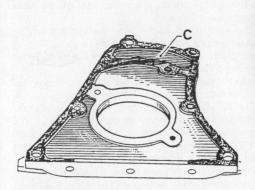

17.24 Smear the cylinder block mating face of the front oil seal housing with sealant, ensuring that the oilway (C) is not blocked

17.25a Fit the crankshaft front oil seal housing . . .

17.25b . . . and tighten the securing bolts

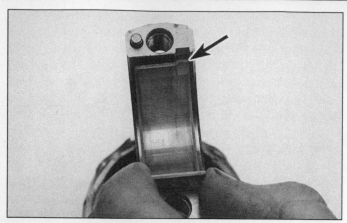

18.2 The locating tabs (arrowed) in the shells engage with the cut-outs in the connecting rods

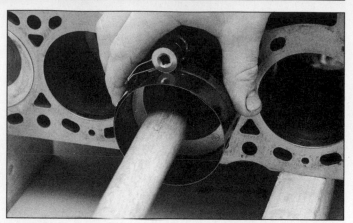

18.4 Fitting a piston/connecting rod assembly to the cylinder block using a piston ring compressor and a hammer handle

18.8 Tightening a big-end bearing cap bolt

18 Piston/connecting rod assemblies - refitting and big-end bearing running clearance check

Note: *A piston ring compressor tool will be required for this operation.*
1   Clean the backs of the big-end bearing shells and the recesses in the connecting rods and big-end caps. If new shells are being fitted, ensure that all traces of the protective grease are cleaned off using paraffin. Wipe the shells and connecting rods dry with a lint-free cloth.
2   Press the big-end bearing shells into the connecting rods and caps, in their correct locations if the original shells are to be re-used. Make sure that the locating tabs are engaged with the cut-outs in the connecting rods **(see illustration)**.

Big-end bearing running clearance check

Note: *Suitable measuring equipment will be required for this check - see text.*
3   Lubricate No 1 piston and piston rings, and check that the ring gaps are spaced at 120° intervals to each other.
4   Fit a ring compressor to No 1 piston, then insert the piston and connecting rod into No 1 cylinder. The combustion chamber in the piston crown should be on the oil filter side of the engine. With No 1 crankpin at its lowest point, drive the piston carefully into the cylinder with the wooden handle of a hammer **(see illustration)**, at the same time guiding the connecting rod onto the crankpin.
5   To measure the big-end bearing running clearance, refer to the information contained in Section 17; the same general procedures apply. If the Plastigage method is being used, ensure that the crankpin journal and the big-end bearing shells are clean and dry, then engage the connecting rod with the crankpin. Place the Plastigage strip on the crankpin, fit the bearing cap in its previously-noted position (see

Section 10), then tighten the bolts to the specified torque. Do not rotate the crankshaft during this operation. Remove the cap and check the running clearance by measuring the Plastigage as previously described.
6   Repeat the above procedures on the remaining piston/connecting rod assemblies.

Final refitting

7   Having checked the running clearance of all the crankpin journals and taken any corrective action necessary, clean off all traces of Plastigage from the bearing shells and crankpin.
8   Liberally lubricate the crankpin journals and big-end bearing shells. Refit the bearing caps once more, ensuring correct positioning as previously described. Tighten the bearing cap bolts to the specified torque, and turn the crankshaft each time to make sure that it is free before moving on to the next assembly **(see illustration)**.
9   On completion, refit the oil pump, sump and cylinder head as described in Chapter 2A.

19 Engine - initial start-up after overhaul

1   With the engine refitted to the vehicle, check the engine oil and coolant levels, and check that the battery is well charged.
2   Prime the fuel system as described in Chapter 4.
3   Prime the engine lubrication circuit by disconnecting the stop solenoid and cranking the engine on the starter motor in several ten-second bursts, pausing for half a minute or so between each burst. Reconnect the solenoid when satisfied that oil pressure has been established (ensure that the oil pressure warning light on the facia extinguishes when the engine is cranked).
4   Fully depress the accelerator pedal, turn the ignition key to position "M" and wait for the preheating warning light to go out.
5   Start the engine. Additional cranking may be necessary to bleed the fuel system before the engine starts.
6   Once started, keep the engine running at fast tickover. Check that the oil pressure light goes out, then check that there are no leaks of oil, fuel and coolant. Do not be alarmed if there are some odd smells and smoke from parts getting hot and burning off oil deposits.
7   Keep the engine idling until hot coolant is felt circulating through the radiator top hose, indicating that the engine is at normal operating temperature, then stop the engine and allow it to cool.
8   Recheck the oil and coolant levels and top up if necessary.
9   Check the fuel injection pump timing and the idle speed as described in Chapters 4 and 1 respectively.
10   If new pistons, rings or bearings have been fitted, the engine must be run-in at reduced speeds and loads for the first 500 miles (800 km) or so. Do not operate the engine at full throttle, or allow it to labour in any gear during this period. It is beneficial to change the engine oil and filter at the end of this period.

Chapter 3
Cooling and heating systems

Contents

3

Specifications

General

Cooling system type	Pressurised, with belt-driven pump, front-mounted radiator and electric cooling fan
Coolant type	See Chapter 1 (*"Lubricants, fluids and capacities"*)
Coolant capacity	See Chapter 1 (*"Lubricants, fluids and capacities"*)
System pressure:	
Brown cap	1.2 bars
Blue cap	1.6 bars

Thermostat

Type	Wax

	Starts to open	Fully open
Opening temperatures	82°C	94°C
Travel (closed to fully open)	7.5 mm	

Temperature gauge/warning light sender unit

Resistance values (typical)

20°C	3550 ± 500 ohms
80°C	335 ± 35 ohms
90°C	240 ± 30 ohms

1   General information and precautions

General information

The cooling system is of the pressurised type. The main components are a belt-driven pump, an aluminium crossflow radiator, an expansion tank, an electric cooling fan, a thermostat, and the associated hoses **(see illustration)**.

The system functions as follows. When the engine is cold, coolant is pumped around the cylinder block and head passages, and the engine oil cooler. After cooling the cylinder bores, combustion surfaces and valve seats, the coolant passes through the heater and fuel heater, and is returned to the water pump. A small proportion of coolant is also circulated through the expansion tank in order to purge any air from the circuit.

When the coolant reaches a predetermined temperature, the thermostat opens, and the hot coolant passes through the top hose to the radiator. As the coolant circulates through the radiator, it is cooled by the inrush of air when the vehicle is in motion. The airflow is supplemented by the action of the electric cooling fan (or twin fans on certain models) when necessary. Upon reaching the bottom of the radiator, the coolant returns to the pump via the radiator bottom hose, and the cycle is repeated.

As the coolant warms up, it expands; the increased volume is accommodated in an expansion tank.

The electric cooling fan (or twin fans on certain models), mounted behind the radiator, is controlled by a thermostatic switch located in the side of the radiator. At a predetermined coolant temperature, the switch contacts close, actuating the fan via a relay.

An engine oil cooler is fitted, mounted between the oil filter and the cylinder block.

Precautions

Warning: *Do not attempt to remove the expansion tank filler cap or disturb any part of the cooling system while the engine is hot, as there is a high risk of scalding. If the expansion tank filler cap must be removed before the engine and radiator have fully cooled (even though this is not recommended) the pressure in the cooling system must first be relieved. Cover the cap with a thick layer of cloth, to avoid scalding, and slowly unscrew the filler cap until a hissing sound can be heard. When the hissing has stopped, indicating that the pressure has reduced, slowly unscrew the filler cap until it can be removed; if more hissing sounds are heard, wait until they have stopped before unscrewing the cap completely. At all times keep well away from the filler cap opening.*
Warning: *Do not allow antifreeze to come into contact with skin or painted surfaces of the vehicle. Rinse off spills immediately with plenty of water. Never leave antifreeze lying around in an open container or in a puddle in the driveway or on the garage floor. Children and pets are attracted by its sweet smell. Antifreeze can be fatal if ingested.*
Warning: *If the engine is hot, the electric cooling fan may start rotating even if the engine is not running, so be careful to keep hands, hair and loose clothing well clear when working in the engine compartment.*

2   Cooling system hoses - renewal

Note: *Refer to the warnings given in Section 1 of this Chapter before proceeding. Hoses should only be disconnected once the engine has cooled sufficiently to avoid scalding.*

1   Before commencing work, make sure that the new hoses are to hand, along with new hose clips if needed. It is good practice to renew the hose clips at the same time as the hoses.
2   Drain the cooling system, saving the coolant if it is fit for re-use (Chapter 1). Squirt a little penetrating oil onto the hose clips if they are rusty.
3   Release the hose clips from the hose concerned. Three types of clip are used: worm-drive, spring and "sardine-can". The worm-drive clip is released by turning its screw anti-clockwise. The spring clip is released by squeezing its tags together with pliers, at the same time

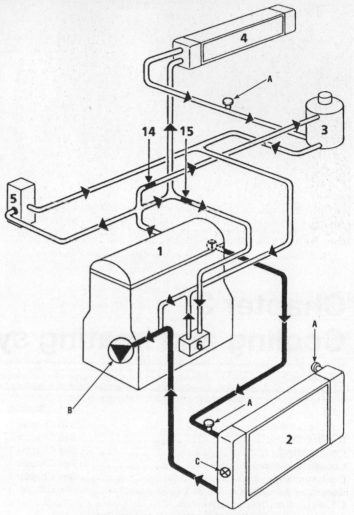

1.1 Cooling system schematic view

1	Engine	14	3 mm diameter restrictor
2	Radiator	15	10 mm diameter restrictor
3	Expansion tank	A	Bleed screws
4	Heater matrix	B	Water pump
5	Fuel filter/heater	C	Cooling fan switch
6	Oil cooler	T	Thermostat

working the clip away from the hose stub **(see illustration)**. The "sardine-can" clip is not re-usable, and is best cut off with snips or side cutters.
4   Unclip any wires, cables or other hoses which may be attached to the hose being removed. Make notes for reference when reassembling if necessary.
5   Release the hose from its stubs with a twisting motion. Be careful not to damage the stubs on delicate components such as the radiator. If the hose is stuck fast, the best course is often to cut it off using a sharp knife, but again be careful not to damage the stubs.
6   Before fitting the new hose, smear the stubs with washing-up liquid or a suitable rubber lubricant to aid fitting. **Do not** use oil or grease, which may attack the rubber.
7   Fit the hose clips over the ends of the hose, then fit the hose over its stubs. Work the hose into position. When satisfied, locate and tighten the hose clips.
8   Refill the cooling system (Chapter 1). Run the engine, and check that there are no leaks.
9   Top up the coolant level if necessary.
10   Recheck the tightness of the hose clips on any new hoses after a few hundred miles.

2.3 Releasing a spring hose clip using self-locking pliers

3.4 Disconnecting the radiator top hose

3 Radiator - removal, inspection, cleaning and refitting

Note: *Refer to the warnings given in Section 1 of this Chapter before proceeding. If the radiator is to be removed for a period of more than 48 hours, precautions must be taken against internal corrosion. Either rinse the radiator with clean water and dry it thoroughly by blowing air through it, or fill it with coolant and plug the hose stubs. If the reason for removing the radiator is concern over coolant loss, note that minor leaks may be repaired by using a proprietary radiator sealant.*

Removal

1   Disconnect the battery earth lead.
2   Remove the cooling fan (Section 6).
3   Drain the cooling system by disconnecting the radiator bottom hose. Save the coolant in a clean container if it is fit for re-use.
4   Release the hose clips and disconnect the remaining hoses from the radiator **(see illustration)**.
5   Remove the two radiator mounting bolts from the top crossmember. Note the position of each mounting (they are not the same) and remove them **(see illustrations)**.
6   If wished, the bonnet may be removed to improve access.
7   Carefully lift the radiator off its bottom mountings until the thermostatic switch wiring plug can be disconnected, then remove it from the engine compartment.
8   Recover the mountings; renew them if they are in poor condition **(see illustration)**.

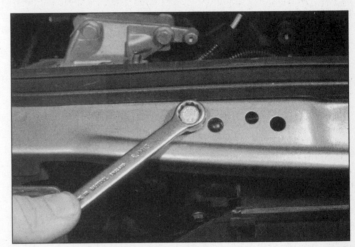

3.5a Removing a radiator mounting bolt

Inspection and cleaning

9   Radiator repair is best left to a specialist, but minor leaks may be sealed without removing the radiator, using a proprietary sealant. The area of a leak can usually be identified by a rusty or crystalline deposit.
10   Clear the radiator matrix of flies and leaves with a soft brush, or by hosing.

3.5b Right-hand mounting has a locating tag (arrowed) . . .

3.5c . . . left-hand mounting does not

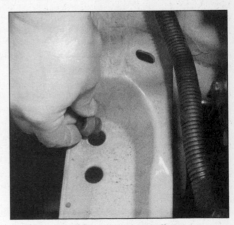

3.8 Removing the radiator bottom mountings

3

5.5a Removing the thermostat

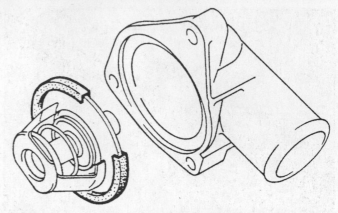

5.5b Thermostat and cover/housing

6.3a Removing the electric cooling fan assembly retaining screws
(models without a shroud)

Refitting

11   Refit by reversing the removal operations. Refill the cooling system on completion (see Chapter 1).

4   Expansion tank - removal, inspection and refitting

Note: *Refer to the warnings given in Section 1 of this Chapter before proceeding.*

Removal

1   With the engine cold, drain some coolant from the system until the expansion tank is empty.
2   Release the strap which secures the tank. Disconnect the hoses and remove the tank.

Inspection

3   Clean the tank and inspect it for cracks and other damage. Renew it if necessary. Also inspect the cap; if there is evidence that coolant has been vented through the cap, renew it.

Refitting

4   Refit by reversing the removal operations. Refill and bleed the cooling system as described in Chapter 1.

5   Thermostat - removal, testing and refitting

Note: *Refer to the warnings given in Section 1 of this Chapter before proceeding. A new sealing ring may be required on refitting.*
1   The thermostat is located in a housing bolted to the left-hand end of the cylinder head.

Removal

2   Where necessary, disconnect the crankcase breather hose and move the hose to one side to improve access to the thermostat cover/housing.
3   Partially drain the cooling system, so that the coolant level is below the thermostat location.
4   For improved access loosen the clip and disconnect the top hose from the thermostat cover/housing.
5   Unbolt the cover/housing, and remove the thermostat **(see illustrations)**.
6   Remove the sealing ring from the thermostat.

Testing

7   To test whether the unit is serviceable, suspend it on a string in a saucepan of cold water, together with a thermometer. Heat the water, and note the temperature at which the thermostat begins to open. Continue heating the water until the thermostat is fully open, and then remove it from the water.
8   The temperature at which the thermostat should start to open is stamped on the unit. If the thermostat does not start to open at the specified temperature, does not fully open in boiling water, or does not fully close when removed from the water, then it must be discarded and a new one fitted.

Refitting

9   Refitting is a reversal of removal, but renew the sealing ring. Refill the cooling system as described in Chapter 1.

6   Electric cooling fan assembly - removal and refitting

Removal

1   Disconnect the battery earth lead.
2   Release the multi-plugs from each side of the fan frame, and disconnect them.
3   Remove the four retaining screws and withdraw the fan assembly. On some models the cooling fan is attached to the radiator shroud **(see illustrations)**. Note which way up it is fitted.
4   Unscrew the nut or extract the retaining clip and slide the fan off the motor shaft.
5   The motor can now be removed by drilling out the retaining rivets, or unscrewing the mounting nuts and bolts, as applicable.

6.3b Radiator shroud mounting bolt (arrowed)

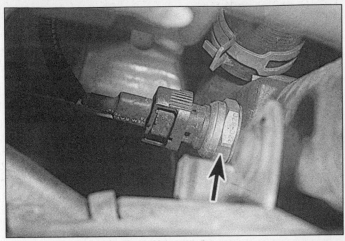

7.1 Fan switch (arrowed) screws into radiator

9.3 Three bolts (arrowed) which secure the water pump pulley

Refitting

6   Refit by reversing the removal operations, but where applicable, use new rivets.

7   Electric cooling fan thermostatic switch - testing, removal and refitting

Testing

1   Free the switch multi-plug and disconnect it **(see illustration)**.
2   With the ignition on, bridge the multi-plug terminals on the wiring harness with a paper clip or a short length of wire. Be careful not to let the bridging link touch earth (bare metal). The fan should run.
3   If there has been a problem of overheating due to the fan not operating, but it runs with the bridge in place, this suggests that the thermostatic switch is defective.
4   If the fan does not run with the bridge in place, there is a fault in the fan itself or in its supply circuit (including the fuse and, if applicable, the relay).
5   The switch can be tested further after removal by immersing it in heated water (refer to Section 5 - testing the thermostat), and using a continuity tester to check that the switch contacts open and close.

Removal

6   Drain the cooling system (Chapter 1).
7   Free the switch multi-plug and disconnect it.
8   Unscrew the switch from the radiator and remove it.

Refitting

9   Apply a little sealant to the threads of the switch, and screw it into position.
10   Reconnect and secure the multi-plug.
11   Refill the cooling system (Chapter 1).

8   Temperature gauge/warning light sender unit - testing, removal and refitting

1   The temperature gauge/warning light sender unit is located at the rear left-hand end of the cylinder head.

Testing

Note: *An ohmmeter will be required for testing.*
2   Disconnect the wiring plug from the sender. Using an ohmmeter, measure the resistance of the sender, and compare it with the values given in the Specifications. If the value obtained is greatly different from that specified, the sender is probably defective.
3   For accurate testing across the temperature range, the sender unit will have to be removed.

Removal

Note: *Refer to the warnings given in Section 1 of this Chapter before proceeding. Suitable sealant will be required when refitting.*
4   Drain the cooling system (see Chapter 1). Alternatively, remove the expansion tank cap to depressurise the system, and have the new sender or a suitable bung to hand.
5   Disconnect the wiring plug and unscrew the sender.

Refitting

6   Apply a little sealant to the sender threads, and screw it into position. Reconnect the wiring plug.
7   Top-up or refill the cooling system as necessary (see Chapter 1).

9   Water pump - removal and refitting

Note: *Refer to the warnings given in Section 1 of this Chapter before proceeding. A new gasket must be used on refitting.*

Removal

1   Disconnect the battery negative lead, then refer to Chapter 1 and drain the cooling system.
2   Remove the alternator as described in Chapter 5.
3   Unscrew the three bolts and remove the pump pulley **(see illustration)**.

3

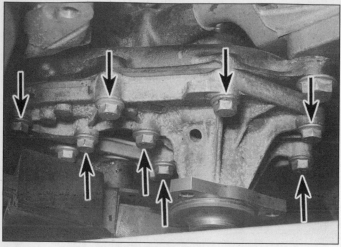

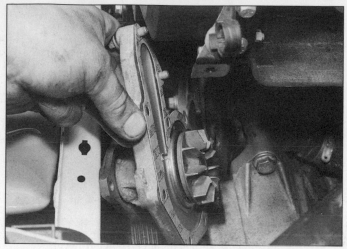

9.4 Water pump securing bolts (arrowed) - not all bolts are visible

9.5 Withdrawing the water pump

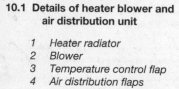

10.1 Details of heater blower and air distribution unit

1   Heater radiator
2   Blower
3   Temperature control flap
4   Air distribution flaps
5   Air distribution control cable
6   Temperature control cable
a   Air inlet
b   Outlet to demisting ducts
c   Outlet to facia vents
d   Outlet to lower vents
X   Scuttle (under-bonnet)
Y   Passenger compartment

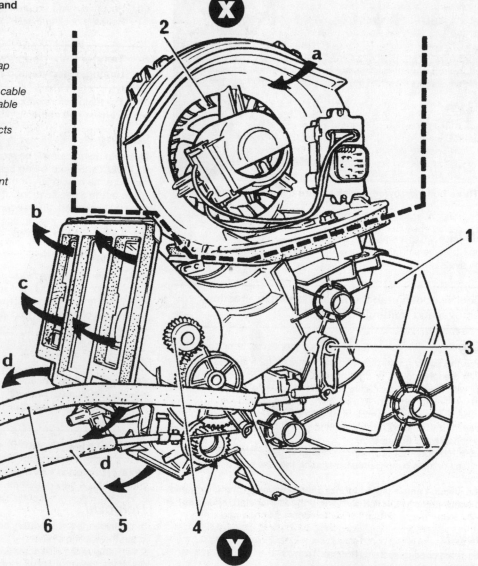

11.4 Removing a heater blower cover screw

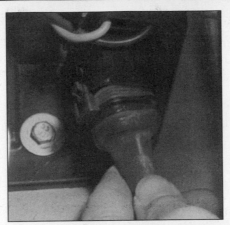

11.5 Disconnecting the multi-plug from the heater blower resistor

11.7a One of the heater blower securing bolts (arrowed)

4   Working through the top of the engine compartment, unscrew the bolts securing the water pump to the cylinder block **(see illustration)**. Note that some of the bolts cannot be removed completely due to limited clearance, and must be removed with the pump.

5   Withdraw the pump from its location **(see illustration)**. It may be necessary to lever the engine slightly away from the right-hand body panel, using a suitable lever, to allow sufficient clearance to remove the pump (the engine should move sufficiently without disconnecting the mountings). If this is done, take care not to damage any of the surrounding components. If the pump is stuck, tap it sharply with a plastic or hide mallet. Remove the gasket.

Refitting

6   Clean the mating faces of the water pump and cylinder block.

7   Locate the water pump on the cylinder block together with a new gasket, and with the relevant bolts fitted to the pump flange. If necessary, lever the engine slightly away from the body as during removal.

8   Insert the remaining bolts and tighten them.

9   Refit the pump pulley and tighten the bolts.

10   Refit the alternator as described in Chapter 5, and tension the drivebelt with reference to Chapter 1.

11   Refill the cooling system (Chapter 1), then re-connect the battery negative lead.

10 Heating system - general information and checks

General information

The heater and fresh air ventilation unit works on the principle of mixing hot and cold air in the proportions selected by means of the central (temperature) control knob **(see illustration)**. Coolant flows through the heater radiator all the time that the engine is running, regardless of the temperature selected.

Air distribution is selected by the left-hand control knob. Additional control is possible by opening, closing or redirecting individual vents in the facia panel.

A three-speed blower is controlled by the right-hand knob.

Checks

Periodically check that all the controls operate as intended. Problems related to the temperature and air distribution controls may be due to cables being broken or disconnected (Section 13).

If the blower does not operate at all, check the fuse and the blower multi-plug before condemning the motor. If one or two speeds do not work, the fault is almost certainly in the dropper resistor (Section 11).

Check the condition and security of the coolant hoses which feed

11.7b Removing the heater blower

the heater radiator. The radiator-to-hose joints are at the bulkhead under the bonnet. If water leaks inside the car seem to be coming from the heater, establish whether the leak is of coolant (indicating a leaking heater radiator) or of rainwater (indicating a defective scuttle seal). Cooling system antifreeze has a distinctive sweet smell.

11 Heater components - removal and refitting

Blower assembly

1   Disconnect the battery earth lead.

2   Remove the windscreen cowl panel (Chapter 11).

3   Remove the vehicle jack.

4   Remove the heater blower cover, which is secured by two screws **(see illustration)**.

5   Disconnect the multi-plug from the resistor on the side of the blower **(see illustration)**.

6   Remove the two bolts which secure the blower.

7   Manipulate the blower and remove it through the scuttle **(see illustrations)**.

8   If the motor is to be renewed, release the clips and separate the half-housings. Use new clips (supplied with a new motor) on reassembly.

9   Check the condition of the seal at the base of the blower. Renew it if its condition is in doubt. **Note:** *If the seal is defective, rainwater entering the scuttle will leak into the passenger compartment.*

10   Refit by reversing the removal operations.

3

11.12 Disconnecting the blower motor multi-plug

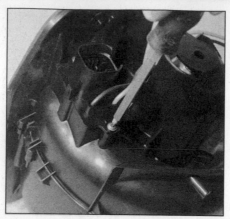

11.13a Remove the screws . . .

11.13b . . . release the clips and withdraw the resistor

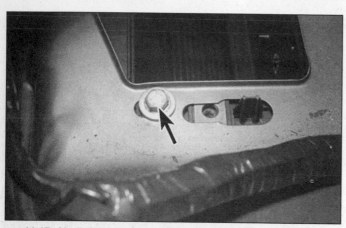

11.17 Air distribution unit retaining screw (arrowed) is only accessible after removing the blower

11.18 Disconnecting the heater hoses at the bulkhead. Hoses are different sizes, so they cannot get mixed up

Blower motor dropper resistor

11   This resistor is located in the right-hand side of the blower casing. It is switched into the circuit at low and intermediate speeds. If it fails, one or more speeds will not be operative.

12   Gain access to the blower assembly as described earlier, and disconnect the multi-plug from the resistor. Also disconnect the multi-plug from the blower motor **(see illustration)**.

13   Remove the two screws, release the clips and withdraw the resistor **(see illustrations)**.

14   Refit by reversing the removal operations.

Air distribution unit

Note: *Refer to the warnings given in Section 1 of this Chapter before proceeding.*

15   Remove the complete facia assembly (Chapter 11).

16   Remove the blower assembly as described earlier. Also remove the windscreen wiper arms.

17   Remove the single retaining screw now accessible from the scuttle **(see illustration)**.

18   Clamp the coolant hoses where they pass through the bulkhead. Alternatively, drain the cooling system. Disconnect the hoses from the heater radiator stubs **(see illustration)**.

19   Remove the two screws and free the duct panel from the air distribution unit, bending the facia central support bracket rearwards if necessary **(see illustration)**.

20   Remove the air distribution unit, complete with control panel and cables, from inside the car **(see illustration)**. Be prepared for coolant spillage from the heater radiator.

21   Refit by reversing the removal operations. Refill and bleed the cooling system (Chapter 1).

11.19 Removing the duct panel from the air distribution unit

Heater radiator

22   Remove the air distribution unit as previously described.

23   Remove the foam seal and the closing plate from the heater radiator stubs **(see illustration)**.

24   Remove the two screws (if fitted), release the clips and withdraw the heater radiator **(see illustrations)**. Be careful not to damage the fins.

25   Refit by reversing the removal operations. If the clips were damaged during removal, secure the radiator using two screws in the holes provided.

11.20 Removing the air distribution unit, control panel and cables

11.23 Removing the foam seal and the closing plate from the heater radiator stubs

11.24a Remove the heater radiator securing screws, if fitted . . .

11.24b . . . release the clips . . .

11.24c . . . and remove the heater radiator

12.1a Remove the screws (two at the bottom and one at the side) . . .

3

12.1b . . . to free the facia side vent

13.3a Removing a heater control panel screw

13.3b Withdrawing the heater control panel

12 Heater ducts and vents - removal and refitting

1   The facia side vents are each secured by three Torx screws - one at the side, and two at the bottom. Remove the screws and withdraw the vent **(see illustrations)**.
2   The centre vent cannot be removed independently of the facia.
3   The removal of the central duct panel is included in the operation to remove the air distribution unit (Section 11).

13 Heater controls - removal and refitting

Control panel and bulb
1   Disconnect the battery earth lead. Remove the radio (Chapter 12).
2   Remove the radio housing, which is secured by four screws (Chapter 11).
3   Remove the two screws which secure the heater control panel. Withdraw the control panel **(see illustrations)**.

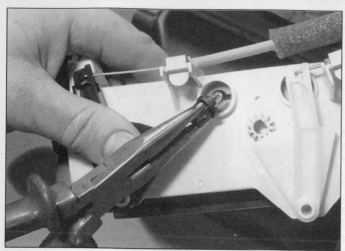

13.4a To renew the heater control panel bulb, free the bulbholder by twisting it a quarter of a turn with pliers . . .

13.4b . . . then separate the bulb and holder

13.8a Remove the heater control cable securing clip . . .

13.8b . . . and disconnect the cable from the lever

4   If the reason for removing the panel is to renew the bulb, this can be done without further dismantling **(see illustrations)**. To remove the panel completely, disconnect the multi-plugs and the cables.
5   Refit by reversing the removal operations. Check that the controls operate over their full range before securing the panel.

Control cables

6   Remove the control panel as just described.
7   Remove the two screws which secure the duct panel to the air distribution unit. Withdraw the duct panel for access to the cables.
8   Remove the cable securing clips. Disconnect each cable from its lever by turning the cable through 90° **(see Illustrations)**. Also disconnect the return spring from the temperature control lever.
9   Remove the cables. Note that they are of different lengths; the longer cable controls the temperature flap.
10   Before refitting, position the flap levers on the distribution unit in the "cold" and "ventilation" positions **(see illustration)**. Turn the control panel knobs fully anti-clockwise to the corresponding positions.
11   Connect the cables and the return spring. Fit the cable securing clips, and check the operation of the controls.
12   Refit the duct panel and the control panel.

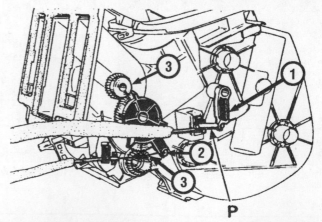

13.10 Correct positions of control flap levers on the heater distribution unit when reconnecting the cables

1	Temperature control flap	3	Gear alignment marks
2	Air distribution flap	P	Spring

Chapter 4
Fuel, exhaust and emission control systems

Contents

Specifications

Note: *The engine code appears on a plate attached to the engine. Refer to "Buying spare parts and vehicle identification numbers" for further details.*

General

System type	Rear-mounted fuel tank, distributor fuel injection pump with integral transfer pump, indirect injection.
Firing order	1-3-4-2 (number 1 at flywheel end)
Fuel type	Diesel
Fuel tank capacity	43 litres
Maximum speed	5200 ± 100 rpm
Fast idle speed:	
Bosch injection pump	1000 ± 50 rpm
Roto-Diesel/Lucas injection pump	Not adjustable (factory set)

Injection pump (Bosch)

Direction of rotation	Clockwise viewed from sprocket end
Static timing:	
Engine position	Number 1 cylinder at TDC (see Section 14)
Pump position:	
F8Q 730 engine	0.82 ± 0.02 mm
F8Q 732 engine	0.70 ± 0.02 mm
Dynamic timing:	
F8Q 730 engine	No information available at time of writing
F8Q 732 engine	12.5 ± 1° BTDC at idle

Injection pump (Roto-Diesel/Lucas/CAV)

Direction of rotation	Clockwise viewed from sprocket end
Static timing:	
Engine position	Number 1 cylinder at TDC (see Section 13)
Pump position	Value shown on pump (see Section 13)
Dynamic timing	No information available at time of writing

Injectors

Type	Pintle
Opening pressure:	
Bosch injection pump	130 + 8 - 5 bars
Roto-Diesel/Lucas injection pump	118 + 7 - 5 bars

Torque wrench settings

	Nm	lbf ft
Fuel gauge sender unit	60 to 70	44 to 52
Fuel injectors to cylinder head	70	52
Fuel pipe union nuts and bolts	25	18
Injection pump timing hole blanking plug:		
Roto-Diesel/Lucas pump	5	4
Bosch pump	10	7
Injection pump mounting nuts and bolts	25	18
Injection pump sprocket securing nut	50	37
Injection pump sprocket adjuster bolts (two-piece adjustable sprocket)	20	15
Fast idle thermostatic actuator-to-cylinder head	35	26

---

1   General information and precautions

General information

1   The fuel system consists of a rear-mounted fuel tank, a fuel filter with integral water separator, a fuel injection pump, injectors and associated components **(see illustration)**. As it passes through the filter, the fuel is heated by coolant flowing through the filter bowl. The exhaust system is conventional.

2   Fuel is drawn from the fuel tank to the fuel injection pump by a vane-type transfer pump incorporated in the fuel injection pump. Before reaching the pump the fuel passes through a fuel filter where foreign matter and water are removed. Excess fuel lubricates the moving components of the pump and is then returned to the tank.

3   The fuel injection pump is driven at half crankshaft speed by the timing belt. The high pressure required to inject the fuel into the compressed air in the swirl chambers is achieved by a cam plate acting on a single piston on the Bosch pump, or by two opposed pistons forced together by rollers running in a cam ring on the Roto-Diesel/Lucas pump **(see illustration)**. The fuel passes through a central rotor with a single outlet drilling which aligns with ports leading to the injector pipes.

4   Fuel metering is controlled by a centrifugal governor which reacts to accelerator pedal position and engine speed. The governor is linked to a metering valve which increases or decreases the amount of fuel

delivered at each pumping stroke.

5   Basic injection timing is determined when the pump is fitted. When the engine is running it is varied automatically to suit the prevailing engine speed by a mechanism which turns the cam plate or ring.

6   A solenoid valve in the pump is used to advance the injection timing briefly after a cold start. The system operates by increasing the pump transfer pressure via a restrictor valve.

7   The four fuel injectors produce a homogeneous spray of fuel into the swirl chambers located in the cylinder head. The injectors are calibrated to open and close at critical pressures to provide efficient and even combustion. Each injector needle is lubricated by fuel which accumulates in the spring chamber and is channelled to the injection pump return hose by leak-off pipes.

8   Roto-Diesel/Lucas or Bosch fuel system components may be fitted, depending on model. Components from the former manufacturer are marked either "Roto-Diesel", "Con-Diesel" or "CAV", depending on their date and place of manufacture. Replacement components must be of the same make as those originally fitted.

9   Cold starting is assisted by preheater or "glow" plugs fitted to each swirl chamber (see Chapter 5 for further details).

10   The fast idle system is operated either by a thermostatic actuator, or a vacuum actuator, depending on model.

11   On models with a thermostatic fast idle actuator, a thermostatic sensor in the cooling system operates a fast idle lever on the injection pump, via a cable, to increase the idling speed when the engine is cold.

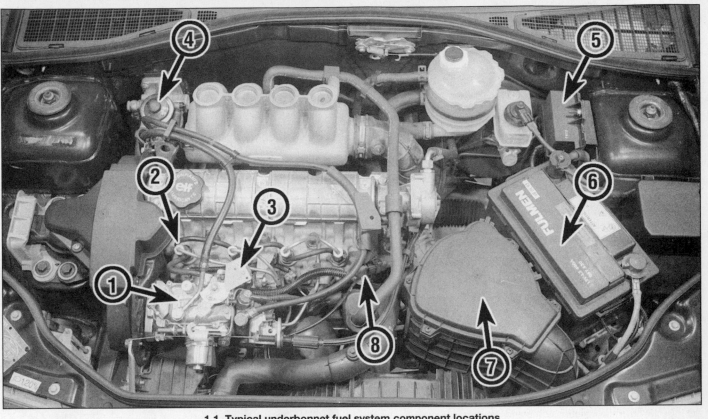

1.1 Typical underbonnet fuel system component locations

1	Injection pump	3	Load micro-switch
2	Fuel injector	4	Fuel filter

5	Preheating control unit	7	Air filter assembly
6	Battery	8	Fast idle thermostatic actuator

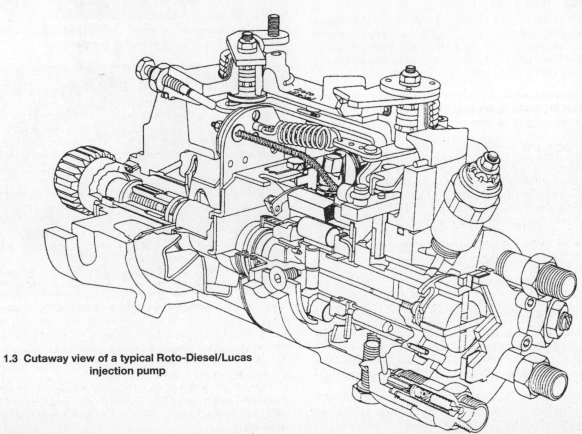

1.3 Cutaway view of a typical Roto-Diesel/Lucas injection pump

4

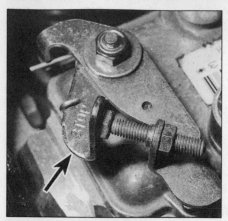

1.13 Hand-operated stop lever (arrowed) - Roto-Diesel/Lucas injection pump

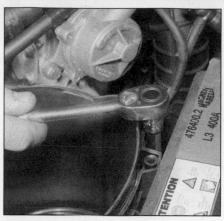

2.2 Removing the air cleaner housing mounting bolts

2.3 Disconnecting the air inlet hose from the air cleaner housing assembly

12   On models with a vacuum actuator, the fast idle cable is operated by a vacuum-controlled (brake servo vacuum) actuator, via a solenoid valve. The solenoid valve is controlled by the preheating system control unit.

13   A stop solenoid cuts the fuel supply to the injection pump rotor when the ignition is switched off, and there is also a hand-operated stop lever for use in an emergency **(see illustration)**.

14   Provided that the specified maintenance is carried out, the fuel injection equipment will give long and trouble-free service. The injection pump itself may well outlast the engine. The main potential cause of damage to the injection pump and injectors is dirt or water in the fuel.

15   Servicing of the injection pump and injectors is very limited for the home mechanic, and any dismantling or adjustment other than that described in this Chapter must be entrusted to a Renault dealer or fuel injection specialist.

Precautions

Warning: *It is necessary to take certain precautions when working on the fuel system components, particularly the fuel injectors. Before carrying out any operations on the fuel system, refer to the precautions given in "Safety first!" at the beginning of this manual, and to any additional warning notes at the start of the relevant Sections.*

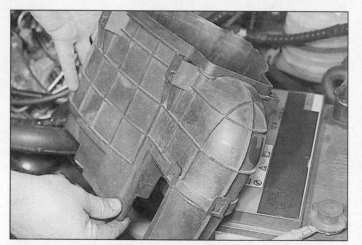

2.4 Withdrawing the air cleaner housing assembly from the engine compartment

---

2   Air cleaner housing assembly - removal and refitting

Removal

1   Remove the air cleaner filter element as described in Chapter 1.

2   Using an extension bar, unscrew the two bolts which secure the air cleaner housing to the battery tray **(see illustration)**.

3   Loosen the clip and disconnect the air inlet hose from the air cleaner housing assembly **(see illustration)**.

4   Withdraw the assembly from the engine compartment **(see illustration)**.

5   Check the condition of the rubber mountings where applicable and renew them as necessary. Also check the hose and hose clip for condition.

Refitting

6   Refitting is a reversal of removal.

---

3   Fuel gauge sender unit - removal and refitting

Note: *Refer to the precautions given in Section 1 before proceeding.*

Removal

1   Disconnect the battery earth lead. Tilt the rear seat, and remove the access cover from the fuel gauge sender hatch.

3.2 Fuel gauge sender unit and connections

2   Disconnect the hose(s) and the multi-plugs from the top of the sender unit, making marks for reference when refitting if there is any possibility of confusion **(see illustration)**.

3   Unscrew the ring nut, using a tool made up to the dimensions shown **(see illustration)**. Remove the ring nut and withdraw the sender unit, allowing any fuel contained in it to drain back into the tank **(see illustration)**.

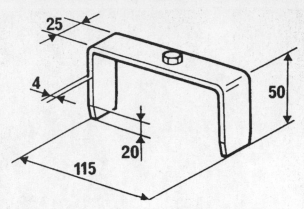

3.3a Ring nut spanner tool dimensions (in mm)

3.3b Removing the fuel gauge sender unit (fuel tank removed)

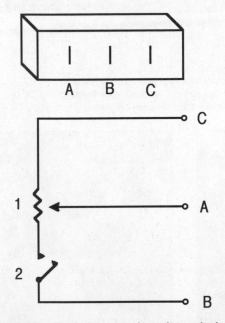

3.5 Identification of fuel gauge sender unit terminals (viewed with sender in upright position) and schematic of internal connections

A	Common	1	Potentiometer
B	Warning light switch	2	Switch
C	Gauge		

4.5 Fuel filler pipe, breather and vent hoses

Testing

4   Invert the sender unit: the float should be heard to move.

5   Connect an ohmmeter across the terminals, two at a time, and observe the changes in resistance between the "empty" position (sender upright and the right way up) and the "full" position (sender upside-down). Refer to the accompanying illustration for the terminal identification **(see illustration)**. The following results were obtained in the workshop:

Terminals	Empty	Full
A — B	10 ohms	Infinity (open-circuit)
A — C	290 ohms	0.7 ohms
B — C	300 ohms	Infinity (open-circuit)

6   If the readings obtained do not change as described, and if erratic operation of the fuel gauge or warning light has been experienced, the sender unit should be renewed.

Refitting

7   Refit by reversing the removal operations. Use a new seal and (if possible) tighten the ring nut to the specified torque.

---

4   Fuel tank - removal and refitting

Note: *Refer to the precautions given in Section 1 before proceeding.*

Removal

1   A drain plug is not provided on the fuel tank, and it is therefore preferable to carry out the removal operation when the tank is nearly empty. Disconnect the battery earth lead. Disconnect the hose(s) and the multi-plug(s) from the fuel gauge sender unit (Section 3).

2   Carefully siphon the remaining fuel from the tank into a suitable container.

3   Raise and support the car. Remove the exhaust system (Section 17) and the centre section heat shield.

4   Disconnect the handbrake cables from the equaliser. Unclip the cables and move them out of the way.

5   Disconnect the fuel filler pipe from the tank. Also disconnect the breather and vent hoses **(see illustration)**. If crimped hose clips have been used, cut them off and obtain worm-drive clips for reassembly.

6   Disconnect the outlet hose from the fuel filter. Be prepared for fuel spillage.

7   Have an assistant support the fuel tank. Remove the five mounting bolts and lower the tank, freeing it from the brake pipe clips. Disconnect any remaining wires or hoses and remove the tank **(see illustration)**.

4

8   The tank is made of plastic. If it is damaged, it should be renewed. Proprietary repair kits are available, but check that they are suitable for use on plastic tanks. A fuel leak is not just expensive, it is dangerous.

Refitting

9   Refit by reversing the removal operations. Adjust the handbrake as described in Chapter 1.

---

5   Fuel tank filler pipe - removal and refitting

Note: *Refer to the precautions given in Section 1 before proceeding.*

Removal

1   A drain plug is not provided on the fuel tank, and it is therefore preferable to carry out the removal operation when the tank is nearly empty. Before proceeding, disconnect the battery earth lead, then syphon or pump the remaining fuel from the tank.
2   Chock the front wheels, then jack up the rear of the car and support it on axle stands. Remove the spare wheel and the right-hand rear wheel. Also remove the mudflap.
3   Loosen the clip and disconnect the filler hose from the filler pipe.
4   Remove the two screws which secure the breather pipe assembly.
5   Mark the positions of the breather pipes, then disconnect them

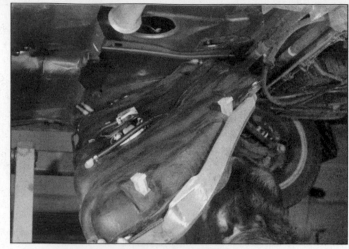

4.7 Removing the fuel tank

from the filler pipe.
6   Open the fuel filler flap and remove the cap.
7   Unscrew the cross-head screws located inside the filler flap recess, and remove the filler pipe assembly.

6.1a Disconnecting the accelerator inner cable from the injection pump (Roto-Diesel/Lucas)

6.1b Accelerator inner cable connection to the injection pump (Bosch)

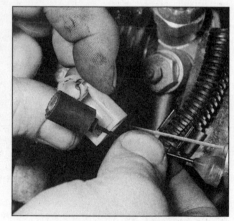

6.2a Remove the balljoint . . .

6.2b . . . to enable the cable to pass through the bracket (Roto-Diesel/Lucas pump)

6.2c Accelerator outer cable connection to the injection pump (Bosch)

6.3 Accelerator cable connection to the pedal

7.1 Remove the nut (arrowed) which secures the accelerator pedal pivot bush

8.3 Loosening the fuel system bleed screw located on the injection pump inlet union

Refitting

8   Refit by reversing the removal operations, using new hose clips when necessary.

6   Accelerator cable - removal, refitting and adjustment

Removal

1   Working in the engine compartment, operate the accelerator lever on the fuel injection pump, and release the inner cable from the lever. Alternatively, on models with a press-fit balljoint cable end fitting, pull the cable end from the lever **(see illustrations)**.
2   Pull the cable outer ferrule from the grommet in the fuel injection pump bracket. Note that on models with a balljoint end fitting, it will be necessary to prise the balljoint from the rubber cable end fitting to enable the cable to pass through the pump bracket **(see illustrations)**. Where necessary remove the wiring harness plastic clip from the ferrule.
3   Working inside the vehicle, release the cable end fitting which is a push fit in the accelerator pedal rod **(see illustration)**.
4   Release the cable from the remaining clips and brackets in the engine compartment, noting its routing.
5   Withdraw the cable through the bulkhead into the engine compartment.

Refitting and adjustment

6   Refitting is a reversal of removal, ensuring that the cable is routed as noted before removal, and on completion, check the cable adjustment as follows.

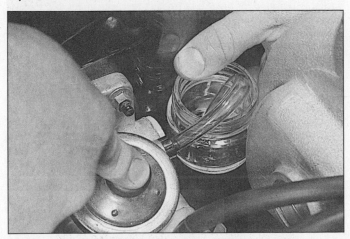

8.4 Pumping the fuel system priming plunger

7   Have an assistant fully depress the accelerator pedal, then check that the accelerator lever on the injection pump is touching the maximum speed adjustment screw. If adjustment is required, remove the spring clip from the adjustment ferrule, reposition the ferrule as necessary, then insert the clip in the next free groove on the ferrule.
8   With the accelerator pedal fully released, check that the accelerator lever is touching the anti-stall adjustment screw.

7   Accelerator pedal - removal and refitting

Removal

1   Remove the nut which secures the accelerator pedal pivot bush **(see illustration)**.
2   Disconnect the accelerator cable from the pedal as described in the previous Section.
3   Remove the pedal and bush.

Refitting

4   Refit by reversing the removal operations.

8   Fuel system - priming and bleeding

Note: *Refer to the precautions given in Section 1 before proceeding.*
1   After disconnecting part of the fuel supply system or running out of fuel, it is necessary to prime the system and bleed off any air which may have entered the system components.
2   All models are fitted with a hand-operated priming pump, operated by a plunger located on the top of the fuel filter head, on the right-hand side of the engine compartment bulkhead.
3   To prime the system, loosen the bleed screw, located on the filter head, or on the injection pump inlet union **(see illustration)**.
4   Fit a piece of pipe to the bleed screw and place the open end in a container to catch the fuel. Pump the priming plunger until fuel free from air bubbles emerges from the bleed screw **(see illustration)**. Retighten the bleed screw, and remove the pipe and container.
5   Switch on the ignition (to activate the stop solenoid) and continue pumping the priming plunger until firm resistance is felt, then pump a few more times.
6   If air has entered the injector pipes, place wads of rag around the injector pipe unions at the injectors (to absorb spilt fuel), then slacken the unions. Crank the engine on the starter motor until fuel emerges from the unions, then stop cranking the engine and retighten the unions. Mop up spilt fuel. **Warning:** *Be prepared to stop the engine if it should fire, to avoid excessive fuel spray and spillage.*
7   Start the engine with the accelerator pedal fully depressed. Additional cranking may be necessary to finally bleed the system before the engine starts.

4

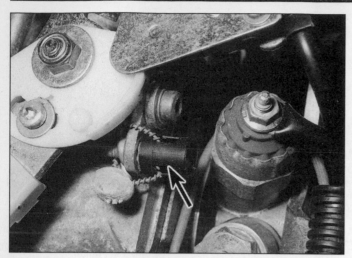

9.3a Maximum speed adjustment screw (arrowed) -
Roto-Diesel/Lucas injection pump

9.3b Maximum speed adjustment screw (arrowed) -
Bosch injection pump

9   Maximum speed - checking and adjustment

Caution: *The maximum speed adjustment screw is sealed by the manufacturers at the factory using paint or a locking wire and a lead seal. There is no reason why it should require adjustment. Do not disturb the screw if the vehicle is still within the warranty period otherwise the warranty will be invalidated. This adjustment requires the use of a tachometer - refer to the following Section for alternative methods.*

1   Run the engine to normal operating temperature.
2   Have an assistant fully depress the accelerator pedal and check that the maximum engine speed is as given in the Specifications. Do not keep the engine at maximum speed for more than two or three seconds.
3   If adjustment is necessary, stop the engine then loosen the locknut, turn the maximum speed adjustment screw as necessary, and retighten the locknut **(see illustrations)**.
4   Repeat the procedure in paragraph 2 to check the adjustment.
5   Stop the engine and disconnect the tachometer.

10   Fast idle thermostatic actuator and cable - removal, refitting, testing and adjustment

Note: *A new sealing ring will be required on refitting.*

Removal

1   The thermostatic actuator is located at the left-hand end of the cylinder head.
2   Partially drain the cooling system as described in Chapter 1.
3   Loosen the clamp screw or nut (as applicable) and slide the fast idle cable end fitting from the inner cable at the fast idle lever on the injection pump **(see illustration)**.
4   Slide the outer cable from the bracket on the fuel injection pump.
5   Using a suitable open-ended spanner, unscrew the thermostatic actuator from the cylinder head, and withdraw the actuator complete with the cable. Recover the sealing ring **(see illustrations)**.

Refitting

6   Fit the actuator, using a new sealing ring, and tighten it.
7   Refill the cooling system as described in Chapter 1.
8   Insert the outer cable through the bracket on the injection pump.
9   Insert the inner cable through the fast idle lever, and position the end fitting on the cable, but do not tighten the clamp screw or nut (as applicable).
10   Adjust the cable as described in the following paragraphs.

10.3 Fast idle cable end fitting (arrowed) -
Roto-Diesel/Lucas injection pump

Testing and adjustment

Bosch injection pump

Note: *During this procedure, it is necessary to measure the engine speed. The usual type of tachometer (rev counter), which works from ignition system pulses, cannot be used on diesel engines. A diagnostic socket is provided for the use of Renault test equipment, but this will not normally be available to the home mechanic. If it is not felt that adjusting the idle speed "by ear" is satisfactory, or that (where fitted) the instrument panel tachometer is not sufficiently reliable, one of the following alternatives may be used.*

a) *Purchase or hire of an appropriate tachometer.*
b) *Delegation of the job to a Renault dealer or other specialist.*
c) *Timing light (strobe) operated by a petrol engine running at the desired speed. If the timing light is pointed at a mark on the camshaft pump pulley, the mark will appear stationary when the two engines are running at the same speed (or multiples of that speed). The pulley will be rotating at half the crankshaft speed but this will not affect the adjustment. (In practice it was found impossible to use this method on the crankshaft pulley due to the acute viewing angle.)*

11   With the engine warm (the cooling fan should have cut in and out once) and running at the correct idle speed (see Chapter 1), proceed as follows.
12   Move the fast idle lever on the injection pump towards the flywheel end of the engine so that it contacts the fast idle adjustment

10.5a Unscrew the thermostatic actuator . . .

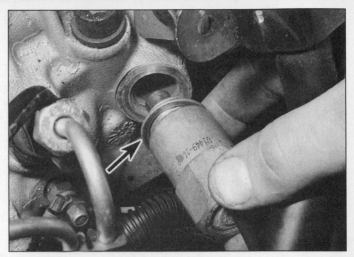

10.5b . . . and withdraw it from the cylinder head. Note the sealing ring (arrowed)

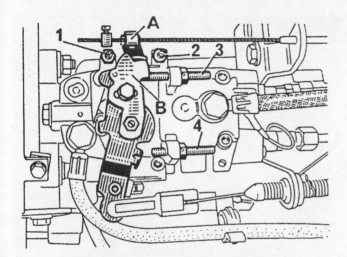

10.12 Bosch injection pump adjustment screws

A   Fast idle lever
B   Accelerator lever
1   Fast idle adjustment screw
2   Idle adjustment screw
3   Anti-stall adjustment screw
4   Maximum speed adjustment screw

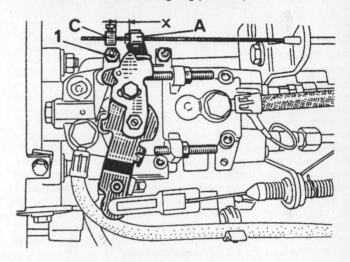

10.17 Bosch injection pump fast idle cable adjustment (thermostatic actuator)

A   Fast idle lever
C   Cable end fitting
1   Fast idle adjustment screw
x = 6.0 mm

screw (see illustration).
13   Check the fast idle speed. If necessary, loosen the locknut and turn the adjustment screw to give the specified fast idle speed. Retighten the locknut on completion.
14   Stop the engine, and disconnect the tachometer where applicable.
15   The fast idle cable should now be adjusted as follows.
16   With the engine still at normal operating temperature, and the fast idle lever in its rest position (resting against the idle speed adjustment screw, **not** the fast idle adjustment screw), gently pull the fast idle cable taught.
17   Position the end fitting on the cable so that the dimension between the end of the fast idle lever and the end fitting is as specified (see illustration).
18   With the end fitting correctly positioned, tighten the clamp screw.
19   When the engine has cooled, check that the cable has pulled the fast idle lever so that it rests against the fast idle adjustment screw. Re-check that with the engine at normal operating temperature the dimension between the end of the fast idle lever and the cable end fitting is as specified. If not, it is likely that the thermostatic actuator is faulty.

Roto-Diesel/Lucas injection pump (up to early 1993 - F8Q 730 engine)

20   The fast idle speed is set at the factory on a test bench and cannot be adjusted.
21   With the engine cold, loosen the cable clamp and push the fast idle lever fully away from the timing end of the engine. This is the fast idling position of the lever.
22   With the lever held in the fast idle position, pull the end of the cable so that it is moderately tensioned, then locate the clamp on the cable so that it is just in contact with the fast idle lever. Tighten the clamp onto the cable.
23   Run the engine until it is at normal operating temperature (the cooling fan should have cut in and out once), then stop the engine. The fast idle lever should now have been fully released by the thermostatic actuator.
24   Pull the end of the cable as in paragraph 22, then use a feeler gauge to check that the clearance between the clamp and the fast idle lever is 2.0 to 3.0 mm. If not, adjust the position of the clamp on the inner cable.

4

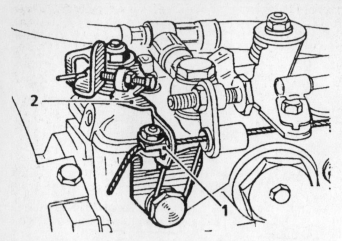

**10.30 Lucas injection pump fast idle cable adjustment
(thermostatic actuator)**

1 Cable clamp	2 Fast idle lever

Roto-Diesel/Lucas injection pump (from early 1993 – F8Q 714 engine)

25   The fast idle speed is set at the factory on a test bench and cannot be adjusted.

26   With the engine cold, note the length of the exposed inner fast idle cable, measured from the end of the cable to the point where it enters the outer cable.

27   Run the engine until it is at normal operating temperature (the cooling fan should have cut in and out once), then stop the engine.

28   Again measure the length of the exposed inner fast idle cable, which should have increased by 7.0 to 8.5 mm. If the cable travel between cold and normal operating temperature is not as specified, it is likely that the thermostatic actuator is faulty.

29   With the engine still at normal operating temperature, and the fast idle lever in the rest position, gently pull the fast idle cable taught.

30   Check that the dimension between the end of the fast idle lever and the clamp is 3.0 ± 1.0 mm **(see illustration)**.

11   Fuel injection pump - removal and refitting

Note: *Refer to the precautions given in Section 1 of this Chapter before proceeding. Be careful not to allow dirt into the pump or injector pipes during this procedure. New sealing rings should be used on the fuel pipe banjo unions when refitting.*

Removal

1   Disconnect the battery negative lead.

2   Apply the handbrake, then jack up the front of the vehicle and support securely on axle stands.

3   Remove the right-hand front roadwheel and the wheel arch liner.

4   Remove the air cleaner housing assembly as described in Section 2 of this Chapter.

5   Remove the electric cooling fan assembly from the rear of the radiator as described in Chapter 3.

6   Remove the alternator as described in Chapter 5.

7   Turn the crankshaft to bring No 1 piston to TDC on the compression stroke, and fit the tool to lock the crankshaft in position, as described in Chapter 2A.

8   Unscrew the securing bolts, and remove the timing belt cover which covers the fuel injection pump sprocket.

9   If a suitable injection pump sprocket locking tool is available (Renault tool Mot.1131 for one-piece sprockets, or Mot.1200 for two-piece adjustable sprockets), remove the crankshaft locking tool, turn the engine back from TDC by one camshaft sprocket tooth, and fit the

11.11 Accelerator cable (1) and fast idle cable (2) on the Bosch injection pump

11.13 Fuel supply hose banjo union (arrowed) on the Bosch injection pump

injection pump sprocket locking tool (turning the engine back by one sprocket tooth will ensure that sufficient adjustment is available to set the pump timing on refitting).

10   If a suitable locking tool is not available, remove the timing belt as described in Chapter 2A.

11   Disconnect the accelerator cable from the injection pump, with reference to Section 6 if necessary **(see illustration)**.

12   Disconnect the fast idle cable from the injection pump, with reference to Section 10 if necessary.

13   Loosen the clip or undo the banjo union, as applicable and disconnect the fuel supply hose from the injection pump **(see illustration)**. Recover the sealing washers from the banjo union, where applicable. Cover the open end of the hose or pipe, and plug the opening in the injection pump to keep dirt out (on models with a banjo union, the banjo bolt can be refitted to the pump and covered).

14   Disconnect the main fuel leak-off return hose (connected to the main fuel return pipe) from the relevant fuel injector **(see illustration)**.

15   Disconnect the main fuel return pipe banjo union from the injection pump **(see illustration)**. Recover the sealing washers from the banjo union. Again, cover the open end of the hose and the banjo bolt to keep dirt out. Take care not to get the inlet and outlet banjo unions mixed up.

16   Unbolt the plastic cover from the front of the injection pump, then disconnect all relevant wiring. Note that on certain pumps, this can be

11.14 Disconnect the main fuel leak-off return hose from the relevant fuel injector

11.15 Main fuel return pipe banjo union (arrowed) on the Bosch injection pump

11.17 Cover the injectors to keep dirt out

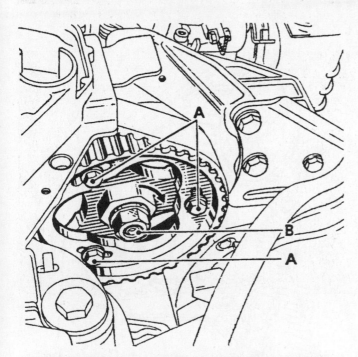

11.20 Two-piece sprocket adjuster bolts (A) and sprocket securing nut (B). Turn sprocket boss in direction arrowed before removing pump

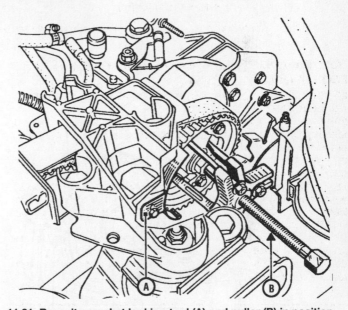

11.21 Renault sprocket locking tool (A) and puller (B) in position - two-piece adjustable sprocket

4

achieved by simply disconnecting the wiring connectors at the brackets on the pump. On some pumps it will be necessary to disconnect the wiring from the individual components (some connections may be protected by rubber covers).

17   Unscrew the union nuts securing the injector pipes to the injection pump and injectors. Counterhold the unions on the pump, when unscrewing the pipe-to-pump union nuts. Remove the pipes as a set. Cover open unions to keep dirt out, using small plastic bags or fingers cut from discarded (but clean!) rubber gloves **(see illustration)**. Note that the leak-off hoses will have to be removed from the fuel injectors to enable the injectors to be covered.

18   Where applicable, remove the alternator plastic shield from below the injection pump. Note the locations of any brackets secured by the shield securing nut and bolt.

19   Loosen the injection pump sprocket securing nut, and unscrew it to the end of the thread on the pump shaft (do not remove the nut at this stage. If a Renault sprocket locking tool is not available (see paragraph 7), counterhold the sprocket using a suitable improvised tool engaged with the holes in the sprocket (**not** the sprocket teeth).

20   On models with a two-piece adjustable pump sprocket, loosen the three sprocket adjuster bolts **(see illustration)**. Using the centre boss, turn the sprocket rear section clockwise, (viewed from the timing belt end of the engine - effectively turning the pump shaft) so that the adjuster bolts are positioned at the ends of the elongated slots. Retighten the adjuster bolts.

21   Fit a suitable puller to the pump sprocket, acting on the sprocket nut, and free the sprocket from the taper on the pump shaft **(see illustration)**. **Note:** *The puller must bear on the sprocket holes (between the two sprocket halves on models with two-piece adjustable sprockets),* **not** *on the teeth.* **Do not** hammer on the end of the pump shaft to free it, as this will damage the internal components of the pump.

22   On models with a one-piece sprocket, mark the sprocket in relation to the end of the pump shaft to ensure correct refitting. This is necessary regardless of whether the timing belt has been removed, because there are two keyways in the sprocket (for use with different injection pump types), and it is possible to refit the sprocket to the pump shaft incorrectly (see Chapter 2A, Section 5).

23   Remove the puller and the sprocket nut. Unless an injection pump sprocket locking tool has been fitted, remove the sprocket.

24   Unscrew the bolts securing the rear injection pump mounting bracket to the cylinder head **(see illustration)**.

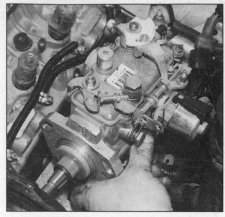

11.24 Unscrew the bolts securing the rear injection pump mounting bracket to the cylinder head

11.27a Remove the securing bolts . . .

11.27b . . . and withdraw the fuel injection pump

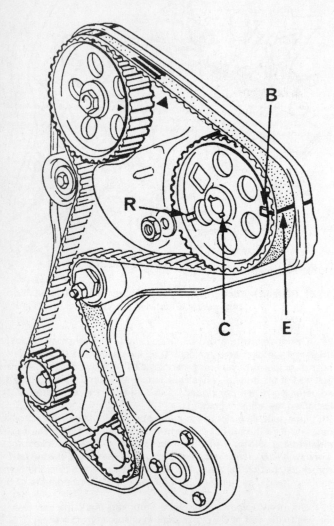

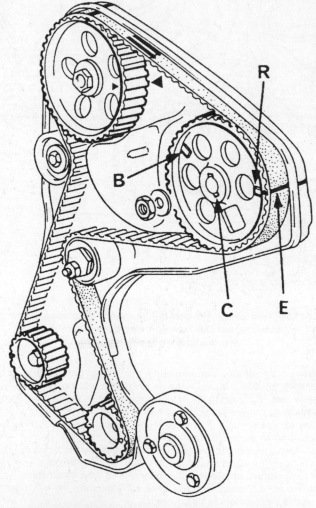

11.32a One-piece injection pump sprocket orientation - Bosch injection pump (engine shown with No 1 piston at TDC)

B	Sprocket alignment mark for Bosch injection pump
C	Position of injection pump shaft Woodruff key
E	Sprocket alignment mark on timing belt
R	Sprocket alignment mark for Roto-Diesel/Lucas injection pump

11.32b One-piece injection pump sprocket orientation - Roto-Diesel/Lucas injection pump (engine shown with No 1 cylinder at TDC)

B	Sprocket alignment mark for Bosch injection pump
C	Position of injection pump shaft Woodruff key
E	Sprocket alignment mark on timing belt
R	Sprocket alignment mark for Roto-Diesel/Lucas injection pump

11.37 Tightening the injection pump sprocket bolt

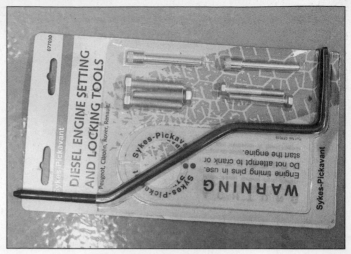

12.3 TDC locking tools for setting injection timing on Renault diesel engines

25 Make a final check to ensure that all relevant pipes, hoses and wires have been disconnected to facilitate pump removal.

26 Make alignment marks between the pump and the mounting bracket. This will aid pump timing on refitting.

27 Unscrew the three pump securing bolts, and withdraw the pump from its mounting bracket, leaving the sprocket engaged with the timing belt, where applicable **(see illustrations)**. Access to the lower pump mounting bolt is most easily obtained from the rear of the pump, using a deep socket and extension.

28 Recover the Woodruff key from the end of the pump shaft if it is loose.

29 If desired, the rear pump mounting bracket can be unbolted from the rear of the pump.

Refitting

30 Where applicable, refit the rear mounting bracket to the rear of the injection pump.

31 Commence refitting by fitting the Woodruff key to the end of the pump shaft, where applicable.

32 Offer the injection pump to the mounting bracket. If the sprocket is still engaged with the timing belt, engage the pump shaft with the sprocket. On models with a one-piece sprocket, align the marks made on the sprocket and the pump shaft before removal (this will ensure that the key engages with the correct keyway in the sprocket - see paragraph 22) **(see illustrations)**. Ensure that the Woodruff key does not fall out of the shaft as the sprocket is engaged.

33 Where applicable, align the marks made on the pump and the mounting bracket before removal. If a new pump is being fitted, transfer the mark from the old pump to give an approximate setting.

34 Refit and lightly tighten the front pump mounting bolts.

35 Refit and tighten the bolts securing the rear pump mounting bracket to the cylinder head.

36 Where applicable, refit the sprocket to the pump shaft, ensuring that the Woodruff key engages correctly. On models with a one-piece sprocket, align the marks made on the sprocket and the pump shaft before removal, to ensure that the key engages with the correct keyway in the sprocket (see paragraph 22).

37 Tighten the pump sprocket securing nut to the specified torque, counterholding the sprocket as during removal **(see illustration)**.

38 If the timing belt has been removed, refit and tension it as described in Chapter 2A.

39 On models with a two-piece adjustable sprocket, loosen the three sprocket adjuster bolts. Using the centre boss, turn the sprocket rear section anti-clockwise (viewed from the timing belt end of the engine - effectively turning the pump shaft) so that the adjuster bolts are positioned at the ends of the elongated slots. Lightly tighten the adjuster bolts.

40 Where applicable, remove the sprocket locking tool, then turn the crankshaft to bring No 1 piston to TDC on the compression stroke, and fit the tool to lock the crankshaft in position, as described in Chapter 2A.

41 Carry out injection timing as described in Sections 12, and 13 or 14, as applicable.

42 Refit the plastic shield under the pump, ensuring that any brackets noted during removal are in place.

43 Refit and reconnect the injector fuel pipes, and tighten the unions. Counterhold the unions on the pump when tightening the pipe-to-pump union nuts.

44 Reconnect all relevant wiring to the pump, then refit the plastic cover to the front of the injection pump.

45 Reconnect the fuel supply and return pipes and hoses, and tighten the unions, as applicable. Use new sealing washers on the banjo unions. Also reconnect the leak-off hoses.

46 Reconnect the accelerator cable and adjust as described in Section 6.

47 Reconnect and adjust the fast idle cable as described in Section 10, noting that final adjustment must be carried out after the engine has been started and reached normal operating temperature.

48 Refit the alternator with reference to Chapter 5.

49 Refit the electric cooling fan assembly with reference to Chapter 3.

50 Refit the air cleaner housing assembly with reference to Section 2 of this Chapter.

51 Refit the right-hand front roadwheel and the wheel arch liner.

52 Lower the vehicle to the ground.

53 Reconnect the battery negative lead.

54 Check the no-load switch adjustment as described in Chapter 5.

55 Prime and bleed the fuel system as described in Section 8.

56 Start the engine, and check the idle speed and anti-stall speed, as described in Chapter 1.

12 Injection timing - checking methods and adjustment

1 Checking the injection timing is not a routine operation. It is only necessary after the injection pump has been disturbed.

2 Dynamic timing equipment does exist, but it is unlikely to be available to the home mechanic. The equipment works by converting pressure pulses in an injector pipe into electrical signals. If such equipment is available, use it in accordance with its makers instructions.

3 Static timing as described in this Chapter gives good results if carried out carefully. A dial test indicator will be needed, with probes and adaptors appropriate to the type of injection pump **(see illustration)**. Read through the procedures before starting work to find out what is involved.

4

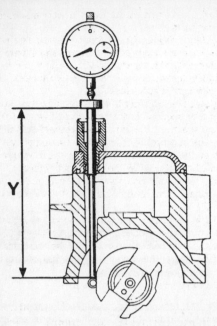

13.4 Timing probe details (Renault tool Mot.1079) - Roto-Diesel/Lucas injection pump

$$Y = 95.5 \pm 0.01 \text{ mm}$$

13.5 Unscrewing the timing inspection plug from the top of a Roto-Diesel/Lucas injection pump

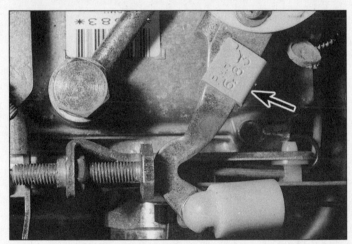

13.9 Injection pump timing value marked on accelerator lever tag (arrowed) - Roto-Diesel/Lucas injection pump

13 Injection timing (Roto-Diesel/Lucas injection pump) - checking and adjustment

Caution: *The maximum engine speed and transfer pressure settings, together with timing access plugs, are sealed by the manufacturers at the factory using locking wire and lead seals. Do not disturb the wire if the vehicle is still within the warranty period otherwise the warranty will be invalidated. Also do not attempt the timing procedure unless accurate instrumentation is available. Suitable special tools for carrying out pump timing are available from motor factors, and a dial test indicator will be required regardless of the method used. Refer to the precautions given in Section 1 of this Chapter before proceeding.*

1   Disconnect the battery negative lead.

2   Apply the handbrake, then jack up the front right-hand corner of the vehicle until the wheel is just clear of the ground. Support the vehicle on an axle stand and engage 4th or 5th gear. This will enable the crankshaft to be turned easily by turning the right-hand wheel. Alternatively, the engine can be turned using an open-ended spanner on the crankshaft pulley bolt.

3   Turn the crankshaft to bring No 1 piston to TDC on the compression stroke, and fit the tool to lock the crankshaft in position, as described in Chapter 2A.

4   A dial test indicator will now be required, along with a suitable special probe (Renault tool Mot.1079, or an alternative available from motor factors). Note that the probe must seal on the sealing washer surface in the timing aperture, **not** on the top surface of the timing aperture. The probe is "waisted" to allow it to clear the pump rotor **(see illustration).**

5   Remove the inspection plug from the top of the pump **(see illustration)**, and recover the sealing washer. Position the timing probe in the aperture so that the tip of the probe rests on the rotor timing piece.

6   Position the dial test indicator securely on the injection pump body, so that it can read the movement of the timing probe. Ensure that the gauge is positioned directly in line with the probe, with the gauge plunger at the mid-point of its travel.

Models with one-piece fixed injection pump sprocket

7   Remove the crankshaft locking tool, then turn the crankshaft approximately a quarter-turn anti-clockwise (viewed from the timing belt end of the engine), and zero the dial test indicator. Check that the timing probe is seated against the sealing washer surface of the timing aperture (see paragraph 4).

8   Turn the crankshaft clockwise slowly until the crankshaft locking tool can be re-inserted (bringing the engine back to TDC).

9   Read the dial test indicator; the reading should correspond to the value marked on the pump. The timing value may be marked on a plastic disc on the front of the pump, or alternatively may appear on a label attached to the top of the pump, or a tag attached to the accelerator pump lever **(see illustration)**.

10   If the reading is not as specified, proceed as follows.

11   Cover the alternator with a plastic bag or rags as a precaution against spillage of diesel fuel.

12   Unscrew the union nuts securing the injector pipes to the fuel injection pump and the fuel injectors. Counterhold the unions on the pump, when unscrewing the nuts. Cover open unions to keep dirt out, using small plastic bags or fingers cut from discarded (but clean!) rubber gloves.

13   Slacken the three front pump mounting bolts, and the two rear pump mounting nuts, and slowly rotate the pump body until the point is found where the specified reading is obtained on the dial gauge. When the pump is correctly positioned, tighten the mounting nuts and bolts, ensuring that the reading on the dial gauge does not change as the fixings are tightened.

14   Withdraw the timing probe slightly, so that it is positioned clear of the pump rotor, and remove the crankshaft locking tool. Rotate the crankshaft through one and three quarter turns clockwise.

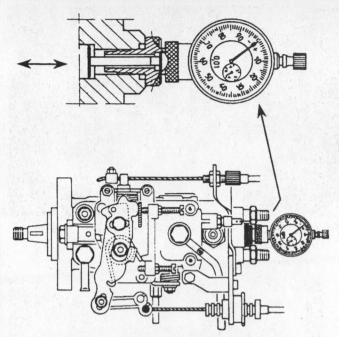

14.5 Dial test indicator and timing probe for use with Bosch injection pump

Note: Pump cable linkages may differ from that shown

15 Slide the timing probe back into position, ensuring that it is correctly seated against the sealing washer surface, as described previously, then zero the dial test indicator.

16 Rotate the crankshaft slowly clockwise until the crankshaft locking tool can be reinserted (bringing No 1 piston back to TDC). Recheck the timing measurement.

17 If adjustment is necessary, slacken the pump mounting nuts and bolts, and repeat the operations described in paragraphs 13 to 16.

18 When the timing is correct, reconnect the fuel injector pipes to the pump and the injectors, and remove the dial test indicator. Remove the probe from the inspection hole, and refit the inspection plug, ensuring that the sealing washer is in place.

19 Where applicable, remove the plastic bag or rags from the alternator.

20 Remove the crankshaft locking tool.

21 Lower the vehicle to the ground and reconnect the battery negative lead.

22 Bleed the fuel system as described in Section 8.

23 Check and if necessary adjust the idle speed and anti-stall speed as described in Chapter 1.

Models with two-piece adjustable injection pump sprocket

24 Remove the crankshaft locking tool, then turn the crankshaft approximately a quarter-turn anti-clockwise (viewed from the timing belt end of the engine), and zero the dial test indicator. Check that the timing probe is seated against the sealing washer surface of the timing aperture (see paragraph 4).

25 Turn the crankshaft clockwise slowly until the crankshaft locking tool can be re-inserted (bringing the engine back to TDC).

26 Read the dial test indicator; the reading should correspond to the value marked on the pump. The timing value may be marked on a plastic disc on the front of the pump, or alternatively may appear on a label attached to the top of the pump, or a tag attached to the accelerator pump lever **(see illustration 13.9)**.

27 If the reading is not as specified, proceed as follows.

28 Loosen the three sprocket adjuster bolts. Using the centre boss, turn the sprocket rear section anti-clockwise (viewed from the timing belt end of the engine - effectively turning the pump shaft) so that the

adjuster bolts are positioned at the ends of the elongated slots. Tighten the adjuster bolts.

29 Zero the dial test indicator. Check that the timing probe is seated against the sealing washer surface of the timing aperture (paragraph 4).

30 Remove the crankshaft locking tool, then turn the crankshaft through two complete turns clockwise, refit the locking tool, and check that the dial test indicator is still zeroed.

31 Loosen the sprocket adjuster bolts, and using the centre boss, turn the sprocket rear section clockwise (viewed from the timing belt end of the engine - effectively turning the pump shaft) until the dial test indicator displays the appropriate timing value marked on the pump. In this position, tighten the sprocket adjuster bolts (the reading on the dial test indicator should not change as the bolts are tightened).

32 Remove the crankshaft locking tool, then turn the crankshaft through two complete turns clockwise, refit the locking tool, and recheck the timing value.

33 If adjustment is necessary, slacken the sprocket adjuster bolts, and repeat the operations described in paragraphs 31 and 32.

34 When the timing is correct, remove the dial test indicator. Remove the probe from the inspection hole, and refit the inspection plug, ensuring that the sealing washer is in place.

35 Proceed as described in paragraphs 20 to 23.

14 Injection timing (Bosch injection pump) - checking and adjustment

Caution: *Some of the injection pump settings and access plugs may be sealed by the manufacturers at the factory using paint or locking wire and lead seals. Do not disturb the seals if the vehicle is still within the warranty period, otherwise the warranty will be invalidated. Also do not attempt the timing procedure unless accurate instrumentation is available. Refer to the precautions given in Section 1 of this Chapter before proceeding.*

1 Disconnect the battery negative lead.

2 Apply the handbrake, then jack up the front right-hand corner of the vehicle until the wheel is just clear of the ground. Support the vehicle on an axle stand and engage 4th or 5th gear. This will enable the engine to be turned easily by turning the right-hand wheel. Alternatively, the engine can be turned using an open ended spanner on the crankshaft pulley bolt.

3 Turn the crankshaft to bring No 1 piston to TDC on the compression stroke, and fit the tool to lock the crankshaft in position, as described in Chapter 2A.

4 Cover the alternator with a plastic bag or rags as a precaution against spillage of diesel fuel.

5 A dial test indicator will now be required, along with a suitable special probe and adaptor to screw into the hole in the rear of the pump (designed specifically for the Bosch pump and available from motor factors) **(see illustration)**.

6 Unscrew the union nuts securing the injector pipes to the fuel injection pump. Counterhold the unions on the pump, when unscrewing the nuts. Cover open unions to keep dirt out, using small plastic bags or fingers cut from discarded (but clean!) rubber gloves.

7 Unscrew the blanking plug from the end of the injection pump between the injector pipe connections. Be prepared for the loss of some fuel.

8 Insert the probe and connect it to the dial test indicator positioned directly over the inspection hole.

Models with one-piece fixed injection pump sprocket

9 Remove the locking tool from the flywheel, and turn the engine approximately a quarter-turn anti-clockwise (viewed from the timing belt end of the engine), and zero the dial test indicator.

10 Turn the crankshaft clockwise slowly until the crankshaft locking tool can be re-inserted (bringing the engine back to TDC).

11 Read the dial test indicator; the reading should correspond to the value given in the Specifications. Note that on some pumps, the timing value may also be marked on the pump accelerator lever.

12 If the reading is not as specified, proceed as follows.

4

14.28 The three adjuster bolts (arrowed) on the two-piece adjustable injection pump sprocket

15.4 Pull the leak-off pipes from the fuel injectors

15.6 Disconnect the fuel pipes from the injectors

13   Slacken the three front pump mounting bolts, and the rear pump mounting nuts, and slowly rotate the pump body until the point is found where the specified reading is obtained on the dial gauge. When the pump is correctly positioned, tighten the mounting nuts and bolts, ensuring that the reading on the dial gauge does not change as the fixings are tightened.

14   Remove the crankshaft locking tool, and rotate the crankshaft through one and three quarter turns clockwise. Check that the dial test indicator is reading zero.

15   Rotate the crankshaft slowly clockwise until the crankshaft locking tool can be reinserted (bringing No 1 piston back to TDC). Recheck the timing measurement.

16   If adjustment is necessary, slacken the pump mounting nuts and bolts, and repeat the operations described in paragraphs 13 to 15.

17   When the timing is correct, remove the dial test indicator, remove the probe from the inspection hole, and refit the blanking plug.

18   Reconnect the fuel injector pipes to the pump.

19   Where applicable, remove the plastic bag or rags from the alternator.

20   Remove the crankshaft locking tool.

21   Lower the vehicle to the ground and reconnect the battery negative lead.

22   Bleed the fuel system as described in Section 8.

23   Check and if necessary adjust the idle speed and anti-stall speed as described in Chapter 1.

Models with two-piece adjustable injection pump sprocket

24   Remove the locking tool from the flywheel, and turn the engine approximately a quarter-turn anti-clockwise (viewed from the timing belt end of the engine), and zero the dial test indicator.

25   Turn the crankshaft clockwise slowly until the crankshaft locking tool can be re-inserted (bringing the engine back to TDC).

26   Read the dial test indicator; the reading should correspond to the value given in the Specifications. Note that on some pumps, the timing value may also be marked on the pump accelerator lever.

27   If the reading is not as specified, proceed as follows.

28   Loosen the three sprocket adjuster bolts **(see illustration)**. Using the centre boss, turn the sprocket rear section anti-clockwise (viewed from the timing belt end of the engine - effectively turning the pump shaft) so that the adjuster bolts are positioned at the ends of the elongated slots. Tighten the adjuster bolts.

29   Zero the dial test indicator.

30   Remove the crankshaft locking tool, then turn the crankshaft through two complete turns, refit the locking tool, and check that the dial test indicator is still zeroed.

31   Loosen the sprocket adjuster bolts, and using the centre boss, turn the sprocket rear section clockwise (viewed from the timing belt

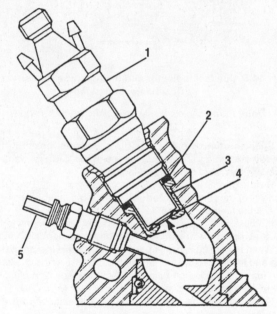

15.7a Cross-section of fuel injector mounting details

1 Fuel injector	4 Fire washer
2 Copper washer	5 Glow plug
3 Sleeve	

end of the engine - effectively turning the pump shaft) until the dial test indicator displays the appropriate timing given in the Specifications. In this position, tighten the sprocket adjuster bolts (the reading on the dial test indicator should not change as the bolts are tightened), then remove the crankshaft locking tool.

32   Turn the crankshaft through two complete turns clockwise, refit the locking tool, and recheck the timing value.

33   If adjustment is necessary, repeat the operations described in paragraphs 31 and 32.

34   When the timing is correct, proceed as described in paragraphs 17 to 23.

15   Fuel injectors - testing, removal and refitting

Warning: *Exercise extreme caution when working on the fuel injectors. Never expose the hands or any part of the body to injector spray, as the high working pressure can cause the fuel to penetrate the skin, with possibly fatal results. You are strongly advised to have any work which*

15.7b Unscrew the injectors . . .

15.7c . . . and withdraw them from the cylinder head

15.8a Recover the copper washers . . .

15.8b . . . and the fire seal washers

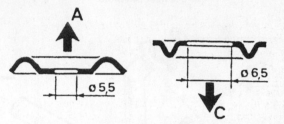

15.12 Fire seal washer fitting details

A   *Early type washer - fits with convex side upwards*
C   *Later type washer - fits with convex side downwards*

involves testing the injectors under pressure carried out by a dealer or fuel injection specialist. Refer to the precautions given in Section 1 of this Chapter before proceeding.

Testing

1   Injectors do deteriorate with prolonged use and it is reasonable to expect them to need reconditioning or renewal after 60 000 miles (100 000 km) or so. Accurate testing, overhaul and calibration of the injectors must be left to a specialist. A defective injector which is causing knocking or smoking can be located without dismantling as follows.
2   Run the engine at a fast idle. Slacken each injector union in turn, placing rag around the union to catch spilt fuel and being careful not to expose the skin to any spray. When the union on the defective injector is slackened, the knocking or smoking will stop.

Removal

Note: *Take great care not to allow dirt into the injectors or fuel pipes during this procedure.*
3   Carefully clean around the injectors and injector pipe union nuts.
4   Pull the leak-off pipes from the injectors **(see illustration)**.
5   Unscrew the union nuts securing the injector pipes to the fuel injection pump. Counterhold the unions on the pump, when unscrewing the nuts. Cover open unions to keep dirt out, using small plastic bags or fingers cut from discarded (but clean!) rubber gloves.
6   Unscrew the union nuts and disconnect the pipes from the injectors **(see illustration)**. If necessary the injector pipes may be

completely removed. Note the locations of any clips attached to the pipes. Cover the ends of the injectors to prevent dirt ingress.
7   Unscrew the injectors using a deep socket or box spanner (27 mm across flats) and remove them from the cylinder head **(see illustrations)**.
8   Recover the copper washers and fire seal washers from the cylinder head. Also recover the sleeves if they are loose **(see illustrations)**.

Refitting

9   Obtain new copper washers and fire seal washers. Also renew the sleeves if they are damaged.
10   Take care not to drop the injectors or allow the needles at their tips to become damaged. The injectors are precision-made to fine limits and must not be handled roughly. In particular, do not mount them in a bench vice.
11   Commence refitting by inserting the sleeves (if removed) into the cylinder head.
12   Fit the new fire seal washers to the cylinder head. Note that two types of fire seal washers have been fitted to the engines covered by this manual. The earlier type of washer has a hole diameter of 5.5 mm, and should be fitted with the convex side upwards (towards the fuel injector). The later type of washer has a hole diameter of 6.5 mm, and should be fitted with the convex side downwards (towards the cylinder head) **(see illustration)**. It is likely that the new washers supplied by a Renault parts centre will be of the later type. Ensure that the washers are fitted correctly, according to type.
13   Fit the copper washers to the cylinder head.
14   Insert the injectors and tighten them to the specified torque.
15   Refit the injector pipes and tighten the union nuts. Position any clips attached to the pipes as noted before removal.
16   Reconnect the leak-off pipes.
17   Start the engine. If difficulty is experienced, bleed the fuel system as described in Section 8.

4

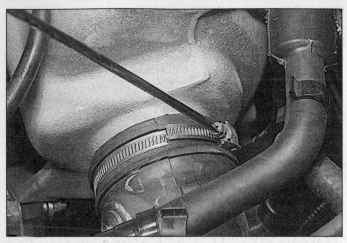

16.3 Releasing the clip securing the air inlet hose to the inlet manifold

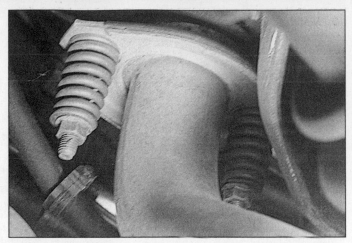

16.6 Exhaust downpipe connection to the exhaust manifold

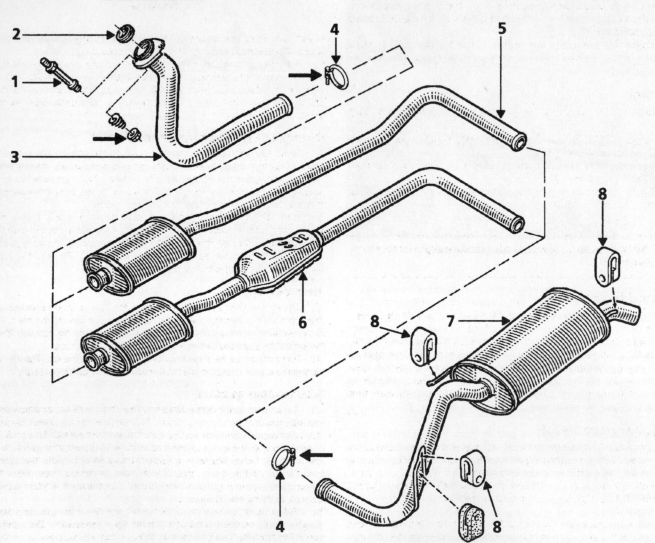

17.1 Typical exhaust system components

1	Stud	5	Intermediate section
2	Sealing ring	6	Intermediate section (with expansion chamber - not
3	Downpipe (front section)		fitted to models covered by this manual)
4	Clamp (note that a two-part version of this clamp is	7	Rear section (silencer)
	also fitted)	8	Rubber mountings

16 Manifolds - removal and refitting

Note: *A new gasket must be used on refitting.*

Removal

1   Although the manifolds are separate, they are retained by the same nuts, since the stud holes are split between the manifold flanges.
2   Note the location of any wiring or hose brackets/clips attached to the manifolds, and remove them.
3   Release the securing clip, and disconnect the air inlet hose from the inlet manifold **(see illustration)**. On models with an exhaust gas recirculation (EGR) system, undo the two bolts securing the EGR hose to the inlet manifold and collect the gasket (where fitted).
4   Where applicable, disconnect the hoses from the oil separator mounted on the inlet manifold. If desired, the oil separator can be unbolted from its bracket.
5   Where applicable, disconnect the breather hose(s) from the inlet manifold.
6   Unscrew and remove the two nuts, then remove the washers, tension springs and sleeves securing the exhaust downpipe to the manifold **(see illustration)**. Slide the flange plate off the manifold studs and separate the joint.
7   Progressively unscrew the nuts securing the inlet and exhaust manifolds and withdraw them from the cylinder head. Recover the manifold gasket.

Refitting

8   Refitting is a reversal of removal, bearing in mind the following points.

   a) *Ensure that the cylinder head and manifold mating surfaces are clean and use a new gasket.*
   b) *Reconnect the exhaust front section to the manifold with reference to Section 17.*
   c) *Ensure that any wiring or hose brackets/clips are positioned as noted before removal.*

17 Exhaust system - general information and component renewal

General information

1   The exhaust system consists of three sections **(see illustration)**.
2   On all models covered in this manual, both the downpipe, the rear section and catalytic converter (where fitted) can be removed leaving the remaining exhaust system in position. To remove the intermediate section, it is recommended that the rear section is removed first, then the intermediate section can be disconnected from the downpipe. In practice, it is often easier to remove the whole system and then separate the sections on the bench.

Component renewal

3   Exhaust system clamps and connections will often be found to be badly rusted. Apply penetrating oil or releasing fluid before starting work, or cut them off if they are to be renewed. The use of a high-temperature anti-seize compound on reassembly will avoid future problems. Exhaust jointing compound should be used on the joints between sections.
4   To remove the system or part of the system, first jack up the front or rear of the car and support it on axle stands. Alternatively, position the car over an inspection pit or on car ramps.

Downpipe - models not fitted with a catalytic converter

5   To remove the downpipe, unscrew and remove the two nuts, then remove the washers, tension springs and sleeves securing the downpipe to the manifold. Slide the flange plate off the manifold studs, then separate the joint, recovering the sealing ring. Release the clamp

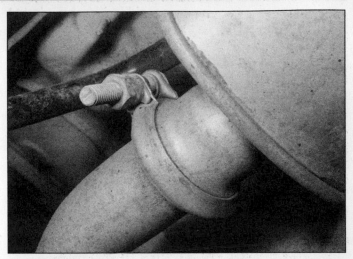

17.5 Clamp securing the intermediate exhaust section to the downpipe

which secures the intermediate section to the downpipe **(see illustration)**. Also unbolt the heat guard if necessary.
6   Refitting of the downpipe is a reversal of removal. Use a new sealing ring at the exhaust manifold. Tighten the manifold nuts to compress the springs until the nuts butt against the spacers on the studs. Tighten the clamp nuts securing the downpipe to the intermediate section.

Downpipe - catalytic converter models

7   Unscrew and remove the two nuts, then remove the washers, tension springs and sleeves securing the downpipe to the manifold. Slide the flange plate off the manifold studs, then separate the joint, recovering the sealing ring. Undo the two bolts securing the front pipe to the catalytic converter and recover the gasket.
8   Refitting of the downpipe is a reversal of removal. Use a new sealing ring at the exhaust manifold and a new gasket at the catalytic converter joint. Tighten the manifold nuts to compress the springs until the nuts butt against the spacers on the studs. Tighten the bolts securing the downpipe to the intermediate section.

Rear section

9   To remove the rear section, release the clamp which secures it to the intermediate section. Slide the rubber mountings off the bars, and if necessary, remove them from the underbody by turning them through 90°. Separate the rear and intermediate sections.
10   Refitting of the rear section is a reversal of removal. Tighten the clamp(s) securely, and renew the rubber mountings if necessary.

Intermediate section

11   To remove the intermediate section, first remove or disconnect the rear section as just described. Release the clamp which secures the intermediate section to the downpipe (models not fitted with a catalytic converter) or undo the two bolts and collect the gasket from the front joint (models with a catalytic converter). Slide the rubber mountings off the bars, and if necessary remove them from the underbody by turning them through 90°. Separate the intermediate section from the downpipe.
12   Refitting is a reversal of removal; tighten the nuts and bolts securely, and renew the rubber mountings if necessary. On catalytic converter models, fit a new gasket to the intermediate pipe to catalytic converter joint.

Complete system

13   When the whole system has been removed, refit it with the various clamps and connections loose. Begin tightening at the exhaust manifold, and work towards the tail pipe, ensuring that the system hangs easily and without strain.

4

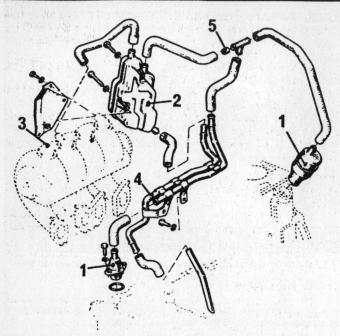

18.1a Dual-separator crankcase emission control system

1   *Auxiliary oil separators*   4   *Return pipe to sump*
2   *Main oil separator*   5   *Calibrated orifice*
3   *Inlet manifold*

18   Emission control systems - general information

Crankcase emission control system

1   A crankcase emission control system (crankcase ventilation system) is fitted to models covered by this manual **(see illustrations)**.
2   Oil fumes and piston blow-by gases (combustion gases which have passed by the piston rings) are drawn from the crankcase through an auxiliary oil separator (two separators, located at the front and rear of the cylinder block on some engines), through the main oil separator, into the air inlet tract. The gases are then drawn into the engine together with the inlet air. Condensed oil vapour is returned from the main oil separator to the engine sump.

Exhaust emission control system

3   This system is fitted to later models fitted with the F8Q 732 engine.
4   To minimise the level of exhaust gas pollutants released into the atmosphere, a catalytic converter is fitted, located in the exhaust system.
5   The catalytic converter consists of a canister containing a fine mesh impregnated with a catalyst material, over which the exhaust gases pass. The catalyst speeds up the oxidation of harmful carbon monoxide, unburnt hydrocarbons and soot, effectively reducing the quantity of harmful products reaching the atmosphere.

Exhaust gas recirculation (EGR) system

6   This system is fitted to later models fitted with the F8Q 732 engine.
7   The system is designed to recirculate small quantities of exhaust gas into the inlet tract, and therefore into the combustion process. This process reduces the level of oxides of nitrogen present in the final exhaust gas which is released into the atmosphere, and also lowers the combustion temperature.
8   The volume of exhaust gas recirculated is controlled by a vacuum-operated exhaust gas recirculation (EGR) valve on the exhaust manifold, via a solenoid valve controlled by a micro-switch mounted on

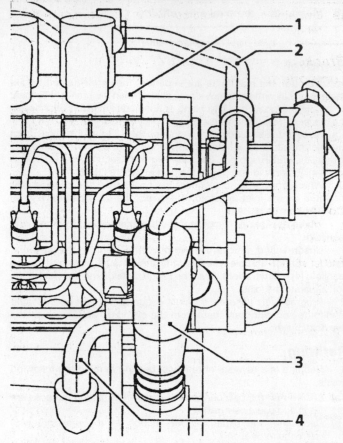

18.1b Single-separator crankcase emission control system

1   *Inlet manifold*   3   *Oil separator*
2   *Hose to inlet manifold*   4   *Return pipe to sump*

the injection pump. A temperature valve fitted in the vacuum supply line cuts off the vacuum supply until the engine has warmed up sufficiently.
9   Between idling speed and a part throttle, the microswitch on the injection pump remains open and supplies power to the solenoid valve. The solenoid valve is then open, allowing vacuum (from the braking system pump) to act on the EGR valve, allowing a small amount of exhaust gas to be recirculated back into the inlet tract. Under full-load conditions, the accelerator lever contacts the switch roller and closes the microswitch, which in turn shuts off the solenoid valve. This cuts off the vacuum supply to the EGR valve and shuts off the exhaust gas recirculation passage. Additional control is provided by the temperature valve, which cuts off the vacuum supply to the until the coolant temperature reaches a predetermined temperature (approximately 20ºC), preventing the EGR valve from opening during the engine warm-up phase.

Cold-start timing advance system

10   This system is fitted to some later Bosch injection pumps.
11   The system consists of an electrically-operated solenoid valve, which is screwed into the side of the injection pump, which is controlled by the preheating system control unit (see Chapter 5).
12   On cold starts, the preheating unit supplies the solenoid valve with current. The solenoid valve then opens and advances the injection timing.
13   The solenoid remains open for between 30 seconds and two and a half minutes, depending on engine temperature (the colder the engine, the longer the time). The control unit switches off the current, shutting the solenoid valve, and injection timing returns to its normal setting.

19 Emission control systems - testing and component renewal

Crankcase emission control system components

Testing

1   If the system is thought to be faulty, firstly, check that the hoses are unobstructed. On high mileage vehicles, particularly when regularly used for short journeys, a jelly-like deposit may be evident inside the system hoses and oil separators. If excessive deposits are present, the relevant component(s) should be removed and cleaned.

2   Periodically inspect the system components for security and damage, and renew them as necessary.

Component renewal

3   Renewal procedures for the hoses and oil separators are self-evident.

Exhaust emission control system

Testing

4   The system can only be tested accurately using a suitable exhaust gas analyser (suitable for use with diesel engines).

Component renewal

5   The catalytic converter is fitted in the exhaust system between the front and intermediate sections.

6   Removal and refitting is described in Section 17.

Exhaust gas recirculation system

Testing

7   Start the engine, and run it until it reaches normal operating temperature (the cooling fan should have cut in and out at least once).

8   With the engine idling, disconnect the vacuum hose from the recirculation valve. As the hose is disconnected, it should be possible to hear the valve click shut. If no click is heard, proceed as follows.

9   Check that vacuum is present at the recirculation valve end of the vacuum hose. If a vacuum gauge is available, check that the vacuum is at least 500 mbars. If vacuum is present, it is likely that the recirculation valve is faulty (jammed or pierced diaphragm). If no vacuum is present, carry out the following checks.

10   Check the security of all vacuum hose connections.

11   Check the electrical feed to the solenoid valve.

12   Check the operation of the temperature valve. This can be done by checking that vacuum will pass through the valve with the engine at normal operating temperature. Stop the engine and disconnect the temperature valve vacuum hoses at the recirculation valve and the solenoid valve, and check that it is possible to blow through the hoses. If not, it is likely that the temperature valve is faulty, or the hoses are obstructed.

13   Check the operation of the EGR microswitch on the injection pump as described in Chapter 5. If it proves impossible to adjust the switch, it is faulty and must be renewed.

Component renewal

Exhaust gas recirculation (EGR) valve

14   The valve is located at the rear of the engine, and is bolted to the exhaust manifold and connected to the inlet manifold via a metal pipe bolted between the valve and the manifold. To improve access to the valve, unbolt the oil separator from the rear of the inlet manifold.

15   Disconnect the vacuum hose from the valve.

16   Remove the retaining bolts, and disconnect the valve pipe from the base of the inlet manifold. Recover the gasket.

17   Unbolt the valve body from the exhaust manifold, and recover the gasket. Remove the valve complete with the pipe.

18   If a new valve is to be fitted, unscrew the securing bolts, and transfer the pipe to the new valve, using a new gasket.

19   Refitting is a reversal of removal, using new gaskets, ensuring all bolts are securely tightened.

Solenoid valve

20   The valve is mounted on the engine compartment bulkhead, directly behind the inlet manifold.

21   Disconnect the wiring plug and the vacuum hoses from the valve.

22   Unscrew the retaining nut(s), and withdraw the valve complete with its bracket.

23   Refitting is a reversal of removal, ensuring that the vacuum hoses are securely reconnected.

Temperature valve

24   The temperature valve is screwed into one of the cooling system hoses near the left-hand end of the cylinder head. To locate the valve, trace the vacuum pipe back from the solenoid valve and then onto the valve.

25   Disconnect the vacuum hoses from the valve then unscrew the valve from the hose and plug the hose aperture to minimise coolant loss. Be prepared for coolant spillage as the switch is removed and wash off any spilt coolant with cold water.

26   Refitting is reversal of removal, ensuring the switch is securely tightened. On completion, top up the coolant level (if necessary) and check for coolant leaks.

Microswitch

27   Refer to Chapter 5.

Cold-start timing advance system

Testing

28   To check the operation of the system, start the engine from cold, and listen for a knocking or harshness, disappearing after between 30 seconds and 2 minutes 45 seconds (depending on engine temperature). This shows that the system is working correctly. (If dynamic timing equipment is available, this can be used to check the advance.)

29   If the system does not seem to be working, check for voltage at the solenoid feed wire with the starter motor cranking, and for 5 to 6 seconds after start-up (the feed to the solenoid is controlled by the preheating system control unit).

30   If voltage is present, but the system is still not working, the solenoid valve is probably faulty, and should be renewed.

Solenoid renewal

Note: *Be careful not to allow dirt into the injection pump during this procedure.*

31   Disconnect the battery negative lead, then disconnect the solenoid wiring connector.

32   Unscrew the solenoid valve from the pump and recover the sealing washer. Take great care not to allow dirt to enter the pump.

33   Refitting is a reversal of removal, using a new sealing washer.

4

Notes

Chapter 5 Engine electrical systems

Contents

Specifications

General

System type	12-volt, negative earth
Battery type	Lead-acid, low-maintenance or "maintenance-free" (sealed-for-life)
Battery capacity (original equipment)	35, 50 or 60 amp-hours, according to model

Alternator

Make	Valeo
Maximum output - at 13.5 volts and 8000 (alternator) rpm	60, 70, 90 or 110 amps
Regulated voltage	13.5 to 14.8 volts

Starter motor

Make and type	Bosch, reduction gear

Glow plugs

Type	Champion CH 155

Solenoid stop valve

Winding resistance	9 ± 1 ohms

Torque wrench setting

	Nm	lbf ft
Glow plugs	20	15
Stop solenoid	20	15
Stop solenoid terminal nut	3.5	3

1 General information and precautions

General information

The engine electrical system includes all charging, starting and pre-heating components and engine oil sensors. Because of their engine-related functions, these components are covered separately from the body electrical devices such as the lights, instruments, etc (which are covered in Chapter 12).

The electrical system is of 12-volt negative earth type.

The battery is charged by the alternator, which is belt-driven from a crankshaft-mounted pulley. Most models are fitted with a "maintenance-free" (sealed-for-life) battery. In certain territories, a low-maintenance battery may be fitted, which will require periodic topping-up of the electrolyte level.

The starter motor is of the pre-engaged reduction gear type, incorporating an integral solenoid. On starting, the solenoid moves the drive pinion into engagement with the flywheel ring gear before the starter motor is energised. Once the engine has started, a one-way clutch prevents the motor armature being driven by the engine until the pinion disengages from the flywheel. The motor is fitted with a reduction gear mechanism, in order to achieve the high torque necessary to turn the engine against the high compression pressures encountered in a diesel engine.

Precautions

Further details of the various systems are given in the relevant Sections of this Chapter. While some repair procedures are given, the usual course of action is to renew the component concerned.

It is necessary to take extra care when working on the electrical system to avoid damage to semi-conductor devices (diodes and transistors), and to avoid the risk of personal injury. In addition to the precautions given in *"Safety first!"* at the beginning of this manual, observe the following when working on the system:

Always remove rings, watches, etc before working on the electrical system. Even with the battery disconnected, capacitive discharge could occur if a component's live terminal is earthed through a metal object. This could cause a shock or nasty burn.

Do not reverse the battery connections. Components such as the alternator, pre-heating electronic control unit, or any other components having semi-conductor circuitry could be irreparably damaged.

If the engine is being started using jump leads and a slave battery, connect the batteries *positive-to-positive* and *negative-to-negative* (see *"Booster battery (jump) starting"*). This also applies when connecting a battery charger.

Never disconnect the battery terminals, the alternator, any electrical wiring or any test instruments when the engine is running.

Do not allow the engine to turn the alternator when the alternator is not connected.

Never "test" for alternator output by "flashing" the output lead to earth.

Never use an ohmmeter of the type incorporating a hand-cranked generator for circuit or continuity testing.

Always ensure that the battery negative lead is disconnected when working on the electrical system. (The battery terminal connectors fitted as original equipment are particularly easy to disconnect. Just unscrew the wing nut on top of the terminal a few turns; there is no need to remove the connector completely.)

Before using electric-arc welding equipment on the car, disconnect the battery, alternator and components such as the pre-heating electronic control unit etc, to protect them from the risk of damage.

The radio/cassette unit fitted as standard equipment by Renault may be equipped with a built-in security code to deter thieves. If the power source to the unit is cut, the anti-theft system will activate. Even if the power source is immediately reconnected, the radio/cassette unit will not function until the correct security code has been entered. Therefore, if you do not know the correct security code for the radio/cassette unit **do not** disconnect the battery negative terminal of the battery or remove the radio/cassette unit from the vehicle. Refer to the manufacturer's handbook supplied with the vehicle for details of how to enter the security code.

2 Electrical fault finding - general information

Refer to Chapter 12.

3 Battery - testing and charging

Note: *Refer to the precautions given in "Safety first!" and in Section 1 of this Chapter before proceeding.*

Testing

1 Most vehicles are fitted with a "maintenance-free" (sealed-for-life) battery, in which case the electrolyte level cannot be checked. In this case, refer to the battery manufacturer's recommendations for maintenance and charging procedures.

2 Where a conventional battery is fitted, the electrolyte level of each cell should be checked, and if necessary topped-up with distilled or de-ionised water, at the intervals given in Chapter 1. On some batteries, the case is translucent, and incorporates minimum and maximum level marks.

3 If the vehicle covers a very small annual mileage, it is worthwhile checking the specific gravity of the electrolyte every three months, to determine the state of charge of the battery. Use a hydrometer to make the check, and compare the results obtained with the following table.

	Above 25°C (77°F)	Below 25°C (77°F)
Fully charged	1.210 to 1.230	1.270 to 1.290
70% charged	1.170 to 1.190	1.230 to 1.250
Fully discharged	1.050 to 1.070	1.110 to 1.130

4 If the battery condition is suspect, where possible, first check the specific gravity of the electrolyte in each cell. A variation of 0.040 or more between cells indicates loss of electrolyte or deterioration of the internal plates.

5 An accurate test of battery condition can be made by a battery specialist, using a heavy-discharge meter. Alternatively, connect a voltmeter across the battery terminals, and disconnect the stop solenoid (see Section 20); operate the starter motor with the headlamps, heated rear window and heater blower switched on. If the voltmeter reading remains above 9.6 volts, the battery condition is satisfactory. If the voltmeter reading drops below 9.6 volts, and the battery has already been charged, it is faulty.

Charging

Note: *The following is intended as a guide only. Always refer to the battery manufacturer's recommendations (often printed on a label attached to the battery) before charging.*

6 In normal use, the battery should not require charging from an external source, unless it is discharged accidentally (for instance by leaving the lights on). Charging can also temporarily revive a failing battery, but if frequent recharging is required (and the alternator output is correct), the battery is worn out.

7 Unless the battery manufacturer advises differently, the charging rate in amps should be no more than one-tenth of the battery capacity in amp-hours (for instance, 6.5 amps for a 65 amp-hour battery). Most domestic battery chargers have an output of 5 amps or so, and these can safely be used overnight. Rapid "boost" charging is not recommended; if it is not carefully controlled, it can cause serious damage to the battery plates through overheating.

8 Both battery terminal leads must be disconnected before connecting the charger leads (disconnect the negative lead first). Connect the charger leads **before** switching on at the mains. When charging is complete, switch off at the mains **before** disconnecting the charger. If this procedure is followed, there is no risk of creating a spark at the battery terminals. Continue to charge the battery until no further rise in specific gravity is noted over a four-hour period, or until vigorous gassing is observed.

9 On completion of charging, check the electrolyte level (if possible) and top-up if necessary, using distilled or de-ionised water.

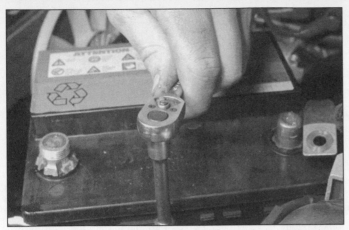

4.4a Unscrew the extended clamp bolt . . .

4.4b . . . and withdraw the battery clamp assembly

4 Battery - removal and refitting

Note: *Refer to the precautions given in "Safety first!" and in Section 1 of this Chapter before proceeding.*

Removal

Note: *Refer to the precautions given in "Safety first!" and in Section 1 of this Chapter.*

1   The battery is located at the front left-hand corner of the engine compartment.
2   Disconnect the lead(s) at the negative (earth) terminal by unscrewing the retaining nut and removing the terminal clamp.
3   Disconnect the positive terminal lead(s) in the same way.
4   Unscrew the extended clamp bolt, remove the clamp assembly, then lift the battery from its location **(see illustrations)**. Keep the battery in an upright position, to avoid spilling electrolyte on the bodywork.

Refitting

5   Refitting is a reversal of removal. Smear petroleum jelly on the terminals when reconnecting the leads. Always reconnect the positive lead first, and the negative lead last.

5 Charging system - testing

Note: *Refer to the warnings given in "Safety first!" and in Section 1 of this Chapter before starting work.*

1   If the ignition (no-charge) warning light fails to illuminate when the ignition is switched on, first check the security of the alternator wiring connections. If satisfactory, check that the warning light bulb has not blown, and that the bulbholder is secure in its location in the instrument panel. If the light still fails to illuminate, check the continuity of the warning light feed wire from the alternator to the bulbholder. If all is satisfactory, the alternator is at fault, and should be renewed or taken to an auto-electrician for testing and repair.
2   If the ignition warning light illuminates when the engine is running, stop the engine and check that the drivebelt is correctly tensioned (Chapter 1) and that the alternator connections are secure. If all is so far satisfactory, check the alternator brushes and slip rings (Section 8). If the fault persists, the alternator should be renewed, or taken to an auto-electrician for testing and repair.
3   If the alternator output is suspect even though the warning light functions correctly, the regulated voltage may be checked as follows.
4   Connect a voltmeter across the battery terminals, and start the engine.
5   Increase the engine speed until the voltmeter reading remains steady; the reading should be between 13.5 and 14.8 volts.
6   Switch on as many electrical accessories (headlights, heated rear

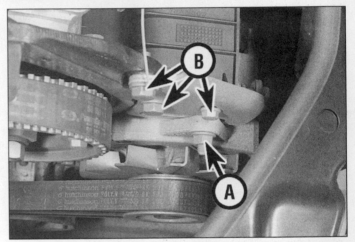

7.4 Alternator tensioner bolt (A) and tensioner bracket bolts (B)

window, heater blower etc) as possible, and check that the alternator maintains the regulated voltage between 13.5 and 14.8 volts. It may be necessary to increase engine speed slightly.
7   If the regulated voltage is not as stated, the fault may be due to worn brushes, weak brush springs, a faulty voltage regulator, a faulty diode, a severed phase winding, or worn or damaged slip rings. The brushes and slip rings may be checked (see Section 8), but if the fault persists, the alternator should be renewed or taken to an auto-electrician for testing and repair.

6 Auxiliary drivebelt - removal, refitting and adjustment

Refer to Chapter 1, Section 10.

7 Alternator - removal and refitting

Note: *Refer to the warnings given in "Safety first!" and in Section 1 of this Chapter before proceeding.*

Removal

1   Disconnect the battery leads (negative lead first).
2   Remove the radiator grille panel and bonnet (see Chapter 11).
3   Remove the front right-hand indicator light and the front right-hand headlight (see Chapter 12).
4   Loosen the alternator tensioner bolt on the bottom of the bracket, then swivel the alternator towards the engine and remove the drivebelt from the alternator pulley **(see illustration)**.

5

7.7a   Disconnecting the alternator wiring plug

7.7b   Remove the rubber cover . . .

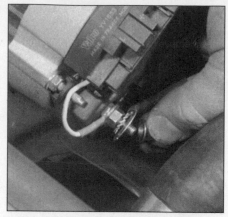

7.7c   . . . then disconnect the alternator main feed wire

7.8   Removing the alternator through the headlight aperture

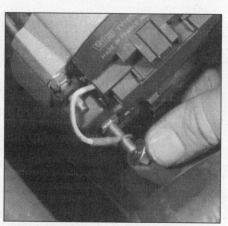

8.2   Disconnecting the brush holder/regulator assembly wire from the rear of the alternator

8.3   Removing the plastic cover from the rear of the alternator

5   Unbolt the alternator tensioning bracket from the injection pump bracket.

6   Unscrew and remove the alternator lower pivot bolt. It may be necessary to disconnect the radiator bottom hose, in which case the cooling system should be drained as described in Chapter 1.

7   Withdraw the alternator sufficiently to disconnect the wiring plug, and/or disconnect the wires from their terminals, as applicable **(see illustrations)**. Note the locations of the wires for reference when refitting.

8   Withdraw the alternator through the headlight aperture **(see illustration)**.

Refitting

9   Refitting is a reversal of the removal procedure, but tension the drivebelt as described in Chapter 1. If the bottom hose was disconnected refill the cooling system with reference to Chapter 1.

8   Alternator brushes and regulator - removal, inspection and refitting

Note: *Refer to the warnings given in "Safety first!" and in Section 1 of this Chapter before proceeding.*

Removal

1   Remove the alternator as described in the previous Section.

2   Note the location of the brush holder/regulator assembly wire on the alternator B+ terminal. Unscrew the nut and disconnect the wire **(see illustration)**.

3   Unclip the plastic cover from the studs on the rear of the alternator, and remove the cover **(see illustration)**.

4   Unscrew the two screws securing the brush holder/regulator assembly to the rear of the alternator **(see illustration)**.

5   Disconnect the remaining wire from the terminal on the rear of the alternator, then lift the brush holder/regulator assembly from the alternator **(see illustration)**.

Inspection

6   Measure the protrusion of each brush from the brush holder **(see illustration)**. No minimum dimension is specified by the manufacturers, but as a rough guide, 5 mm should be regarded as a minimum. If either brush is worn below this dimension, the complete brush holder/regulator assembly must be renewed. If the brushes are still serviceable, clean them with a fuel-moistened cloth. Check that the brush spring tension is equal for both brushes and provides a reasonable pressure. The brushes must move freely in their holders.

7   Clean the alternator slip rings with a petrol-moistened cloth. Check for signs of scoring, burning or severe pitting on the surface of the slip rings. It may be possible to have the slip rings renovated by an electrical specialist.

Refitting

8   Refit the brush holder/regulator assembly using a reversal of the removal procedure.

9   Refit the alternator with reference to Section 7.

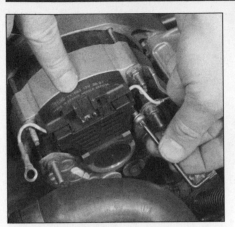

8.4 Unscrewing a brush holder/regulator assembly securing screw

8.5 Removing the brush holder/regulator assembly

8.6 Measuring the alternator brush protrusion

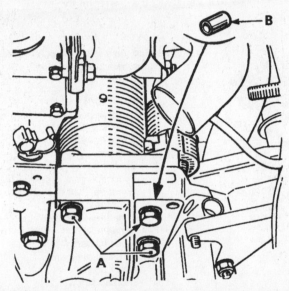

10.3 Starter motor securing bolts (A) and locating dowel (B)

9 Starting system - testing

Note: *Refer to the precautions given in "Safety first!" and in Section 1 of this Chapter before starting work.*

1   If the starter motor fails to operate when the ignition key is turned to the appropriate position, the possible causes are as follows:

  a) *The battery is faulty.*
  b) *The electrical connections between the switch, solenoid, battery and starter motor are somewhere failing to pass the necessary current from the battery through the starter to earth.*
  c) *The solenoid is faulty.*
  d) *The starter motor is mechanically or electrically defective.*

2   To check the battery, switch on the headlights. If they dim after a few seconds, this indicates that the battery is discharged - recharge (see Section 3) or renew the battery. If the headlights glow brightly, operate the starter switch and observe the lights. If they dim, then this indicates that current is reaching the starter motor, therefore the fault must lie in the starter motor. If the lights continue to glow brightly (and no clicking sound can be heard from the starter motor solenoid), this indicates that there is a fault in the circuit or solenoid - see the following paragraphs. If the starter motor turns slowly when operated, but the battery is in good condition, then this indicates either that the starter motor is faulty, or there is considerable resistance somewhere in the circuit.

3   If a fault in the circuit is suspected, disconnect the battery leads (including the earth connection to the body), the starter/solenoid wiring and the engine/transmission earth strap. Thoroughly clean the connections, and reconnect the leads and wiring. Use a voltmeter or test light to check that full battery voltage is available at the battery positive lead connection to the solenoid. Smear petroleum jelly around the battery terminals to prevent corrosion - corroded connections are among the most frequent causes of electrical system faults.

4   If the battery and all connections are in good condition, check the circuit by disconnecting the wire from the solenoid blade terminal. Connect a voltmeter or test light between the wire end and a good earth (such as the battery negative terminal), and check that the wire is live when the ignition switch is turned to the "start" position. If it is, then the circuit is sound - if not, there is a fault in the ignition/starter switch or wiring.

5   The solenoid contacts can be checked by connecting a voltmeter or test light between the battery positive feed connection on the starter side of the solenoid, and earth. When the ignition switch is turned to the "start" position, there should be a reading or lighted bulb, as applicable. If there is no reading or lighted bulb, the solenoid is faulty and should be renewed.

6   If the circuit and solenoid are proved sound, the fault must lie in the starter motor. Begin checking the starter motor by removing it (Section 10), and checking the brushes (Section 11). If the fault does not lie in the brushes, the motor windings must be faulty. In this event, the starter motor must be renewed, unless an auto-electrical specialist can be found who will overhaul the unit at a cost significantly less than that of a new or exchange starter motor.

10 Starter motor - removal and refitting

Note: *Refer to the precautions given in "Safety first!" and in Section 1 of this Chapter before proceeding.*

Removal

1   Open the bonnet and disconnect the battery negative lead. For improved access remove the battery completely as described in Section 4.

2   Remove the air cleaner housing assembly as described in Chapter 4, Section 2.

3   Unscrew the three bolts securing the starter motor to the gearbox bellhousing. Where applicable, note the location of any wiring brackets secured by the bolts. Note the location of the dowel in the upper rear bolt hole **(see illustration)**.

4   Apply the handbrake, then jack up the front of the vehicle and support it securely on axle stands. For improved access, remove the right-hand roadwheel.

5   Unbolt and remove the heat shield from the rear of the starter motor.

5

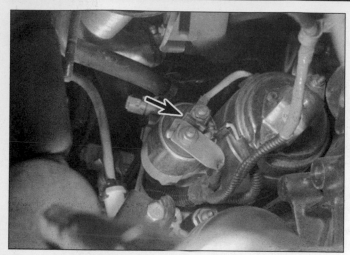

**10.7 Starter motor wiring (arrowed) viewed from
under the vehicle**

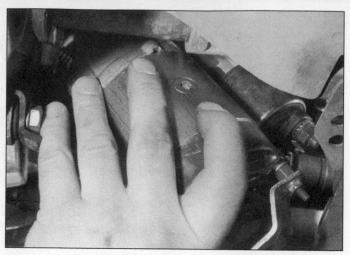

10.8 Removing the starter motor

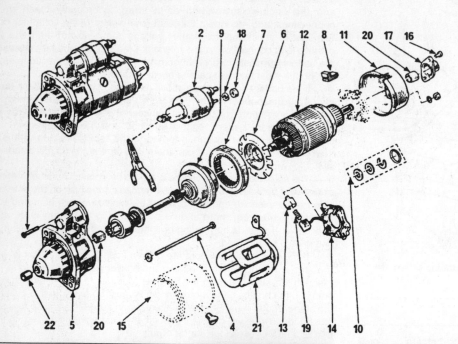

**11.1 Exploded view of the Bosch reduction
gear type starter motor**

1   Bolt
2   Solenoid
4   Through-bolt
5   Drive end housing
6   Armature retaining plate
7   Ring gear
8   Rubber wiring grommet
9   Reduction gear assembly
10 Armature shaft end circlips
    and shims
11 Armature end cover
12 Armature
13 Brush holder
14 Brush holder plate
15 Motor body
16 End cap screw
17 Armature shaft end cap
18 Terminal nut and washer
19 Brush spring
20 Bush
21 Field windings
22 Bush

**11.3 Removing the mounting bracket from the rear
of the starter motor**

11.4a Unscrew the securing screws . . .

11.4b . . . and remove the armature
shaft end cap

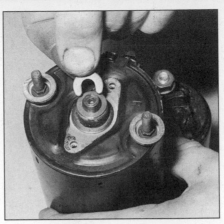

11.5a Remove the circlip . . .

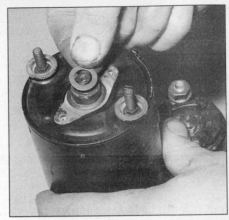

11.5b . . . and recover the washers
and spacers

11.6 Remove the nut securing the field
wiring to the solenoid

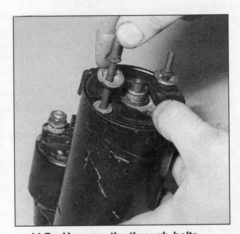

11.7a Unscrew the through-bolts . . .

11.7b . . . and withdraw the armature
end cover

6   Remove the starter motor rear mounting bracket by unscrewing the two bolts and nut on the cylinder block and the two nuts to the rear of the starter.

7   Disconnect the wiring from the terminals on the starter motor solenoid **(see illustration)**.

8   Withdraw the starter motor from the engine **(see illustration)**.

Refitting

9   Refitting is a reversal of removal, bearing in mind the following points.

a) *Ensure that the locating dowel is correctly positioned in the bellhousing bolt hole, as noted during removal.*

b) *When reconnecting the wiring to the motor, make sure that the terminal on the end of the wire is positioned clear of the starter motor body and surrounding components.*

c) *Where applicable, refit the any wiring brackets to the starter motor mounting bolts.*

11 Starter motor - brush renewal

1   With the starter motor removed from the vehicle as described in Section 10, proceed as follows **(see illustration)**.

2   Make alignment marks on the armature end cover and the motor body.

3   Where applicable, unscrew the two securing nuts, and remove the mounting bracket from the rear of the starter motor **(see illustration)**.

4   Unscrew the securing screws, and remove the armature shaft end cap **(see illustrations)**.

5   Remove the circlip from the end of the armature shaft. Recover the washers and spacers, noting their orientation **(see illustrations)**.

6   Remove the nut securing the field wiring to the solenoid **(see illustration)**.

7   Unscrew the two through-bolts and withdraw the armature end cover, along with the mounting bracket, when fitted **(see illustrations)**.

8   Withdraw the brush plate assembly from the rear of the starter motor, pulling the rubber wiring grommet from the motor casing as it is withdrawn.

9   Withdraw the brushes and the springs from the brush holders, then unclip the brush holders from the brush plate **(see illustrations)**.

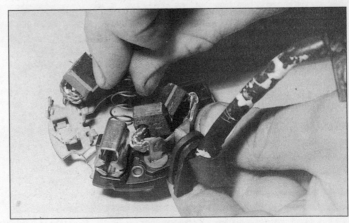

11.9a Withdraw the brushes . . .

11.9b . . . springs . . .

11.9c . . . and brush holders from the brush plate

11.13 Use a socket to hold the brushes in position

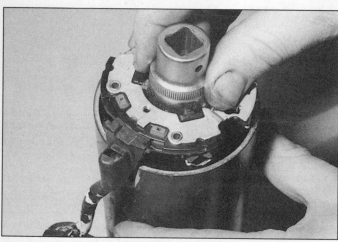

11.14 Fitting the brush plate over the armature shaft

the brushes to the brush holders. Ensure that the brushes move freely in their holders. Ensure that the brush springs provide adequate pressure on the brushes, and renew any worn springs.

13   Push the brushes into the brush holders, and use a socket to hold them in position as shown **(see illustration)**.

14   Position the brush plate over the rear of the armature shaft, then withdraw the socket so that the brushes contact the commutator **(see illustration)**.

15   Further refitting is a reversal of removal, bearing in mind the following points.

a) *Align the marks made on the end cover and the motor body before removal.*

b) *Ensure that the washers and spacers on the end of the armature shaft are fitted as noted before removal.*

c) *Refit the starter motor as described in Section 10.*

12   Ignition switch - removal and refitting

Removal

1   Disconnect the battery negative lead.

2   Remove the steering column shrouds as described in Chapter 11, Section 26.

3   Follow the switch wiring behind the facia, and disconnect the wiring connectors **(see illustration)**. If necessary, lower the driver's side facia panel for access, as described in Chapter 11, Section 26. Take note of the routing of the wiring.

4   Insert the ignition key into the switch, and turn it to position "M" (or "3").

10   Examine the brushes for wear and damage. If they are damaged, or worn to the extent where the springs are unable to exert sufficient pressure to maintain good contact with the commutator, they should be renewed. If renewal is necessary, unsolder the old brushes, and solder new ones into place.

11   Clean the brush holder assemblies, and wipe the commutator with a petrol-moistened cloth. If the commutator is dirty, it may be cleaned with fine glass paper, then wiped with the cloth.

12   Fit the brush holders to the brush plate, then refit the springs and

12.3 Disconnecting a wiring connector from the ignition switch

12.5 Unscrewing the ignition switch grub screw

12.6a Depressing the ignition switch securing clip

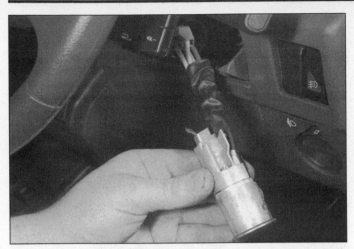

12.6b Withdrawing the ignition switch

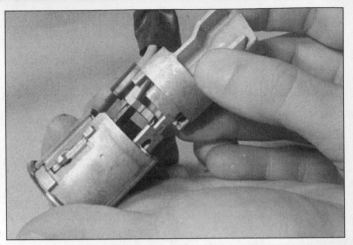

12.7a Removing the ignition switch rear cover . . .

5   Reach up behind the switch, and using a Torx key, remove the grub screw securing the switch assembly to the steering column **(see illustration)**.

6   Using a screwdriver, depress the securing clip located at the bottom of the switch assembly, then pull the assembly from the steering column using the key. Feed the wiring through the steering column as the switch is withdrawn **(see illustrations)**.

7   To separate the switch from the lock assembly, remove the two securing screws from the rear of the housing, and lift off the rear cover. The switch can now be withdrawn from the lock **(see illustrations)**.

Refitting

8   Refitting is a reversal of removal, bearing in mind the following points.

a) *When refitting the switch to the lock assembly, make sure that the lugs on the lock engage with the cut-outs in the switch. Note that the switch will only fit in one position.*

b) *Ensure that the switch wiring is routed as noted before removal.*

13 Oil pressure warning light switch - removal and refitting

Removal

1   The oil pressure warning light switch is located at the lower front right-hand side of the cylinder block.

12.7b . . . and withdrawing the switch from the lock

2   Disconnect the battery negative lead, then release the wiring connector from the switch.

3   Carefully unscrew the switch and withdraw it from the cylinder block. Be prepared for some oil spillage.

4   Recover the sealing ring, where applicable.

Refitting

5   Refitting is a reversal of removal, but clean the threads of the switch before screwing it into the cylinder block, and where applicable, use a new sealing ring.

14 Oil level sensor - removal and refitting

Where fitted, the oil level sensor is located in the front lower face of the cylinder block or in the side of the sump. Removal and refitting details are as described for the oil pressure warning light switch in Section 13.

15 Preheating system - description and testing

Description

1   Each swirl chamber has a heater plug (commonly called a glow plug) screwed into it. The plugs are electrically operated before, during, and a short time after start-up when the engine is cold. Electrical feed to the glow plugs is controlled by the preheating control unit.

2   The "post-heating" function of the glow plugs allows them to remain switched on for a period after the engine has started. Once the starter has been switched off, the glow plugs are supplied with full current for 5 to 10 seconds, then the plugs are supplied with half the "preheating" current, alternately, in pairs, for up to 3 minutes. The exact "post-heating" time is controlled by the preheating control unit, and is dependant on the prevailing engine operating conditions. The supply to the plugs will be interrupted by:

a) *Opening of the post-heating cut-out switch. The supply is cut off 3 seconds after the switch opens (ie 3 seconds after the accelerator pedal is depressed). The current supply is restored as soon as the switch closes.*

b) *A coolant temperature of more than 60°C.*

3   A warning light in the instrument panel tells the driver that preheating is taking place. When the light goes out, the engine is ready to be started. The voltage supply to the glow plugs continues for several seconds after the light goes out. If no attempt is made to start, the timer then cuts off the supply in order to avoid draining the battery and overheating of the glow plugs.

5

16.2 Unscrew the securing nut (arrowed) . . .

16.3 . . . then withdraw the preheating system control unit and disconnect the wiring

Testing

4   If the system malfunctions, testing is ultimately by substitution of known good units, but some preliminary checks may be made as follows.

5   Connect a voltmeter or 12 volt test light between the glow plug supply cable (disconnected) and earth (engine or vehicle metal). Make sure that the live connection is kept clear of the engine and bodywork.

6   Have an assistant switch on the ignition and check that voltage is applied to the glow plugs. Note the time for which the warning light is lit and the total time for which voltage is applied before the system cuts out. Switch off the ignition.

7   At an under-bonnet temperature of 20°C typical times noted should be 5 or 6 seconds for warning light operation, followed by a further 4 to 5 seconds supply after the light goes out (provided the starter motor is not operated). Warning light time will increase with lower temperatures and decrease with higher temperatures.

8   If there is no supply at all, the relay or associated wiring is at fault.

9   To locate a defective glow plug, disconnect the main supply cable and the interconnecting wire or strap from the top of the glow plugs. Be careful not to drop the nuts and washers.

10   Use a continuity tester, or a 12 volt test light connected to the battery positive terminal, to check for continuity between each glow plug terminal and earth. The resistance of a glow plug in good condition is very low (less than 1 ohm), so if the test light does not light or the continuity tester shows a high resistance the glow plug is certainly defective.

11   If an ammeter is available, the current draw of each glow plug can be checked. After an initial surge of around 15 to 20 amps, each plug should draw around 10 amps. Any plug which draws much more or less than this is probably defective.

12   As a final check the glow plugs can be removed and inspected as described in Section 17.

16 Preheating system control unit - removal and refitting

Removal

1   The unit is located on the left-hand suspension tower, to the rear of the battery. Disconnect the battery negative lead.

2   Unscrew the securing nut **(see illustration)**, and withdraw the unit from the bracket.

3   Disconnect the wiring from the base of the unit, noting the connector locations **(see illustration)**.

Refitting

4   Refitting is a reversal of removal, ensuring that the wiring connectors are correctly connected.

17 Glow plugs - removal, inspection and refitting

Removal

Caution: *If the preheating system has just been energised, or if the engine has been running, the glow plugs may be very hot.*

1   Disconnect the battery negative lead.

2   Unscrew the nuts from the glow plug terminals, and recover the washers. Disconnect the wiring **(see illustration)**. Note that the main electrical feed wiring is connected to two of the plugs.

3   Where applicable, carefully move any obstructing pipes or wires to one side to enable access to the glow plugs.

4   Unscrew the glow plugs and remove them from the cylinder head **(see illustrations)**.

Inspection

5   Inspect the glow plugs for physical damage. Burnt or eroded glow

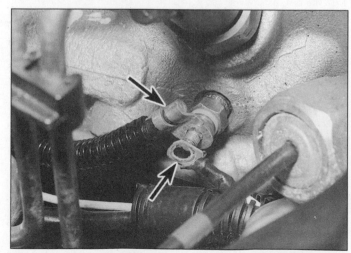

17.2 Disconnect the wiring (arrowed) from the glow plug terminal

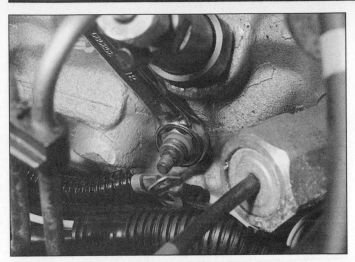

17.4a Unscrew the glow plug . . .

17.4b . . . and remove it from the cylinder head

plug tips can be caused by a bad injector spray pattern. Have the injectors checked if this sort of damage is found.

6   If the glow plugs are in good physical condition, check them electrically using a 12 volt test light or continuity tester as described in the previous Section.

7   The glow plugs can be energised by applying 12 volts to them to verify that they heat up evenly and in the required time. Observe the following precautions:

a) *Support the glow plug by clamping it carefully in a vice or self-locking pliers. Remember it will become red-hot.*

b) *Make sure that the power supply or test lead incorporates a fuse or overload trip to protect against damage from a short-circuit.*

c) *After testing, allow the glow plug to cool for several minutes before attempting to handle it.*

8   A glow plug in good condition will start to glow red at the tip after drawing current for 5 seconds or so. Any plug which takes much longer to start glowing, or which starts glowing in the middle instead of at the tip, is defective.

Refitting

9   Refit by reversing the removal operations. Apply a smear of copper-based anti-seize compound to the plug threads and tighten the

glow plugs to the specified torque. Do not overtighten, as this can damage the glow plug element.

18 Injection pump microswitch(es) - testing, adjustment, removal and refitting

Note: *The engine code appears on a plate attached to the engine. Refer to "Buying spare parts and vehicle identification numbers" for further details.*

F8Q 714 and F8Q 730 engines

Testing and adjustment

Note: *A continuity tester or an ohmmeter will be required for testing.*

1   On these engines, the microswitch performs the post-heating cut-out facility and is sometimes referred to as the "no-load" switch. To adjust the switch, first disconnect the switch wiring connector **(see illustration)**.

2   Connect a continuity tester or an ohmmeter across wiring connector terminals "B" and "C" **(see illustration)**.

3   Insert feeler gauges of different thicknesses between the injection

5

18.1 Disconnecting the no-load switch wiring connector - Roto-Diesel/Lucas injection pump

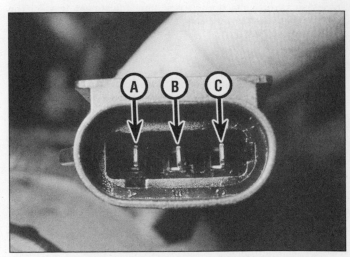

18.2 No-load switch wiring connector terminal identification - Roto-Diesel/Lucas injection pump

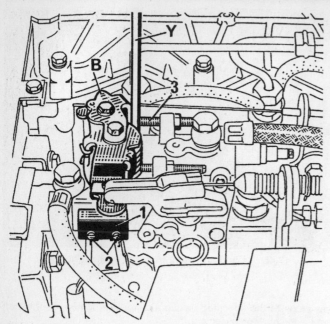

18.3a Adjusting the post-heating cut-out microswitch - F8Q 714 and F8Q 730 engines with Bosch injection pump

B	Accelerator lever	2	Mounting screws
Y	Feeler gauge	3	Anti-stall adjustment
1	Microswitch		screw

pump accelerator lever and the anti-stall adjustment screw, and note the readings on the continuity tester or ohmmeter, as applicable **(see illustrations)**. The readings obtained should be as follows.

Bosch injection pump

Spacer thickness	Test reading
Up to 9.7 mm	Continuity/zero resistance
10.7 mm or more	No continuity/infinite resistance

Roto-Diesel/Lucas injection pump

Spacer thickness	Test reading
Up to 8.0 mm	Continuity/zero resistance
12.0 mm or more	No continuity/infinite resistance

4   If the switch does not behave as described, slacken its mounting screws and reposition it as necessary. Note that on certain Roto-Diesel/Lucas fuel injection pumps, the adjustment is made by loosening the screw and adjusting the position of the cam in relation to the accelerator lever.

5   If the switch is permanently open or closed, renew it.

Removal

6   Disconnect the switch wiring connector, then remove the two securing screws, and withdraw the switch from its bracket on the injection pump.

Refitting

7   Refitting is a reversal of removal, but where applicable, before tightening the securing screws adjust the switch as described previously.

F8Q 732 engine

8   On F8Q 732 engines there are two microswitches on the injection pump, the inner microswitch is the post-heating cut-out switch and the outer switch is the exhaust gas recirculation (EGR) system microswitch. Both switches are of the "full-load" type.

Testing and adjustment

9   To adjust a switch, first disconnect the relevant wiring connector.

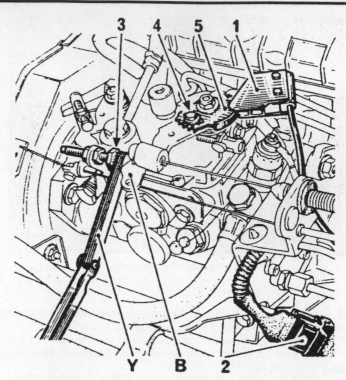

18.3b Adjusting the post-heating cut-out microswitch - F8Q 714 and F8Q 730 engines with Roto-Diesel/Lucas injection pump

B	Accelerator lever	3	Anti-stall adjustment
Y	Feeler gauges		screw
1	Microswitch	4	Bolt
2	Switch wiring connector	5	Cam

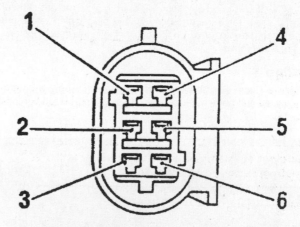

18.10 Injection pump microswitch wiring connector terminal details - F8Q 732 engines

1	Cold start advance solenoid terminal
2 and 3	Post heating microswitch terminals
4	Not used
5 and 6	EGR system switch

10   Connect a continuity tester or an ohmmeter across the relevant wiring connector terminals **(see illustration)**.

11   Insert feeler gauges of different thicknesses between the injection pump accelerator lever and the anti-stall adjustment screw, and note the readings on the continuity tester or ohmmeter, as applicable. The readings obtained should be as follows.

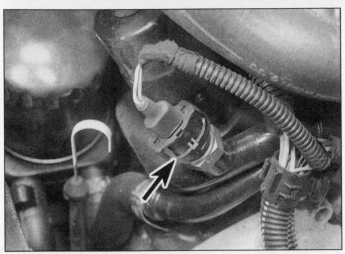

19.9 Coolant temperature switch (post-heating cut-off) (arrowed)

20.4 Disconnecting the stop solenoid wiring -
Roto-Diesel/Lucas injection pump

Post-heating switch

Spacer thickness	Test reading
Up to 7 mm	*Continuity/zero resistance*
8 mm or more	*No continuity/infinite resistance*

EGR system switch

Spacer thickness	Test reading
Up to 13.5 mm	*Continuity/zero resistance*
14.5 mm or more	*No continuity/infinite resistance*

12   If the switch does not behave as described, slacken its mounting screws and reposition it as necessary.
13   If the switch is permanently open or closed, renew it.

Removal

14   Disconnect the switch wiring connector, then remove the two securing screws, and withdraw the switch from its bracket on the injection pump. In order to remove the post-heating cut-out (inner) switch, it will be necessary to first remove the EGR system (outer) switch.

Refitting

15   Refitting is a reversal of removal, but where applicable, before tightening the securing screws adjust the switch(es) as described previously.

19 Coolant temperature switch (post-heating cut-off) - testing, removal and refitting

Testing

Note: *A continuity tester or an ohmmeter will be required for testing.*
1   Remove the switch as described in paragraphs 7 to 9.
2   Connect a continuity tester or an ohmmeter across the switch terminals. There should be continuity/zero resistance between the terminals.
3   Now suspend the switch in a container of water (using wire or string), along with a thermometer.
4   Gently heat the water, keeping note of the rise in temperature.
5   Periodically remove the switch from the water, ensure that the terminals are dry, and again check for continuity/resistance. The results obtained should be as follows.
   Water temperature below 55°C ± 2°C - Continuity/zero resistance
   Water temperature above 65°C ± 2°C - No continuity/infinite resistance
6   If the results obtained are not as specified, the switch is proved faulty and should be renewed.

Removal

7   The switch is located in a housing in the coolant hose at the left-hand front corner of the engine.
8   Drain the cooling system as described in Chapter 1. Alternatively have the new switch or a suitable bung to hand.
9   Disconnect the switch wiring plug, then unscrew and remove the switch **(see illustration)**. Recover the sealing ring, where applicable.

Refitting

10   Refitting is a reversal of removal, using a new sealing ring, where applicable.
11   On completion, check the coolant level, and top up or refill and bleed the cooling system, as necessary, as described in Chapter 1.

20 Stop solenoid - description, removal and refitting

Description

1   The stop solenoid is located on the end of the fuel injection pump. Its purpose is to cut the fuel supply when the ignition switch is switched off. If an open circuit occurs in the solenoid or supply wiring it will be impossible to start the engine, as the fuel will not reach the injectors. The same applies if the solenoid plunger jams in the "stop" position. If the solenoid jams in the "run" position, the engine will not stop when the ignition is switched off.
2   If the solenoid has failed and the engine will not run, a temporary repair may be made by removing the solenoid as described in the following paragraphs. Refit the solenoid body without the plunger and spring. Tape up the wire so that it cannot touch earth. The engine can now be started as usual, but it will be necessary to use the manual stop lever on the fuel injection pump (or to stall the engine in gear) to stop it.

Removal

Caution : *Be careful not to allow dirt into the injection pump during this procedure. A new sealing washer or O-ring must be used on refitting.*
3   Disconnect the battery negative lead.
4   Withdraw the rubber boot (where applicable), then unscrew the terminal nut and disconnect the wire from the top of the solenoid **(see illustration)**.
5   Carefully clean around the solenoid, then unscrew and withdraw the solenoid, and recover the sealing washer or O-ring (as applicable). Recover the solenoid plunger and spring if they remain in the pump. Operate the hand priming pump as the solenoid is removed to flush away any dirt.

Refitting

6   Before refitting the solenoid, check that the aperture in the injection pump is completely free of dust or dirt. On the Roto-Diesel/Lucas injection pump Instances have been known of a small piece of metal swarf preventing the valve from fully closing when the ignition switch is turned off. Insert a small magnet in the aperture to collect any swarf - do not blow into the aperture otherwise the swarf may enter the fuel circuit. Refitting is a reversal of removal, using a new sealing washer or O-ring. When refitting the terminal wire on Roto-Diesel/Lucas injection pumps, make sure that the fan-shaped washer is located under the wire end fitting. Failure to fit the washer may cause the engine to stop while driving, or prevent the engine from being started.

Chapter 6 Clutch

Contents

6

Specifications

General

Clutch type	Single dry plate, diaphragm spring, cable-operated
Adjustment	Automatic

Clutch disc

Diameter	200.0 mm
Lining thickness (new, and in compressed position)	7.7 mm
Number of springs	6

Torque wrench settings

	Nm	lbf ft
Clutch cover bolts:		
7 mm diameter	25	18
8 mm diameter	30	22

1   General information

All models are equipped with a cable-operated clutch. The unit consists of a steel cover which is dowelled and bolted to the rear face of the flywheel, and contains the pressure plate and diaphragm spring **(see illustration)**.

The clutch disc is free to slide along the gearbox splined input shaft. The disc is held in position between the flywheel and the pressure plate by the pressure of the diaphragm spring. Friction lining material is riveted to the clutch disc, which has a spring-cushioned hub to absorb transmission shocks and help ensure a smooth take-up of the drive.

The clutch is actuated by a cable, controlled by the clutch pedal. The clutch release mechanism consists of a release arm and bearing which is in permanent contact with the fingers of the diaphragm spring.

Depressing the clutch pedal actuates the release arm by means of the cable **(see illustration)**. The arm pushes the release bearing against the diaphragm fingers, so moving the centre of the diaphragm spring inwards. As the centre of the spring is pushed in, the outside of the spring pivots out, so moving the pressure plate backwards and disengaging its grip on the clutch disc.

When the pedal is released, the diaphragm spring forces the pressure plate into contact with the friction linings on the clutch disc. The disc is now firmly sandwiched between the pressure plate and the flywheel, thus transmitting engine power to the gearbox.

Wear of the friction material on the clutch disc is automatically compensated for by a self-adjusting mechanism attached to the clutch pedal. The mechanism consists of a serrated quadrant, a notched cam and a tension spring. One end of the clutch cable is attached to the quadrant, which is free to pivot on the pedal, but is kept in tension by a spring. When the pedal is depressed, the notched cam contacts the quadrant, thus locking it and allowing the pedal to pull the cable and operate the clutch. When the pedal is released, the tension spring causes the notched cam to move free of the quadrant; at the same time tension is maintained on the cable, keeping the release bearing in contact with the diaphragm spring. As the friction material on the disc wears, the self-adjusting quadrant will rotate when the pedal is released, and the pedal free play will be maintained between the notched cam and the quadrant.

2   Clutch cable - removal and refitting

Removal

1   Disconnect the battery negative terminal.
2   In order to gain access to the clutch cable on the gearbox bellhousing, remove the air cleaner and air inlet ducting with reference to Chapter 4.

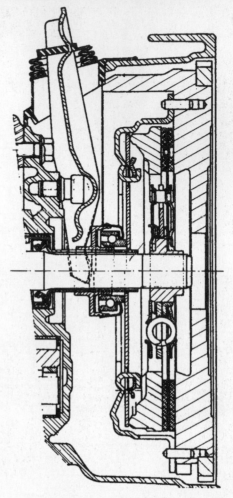

1.1 Cross-section of the clutch components

3   Disengage the inner cable from the release fork, then withdraw the outer cable from the bracket on the bellhousing **(see illustrations)**.
4   Working inside the car, remove the lower facia panel. Press the clutch pedal to the floor. Release the pedal, and free the inner cable end from the serrated quadrant on the self-adjusting mechanism **(see illustration)**.
5   Using a screwdriver, tap out the inner cable guide from the top of the pedal.

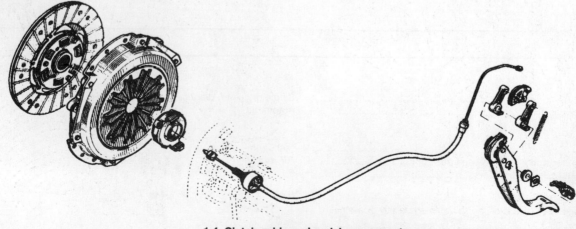

1.4 Clutch cable and pedal components

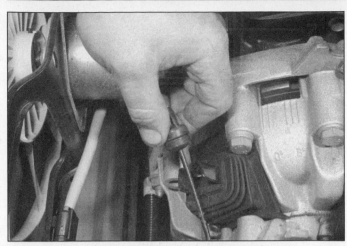

2.3a Disconnecting the clutch inner cable from the release fork

2.3b Withdrawing the clutch outer cable from the bracket on the bellhousing

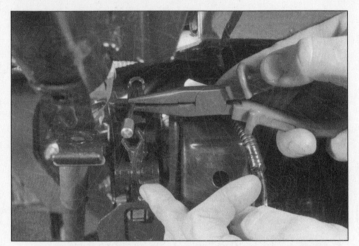

2.4 Disconnecting the inner cable end from the quadrant

6   With the inner cable released, push the outer cable out of its location in the bulkhead.

7   Pull the cable through into the engine compartment, detach it from the support clips and remove it from the car.

Refitting

8   To refit the cable, thread it through from the engine compartment, place it over the self-adjusting cam, and connect the inner cable end to the quadrant **(see illustration)**. Make sure that the self-adjusting cam support arms return to their rest position freely under the tension of the return spring.

9   Refit the inner cable guide to the top of the pedal.

10   Working in the engine compartment, slip the other end of the cable through the bellhousing bracket, and connect the inner cable to the release fork. Refit the cable to the support clips.

11   Depress the clutch pedal to draw the outer cable into its locating hole in the bulkhead, ensuring that it locates properly. At the same time, the inner cable guide will be automatically pulled onto the top of the pedal to hold the inner cable in position.

12   Depress the clutch pedal several times in order to allow the self-adjusting mechanism to set the correct free play.

13   When the self-adjusting mechanism on the clutch pedal is functioning correctly, there should be a minimum of 20 mm slack in the cable. To check this dimension, pull out the inner cable near the release fork on the gearbox **(see illustration)**. If there is less than the minimum slack in the cable, the self-adjusting quadrant should be checked for seizure or possible restricted movement.

6

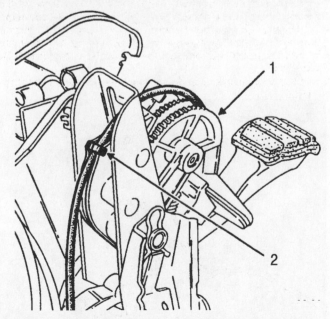

2.8 Clutch inner cable location on the self-adjusting quadrant

1   Quadrant *2   Guide*

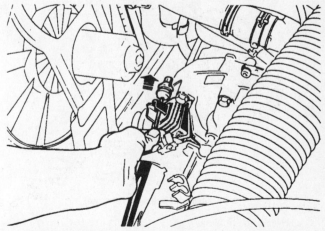

2.13 Checking the clutch inner cable slack at the release fork end

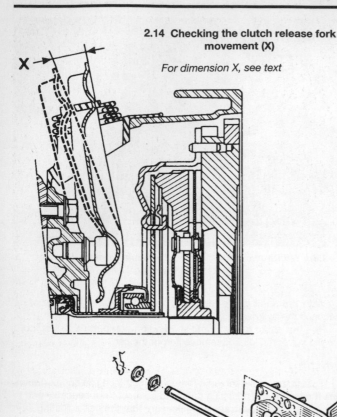

2.14 Checking the clutch release fork movement (X)

For dimension X, see text

14   Depress the clutch pedal fully, and check that the total movement at the top of the release fork is between 17 and 18 mm **(see illustration)**. This movement ensures that the clutch pedal stroke is correct. If not, make sure that the quadrant and support arms are free to turn on their respective pivots, and that the spring has not lost its tension. If necessary, check the free length of the spring against a new one. Also check that the inner cable is not seizing in the outer cable.

15   Finish by refitting the lower facia panel.

3   Clutch pedal - removal and refitting

Removal

1   Disconnect the battery negative terminal.

2   Proceed as described for cable removal in the previous Section, but without actually removing the cable from the bulkhead.

3   Extract the retaining clips from both ends of the clutch/brake

3.3a Pedal components and bracket

Right-hand drive shown

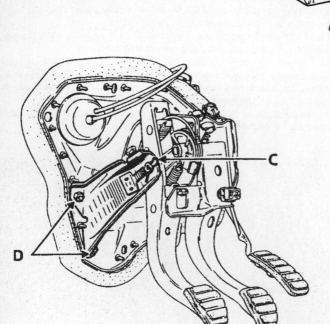

3.3b Support bracket removal

Left-hand drive shown

   D   Mounting nuts   C   Retaining clips

3.3c Remove the pedal cross-shaft retaining clip (arrowed) ...

3.3d . . . and washer

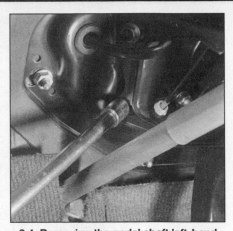

3.4 Removing the pedal shaft left-hand support bracket

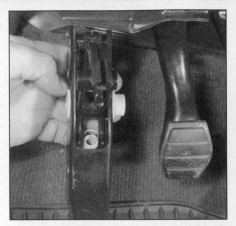

3.5a Removing the clutch pedal

pedal cross-shaft, and recover the washers. Note that the clip ends engage with the pedal bracket **(see illustrations)**.

4   Unscrew the mounting nuts, and remove the pedal shaft left-hand support bracket from the left-hand side of the clutch pedal. Remove the spring washer **(see illustration)**.

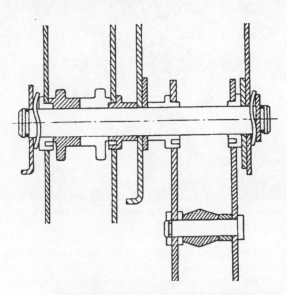

3.5b Cross-section of the pedal bushes

5   Partially withdraw the clutch/brake pedal cross-shaft to the right-hand side, and remove the pedal together with the self-adjusting mechanism and bushes. Note that the thicker bush is on the right-hand side **(see illustrations)**.

6   With the pedal removed, unhook and remove the self-adjusting quadrant return spring. Note the fitted position of the self-adjusting components for correct refitting.

7   Remove the bushes and withdraw the self-adjusting support arms and quadrant **(see illustration)**. Inspect these components and renew them if worn.

Refitting

8   Apply some multi-purpose grease to the bushes, and to the bearing surfaces of the support arms, quadrant and pedal shaft.

9   Locate the plastic bushes in the clutch pedal, making sure that the largest bush is at the brake pedal side, and ensuring that the lugs on the bushes locate in the cut-outs in the pedal **(see illustration)**. Reconnect the self-adjusting quadrant return spring.

10   To facilitate the refitting procedure, and to hold the bushes and support arms together, it is helpful to assemble the pedal on a dummy shaft. If a suitable shaft is not available, the pedal can still be refitted, but it will be necessary to hold the bushes together until the retaining clips are in place.

11   Locate the pedal assembly in the bracket, and push the pedal shaft through from the right-hand side **(see illustration)**. Refit the right-hand retaining spring clip and washer, making sure that the clip engages correctly in the bracket aperture.

12   Fit the spring washer and support bracket on the left-hand end of the shaft. Screw on the bracket mounting nuts hand-tight only at this stage.

6

3.7 Removing the self-adjusting mechanism from the pedal

3.9 Plastic bushes and self-adjusting mechanism located in the pedal

3.11 Locating the pedal assembly in the bracket

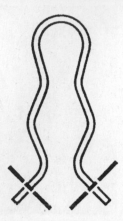

3.13 The ends of the retaining clip may be shortened as shown to make fitting easier

4.2a Unscrewing the clutch cover retaining bolts, showing a screwdriver engaged with the starter ring gear

4.2b Removing the clutch cover retaining bolts. Note that the gearbox has not been removed, just moved to one side

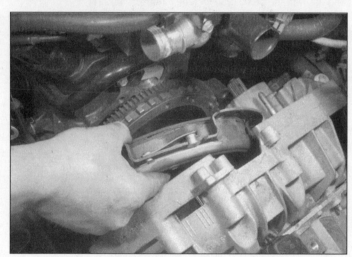

4.3 Removing the clutch cover and disc from the flywheel

13   Using a G-clamp or similar tool, clamp the sides of the bracket together and fit the retaining clip in its groove, also making sure that the ends of the clip engage the aperture in the support bracket. The ends of the clip may be shortened by 2.0 mm if necessary in order to make it easier to fit, but make sure that this has not already been done **(see illustration)**.

14   Remove the G-clamp and fully tighten the support bracket mounting nuts. Note that the support bracket has a locking notch to prevent the shaft from rotating.

15   Reconnect the cable, and check the operation of the self-adjusting mechanism as described in the previous Section.

---

4   Clutch assembly - removal, inspection and refitting

Warning: *Dust created by clutch wear and deposited on the clutch components may contain asbestos which is a health hazard. DO NOT blow it out with compressed air or inhale any of it. DO NOT use petrol or petroleum-based solvents to clean off the dust. Brake system cleaner or methylated spirit should be used to flush the dust into a suitable receptacle. After the clutch components are wiped clean with rags, dispose of the contaminated rags and cleaner in a sealed, marked container.*

Removal

1   Access to the clutch may be gained in one of two ways. Either the gearbox may be removed independently, as described in Chapter 7, or

the engine/gearbox unit may be removed as described in Chapter 2, and the gearbox separated from the engine on the bench. If the gearbox is being removed independently, it need only be moved to one side for access to the clutch.

2   Having separated the gearbox from the engine, unscrew and remove the clutch cover retaining bolts. Work in a diagonal sequence and slacken the bolts only a few turns at a time. Hold the flywheel stationary by positioning a screwdriver over the dowel on the cylinder block and engaging it with the starter ring gear **(see illustrations)**.

3   Ease the clutch cover off its locating dowels. Be prepared to catch the clutch disc, which will drop out as the cover is removed. Note which way round the disc is fitted **(see illustration)**.

Inspection

4   With the clutch assembly removed, clean off all traces of asbestos dust using a dry cloth. This is best done outside or in a well-ventilated area; refer to the warning at the beginning of this Section.

5   Examine the linings of the clutch disc for wear or loose rivets, and the disc rim for distortion, cracks, broken torsion springs and worn splines **(see illustration)**. The surface of the friction linings may be highly glazed, but as long as the friction material pattern can be clearly seen, this is satisfactory. If there is any sign of oil contamination, indicated by shiny black discoloration, the disc must be renewed and the source of the contamination traced and rectified. This will be a leaking crankshaft oil seal, gearbox input shaft oil seal, or both. The

4.5 Inspect the clutch disc linings (A), springs (B) and splines (C)

4.6a Check the machined face of the pressure plate (arrowed) . . .

4.6b . . . and the diaphragm spring, paying particular attention to the tips (arrowed)

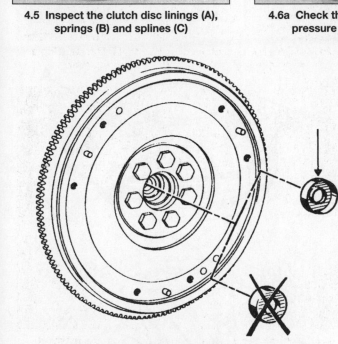

4.9 Fit the dummy bush in the crankshaft bore with the open end facing outwards

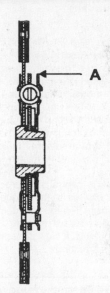

4.12 Clutch disc offset (A) faces away from flywheel

renewal procedure for the former is given in Chapter 2. Renewal of the gearbox input shaft oil seal should be entrusted to a Renault garage, as it involves dismantling the gearbox and the renewal of the clutch release bearing guide tube using a press. The disc must also be renewed if the linings have worn down to, or just above, the level of the rivet heads.

6   Check the machined faces of the flywheel and pressure plate. If either is grooved, or heavily scored, renewal is necessary. The pressure plate must also be renewed if any cracks are apparent, or if the diaphragm spring is damaged or its pressure suspect **(see illustrations)**.

7   Take the opportunity to check the condition of the release bearing, as described in Section 5.

8   It is good practice to renew the clutch disc, pressure plate and release bearing as an assembly. Renewing the disc alone is not always satisfactory. A clutch repair kit can be obtained containing the new components.

9   Renault clutch kits contain a special dummy bush which may be fitted in the crankshaft bore to enable the use of the clutch centring tool also supplied in the kit. To fit this bush, first clean the bore in the end of the crankshaft and apply locking fluid to the outer surface of the bush. Press the bush fully into the crankshaft using a length of tubing of 38 mm outside diameter, making sure that the open end of the bush faces outwards **(see illustration)**.

Refitting

10   Before commencing the refitting procedure, apply a little high-melting-point grease to the splines of the gearbox input shaft. (A sachet of suitable grease may be supplied with the clutch kit.) Distribute the grease by sliding the clutch disc on and off the splines a few times. Remove the disc and wipe away any excess grease.

11   It is important that no oil or grease is allowed to come into contact with the friction material of the clutch disc or the pressure plate and flywheel faces. It is advisable to refit the clutch assembly with clean hands, and to wipe the pressure plate and flywheel faces with a clean dry rag before assembly begins.

12   Begin reassembly by placing the clutch disc against the flywheel, with the side having the larger offset facing away from the flywheel **(see illustration)**.

13   Place the clutch cover over the dowels. Refit the retaining bolts and tighten them finger-tight so that the clutch disc is gripped, but can still be moved.

14   The clutch disc must now be centralised so that, when the engine and gearbox are mated, the splines of the gearbox input shaft will pass through the splines in the centre of the clutch disc hub. If this is not done accurately, it will be impossible to refit the gearbox.

15   Centralisation can be carried out quite easily by inserting a round bar through the hole in the centre of the clutch disc, so that the end of the bar rests in the hole in the end of the crankshaft. Note that a plastic

6

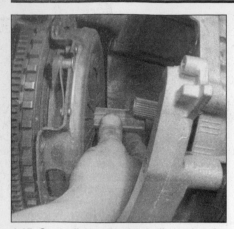

4.15 Centralising the clutch disc using the special tube supplied with Renault clutch kits

4.17 Using a clutch alignment tool to centralise the clutch disc

4.18 Tightening the clutch cover bolts

centralising tube is supplied with Renault clutch kits, making the use of a bar unnecessary **(see illustration)**.

16   If a bar is being used, move it sideways or up and down until the clutch disc is centralised. Centralisation can be judged by removing the bar and viewing the clutch disc hub in relation to the bore in the end of the crankshaft. When the bore appears exactly in the centre of the clutch disc hub, all is correct.

17   If a non-Renault clutch is being fitted, an alternative and more accurate method of centralisation is to use a commercially-available clutch aligning tool obtainable from most accessory shops **(see illustration)**.

18   Once the clutch is centralised, progressively tighten the cover bolts in a diagonal sequence to the torque setting given in the Specifications **(see illustration)**. Remove the centralising device.

19   The gearbox can now be refitted to the engine, referring to the appropriate Chapter of this manual. Check the functioning of the clutch pedal as described in Section 2.

---

5   Clutch release bearing - removal, inspection and refitting

Removal

1   To gain access to the release bearing, it is necessary to separate the engine and gearbox as described at the beginning of the previous Section.

2   With the gearbox removed from the engine, tilt the release fork and slide the bearing assembly off the gearbox input shaft guide tube.

3   To remove the release fork, disengage the rubber cover and then pull the fork off its pivot ball stud. Note the location of the retaining spring beneath the stud.

Inspection

4   Check the bearing for smoothness of operation. Renew it if there is any roughness or harshness as the bearing is spun. It is good practice to renew the bearing as a matter of course during clutch overhaul, regardless of its apparent condition.

Refitting

5   Refitting the release fork and release bearing is the reverse

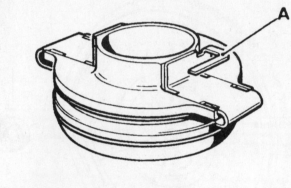

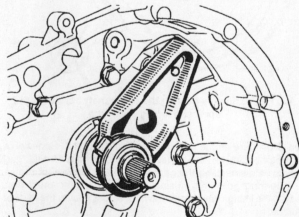

5.5 Clutch release components. Clip (A) on bearing carrier must engage with release fork

sequence to removal, but note the following points **(see illustration)**.

a) *Lubricate the release fork pivot ball stud and the release bearing-to-diaphragm spring contact areas sparingly with molybdenum disulphide grease.*

b) *Ensure that the clip on the bearing carrier engages with the release fork.*

Chapter 7 Manual gearbox

Contents

Specifications

7

General

Type	Five forward speeds (all synchromesh) and reverse. Final drive differential integral with main gearbox
Designation	JB3

Gear ratios (typical):

1st	3.7 : 1
2nd	2.1 : 1
3rd	1.3 : 1
4th	0.97 : 1
5th	0.79:1
Reverse	3.6 : 1
Final drive	3.3 : 1

Torque wrench settings

	Nm	lbf ft
Gearbox mounting nuts/bolts	40 to 50	30 to 37
Clutch bellhousing to engine	50	37
Gearchange casing nuts	15	11
Gearchange link rod clamp nuts and bolts	30	22

1   General information

The manual gearbox is of five-speed (JB3) type, with one reverse gear. Baulk ring synchromesh gear engagement is used on all the forward gears. The final drive (differential) unit is integral with the main gearbox, and is located between the mechanism casing and the clutch and differential housing. The gearbox and differential both share the same lubricating oil **(see illustrations)**.

Gearshift is by means of a floor-mounted lever, connected by a remote control housing and gearchange rod to the gearbox fork contact shaft **(see illustrations)**.

2   Gearchange linkage/mechanism - adjustment

1   Apply the handbrake, then jack up the front of the car and support it on axle stands.

2   Unbolt and remove the splash guard from under the gearbox.

3   Select 1st gear on the gearbox by moving the lever to the correct position **(see illustration 1.2b)**. Renault technicians use a special tool to hold the lever in position and take up any free play **(see illustration)**; a suitable alternative tool can be made from flat metal bar or wood.

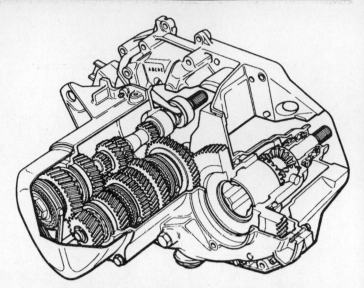

1.1a Cutaway view of the JB3 five-speed gearbox

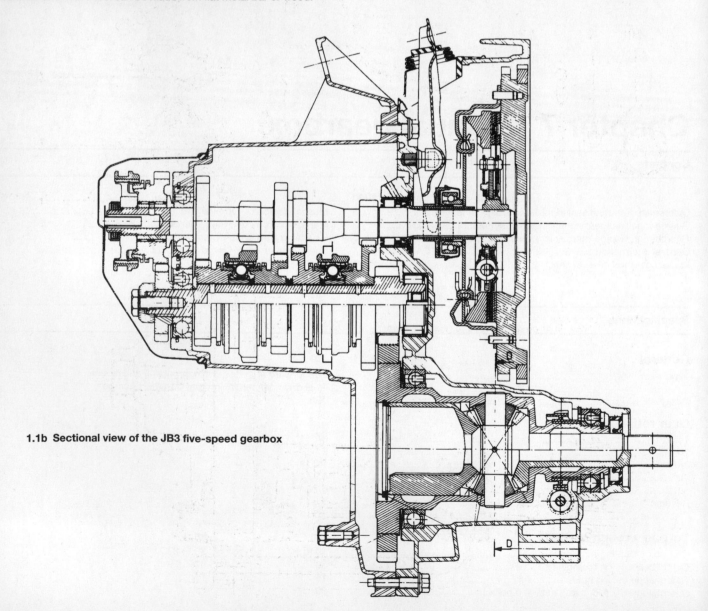

1.1b Sectional view of the JB3 five-speed gearbox

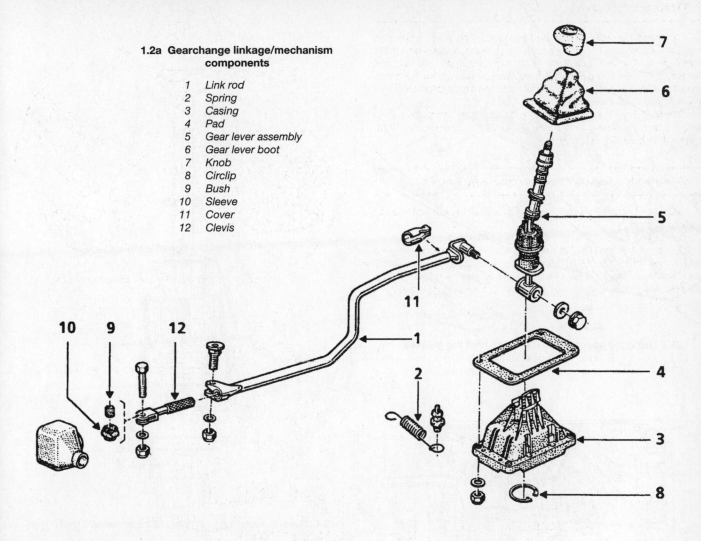

1.2a Gearchange linkage/mechanism
        components

1   Link rod
2   Spring
3   Casing
4   Pad
5   Gear lever assembly
6   Gear lever boot
7   Knob
8   Circlip
9   Bush
10 Sleeve
11 Cover
12 Clevis

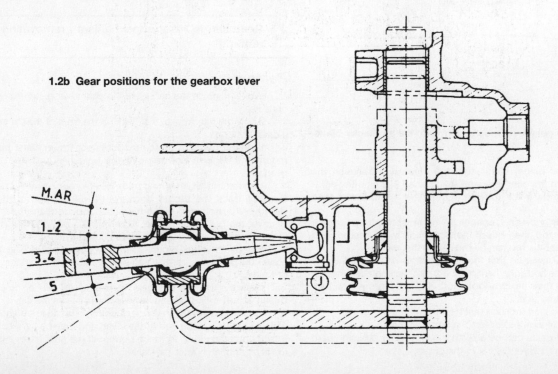

1.2b Gear positions for the gearbox lever

7

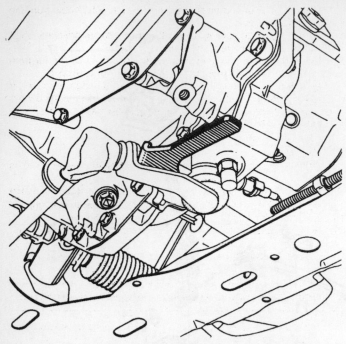

2.3 Using the special Renault tool to hold the gearbox lever in 1st gear position

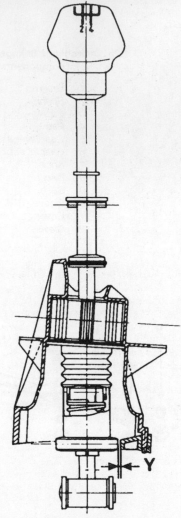

2.4 The adjustment gap (Y) should be between 2 and 5 mm

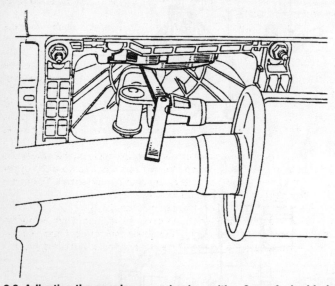

2.6 Adjusting the gear lever mechanism with a 2 mm feeler blade

4   Using a feeler blade, check that the clearance between the reverse stop-ring on the gear lever and the inclined plane on the right-hand side of the gear lever housing is between 2 and 5 mm **(see illustration)**.

5   If adjustment is necessary, unhook the return spring from the gear lever end of the link rod, then loosen the clamp bolt at the gearbox end of the link rod so that the rod can be moved on the clevis.

6   Move the gear lever so that the reverse stop-ring is against the inclined plane on the housing, then insert a 2 mm feeler blade between the ring and plane **(see illustration)**. Hold the lever in this position, then tighten the clamp bolt.

7   Remove the holding tool and refit the return spring.

8   Recheck the clearance described in paragraph 4.

9   Check that all gears can be selected, then refit the splash guard and tighten the bolts. Lower the car to the ground.

3   Gearchange linkage/mechanism - removal and refitting

Removal

1   Working inside the car, prise the gear lever gaiter from the centre console.

2   Apply the handbrake, then jack up the front of the car and support it on axle stands.

3   Working beneath the car, disconnect the exhaust pipe flexible mountings. Unbolt and remove the splash guard from under the gearbox.

4   Unhook the return spring from the link rod.

5   Pull back the rubber boot from the front end of the link rod. Remove the bolt and disconnect the rod from the gearbox lever. Recover the bush and sleeve. Note that the clevis at the front end of the rod is offset, and must be refitted correctly.

6   Remove the nuts securing the casing assembly to the underbody. Lower the assembly, at the same time pulling the exhaust system to one side.

7   Mark the link rod and gear lever clevis in relation to each other. Unscrew the pinch-bolt and remove the rod from the clevis.

8   Grip the gear lever in a vice, then remove the knob and gear lever gaiter. The knob is bonded to the lever, and may be hard to remove.

9   Extract the circlip from the bottom of the gear lever, and withdraw the lever and latch from the casing.

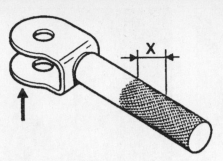

3.12 Area of the clevis to be showing when reconnecting the link rod

X = 10 to 12 mm

Refitting

10 Refitting is a reversal of removal, noting the points in the following paragraphs.
11 Lubricate the pivot points with grease, and use a suitable adhesive to bond the knob to the lever.
12 Make sure that the clevis on the front end of the link rod is fitted with the offset towards the gearbox **(see illustration)**. If the clevis has been removed or if a new clevis is being fitted, connect the link rod to the clevis leaving 10 to 12 mm of the knurled area showing. This will locate the gear lever in its correct longitudinal position.
13 Adjust the gearchange mechanism as described in Section 2.

4 Speedometer drive - removal and refitting

Note: *On some later models, the speedometer drive is taken from the right-hand side of the gearbox, just above the driveshaft. It is not possible to remove the drive on this type. The later type can be identified by the plastic cable connection to the gearbox instead of the clip type connection on earlier models* **(see illustration)**.

Removal

1 Disconnect the left-hand driveshaft at the gearbox end - refer to Chapter 8. There is no need to disturb the hub end of the driveshaft; the driveshaft/swivel hub assembly can be removed together, as described for engine removal (Chapter 2, Part B).
2 Extract the circlip and thrustwasher, then withdraw the left-hand sun wheel from the differential. The sun wheel also acts as the driveshaft spider housing.
3 Turn the differential until the planet wheels are in a vertical plane so that the speedometer drivegear is visible **(see illustration)**.

4 Pull out the clip and disconnect the speedometer cable from the outside of the gearbox.
5 Using long-nosed pliers, extract the speedometer drivegear shaft vertically from the outside of the gearbox.
6 Using the same pliers, extract the speedometer drivegear from inside the differential housing, being very careful not to drop it.
7 Examine the drivegear teeth for wear and damage. Renew it if necessary. Note that if the drivegear teeth on the differential are worn or damaged, it will be necessary to dismantle the gearbox - this work should be entrusted to a Renault dealer.

Refitting

8 Using long-nosed pliers, insert the speedometer drivegear into its location.
9 From outside the gearbox, refit the drivegear shaft. Make sure that it engages with the gear location notches correctly **(see illustration)**.
10 Refit the speedometer cable, and secure with the clip.
11 Insert the differential sun wheel, then refit the thrustwasher and circlip.
12 Reconnect the left-hand driveshaft with reference to Chapter 8.

5 Differential output oil seal (right-hand side) - renewal

1 Apply the handbrake, then jack up the front of the car and support it on axle stands. Remove the right-hand wheel.
2 Position a suitable container beneath the gearbox, then unscrew the drain plug and allow the oil to drain. (On some models, it may be necessary to remove a splash guard from the bottom of the gearbox first.) When most of the oil has drained, clean and refit the drain plug, tightening it securely.
3 Using a pin punch (5 mm diameter), drive out the double roll pins securing the inner end of the right-hand driveshaft to the differential side gear. New pins will be required when reassembling.
4 Unscrew the nut securing the steering track rod end to the steering arm. Use a balljoint removal tool to separate the balljoint taper.
5 Refer to Chapter 9 and unbolt the brake caliper from the swivel hub. Do not disconnect the hydraulic hose from the caliper. Tie the caliper to the suspension coil spring without straining the hydraulic hose.
6 Loosen (but do not remove) the lower bolt securing the swivel hub to the bottom of the suspension strut. Unscrew and remove the upper bolt, then tilt the swivel hub and disconnect the driveshaft. Take care not to damage the driveshaft rubber bellows.
7 Recover the O-ring from the side gear shaft.
8 Wipe clean the old oil seal, and measure its fitted depth below the casing edge. This is necessary to determine the correct fitted position of the new oil seal if the special Renault fitting tool is not being used.

7

4.0 Speedometer drive plastic connection (arrowed) on later models

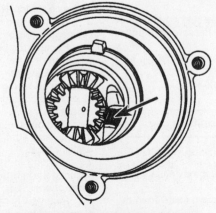

4.3 View of the speedometer drivegear (arrowed) with the differential sun wheel removed

4.9 Notches in the speedometer drivegear engage with the shaft

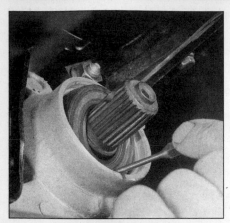

5.9 Tap the old differential output oil seal with a small drift to remove it

5.13a Position the new differential output oil seal on the gearbox . . .

5.13b . . . and drive it in with a socket or metal tube

9   Free the old oil seal, using a small drift to tap the outer edge of the seal inwards so that the opposite edge of the seal tilts out of the casing **(see illustration)**. A pair of pliers or grips can then be used to pull out the oil seal. Take care not to damage the splines of the differential side gear.

10   Wipe clean the oil seal seating in the casing.

11   Before fitting the new oil seal, it is necessary to cover the splines on the side gear to prevent damage to the oil seal lips. Ideally, a close-fitting plastic cap should be located on the splines. If this is not available, wrap some adhesive tape over the splines.

12   Smear a little grease on the lips of the new oil seal and on the protective cap or tape.

13   Carefully locate the new oil seal over the side gear, and enter it squarely into the casing. Using a piece of metal tube or a socket, tap the oil seal into position to its correct depth, as noted previously **(see illustrations)**. Renault use a special tool to ensure that the oil seal is fitted to the correct depth; it may be possible to hire this tool from a Renault garage or tool hire shop.

14   Remove the plastic cap or adhesive tape, and apply a little grease to the splines of the side gear. Fit a new O-ring to the side gear shaft.

15   Engage the driveshaft with the splines on the side gear so that the roll pin holes are correctly aligned. Tilt the swivel hub and slide the driveshaft onto the side gear, making sure that it enters the oil seal centrally.

16   With the holes aligned, tap the new roll pins into position. Seal the ends of the roll pins with a suitable sealant.

17   Refit the upper bolt securing the swivel hub to the bottom of the suspension strut, then tighten both upper and lower bolts to the specified torque (see Chapter 10).

18   Refit the brake caliper to the swivel hub, and tighten the bolts to the specified torque with reference to Chapter 9.

19   Clean the track rod end balljoint taper and the steering arm, then refit the balljoint to the arm and tighten the nut to the specified torque (see Chapter 10).

20   Refill the gearbox with the correct quantity and grade of oil, with reference to Chapter 1. Refit the splash guard where necessary.

21   Refit the roadwheel and lower the car to the ground.

6   Reversing light switch - removal and refitting

Removal

1   Apply the handbrake, then jack up the front of the car and support it on axle stands.

2   Where applicable, unbolt and remove the splash guard from the bottom of the gearbox.

3   Position a suitable container beneath the gearbox, then unscrew the drain plug and allow the oil to drain. When all of the oil has drained,

clean and refit the drain plug, tightening it securely.

4   The switch is located on the left-hand side of the gearbox, next to the driveshaft. Disconnect the wiring from the switch.

5   Unscrew the switch from the gearbox, and remove the washer.

Refitting

6   Clean the location in the gearbox and the threads of the switch.

7   Insert the switch together with a new washer, and tighten it securely.

8   Reconnect the wiring.

9   Refill the gearbox with the correct quantity and grade of oil, with reference to Chapter 1.

10   Refit the gearbox splash guard, where applicable.

11   Lower the car to the ground.

7   Manual gearbox - removal and refitting

Note: *This Section describes the removal of the gearbox, leaving the engine in the car. If adequate lifting gear is available, it may be easier to remove the engine and gearbox together, as described in Chapter 2, and to separate them on the bench.*

Removal

1   The gearbox is removed upwards from the engine compartment, after disconnecting it from the engine. Due to the weight of the unit, it will be necessary to have suitable lifting equipment available, such as an engine crane or hoist, to enable the unit to be removed in this way.

2   Apply the handbrake, then jack up the front of the car and support it on axle stands. Remove both the front roadwheels.

3   Remove the battery with reference to Chapter 5, and the air cleaner housing assembly with reference to Chapter 4.

4   Remove the bonnet with reference to Chapter 11.

5   Remove the plastic cover from the bottom of the gearbox. Position a suitable container beneath the gearbox, then unscrew the drain and filler plugs and allow the oil to drain **(see illustrations)**. When all of the oil has drained, clean and refit the drain plug, tightening it securely.

6   Unscrew the nut securing the left-hand steering track-rod end to the steering arm, then use a balljoint removal tool to separate the balljoint taper.

7   Working in the engine compartment, unscrew the three bolts securing the left-hand driveshaft inner rubber boot to the gearbox **(see illustration)**.

8   Refer to Chapter 9 and unbolt the left-hand brake caliper from the swivel hub **(see illustration)**. Do not disconnect the hydraulic hose from the caliper. Tie the caliper to the suspension coil spring without straining the hose.

7.5a Removing the plastic cover from the bottom of the gearbox

7.5b Unscrew the drain plug . . .

7.5c . . . and drain the oil

7.5d Oil filler plug (arrowed) on the front of the gearbox

7.7 Bolts securing the left-hand driveshaft inner rubber boot to the gearbox

7.8 Left-hand brake caliper retaining bolts (arrowed)

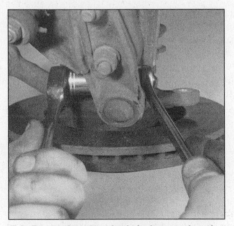

7.9 Removing the pinch-bolt securing the lower balljoint to the swivel hub

7.10a Unscrewing the bolts securing the swivel hub to the bottom of the suspension strut

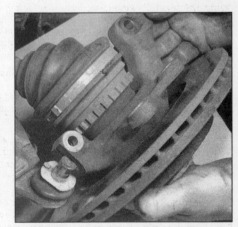

7.10b Disconnecting the swivel hub from the lower balljoint

7   7

9   Unscrew and remove the pinch-bolt securing the front left lower balljoint to the bottom of the swivel hub **(see illustration)**.
10   Support the weight of the swivel hub and driveshaft on a trolley jack. Unscrew the two bolts, and separate the swivel hub from the bottom of the suspension strut and from the lower balljoint **(see illustrations)**.
11   Withdraw the left-hand driveshaft and swivel hub from the gearbox. Make sure that the tripod components remain in position on the inner end of the driveshaft, otherwise they may fall into the gearbox.
12   Working on the right-hand side driveshaft, use a 5 mm diameter pin punch to drive out the roll pins.
13   Loosen (but do not remove) the lower bolt securing the right-hand swivel hub to the bottom of the suspension strut. Unscrew and remove the upper bolt, then tilt the swivel hub and disconnect the driveshaft from the gearbox.

7.14a Pull back the rubber boot on the gearchange rod . . .

7.14b . . . unscrew and remove the bolt . . .

7.14c . . . and recover the bush from inside the lever

7.15a Rivets (arrowed) holding the inner wing protective cover

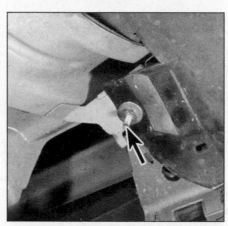

7.15b Inner wing protective cover bottom bolt (arrowed)

7.16 Engine-to-gearbox tie-rod bracket (arrowed)

14 Cut the plastic tie and pull back the rubber boot, then disconnect the gearchange rod from the lever on the gearbox by unscrewing the nut and removing the bolt. Recover the bush from inside the lever **(see illustrations)**. Do not separate the gearchange rod at the clamp, otherwise it will be necessary to adjust the gear lever position on refitting.

15 Unbolt the front left-hand inner wing protective cover (where necessary, drill out the retaining rivets) **(see illustrations)**.

16 Unscrew the engine-to-gearbox tie-rod bracket mounting bolts,

and remove the bracket **(see illustration)**.

17 Unscrew the engine-to-gearbox mounting nut located near the right-hand gearbox output shaft **(see illustration)**.

18 Squeeze together the plastic clip, and disconnect the speedometer cable from the rear of the gearbox, near the rear mounting **(see illustration)**.

19 Refer to Chapter 6, Section 2 and disconnect the clutch cable from the gearbox.

20 Unbolt the earth cable from the gearbox casing and from the

7.17 Engine-to-gearbox mounting nut (arrowed) located on the rear of the engine

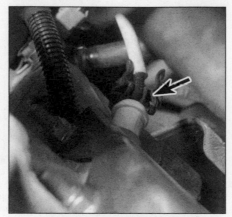

7.18 Speedometer cable connection (arrowed) at the rear of the gearbox

7.20a Wiring harness support on the gearbox

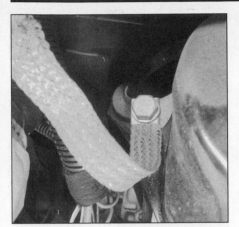
7.20b Earth strap attachment to the gearbox casing

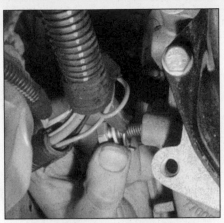
7.20c Wiring harness earth wire attachment to the gearbox casing

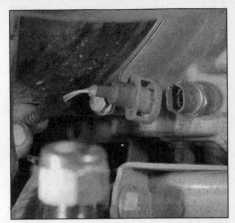
7.21 Disconnecting the wiring from the reversing light switch

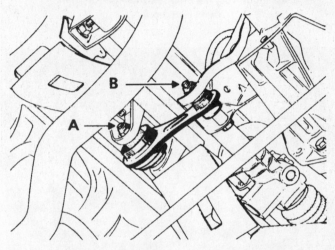
7.22 Engine/gearbox rear mounting link

A Rear mounting bolt
B Front mounting bolt

cylinder block. Also unbolt the wiring harness supports and the earth strap from the gearbox and gearbox mountings, as applicable **(see illustrations)**.

21   Pull the wiring connector from the reversing light switch on the gearbox casing **(see illustration)**.

22   Loosen (but do not remove) bolt (A), then unscrew and remove bolt (B) from the rear mounting link **(see illustration)**. Swivel the link down.

23   To prevent damage to the radiator, drain the cooling system and remove the radiator, referring to Chapters 1 and 3.

24   Disconnect the radiator top hose from the engine.

25   Where applicable, unclip the wiring harness from the gearbox mounting.

26   Disconnect the wiring for the engine from inside the plastic box on the left-hand side of the engine compartment.

27   Disconnect the wiring from the starter motor. Detach the wiring bracket from the rear of the cylinder block, and feed it through the starter cover. Remove the starter motor (see Chapter 5), and pull the engine wiring loom through the hole in the bellhousing **(see illustration)**.

28   Connect a suitable hoist to the engine, and lift it slightly. Alternatively, the engine may be supported on a trolley jack so that the hoist can be used to remove the gearbox.

29   Support the weight of the gearbox.

30   Remove the remaining nuts and bolts which secure the gearbox mounting/battery tray to the bodywork. Remove the bolts which secure the mounting bracket to the gearbox, and lift out the mounting assembly **(see illustration)**.

31   Unbolt the short brace from the left-hand side of the engine subframe **(see illustration)**.

32   Remove the air inlet duct from the left-hand front corner of the engine compartment.

33   Loosen (but do not remove) the front bumper lower mounting bolt on the left-hand side.

7

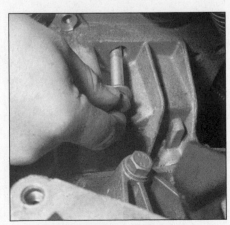
7.27 Removing a starter motor mounting bolt

7.30 Removing the gearbox mounting assembly

7.31 Short brace on the left-hand side of the subframe

**7.34 Subframe lowered to the extent of the mounting bolts
(exposed thread arrowed)**

**7.35a Removing the gearbox-to-engine mounting
bolts (arrowed) . . .**

7.35b . . . and nuts

7.38 Lifting the gearbox out of the engine compartment

34   Loosen (but do not remove) the two left-hand subframe nuts, and lower the subframe to the extent permitted by the length of the bolts **(see illustration)**. This will give the extra room necessary to manoeuvre the gearbox.

35   Unscrew and remove all of the gearbox-to-engine bolts and nuts, noting the location of the washers **(see illustrations)**.

36   Disconnect the gearbox from the engine, sliding the gearbox end housing between the engine subframe and the front wing side panel. Careful use of a wide-bladed screwdriver may be necessary to free the bellhousing from the location dowels. Do not allow the weight of the gearbox to hang on the input shaft.

37   With the gearbox moved as far to the left-hand side of the engine compartment as possible, refer to Chapter 6 and remove the clutch. This is necessary in order to give additional room to manoeuvre the gearbox from the engine compartment.

38   Pivot the gearbox forwards to release the final drive section. Lift the gearbox upwards from the engine compartment, bellhousing end first. If the hoist is being used, attach it to the bellhousing mounting bolt holes **(see illustration)**.

Refitting

39   Refitting is a reversal of removal, noting the following additional points.

a) Before assembling the gearbox to the engine, position a length of wood or similar distance piece between the end of the clutch release fork and the outer cable bracket on the gearbox casing, in order to hold the fork in its released position. This will prevent the release bearing from becoming detached from the end of the release fork during the refitting procedure.

b) Make sure that the location dowels are correctly positioned in the gearbox.

c) Apply a little high-melting-point grease to the splines of the gearbox input shaft. Do not apply too much, otherwise there is the possibility of the grease contaminating the clutch friction disc.

d) Make sure that the centring bush for the starter motor is correctly fitted. Refer to Chapter 5 if necessary.

e) Use new roll pins when reconnecting the right-hand driveshaft, and seal the ends using a suitable sealant.

f) Refit and tighten the brake caliper mounting bolts with reference to Chapter 9.

g) Check the engine mounting adjustment dimensions, as given in Chapter 2.

h) Refill the gearbox with oil, and check the level with reference to Chapter 1.

i) Tighten all nuts and bolts to the specified torque.

j) Refill the cooling system with reference to Chapter 1.

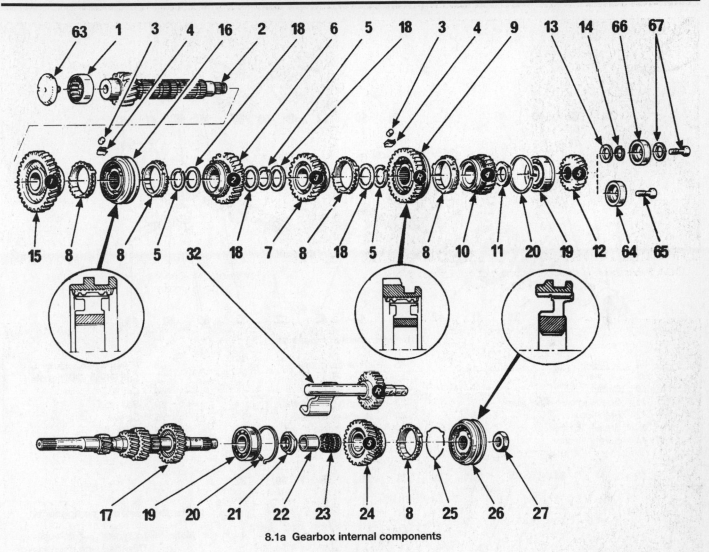

8.1a Gearbox internal components

1	Roller race	13	Washer	24	5th speed gear (primary)
2	Output shaft	14	5th speed circlip	25	5th speed spring
3	Roller	15	1st speed gear	26	5th speed gear hub
4	Spring	16	1st/2nd gear hub	27	5th speed nut
5	Circlip	17	Input shaft	32	Reverse shaft and gear
6	2nd speed gear	18	Splined ring	63	Oil baffle
7	3rd speed gear	19	Ball race	64	Thrustwasher
8	Synchro-ring	20	Circlip	65	5th speed end bolt on
9	3rd/4th gear hub	21	Washer		output shaft
10	4th speed gear	22	5th speed ring	66	Shouldered washer
11	Washer	23	Needle race	67	Retaining bolt and washer
12	5th speed gear				

8 Manual gearbox overhaul - general information

Overhauling a manual gearbox is a difficult and involved job for the DIY home mechanic. In addition to dismantling and reassembling many small parts, clearances must be precisely measured and, if necessary, changed by selecting shims and spacers **(see illustrations)**. Gearbox internal components are also often difficult to obtain, and in many instances, extremely expensive. Because of this, if the gearbox develops a fault or becomes noisy, the best course of action is to have the unit overhauled by a specialist repairer, or to obtain an exchange reconditioned unit.

Nevertheless, it is not impossible for the more experienced mechanic to overhaul a gearbox, provided the special tools are available and the job is done in a deliberate step-by-step manner so that nothing is overlooked.

The tools necessary for an overhaul include internal and external circlip pliers, bearing pullers, a slide-hammer, a set of pin punches, a dial test indicator, and possibly a hydraulic press. In addition, a large, sturdy workbench and a vice will be required.

During dismantling of the gearbox, make careful notes of how each component is fitted, to make reassembly easier and more accurate.

Before dismantling the gearbox, it will help if you have some idea what area is malfunctioning. Certain problems can be closely related to specific areas in the gearbox, which can make component examination and replacement easier. Refer to the *Fault diagnosis* Section at the beginning of this manual for more information.

7

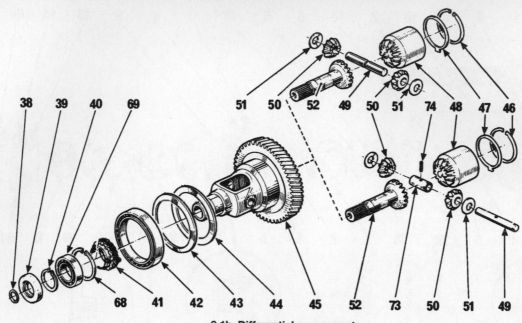

8.1b Differential components

38	O-ring	45	Differential housing	51	Planet wheel washer
39	Oil seal	46	Circlip	52	Sun wheel with tail shaft
40	Circlip	47	Shim	68	Circlip
41	Speedometer drivegear	48	Spider-type sun wheel	69	Ball race
42	Ball race	49	Planet wheel shaft	73	Sleeve
43	Spacer washer	50	Planet wheels	74	Pin
44	Spring washer				

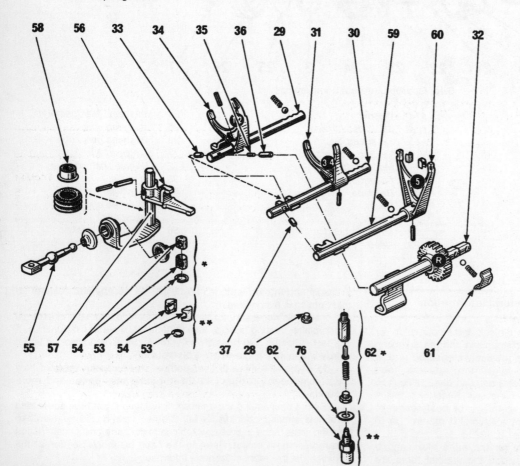

8.1c Gear selector components

Note: * = 1st type, ** = 2nd type

28	Threaded stop (four-speed)
29	1st/2nd shift rod
30	3rd/4th shift rod
31	3rd/4th gear fork
32	Reverse shaft
33	Plunger between 1st/2nd and 3rd/4th
34	1st/2nd shift fork
35	1st/2nd plunger
36	Plunger between 1st/2nd and reverse
37	5th speed plunger (five-speed)
53	Circlip
54	Link support
55	Link
56	Selector finger
57	Input shaft
58	Bush
59	5th speed rod (five-speed)
60	5th speed shift fork (five-speed)
61	Reverse stirrup
62	5th speed detent assembly (five-speed)
76	5th speed detent shim washer

Chapter 8 Driveshafts

Contents

8

Specifications

General

Driveshaft type .... Equal-length solid steel shafts, splined to inner and outer constant velocity joints, vibration damper fitted on some shafts

Lubricant type/specification .... Special grease supplied in sachets with gaiter kits - joints are otherwise pre-packed with grease and sealed

Torque wrench settings

	Nm	lbf ft
Driveshaft retaining nut (renew every time)	250	185
Left-hand driveshaft gaiter retaining plate bolts	25	18
Roadwheel bolts	90	66

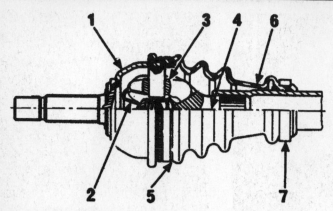

1.1a Sectional view of the spider-and-yoke type outer constant velocity joint

1	Outer member	5	Outer retaining clip
2	Thrust plunger	6	Gaiter
3	Driveshaft spider	7	Inner retaining clip
4	Driveshaft		

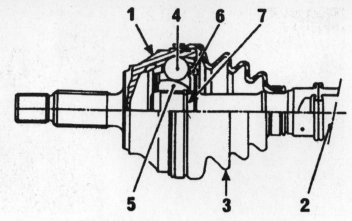

1.1b Sectional view of the ball-and-cage type outer constant velocity joint

1	Outer member	5	Inner member
2	Driveshaft	6	Ball cage
3	Gaiter	7	Circlip
4	Ball		

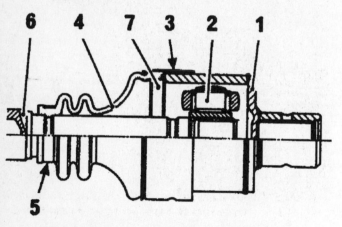

1.2 Sectional view of a right-hand inner constant velocity joint - RC490 type

1	Outer member	5	Inner retaining clip
2	Tripod joint	6	Driveshaft
3	Metal cover	7	Metal insert
4	Gaiter		

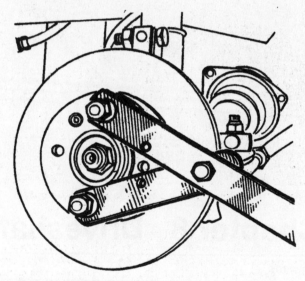

2.2a Using a fabricated tool to hold the front hub stationary whilst the driveshaft retaining nut is slackened

1 General information

Drive is transmitted from the differential to the front wheels by means of two, equal-length, open driveshafts. Both driveshafts are fitted with a constant velocity (CV) joint at their outer ends, which may be of the spider-and-yoke type or of the ball-and-cage type. Each joint has an outer member, which is splined at its outer end to accept the wheel hub and is threaded so that it can be fastened to the hub by a large nut. The joint contains either a spring-loaded plunger or six balls within a cage, which engage with the inner member. The complete assembly is protected by a flexible gaiter secured to the driveshaft and joint outer member (see illustrations).

A different inner constant velocity joint arrangement is fitted to each driveshaft. On the right-hand side, the driveshaft is splined to engage with a tripod joint, containing needle roller bearings and cups. The tripod joint is free to slide within the yoke of the joint outer member, which is splined and retained by a roll pin to the differential sun wheel stub shaft. As on the outer joints, a flexible gaiter secured to the driveshaft and outer member protects the complete assembly (see illustration). On the left-hand side, the driveshaft also engages with a tripod joint, but the yoke in which the tripod joint is free to slide is an

integral part of the differential sun wheel. On this side, the gaiter is secured to the gearbox casing with a retaining plate, and to a ball-bearing on the driveshaft with a retaining clip. The bearing allows the driveshaft to turn within the gaiter, which does not revolve.

2 Driveshaft - removal and refitting

Removal

1   Apply the handbrake, then jack up the front of the vehicle and support it on axle stands. Remove the appropriate front roadwheel.
2   Refit at least two roadwheel bolts to the front hub, and tighten them securely. Have an assistant firmly depress the brake pedal to prevent the front hub from rotating. Using a socket and a long extension bar, slacken and remove the driveshaft retaining nut and washer. This nut is extremely tight. Alternatively, a tool can be fabricated from two lengths of steel strip (one long, one short) and a nut and bolt; the nut and bolt form the pivot of a forked tool (see illustrations). Bolt the tool to the hub using two wheel bolts, and hold the tool to prevent the hub from rotating as the driveshaft retaining nut is undone. Discard the driveshaft nut; a

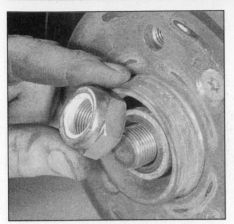

2.2b Removing the driveshaft retaining nut and washer

2.4 Using a balljoint separator to release the track rod end balljoint from the swivel hub

2.5 Withdraw the upper bolt, noting which way around it is fitted

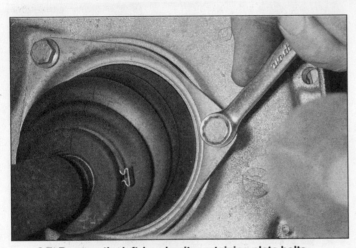

2.7 Remove the left-hand gaiter retaining plate bolts . . .

2.8 . . . and release the tripod joint from the gearbox

new one should be used on refitting.

3   Unscrew the two bolts securing the brake caliper assembly to the swivel hub, and slide the caliper assembly off the disc. Using a piece of wire or string, tie the caliper to the front suspension coil spring, to avoid placing any strain on the hydraulic brake hose.

4   Slacken and remove the nut securing the steering gear track rod end balljoint to the swivel hub. Release the balljoint tapered shank using a universal balljoint separator **(see illustration)**.

5   Slacken and remove the two nuts and washers from the bolts securing the swivel hub to the suspension strut, noting that the nuts are positioned on the rear side of the strut. Withdraw the upper bolt, but leave the lower bolt in position at this stage **(see illustration)**. Now proceed as described under the relevant sub-heading.

Left-hand driveshaft

6   Position a suitable container beneath the drain plug, then remove the drain plug and allow the oil to drain from the gearbox. Once the oil has drained, wipe the threads of the drain plug clean, refit it to the gearbox and tighten it securely.

7   Slacken and remove the three bolts securing the flexible gaiter retaining plate to the side of the gearbox **(see illustration)**.

8   Pull the top of the swivel hub outwards until the driveshaft tripod joint is released from its yoke; be prepared for some oil spillage as the joint is withdrawn **(see illustration)**. Be careful that the rollers on the end of the tripod do not fall off.

9   Remove the lower bolt securing the swivel hub to the suspension strut.

10   Taking care not to damage the driveshaft gaiters, release the outer constant velocity joint from the hub and remove the driveshaft.

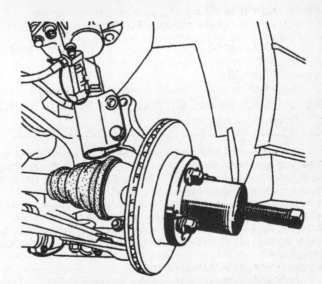

2.10 Using an extractor to press the driveshaft out of the front hub

Note that locking fluid is applied to the outer constant velocity joint splines during assembly, so it is likely that they will be a tight fit in the hub splines. Use a hammer and a soft metal drift to tap the joint out of the hub, or use an extractor to push the driveshaft out of the hub **(see illustration)**.

8

2.11 Drive out the roll pins with a suitable pin punch

2.23 Tighten the driveshaft retaining nut to the specified torque

2.26 Fit the new O-ring onto the sun wheel shaft . . .

Right-hand driveshaft

11   Rotate the driveshaft until the double roll pin, securing the inner constant velocity joint to the sun wheel shaft, is visible. Using a hammer and a 5 mm diameter pin punch, drive out the double roll pin **(see illustration)**. New roll pins must be used on refitting.

12   Pull the top of the swivel hub outwards until the inner constant velocity joint splines are released from the sun wheel shaft. Remove the O-ring from the sun wheel shaft splines.

13   Remove the driveshaft as described in paragraph 10.

Refitting

14   All new driveshafts supplied by Renault are equipped with cardboard or plastic protectors to prevent damage to the gaiters. Even the slightest knock to the gaiter can puncture it, allowing the entry of water or dirt at a later date, which may lead to the premature failure of the joint. If the original driveshaft is being refitted, it is worthwhile making up some cardboard protectors as a precaution. They can be held in position with elastic bands. The protectors should be left on the driveshafts until the end of the refitting procedure.

Left-hand driveshaft

15   Wipe clean the side of the gearbox. Insert the tripod joint into the sun wheel yoke, keeping the driveshaft horizontal as far as possible.

16   Align the gaiter retaining plate with its bolt holes. Refit the retaining bolts, and tighten them to the specified torque. Ensure that the gaiter is not twisted.

17   Check that the splines on the driveshaft outer constant velocity joint and hub are clean and dry. Apply a coat of locking fluid to the splines.

18   Move the top of the swivel hub inwards, at the same time engaging the driveshaft with the hub.

19   Slide the hub fully onto the driveshaft splines, then insert the two suspension strut mounting bolts from the front side of the strut. Refit the washers and nuts to the rear of the bolts, and tighten them to the specified torque (Chapter 10 Specifications).

20   Slide on the washer, then fit the new driveshaft retaining nut, tightening it by hand only at this stage.

21   Reconnect the steering track rod balljoint to the swivel hub, and tighten its retaining nut to the specified torque (Chapter 10 Specifications).

22   Slide the brake caliper assembly into position over the brake disc. Refit the caliper mounting bolts, having first applied a few drops of locking fluid to their threads, and tighten them to the specified torque (Chapter 9 Specifications).

23   Using the method employed during removal to prevent the hub from rotating, tighten a new driveshaft retaining nut to the specified torque **(see illustration)**. Check that the hub rotates freely, then remove the protectors from the driveshaft, taking great care not to damage the flexible gaiters.

24   Refit the roadwheel. Lower the car to the ground and tighten the

2.27 . . . and engage the driveshaft, ensuring that the roll pin holes (arrowed) are correctly aligned

roadwheel bolts to the specified torque.

25   Refill the gearbox with oil; refer to Chapter 1 for details.

Right-hand driveshaft

26   Ensure that the inner constant velocity joint and sun wheel shaft splines are clean and dry. Apply a smear of molybdenum disulphide grease to the splines. Fit a new O-ring over the end of the sun wheel shaft, and slide the O-ring along the shaft until it abuts the transmission oil seal **(see illustration)**.

27   Engage the driveshaft splines with those of the sun wheel shaft, making sure that the roll pin holes are in alignment **(see illustration)**. Slide the driveshaft onto the sun wheel shaft until the roll pin holes are aligned.

28   Drive in new roll pins with their slots 90° apart, then seal the ends of the pins with sealing compound (Renault CAF 4/60 THIXO paste or equivalent) **(see illustrations)**.

29   Carry out the procedures described in paragraphs 17 to 24.

3   Outer constant velocity joint gaiter - renewal

1   Remove the driveshaft as described in Section 2.

2   Cut through the gaiter retaining clip(s) or release the retaining spring and inner collar (as applicable), then slide the gaiter down the shaft to expose the outer constant velocity joint.

3   Scoop out as much grease as possible from the joint, and determine which type of constant velocity joint is fitted. Proceed as described under the relevant sub-heading.

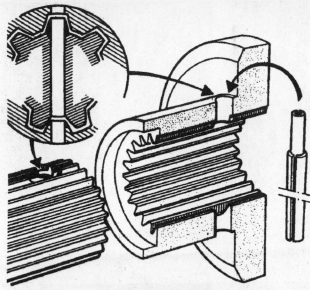

2.28a Right-hand driveshaft inner constant velocity joint roll pin arrangement

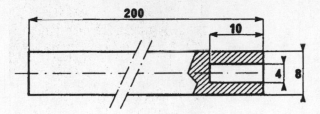

3.12 Using two lengths of hollow metal tubing to install the gaiter retaining spring. Tube dimensions in mm

2.28b Seal the ends of the roll pins with a sealing compound

3.15 Removing the vibration damper from the driveshaft

Ball-and-cage type joint

4   Using circlip pliers, expand the joint internal circlip. At the same time, tap the exposed face of the ball hub with a mallet to separate the joint from the driveshaft. Slide off the gaiter and rubber collar.

5   With the constant velocity joint removed from the driveshaft, clean the joint using paraffin, or solvent, and dry it thoroughly. Carry out a visual inspection of the joint.

6   Move the inner splined driving member from side to side, to expose each ball in turn at the top of its track. Examine the balls for cracks, flat spots or signs of surface pitting.

7   Inspect the ball tracks on the inner and outer members. If the tracks have widened, the balls will no longer be a tight fit. At the same time, check the ball cage windows for wear or cracking between the windows.

8   If on inspection any of the constant velocity joint components are found to be worn or damaged, it will be necessary to renew the complete driveshaft assembly, since no components are available separately. If the joint is in satisfactory condition, obtain a repair kit from your Renault dealer consisting of a new gaiter, rubber collar,

retaining spring, and the correct type and quantity of grease.

9   Tape over the splines on the end of the driveshaft, then slide the rubber collar and gaiter onto the shaft. Locate the inner end of the gaiter on the driveshaft, and secure it in position with the rubber collar.

10   Remove the tape, then slide the constant velocity joint coupling onto the driveshaft until the internal circlip locates in the driveshaft groove.

11   Check that the circlip holds the joint securely on the driveshaft, then pack the joint with the grease supplied. Work the grease well into the ball tracks, and fill the gaiter with any excess.

12   Locate the outer lip of the gaiter in the groove on the joint outer member. With the coupling aligned with the driveshaft, lift the lip of the gaiter to equalise the air pressure. Secure the gaiter in position with the large retaining spring, using two lengths of hollow metal tubing to ease the spring into position **(see illustration)**.

13   Check that the constant velocity joint moves freely in all directions, then refit the driveshaft to the vehicle as described in Section 2.

Spider-and-yoke type joint

14   Remove the inner constant velocity joint, bearing and gaiter (as applicable), as described in Section 4 or 5 of this Chapter.

15   Where a vibration damper is fitted, clearly mark the position of the damper on the driveshaft, then use a puller or press to remove it from the inner end of the driveshaft, noting which way around it is fitted **(see illustration)**. Ensure that the legs of the puller or support plate rest only on the damper inner rubber bush, otherwise the damper will distort and break away from the outer metal housing as it is removed.

8

3.19 Renault driveshaft gaiter repair kit

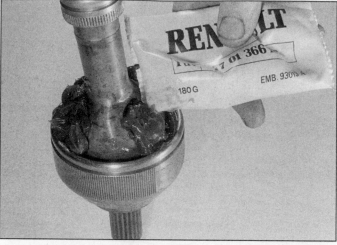

3.21 Pack the joint with the grease supplied in the repair kit . . .

16   Slide the outer constant velocity joint gaiter off the inner end of the driveshaft.

17   Clean the outer constant velocity joint using paraffin or solvent, and dry it thoroughly. Carry out a visual inspection of the joint.

18   Check the driveshaft spider and outer member yoke for signs of wear, pitting or scuffing on their bearing surfaces. Also check that the outer member pivots smoothly and easily, with no traces of roughness.

19   If inspection reveals signs of wear or damage, it will be necessary to renew the driveshaft complete, since no components are available separately. If the joint components are in satisfactory condition, obtain a repair kit consisting of a new gaiter, retaining clips, and the correct type and quantity of grease **(see illustration)**.

20   Tape over the splines on the inner end of the driveshaft, then carefully slide the outer gaiter onto the shaft.

21   Pack the joint with the grease supplied in the repair kit. Work the grease well into the joint, and fill the gaiter with any excess **(see illustration)**.

22   Ease the gaiter over the joint, and ensure that the gaiter lips are correctly located in the grooves on the driveshaft and on the joint **(see illustration)**. With the coupling aligned with the driveshaft, lift the lip of the gaiter to equalise the air pressure.

23   Fit the large metal retaining clip to the gaiter. Remove any slack in the gaiter retaining clip by carefully compressing the raised section of the clip. In the absence of the special tool, a pair of pincers may be

3.22 . . . then slide the gaiter into position over the joint

used. Secure the small retaining clip using the same procedure **(see illustrations)**. Check that the constant velocity joint moves freely in all directions before proceeding further.

3.23a Fit the large retaining clip . . .

3.23b . . . and the small retaining clip. Note use of pincers to secure the clip

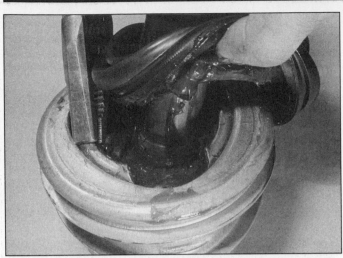

4.4 Bend up the anti-separation tangs with pliers to release the joint outer member (GI62 type)

4.5 Remove the circlip . . .

4.6 . . . and withdraw the tripod joint from the driveshaft end

24 To refit the vibration damper (when applicable), lubricate the driveshaft with a solution of soapy water. Press or drive the vibration damper along the shaft, using a tubular spacer which bears only on the damper inner bush, until it is aligned with the mark made prior to removal.

25 Refit the inner constant velocity joint components as described in Section 4 or 5 (as applicable), then refit the driveshaft to the vehicle as described in Section 2.

4 Right-hand driveshaft inner gaiter - renewal

1 Remove the driveshaft as described in Section 2.
2 On these models, two different types of inner constant velocity joint are used on the right-hand driveshaft: type GI62 and type RC490. The joints can be identified by the shape of their outer members. The GI62 joint has a smooth, circular outer member; the RC490 joint has a recessed outer member which appears clover-shaped when viewed end-on. Identify the type of joint fitted, then proceed as described under the relevant sub-heading.

GI62-type joint

3 Release the large retaining spring and the inner retaining collar, then slide the gaiter down the shaft to expose the joint.
4 Using pliers, carefully bend up the anti-separation plate tangs at

their corners (see illustration). Slide the outer member off the tripod joint. Be prepared to hold the rollers in place, otherwise they may fall off the tripod ends as the outer member is withdrawn. If necessary, secure the rollers in place using tape after removal of the outer member. The rollers are matched to the tripod joint stems, and it is important that they are not interchanged.
5 Using circlip pliers, extract the circlip securing the tripod joint to the driveshaft (see illustration). Note that on some models, the joint may be staked in position; if so, relieve the staking using a file. Mark the position of the tripod in relation to the driveshaft, using a dab of paint or a punch.
6 The tripod joint can now be removed (see illustration). If it is tight, draw the joint off the driveshaft end using a puller. Ensure that the legs of the puller are located behind the joint inner member and do not contact the joint rollers. Alternatively, support the inner member of the tripod joint, and press the shaft out using a hydraulic press, again ensuring that no load is applied to the joint rollers.
7 With the tripod joint removed, slide the gaiter and inner retaining collar off the end of the driveshaft.
8 Wipe clean the joint components, taking care not to remove the alignment marks made on dismantling. **Do not** use paraffin or other solvents to clean this type of joint.
9 Examine the tripod joint, rollers and outer member for any signs of scoring or wear. Check that the rollers move smoothly on the tripod stems. If wear is evident, the tripod joint and roller assembly can be renewed, but it is not possible to obtain a replacement outer member. Obtain a new gaiter, retaining spring/collar and a quantity of the special lubricating grease. These parts are available in the form of a repair kit from your Renault dealer.
10 Tape over the splines on the end of the driveshaft, then carefully slide the inner retaining collar and gaiter onto the shaft.
11 Remove the tape, then, aligning the marks made on dismantling, engage the tripod joint with the driveshaft splines. Use a hammer and soft metal drift to tap the joint onto the shaft, taking great care not to damage the driveshaft splines or joint rollers. Alternatively, support the driveshaft, and press the joint into position using a hydraulic press and suitable tubular spacer which bears only on the joint inner member.
12 Secure the tripod joint in position with the circlip, ensuring that it is correctly located in the driveshaft groove. Where no circlip is fitted, secure the joint in position by staking the end of the driveshaft in three places, at intervals of 120°, using a hammer and punch.
13 Evenly distribute the grease contained in the repair kit around the tripod joint and inside the outer member. Pack the gaiter with the remainder of the grease.
14 Slide the outer member into position over the tripod joint.
15 Using a piece of 2.5 mm thick steel or similar material, make up a support plate (see illustration).

8

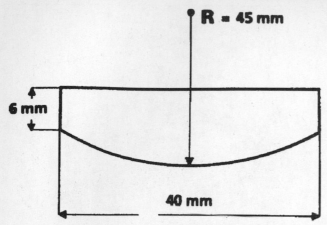

4.15 Support plate dimensions for re-forming the anti-separation plate tangs (GI62 type joint)

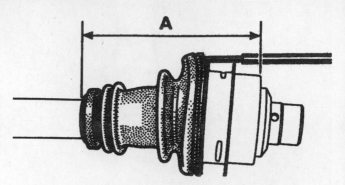

4.19 Fitting dimension for the right-hand driveshaft inner constant velocity joint gaiter (GI62 type joint)

A = 153.5 ± 1 mm

4.24 Removing the metal cover from the right-hand driveshaft inner constant velocity joint - RC490 type

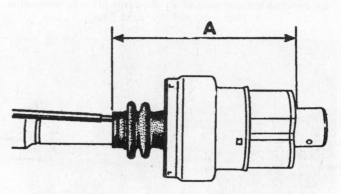

4.32 Fitting dimension for the right-hand driveshaft inner constant velocity joint gaiter - RC490 type joint

A = 156 ± 1 mm

16   Position the support plate under each anti-separation plate tang in the outer member in turn, and tap the tang down onto the support plate. Remove the plate when all the tangs have been returned to their original shape.

17   Slide the gaiter up the driveshaft. Locate the gaiter in the grooves on the driveshaft and outer member.

18   Slide the inner retaining collar into place over the inner end of the gaiter.

19   Using a blunt rod, carefully lift the outer lip of the gaiter to equalise the air pressure. With the rod in position, compress the joint until the dimension from the inner end of the gaiter to the flat end face of the outer member is as shown **(see illustration)**. Hold the outer member in this position and withdraw the rod.

20   Slip the new retaining spring into place to secure the outer lip of the gaiter to the outer member. Take care to ensure that the retaining spring is not overstretched during the fitting process.

21   Check that the constant velocity joint moves freely in all directions, then refit the driveshaft as described in Section 2.

RC490-type joint

22   Using a pair of grips, bend up the metal joint cover at the points where it has been staked into the outer member recesses.

23   Using a pair of snips, cut the gaiter inner retaining clip.

24   Using a soft metal drift, tap the metal joint cover off the outer member **(see illustration)**. Slide the outer member off the end of the tripod joint. Be prepared to hold the rollers in place, otherwise they may fall off the tripod ends as the outer member is withdrawn. If necessary, secure the rollers in place using tape after removal of the outer member. The rollers are matched to the tripod joint stems, and it

is important that they are not interchanged.

25   Remove the tripod joint and gaiter assembly, and examine the joint components for wear, using the information given in paragraphs 6 to 9 of this Section. Obtain a repair kit consisting of a gaiter, retaining clip, metal insert and joint cover, and the correct type and amount of special grease.

26   Fit the metal insert into the inside of the gaiter, then locate the gaiter assembly inside the metal joint cover.

27   Tape over the driveshaft splines, and slide the gaiter and joint cover assembly onto the driveshaft.

28   Refit the tripod joint as described in paragraphs 11 and 12.

29   Evenly distribute the special grease contained in the repair kit around the tripod joint and inside the outer member. Pack the gaiter with the remainder of the grease.

30   Slide the outer member into position over the tripod joint.

31   Slide the metal joint cover onto the outer member until it is flush with the outer member guide panel. Secure the joint cover in position by staking it into the recesses in the outer member, using a hammer and a round-ended punch.

32   Using a blunt rod, carefully lift the inner lip of the gaiter to equalise the air pressure. With the rod in position, compress the joint until the dimension from the inner end of the gaiter to the flat end face of the outer member is as shown **(see illustration)**. Hold the outer member in this position and withdraw the rod.

33   Fit the small retaining clip to the inner end of the gaiter. Remove any slack in the gaiter retaining clip by carefully compressing the raised section of the clip. In the absence of the special tool, a pair of pincers may be used.

34   Check that the constant velocity joint moves freely in all directions, then refit the driveshaft as described in Section 2.

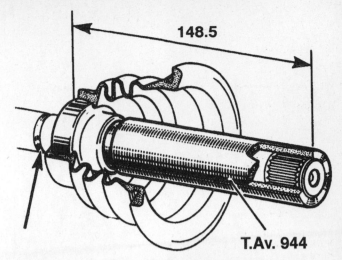

**5.8b Fitting dimension (in mm) for the left-hand driv
shaft inner bearing/gaiter**

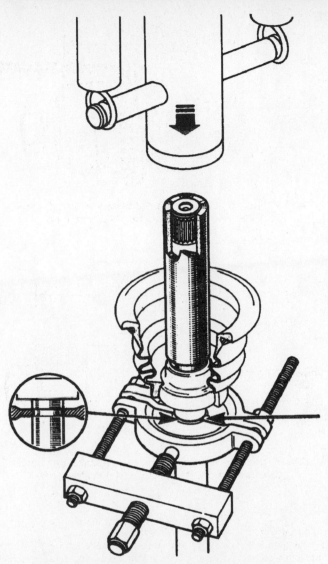

**5.8a Pressing the inner bearing/gaiter onto the end
of the left-hand driveshaft**

5 Left-hand driveshaft inner gaiter - renewal

1   Remove the driveshaft as described in Section 2.
2   Using circlip pliers, extract the circlip securing the tripod joint to the driveshaft. Note that on some models, the joint may be staked in position; if so, relieve the stakings using a file. Using a dab of paint or a hammer and punch, mark the position of the tripod joint in relation to the driveshaft, to use as a guide to refitting.
3   The tripod joint can now be removed. If it is tight, draw the joint off the driveshaft end using a puller. Ensure that the legs of the puller are located behind the joint inner member and do not contact the joint rollers. Alternatively, support the inner member of the tripod joint and press the shaft out of the joint, again ensuring that no load is applied to the joint rollers.
4   The gaiter and bearing assembly is removed in the same way, either by drawing the bearing off the driveshaft, or by pressing the driveshaft out of the bearing. Remove the retaining plate, noting which way round it is fitted.
5   Obtain a new gaiter, which is supplied complete with the small bearing.
6   Owing to the lip-type seal used in the bearing, the bearing and

gaiter must be pressed into position. If a hammer and tubular drift are used to drive the assembly onto the driveshaft, there is a risk of distorting the seal.
7   Refit the retaining plate to the driveshaft, ensuring that it is fitted the correct way around.
8   Support the driveshaft, and press the gaiter bearing onto the shaft, using a tubular spacer which bears only on the bearing inner race **(see illustration)**. Position the bearing so that the distance from the end of the driveshaft to the inner face of the bearing is as shown **(see illustration)**.
9   Align the marks made on dismantling, and engage the tripod joint with the driveshaft splines. Use a hammer and soft metal drift to tap the joint onto the shaft, taking care not to damage the driveshaft splines or joint rollers. Alternatively, support the driveshaft, and press the joint into position using a tubular spacer which bears only on the joint inner member.
10   Secure the tripod joint in position with the circlip, ensuring that it is correctly located in the driveshaft groove. Where no circlip is fitted, secure the joint in position by staking the end of the driveshaft in three places, at intervals of 120°, using a hammer and punch.
11   Refit the driveshaft to the vehicle as described in Section 2.

6 Driveshaft overhaul - general information

1   If any of the checks described in Chapter 1 reveal wear in a driveshaft joint, first remove the roadwheel trim or centre cap (as appropriate) and check that the driveshaft retaining nut is still correctly tightened; if in doubt, use a torque wrench to check it. Refit the centre cap or trim, and repeat the check on the other driveshaft.
2   Road test the vehicle, and listen for a metallic clicking from the front as the vehicle is driven slowly in a circle on full-lock. If a clicking noise is heard, this indicates wear in the outer constant velocity joint.
3   If vibration, consistent with road speed, is felt through the vehicle when accelerating, there is a possibility of wear in the inner constant velocity joints.
4   Constant velocity joints can be dismantled and inspected for wear as described in Sections 3, 4 and 5.
5   Wear in the outer constant velocity joint can only be rectified by renewing the driveshaft. This is necessary since no outer joint components are available separately. For the inner joint, the tripod joint and roller assembly is available separately, but wear in any of the other components will also necessitate driveshaft renewal.

8

Notes

Chapter 9 Braking system

Contents

Specifications

General

System type	Dual hydraulic circuit, split diagonally, with servo assistance
Front brakes	Disc, with single-piston sliding caliper
Rear brakes	Self-adjusting drum
Handbrake	Cable-operated, to rear wheels

Front brakes

Disc diameter	238 mm
Disc thickness:	
New	12.0 mm
Minimum	10.5 mm
Disc run-out	0.07 mm maximum
Brake pad minimum thickness (friction material and backing plate)	6.0 mm

Rear drum brakes

Drum diameter:	
New	180.25 mm
Maximum diameter after machining	181.25 mm
Brake shoe thickness (friction material and shoe):	
New	6.5 mm
Minimum	2.5 mm

9

Torque wrench settings

	Nm	lbf ft
Vacuum servo unit mounting nuts	23	17
Flexible brake hose union	13	10
Master cylinder to servo unit nuts	23	17
Master cylinder brake pipe union nuts	13	10
Bendix front brake caliper mounting bolts	100	74
Girling brake caliper:		
Guide pin bolts*	35	26
Mounting bracket-to-swivel hub bolts	100	74
Rear hub nut*	160	118
Roadwheel bolts	90	66

*Renew every time

1   General information

The braking system is of the servo-assisted, dual circuit hydraulic type. The arrangement of the hydraulic system is such that each circuit operates one front and one rear brake from a tandem master cylinder. Under normal circumstances, both circuits operate in unison. However, in the event of hydraulic failure in one circuit, full braking force will still be available at two wheels.

All models covered by this manual are fitted with front disc brakes and self-adjusting rear drum brakes.

The front disc brakes are actuated by single-piston sliding type calipers, which ensure that equal pressure is applied to each disc pad.

The rear brakes incorporate leading and trailing shoes, which are actuated by twin-piston wheel cylinders (one cylinder per drum). The wheel cylinders incorporate integral pressure-regulating valves, which control the hydraulic pressure applied to the rear brakes. The regulating valves help to prevent rear wheel lock-up during emergency braking. As the brake shoe linings wear, footbrake operation automatically operates a self-adjuster mechanism, which effectively lengthens the strut between the shoes and reduces the lining-to-drum clearance.

The cable-operated handbrake provides an independent mechanical means of rear brake application.

Note: *When servicing any part of the system, work carefully and methodically; also observe scrupulous cleanliness when overhauling any part of the hydraulic system. Always renew components (in axle sets, where applicable) if in doubt about their condition, and use only genuine Renault replacement parts, or at least those of known good quality. Note the warnings given in "Safety first!" and at relevant points in this Chapter, concerning the dangers of asbestos dust and hydraulic fluid.*

2   Brake pedal - removal and refitting

Removal

1   Remove the clutch pedal as described in Chapter 6.
2   Extract the spring clip, then withdraw the clevis pin securing the servo unit pushrod to the brake pedal. Note the spacer which is located on the inside of the pedal.
3   Fully withdraw the pedal cross-shaft and manoeuvre the brake pedal out of the pedal mounting bracket, noting the fitted positions of the pivot bushes **(see illustration)**.
4   Inspect the bushes for signs of wear or damage, and renew as necessary.

Refitting

5   Apply a smear of multi-purpose grease to the contact surfaces of the pivot bushes. Fit the bushes to the brake pedal, noting that the thicker bush is fitted on the left-hand side of the pedal. Also ensure that the lug on each bush is correctly located in the pedal cut-out **(see illustration)**.
6   Slide the pedal and bush assembly into position in the mounting bracket. Ensure that the pedal is correctly engaged with the servo

pushrod, then insert the cross-shaft from the right-hand side of the mounting bracket.
7   Position the spacer on the inside of the pedal. Refit the clevis pin, and secure it in position with the spring clip.
8   Refit the clutch pedal as described in Chapter 6.

3   Vacuum servo unit - testing, removal and refitting

Testing

1   To test the operation of the servo unit, depress the footbrake several times to exhaust the vacuum, then start the engine whilst keeping the pedal firmly depressed. As the engine starts, there should be a noticeable "give" in the brake pedal as the vacuum builds up. Allow the engine to run for at least two minutes, then switch it off. If the brake pedal is now depressed it should feel normal, but further applications should result in the pedal feeling firmer, with the pedal stroke decreasing with each application.
2   If the servo does not operate as described, inspect the servo unit check valve as described in Section 4. If the check valve is OK, try renewing the servo air filter (Section 5).
3   If the servo unit still fails to operate satisfactorily, the fault lies within the unit itself. Apart from external components, no spares are available, so a defective servo must be renewed.

Removal

4   Remove the master cylinder as described in Section 8.
5   Slacken the retaining clip, and disconnect the vacuum hose from the check valve on the servo unit. If the original Renault clip is still fitted, cut the clip and discard it; use a standard worm-drive hose clip on refitting.
6   Release the retaining clips and remove the servo unit insulation cover from the engine compartment bulkhead.
7   Working inside the vehicle, extract the spring clip and withdraw the clevis pin securing the servo unit pushrod to the brake pedal. Note the spacer which is located on the inside of the pedal **(see illustrations)**.
8   Remove the four nuts and washers securing the servo unit to the engine compartment bulkhead. Return to the engine compartment and remove the servo, noting the gasket which is fitted to the rear of the unit.

Refitting

9   Prior to refitting, check that the servo unit pushrod is correctly adjusted as follows. With the gasket removed, check the dimensions **(see illustration)**. If adjustment is necessary, dimension "L" can be altered by slackening the locknut and repositioning the pushrod clevis, and dimension "X" can be altered by repositioning the nut (P). After adjustment ensure that the clevis locknut is securely tightened.
10   Inspect the check valve sealing grommet for signs of damage or deterioration, and renew if necessary.
11   Fit a new gasket to the rear of the servo unit, and reposition the unit in the engine compartment.
12   Working inside the vehicle, ensure that the servo unit pushrod is

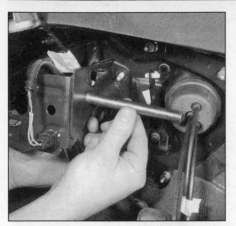

2.3 Withdraw the cross-shaft and manoeuvre the brake pedal out of the mounting bracket

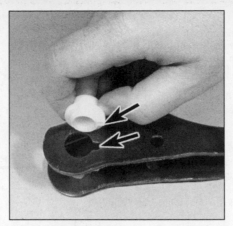

2.5 Ensure that the lugs on the mounting bushes are correctly engaged with the pedal cut-outs (arrows)

3.7a Remove the spring clip (arrowed) . . .

3.7b . . . then withdraw the servo pushrod-to-brake pedal clevis pin. Note the servo mounting nuts (arrowed)

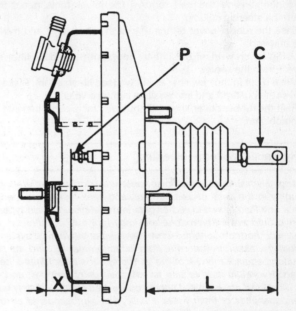

3.9 Vacuum servo unit adjustment dimensions

C   Pushrod clevis   P   Pushrod nut
L   110 mm   X   22.3 mm

correctly engaged with the brake pedal. Refit the servo unit mounting nuts (and washers), and tighten them to the specified torque.

13   Position the spacer on the inside of the pedal. Refit the clevis pin, and secure it in position with the spring clip.

14   Refit the servo unit insulation cover to the bulkhead and secure it in position with all the necessary retaining clips.

15   Reconnect the vacuum hose to the servo unit check valve, and securely tighten its retaining clip.

16   Refit the master cylinder as described in Section 8 of this Chapter.

17   On completion, start the engine and check that there are no air leaks at the servo vacuum hose connection. Check the operation of the servo as described at the beginning of this Section.

4   Vacuum servo unit check valve - removal, testing and refitting

Removal

1   Slacken the retaining clip, and disconnect the vacuum hose from the check valve on the servo unit (see illustration). If the original Renault clip is still fitted, cut the clip and discard it; use a standard worm-drive hose clip on refitting.

2   Withdraw the valve from its rubber sealing grommet, using a pulling and twisting motion. Remove the grommet from the servo.

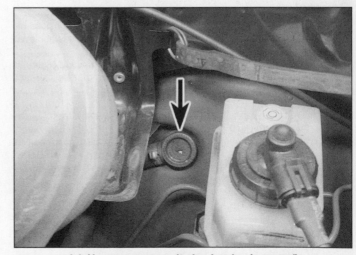

4.1 Vacuum servo unit check valve (arrowed)

Testing

3   Examine the check valve for signs of damage, and renew if necessary. The valve may be tested by blowing through it in both directions. Air should flow through the valve in one direction only - when blown through from the servo unit end of the valve. Renew the valve if this is not the case.

4   Examine the rubber sealing grommet and flexible vacuum hose for signs of damage or deterioration, and renew as necessary.

Refitting

5   Fit the sealing grommet into position in the servo unit.

6   Ease the check valve into position, taking care not to displace or damage the grommet. Reconnect the vacuum hose to the valve, and securely tighten its retaining clip.

7   On completion, start the engine and check that there are no air leaks.

5   Vacuum servo unit air filter - renewal

1   Working inside the car, remove the lower facia panel from beneath the steering column.

2   Ease the rubber cover off the rear of the servo unit, and move it up the pushrod.

3   Using a screwdriver or scriber, hook out the old air filter and remove it from the servo.

4   Make a cut in the new filter as shown **(see illustration)**. Place the filter over the pushrod and into position in the servo end.

5   Refit the rubber cover, then refit the lower facia panel beneath the steering column.

6   Hydraulic system - bleeding

Warning: *Hydraulic fluid is poisonous; wash off immediately and thoroughly in the case of skin contact, and seek immediate medical advice if any fluid is swallowed or gets into the eyes. Certain types of hydraulic fluid are inflammable, and may ignite when allowed into contact with hot components; when servicing any hydraulic system, it is safest to assume that the fluid is inflammable, and to take precautions against the risk of fire as though it is petrol that is being handled. Hydraulic fluid is also an effective paint stripper, and will attack plastics; if any is spilt, it should be washed off immediately using copious quantities of fresh water. Finally, it is hygroscopic (it absorbs moisture from the air) - old fluid may be contaminated and unfit for further use. When topping-up or renewing the fluid, always use the recommended type (see Chapter 1), and ensure that it comes from a freshly-opened, previously-sealed container.*

General

1   The correct operation of any hydraulic system is only possible after removing all air from the components and circuit; this is achieved by bleeding the system.

2   During the bleeding procedure, add only clean, unused hydraulic fluid of the recommended type; never re-use fluid that has already been bled from the system. Ensure that sufficient fluid is available before starting work.

3   If there is any possibility of incorrect fluid being already in the system, the system must be flushed completely with uncontaminated, correct fluid, and new seals should be fitted to the various components.

4   If air has entered the hydraulic system because of a leak, ensure that the fault is cured before proceeding further.

5   Park the vehicle on level ground, switch off the engine and select first or reverse gear. Chock the wheels and release the handbrake.

6   Check that all pipes and hoses are secure, unions tight and bleed screws closed. Clean any dirt from around the bleed screws.

7   Unscrew the master cylinder reservoir cap and top the master cylinder reservoir up to the "MAX" level line; refit the cap loosely. Remember to maintain the fluid level at least above the "MIN" level line

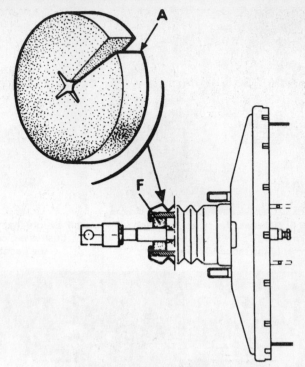

5.4 Vacuum servo unit air filter renewal

A   Cut the new filter as shown
F   Correct fitted position of filter in servo unit

throughout the procedure, or there is a risk of further air entering the system.

8   There are a number of one-man, do-it-yourself brake bleeding kits currently available from motor accessory shops. It is recommended that one of these kits is used whenever possible, as they greatly simplify the bleeding operation, and also reduce the risk of expelled air and fluid being drawn back into the system. If such a kit is not available, the basic (two-man) method must be used, which is described in detail below.

9   If a kit is to be used, prepare the vehicle as described previously, and follow the kit manufacturer's instructions. The procedure may vary slightly according to the type of kit being used; general procedures are as outlined below in the relevant sub-section.

10   Whichever method is used, the same sequence must be followed (paragraphs 11 and 12) to ensure the removal of all air from the system.

Bleeding sequence

11   If the system has been only partially disconnected, and suitable precautions were taken to minimise fluid loss, it should be necessary only to bleed that part of the system (ie the primary or secondary circuit).

12   If the complete system is to be bled, then it should be done working in the following sequence:

a) *Right-hand rear brake.*
b) *Left-hand front brake.*
c) *Left-hand rear brake.*
d) *Right-hand front brake.*

Bleeding - basic (two-man) method

13   Collect a clean glass jar, a suitable length of plastic or rubber tubing which is a tight fit over the bleed screw, and a ring spanner to fit the screw. The help of an assistant will also be required.

14   Remove the dust cap from the first screw in the sequence. Fit the spanner and tube to the screw, place the other end of the tube in the jar, and pour in sufficient fluid to cover the end of the tube.

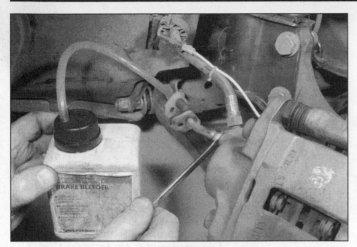

6.21 Bleeding a front brake caliper

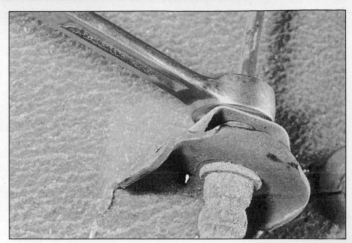

7.2a Using a brake pipe spanner to unscrew a hydraulic union nut

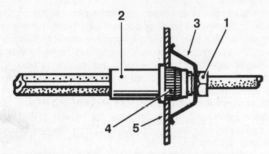

7.2b Hydraulic pipe connection to a flexible hose

1 Union nut	4 Splined end fitting
2 Flexible hose	5 Bodywork
3 Spring clip support	

15   Ensure that the master cylinder reservoir fluid level is maintained at least above the "MIN" level line throughout the procedure.

16   Have the assistant fully depress the brake pedal several times to build up pressure, then maintain it on the final stroke.

17   While pedal pressure is maintained, unscrew the bleed screw (approximately one turn) and allow the compressed fluid and air to flow into the jar. The assistant should maintain pedal pressure, following it down to the floor if necessary, and should not release it until instructed to do so. When the flow stops, tighten the bleed screw again. Have the assistant release the pedal slowly.

18   Repeat the steps given in paragraphs 16 and 17 until the fluid emerging from the bleed screw is free from air bubbles. Remember to recheck the fluid level in the master cylinder reservoir every five strokes or so. If the master cylinder has been drained and refilled, and air is being bled from the first screw in the sequence, allow approximately five seconds between strokes for the master cylinder passages to refill.

19   When no more air bubbles appear, tighten the bleed screw securely, remove the tube and spanner, and refit the dust cap. Do not overtighten the bleed screw.

20   Repeat the procedure on the remaining screws in the sequence until all air is removed from the system and the brake pedal feels firm.

Bleeding - using a one-way valve kit

21   As their name implies, these kits consist of a length of tubing with a one-way valve fitted, to prevent expelled air and fluid being drawn back into the system; some kits include a translucent container, which can be positioned so that the air bubbles can be more easily seen flowing from the end of the tube **(see illustration)**.

22   The kit is connected to the bleed screw, which is then opened. The user returns to the driver's seat and depresses the brake pedal with a smooth, steady stroke and slowly releases it; this is repeated

until the expelled fluid is clear of air bubbles.

23   Note that these kits simplify work so much that it is easy to forget the master cylinder reservoir fluid level; ensure that this is maintained at least above the "MIN" level line at all times.

Bleeding - using a pressure-bleeding kit

24   These kits are usually operated by the reservoir of pressurised air contained in the spare tyre, although it may be necessary to reduce the pressure to lower than normal; refer to the instructions supplied with the kit.

25   By connecting a pressurised, fluid-filled container to the master cylinder reservoir, bleeding can be carried out simply by opening each screw in turn (in the specified sequence) and allowing the fluid to flow out until no more air bubbles can be seen in the expelled fluid.

26   This method has the advantage that the large reservoir of fluid provides an additional safeguard against air being drawn into the system during bleeding.

27   Pressure-bleeding is particularly effective when bleeding "difficult" systems, or when bleeding the complete system at the time of routine fluid renewal.

All methods

28   When bleeding is complete and firm pedal feel is restored, wash off any spilt fluid, tighten the bleed screws securely and refit their dust caps.

29   Check the hydraulic fluid level, and top-up if necessary (Chapter 1).

30   Discard any hydraulic fluid that has been bled from the system; it will not be fit for re-use.

31   Check the feel of the brake pedal. If it feels at all spongy, air must still be present in the system, and further bleeding is required. Failure to bleed satisfactorily after several repetitions of the bleeding procedure may be due to worn master cylinder seals.

---

7   Hydraulic pipes and hoses - renewal

9

Note: *Before starting work, refer to the warning at the beginning of Section 6 concerning the dangers of hydraulic fluid.*

1   If any pipe or hose is to be renewed, minimise fluid loss by removing the master cylinder reservoir cap and then tightening it down onto a piece of polythene (taking care not to damage the sender unit) to obtain an airtight seal. Alternatively, flexible hoses can be sealed, if required, using a proprietary brake hose clamp; metal brake pipe unions can be plugged (if care is taken not to allow dirt into the system) or capped immediately they are disconnected. Place a wad of rag under any union that is to be disconnected, to catch any spilt fluid.

2   If a flexible hose is to be disconnected, unscrew the brake pipe union nut before removing the spring clip which secures the hose to its mounting bracket **(see illustrations)**.

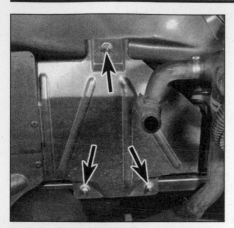

8.1a Undo the heat shield retaining nuts (arrowed) . . .   **8.1b . . . undo the two retaining nuts . . .**   **8.1c . . . and remove the cable retaining bracket (engine removed for clarity)**

3   To unscrew the union nuts, it is preferable to obtain a brake pipe spanner of the correct size (11 mm/13 mm split ring); these are available from motor accessory shops. Failing this, a close-fitting open-ended spanner will be required, though if the nuts are tight or corroded, their flats may be rounded off if the spanner slips. In such a case, a self-locking wrench is often the only way to unscrew a stubborn union, but it follows that the pipe and the damaged nuts must be renewed on reassembly. Always clean a union and surrounding area before disconnecting it. If disconnecting a component with more than one union, make a careful note of the connections before disturbing any of them.

4   If a brake pipe is to be renewed, it can be obtained, cut to length and with the union nuts and end flares in place, from Renault dealers. All that is then necessary is to bend it to shape, following the line of the original, before fitting it to the car. Alternatively, most motor accessory shops can make up brake pipes from kits, but this requires very careful measurement of the original to ensure that the replacement is of the correct length. The safest answer is usually to take the original to the shop as a pattern.

5   On refitting, do not overtighten the union nuts. The specified torque wrench settings (where given) are not high, and it is not necessary to exercise brute force to obtain a sound joint.

6   Ensure that the pipes and hoses are correctly routed with no kinks, and that they are secured in the clips or brackets provided. In the case of flexible hoses, make sure that they cannot contact other components during movement of the steering and/or suspension assemblies.

7   After fitting, remove the polythene from the reservoir (or remove the plugs or clamps, as applicable), and bleed the hydraulic system as described in Section 6. Wash off any spilt fluid, and check carefully for fluid leaks.

8   Master cylinder - removal and refitting

Note: *Before starting work, refer to the warning at the beginning of Section 6 concerning the dangers of hydraulic fluid.*

Removal

1   Remove the nuts securing the brake servo heat shield to the engine compartment bulkhead. Manoeuvre the heat shield out of the engine compartment. Undo the two nuts securing the cable retaining bracket to the master cylinder studs, and position the bracket clear of the master cylinder **(see illustrations)**.

2   Remove the master cylinder reservoir cap, having disconnected the sender unit wiring connector, and syphon the hydraulic fluid from the reservoir. **Note:** *Do not syphon the fluid by mouth, as it is poisonous; use a syringe or an old poultry baster.* Alternatively, open any convenient pair of bleed screws in the system (one in each hydraulic circuit) and gently pump the brake pedal to expel the fluid through plastic tubes connected to the screws (see Section 6).

3   Once drained, remove the reservoir from the master cylinder by

pulling it upwards.

4   Wipe clean the area around the brake pipe unions on the side of the master cylinder, and place absorbent rags beneath the pipe unions to catch any surplus fluid. Make a note of the correct fitted positions of the unions, then unscrew the union nuts and carefully withdraw the pipes. Plug or tape over the pipe ends and master cylinder orifices, to minimise the loss of brake fluid and to prevent the entry of dirt into the system. Wash off any spilt fluid immediately with cold water.

5   Slacken and remove the two nuts securing the master cylinder to the vacuum servo unit, then withdraw the master cylinder from the engine compartment. Remove the O-ring from the rear of the master cylinder, and discard it.

6   It is not possible to obtain seals or internal components for the master cylinder, therefore if it is faulty, it must be renewed as a complete unit. The reservoir mounting bush seals may be renewed if necessary. The O-ring fitted between the master cylinder and the vacuum servo must be renewed as a matter of course whenever the unit is removed, as a leak at this point will allow atmospheric pressure into the servo unit.

Refitting

7   Before refitting the master cylinder, check that the distance between the tip of the master cylinder end of the pushrod and the front of the servo unit, dimension "X", is as shown **(see illustration 3.9)**. If necessary, adjust by repositioning the pushrod nut "P".

8   Remove all traces of dirt from the master cylinder and servo unit mating surfaces. Fit a new O-ring to the groove on the master cylinder body.

9   Fit the master cylinder to the servo, ensuring that the servo pushrod enters the master cylinder bore centrally. Refit the master cylinder mounting nuts, and tighten them to the specified torque.

10   Wipe clean the brake pipe unions, then refit them to the master cylinder ports. Tighten the union nuts to the specified torque.

11   Carefully align the reservoir with the mounting bush seals. Push the reservoir firmly into position.

12   Locate the cable retaining plate on the master cylinder studs, and securely tighten its retaining nuts. Refit the heat shield to the bulkhead and secure it.

13   Refill the master cylinder reservoir with new fluid, and bleed the hydraulic system as described in Section 6.

9   Front brake pads - renewal

Warning: *Renew both sets of front brake pads at the same time - never renew the pads on only one wheel, as uneven braking may result. Note that the dust created by wear of the pads may contain asbestos, which is a health hazard. Never blow it out with compressed air, and don't inhale any of it. An approved filtering mask should be worn when working on the brakes. DO NOT use petroleum-based solvents to clean brake parts - use brake cleaner or methylated spirit only.*

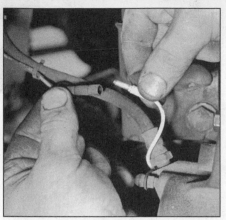

9.2 Disconnecting the pad wear sensor wiring connector (Girling caliper shown)

9.4a On Bendix calipers remove the spring clip . . .

9.4b . . . and remove the pad retaining plate

9.5a Withdraw the outer brake pad . . .

9.5b . . . and the inner brake pad

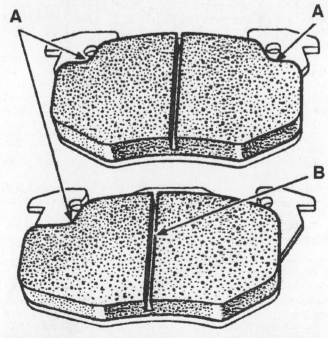

9.7 Bendix caliper symmetrical-lining pad (top) and offset-lining pad (bottom). Offset lining has only a single cut-out (A) and the groove in the friction material (B) is not central

1   Apply the handbrake, then jack up the front of the vehicle and support it on axle stands. Remove the front roadwheels.
2   Trace the brake pad wear sensor wiring back from the inner pad, and disconnect it at the wiring connector **(see illustration)**.
3   Push the piston into its bore by pulling the caliper outwards.

Bendix calipers

4   Extract the small spring clip from the pad retaining plate, and then slide the plate out of the caliper **(see illustrations)**.
5   Using pliers if necessary, withdraw the pads from the caliper **(see illustrations)**. Make a note of the correct fitted position of the anti-rattle spring, and remove the spring from each pad.
6   First measure the thickness of each brake pad (friction material and backing plate). If any pad is worn at any point to the specified minimum thickness or less, all four pads must be renewed. Also, the pads should be renewed if any are fouled with oil or grease; there is no satisfactory way of degreasing friction material once contaminated. If any of the brake pads are worn unevenly or fouled with oil or grease, trace and rectify the cause before reassembly. New brake pads and spring kits are available from Renault dealers.
7   Note that there are two different types of brake pad available for the Bendix caliper. The correct pad type depends on the brake caliper bore/piston diameter. Calipers with a 45 mm diameter bore/piston require pads with symmetrical linings, whereas calipers with a 48 mm diameter bore/piston require pads with offset linings (groove in the friction material not central). The pad types can also be distinguished by the cut-outs in the upper corners of the friction material **(see illustration)**; symmetrical linings have two cut-outs, whereas the offset linings have only a single cut-out.

9

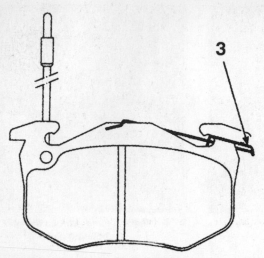

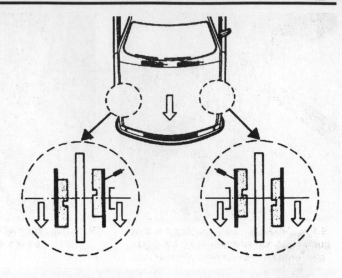

9.11 Anti-rattle spring (3) correctly fitted to Bendix inner brake pad

8   If the brake pads are still serviceable, carefully clean them using a clean, fine wire brush or similar, paying particular attention to the sides and back of the metal backing. Clean out the grooves in the friction material, and pick out any large embedded particles of dirt or debris. Carefully clean the pad locations in the caliper body/mounting bracket.

9   Prior to fitting the pads, check that the guide sleeves are free to slide easily in the caliper body, and check that the rubber guide sleeve gaiters are undamaged. Brush the dust and dirt from the caliper and piston, but *do not inhale it as it is injurious to health*. Inspect the dust seal around the piston for damage, and the piston for evidence of fluid leaks, corrosion or damage. If attention to any of these components is necessary, refer to Section 10. Also inspect the brake disc as described in Section 11.

10   If new brake pads are to be fitted, the caliper piston must be pushed back into the cylinder to make room for them. Either use a G-clamp or similar tool, or use suitable pieces of wood as levers. Provided that the master cylinder reservoir has not been overfilled with hydraulic fluid, there should be no spillage, but keep a careful watch on the fluid level while retracting the piston. If the fluid level rises above the "MAX" level line at any time, the surplus should be syphoned off (not by mouth - use an old syringe or a poultry baster) or ejected via a plastic tube connected to the bleed screw (see Section 6).

11   Fit the anti-rattle springs to the pads, so that when the pads are installed in the caliper, the spring end will be located at the opposite end of the pad to the pad retaining plate **(see illustration)**.

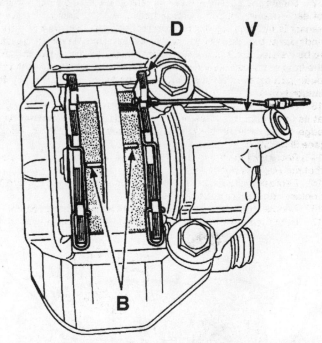

9.12a Correct fitting of Bendix offset lining brake pads

B   *Grooves*
D   *Pad retaining plate spring clip location*
V   *Bleed screw*

9.12b Correct fitted positions of the Bendix offset lining brake pads

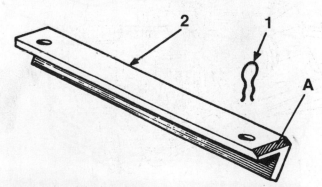

9.13 Bendix disc pad retaining plate (2) and spring clip (1) showing filed chamfer (A)

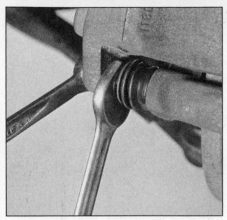

9.19a On Girling calipers, slacken the guide pin bolts whilst holding the guide pins with an open-ended spanner . . .

9.19b . . . then withdraw the bolts and lift off the brake caliper

9.22 Ensure that the brake pads are fitted the correct way round, with friction material facing the disc

12 Locate the pads in the caliper, ensuring that the friction material of each pad is against the brake disc, and the pad with the wear sensor is fitted on the inside. Also recheck that the anti-rattle spring ends are at the opposite end of the pad to which the retaining plate is to be inserted. On models with offset linings, looking at the pads from the front of the car, the innermost pad groove must be higher than the outer pad groove. Make sure that the pads are fitted correctly (see illustrations).

13 Slide the retaining plate into place, and install the small spring clip at its inner end. It may be necessary to file an entry chamfer on the edge of the retaining plate, to enable it to be fitted without difficulty (see illustration).

14 Reconnect the brake pad wear sensor wiring connector, ensuring that the wire is correctly routed.

15 Depress the brake pedal several times to bring the pads into firm contact with the brake disc.

16 Repeat the above procedure on the other front brake caliper.

17 Refit the roadwheels, then lower the vehicle to the ground and tighten the roadwheel bolts to the specified torque.

18 Check the hydraulic fluid level as described in Chapter 1.

Girling calipers

19 Slacken and remove the caliper upper and lower guide pin bolts, using a slim open-ended spanner to prevent the guide pin itself from rotating (see illustrations). Discard the guide pin bolts; new bolts must be used on refitting. If genuine Renault brake pads are purchased, the bolts will be supplied with the pad set.

20 With the guide pins removed, lift the caliper away from the brake pads and mounting bracket, and tie it to the suspension strut using a suitable piece of wire. Do not allow the caliper to hang unsupported on the flexible hose.

21 Withdraw the two brake pads from the caliper mounting bracket, and examine them as described above in paragraph 6 and paragraphs 8 to 10, ignoring paragraph 7, which is only applicable to the Bendix caliper.

22 Install the pads in the caliper mounting bracket, ensuring that the friction material of each pad is against the brake disc. The pad with the wear sensor is fitted on the inside (see illustration).

23 Position the caliper over the pads. Coat the threads of the new lower guide pin bolt with locking fluid, and fit the bolt. Apply locking fluid to the new upper guide pin bolt, press the caliper into position, and fit the bolt. Check that the anti-rattle springs are correctly located (see illustration), then tighten the guide pin bolts to the specified torque, starting with the lower bolt.

24 Carry out the operations described above in paragraphs 14 to 18.

All calipers

25 If new pads have been fitted, full braking efficiency will not be obtained until the linings have bedded-in. Be prepared for longer stopping distances, and avoid harsh braking as far as possible for the first hundred miles or so after fitting new pads.

10 Front brake caliper - removal, overhaul and refitting

Note: Before starting work, refer to the warnings at the beginning of Sections 6 and 9 concerning the dangers of hydraulic fluid and asbestos dust.

Removal

1 Apply the handbrake, then jack up the front of the vehicle and support it on axle stands. Remove the appropriate roadwheel.

2 Minimise fluid loss, either by removing the master cylinder reservoir cap and then tightening it down onto a piece of polythene to obtain an airtight seal (taking care not to damage the sender unit), or by using a brake hose clamp, a G-clamp or a similar tool with protected jaws to clamp the flexible hose.

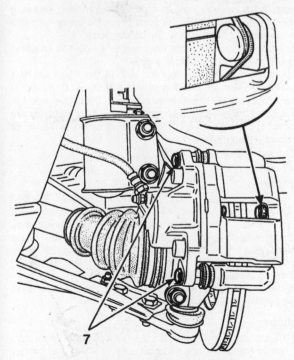

9.23 Girling caliper showing guide pin bolts (7) and correct fitted position of anti-rattle spring

9

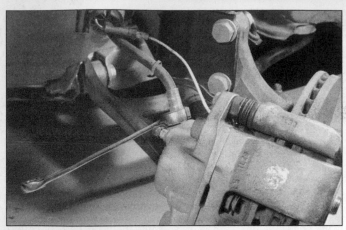

**10.6 Slackening the front brake caliper hose union nut
(Girling caliper shown)**

Bendix caliper

3   Remove the brake pads as described in Section 9, paragraphs 2 to 5.
4   Clean the area around the union, then loosen the brake hose union nut.
5   Slacken the two bolts securing the caliper assembly to the swivel hub, and remove them along with the mounting plate, noting which way around the plate is fitted. Lift the caliper assembly away from the brake disc, and unscrew it from the end of the brake hose.

Girling caliper

6   Clean the area around the hose union, then loosen the brake hose union nut **(see illustration)**.
7   Slacken and remove the upper and lower caliper guide pin bolts, using a slim open-ended spanner to prevent the guide pin itself from rotating. Discard the guide pin bolts; new bolts must be used on refitting. With the guide pin bolts removed, lift the caliper away from the brake disc, then unscrew the caliper from the end of the brake hose. Note that the brake pads need not be disturbed, and can be left in position in the caliper mounting bracket.

Overhaul

8   With the caliper on the bench, wipe away all traces of dust and dirt, but *avoid inhaling the dust, as it is injurious to health.*
9   On the Girling caliper, using a small flat-bladed screwdriver, carefully prise the dust seal retaining clip out of the caliper bore.
10   On all calipers, withdraw the partially-ejected piston from the caliper body and remove the dust seal. The piston can be withdrawn by hand, or if necessary forced out by applying compressed air to the union bolt hole. **Caution:** *The piston may be ejected with some force.* Only low pressure should be required, such as is generated by a foot pump.
11   Extract the piston hydraulic seal using a blunt instrument such as a knitting needle or a crochet hook, taking care not to damage the caliper bore.
12   Withdraw the guide sleeves or pins from the caliper body or mounting bracket (as applicable) and remove the rubber gaiters.
13   Thoroughly clean all components using only methylated spirit, isopropyl alcohol or clean hydraulic fluid as a cleaning medium. Never use mineral-based solvents, such as petrol or paraffin, which will attack the hydraulic system rubber components. Dry the components immediately, using compressed air or a clean, lint-free cloth. Use compressed air to blow clear the fluid passages.
14   Check all components and renew any that are worn or damaged. Check particularly the cylinder bore and piston; if they are scratched, worn or corroded in any way, they must be renewed (note that this means the renewal of the complete body assembly). Similarly check the condition of the guide sleeves or pins and their bores; they should be undamaged and (when cleaned) a reasonably tight sliding fit in the body or mounting bracket bores. If there is any doubt about the

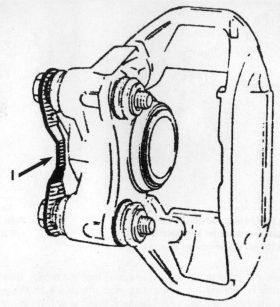

**10.22 On Bendix caliper, ensure mounting plate (1) is fitted so
that its bend curves towards the caliper body**

condition of a component, renew it.
15   If the assembly is fit for further use, obtain the appropriate repair kit; the components are available from Renault dealers, in various combinations.
16   Renew all rubber seals, dust covers and caps disturbed on dismantling as a matter of course; these should never be re-used.
17   Before commencing reassembly, ensure that all components are absolutely clean and dry.
18   Dip the piston and the new piston (fluid) seal in clean hydraulic fluid. Smear clean fluid on the cylinder bore surface.
19   Fit the new piston (fluid) seal, using only the fingers to manipulate it into the cylinder bore groove. Fit the new dust seal to the piston. Refit the piston to the cylinder bore using a twisting motion, ensuring that the piston enters squarely into the bore. Press the piston fully into the bore, then press the dust seal into the caliper body.
20   On the Girling caliper, install the dust seal retaining clip, ensuring that it is correctly seated in the caliper groove.
21   On all calipers, apply the grease supplied in the repair kit, or a good quality high-temperature brake grease or anti-seize compound to the guide sleeves or pins. Fit the sleeves or pins to the caliper body or mounting bracket. Fit the new rubber gaiters, ensuring that they are correctly located in the grooves on both the sleeve or pin, and body or mounting bracket (as applicable).

Refitting

Bendix caliper

22   Screw the caliper fully onto the flexible hose union nut. Position the caliper over the brake disc, then refit the two caliper mounting bolts and the mounting plate. Note that the mounting plate must be fitted so that its bend curves towards the caliper body **(see illustration)**; this is necessary to prevent the plate contacting the driveshaft gaiter when the steering is on full-lock. With the plate correctly positioned, tighten the caliper bolts to the specified torque setting.
23   Tighten the brake hose union nut to the specified torque, then refit the brake pads as described in Section 9.

Girling caliper

24   Screw the caliper body fully onto the flexible hose union nut. Check that the brake pads are still correctly fitted in the caliper mounting bracket.
25   Position the caliper over the pads. Coat the threads of the new lower guide pin bolt with locking fluid, and fit the bolt. Apply locking

11.3 Measuring brake disc thickness with a micrometer

11.4 Measuring brake disc run-out with a dial gauge

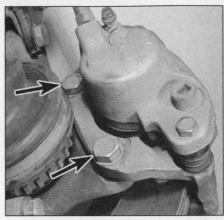

11.6a Undo the two bolts (arrowed) securing the caliper to the swivel hub . . .

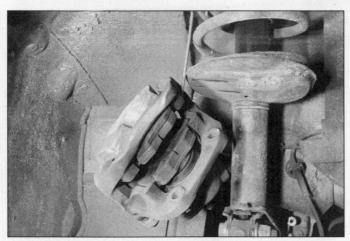

11.6b . . . then slide the caliper off the disc, and suspend it from the suspension strut spring (Girling caliper shown)

fluid to the new upper guide pin bolt, press the caliper into position, and fit the bolt. Check that the anti-rattle springs are correctly located (see illustration 9.23), then tighten the guide pin bolts to the specified torque, starting with the lower bolt.

26 Tighten the brake hose union nut to the specified torque.

All calipers

27 Remove the brake hose clamp or polythene, where fitted, and bleed the hydraulic system as described in Section 6. Providing the precautions described were taken to minimise brake fluid loss, it should only be necessary to bleed the relevant front brake.

28 Refit the roadwheel, then lower the vehicle to the ground and tighten the roadwheel bolts to the specified torque.

11 Front brake disc - inspection, removal and refitting

Note: *Before starting work, refer to the warning at the beginning of Section 9 concerning the dangers of asbestos dust. If either disc requires renewal, both should be renewed at the same time, to ensure even and consistent braking. In principle, new pads should be fitted also.*

Inspection

1   Chock the rear wheels, firmly apply the handbrake, jack up the front of the vehicle and support on axle stands. Remove the appropriate front roadwheel.

2   Slowly rotate the brake disc so that the full area of both sides can be checked; remove the brake pads, as described in Section 9, if

better access is required to the inboard surface. Light scoring is normal in the area swept by the brake pads, but if heavy scoring is found, the disc must be renewed.

3   It is normal to find a lip of rust and brake dust around the disc's perimeter; this can be scraped off if required. If, however, a lip has formed due to wear of the brake pad swept area, the disc thickness must be measured using a micrometer (see illustration). Take measurements at several places around the disc at the inside and outside of the pad swept area; if the disc has worn at any point to the specified minimum thickness or less, it must be renewed.

4   If the disc is thought to be warped, it can be checked for run-out, ideally by using a dial gauge mounted on any convenient fixed point, while the disc is slowly rotated (see illustration). In the absence of a dial gauge, use feeler blades to measure (at several points all around the disc) the clearance between the disc and a fixed point such as the caliper mounting bracket. If the measurements obtained are at the specified maximum or beyond, the disc is excessively warped, and must be renewed; however, it is worth checking first that the hub bearing is in good condition (Chapters 1 and 10). Also try the effect of removing the disc and turning it through 180° to reposition it on the hub; if run-out is still excessive, the disc must be renewed.

5   Check the disc for cracks (especially around the wheel bolt holes), and for any other wear or damage. Renew the disc if necessary.

Removal

6   Unscrew the two bolts securing the brake caliper to the swivel hub, and slide the caliper assembly off the disc. Using a piece of wire or string, tie the caliper to the front suspension coil spring, to avoid placing any strain on the hydraulic brake hose (see illustrations).

7   If the same disc is to be refitted, use chalk or paint to mark the relationship of the disc to the hub. Remove the two screws securing the brake disc to the hub, and remove the disc. If it is tight, lightly tap its rear face with a hide or plastic mallet.

Refitting

8   Refitting is the reverse of the removal procedure, noting the following points:

a)   *Ensure that the mating surfaces of the disc and hub are clean and flat.*

b)   *If applicable, align the marks made on removal.*

c)   *Securely tighten the disc retaining screws.*

d)   *If a new disc has been fitted, use a suitable solvent to wipe any preservative coating from the disc before refitting the caliper.*

e)   *Apply locking fluid to the threads of the brake caliper mounting bolts, and tighten them to the specified torque.*

f)   *Refit the roadwheel, then lower the vehicle to the ground and tighten the roadwheel bolts to the specified torque. On completion, depress the brake pedal several times to bring the brake pads into contact with the disc.*

9

12.2 Lever out the cap from the centre of the brake drum . . .

12.3 . . . then remove the rear hub nut and thrustwasher

12 Rear brake drum - removal, inspection and refitting

Note: *Before starting work, refer to the warning at the beginning of Section 13 concerning the dangers of asbestos dust. If either drum requires renewal or refinishing, both should be dealt with at the same time, to ensure even and consistent braking. In principle, new shoes should be fitted also.*

Removal

1   Chock the front wheels, engage reverse gear and release the handbrake. Jack up the rear of the vehicle and support it on axle stands. Remove the appropriate rear wheel.
2   Using a hammer and suitable large flat-bladed screwdriver, carefully tap and prise the cap out of the centre of the brake drum **(see illustration)**.
3   Using a socket and long bar, slacken and remove the rear hub nut, and withdraw the thrustwasher **(see illustration)**. Discard the hub nut; a new nut must used on refitting.
4   It should now be possible to withdraw the brake drum and hub bearing assembly from the stub axle by hand. It may be difficult to remove the drum due to the tightness of the hub bearing on the stub axle, or due to the brake shoes binding on the inner circumference of the drum. If the bearing is tight, tap the periphery of the drum using a hide or plastic mallet, or use a universal puller, secured to the drum with the wheel bolts, to pull it off. If the brake shoes are binding, proceed as follows.
5   First ensure that the handbrake is fully off. From underneath the vehicle, slacken the handbrake cable adjuster locknut, then back off the adjuster nut on the handbrake lever rod. Note that on some models, it will first be necessary to remove the mounting nut(s) and lower the exhaust heat shield to gain access to the adjuster nut.
6   Insert a screwdriver through one of the wheel bolt holes in the brake drum, so that it contacts the handbrake operating lever on the trailing brake shoe **(see illustrations)**. Push the lever until the stop-peg slips behind the brake shoe web, allowing the brake shoes to retract fully. Withdraw the brake drum, and slide the spacer off the stub axle.

Inspection

7   Working carefully, remove all traces of brake dust from the drum, but *avoid inhaling the dust, as it is injurious to health.*
8   Scrub clean the outside of the drum, and check it for obvious signs of wear or damage such as cracks around the roadwheel bolt holes; renew the drum if necessary.
9   Examine carefully the inside of the drum. Light scoring of the friction surface is normal, but if heavy scoring is found, the drum must be renewed. It is usual to find a lip on the drum's inboard edge which consists of a mixture of rust and brake dust; this should be scraped away to leave a smooth surface which can be polished with fine (120

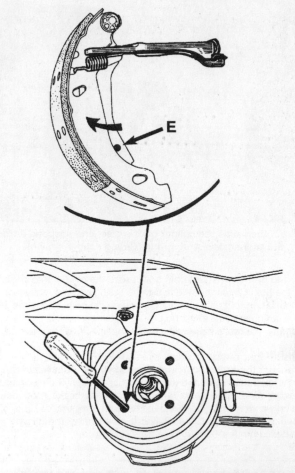

12.6a Using a screwdriver inserted through the brake drum to release the handbrake operating lever

E   Handbrake operating lever stop-peg location

to 150 grade) emery paper. If the lip is due to the friction surface being recessed by wear, then the drum must be refinished (within the specified limits) or renewed.
10   If the drum is thought to be excessively worn or oval, its internal diameter must be measured at several points using an internal micrometer. Take measurements in pairs, the second at right-angles the first, and compare the two to check for signs of ovality. Minor ovality can be corrected by machining; otherwise, renew the drum.

12.6b Release the handbrake operating lever as described in the text

12.12 Check that the handbrake lever stop-peg is correctly positioned against the trailing shoe edge

13.6 Removing a shoe retainer spring cup

13.7 On Bendix rear brakes, ease the shoes out of the lower pivot point and disconnect the lower return spring

Refitting

11   If a new brake drum is to be installed, use a suitable solvent to remove any preservative coating that may have been applied to its interior.

12   Ensure that the handbrake lever stop-peg is correctly repositioned against the edge of the brake shoe web (see illustration). Apply a smear of gear oil to the stub axle, and slide on the spacer and brake drum, being careful not to get oil onto the brake shoes or the friction surface of the drum. Fit the thrustwasher and a new hub nut; tighten the nut to the specified torque. Tap the hub cap into place in the centre of the brake drum.

13   Depress the footbrake several times to operate the self-adjusting mechanism.

14   Repeat the above procedure on the remaining rear brake assembly (if necessary), then adjust the handbrake as described in Chapter 1.

15   On completion, refit the roadwheel(s), lower the vehicle to the ground and tighten the wheel bolts to the specified torque.

13   Rear brake shoes - inspection and renewal

Warning: *Brake shoes must be renewed on both rear wheels at the same time - never renew the shoes on only one wheel, as uneven braking may result. Also, the dust created by wear of the shoes may contain asbestos, which is a health hazard. Never blow it out with compressed air, and don't inhale any of it. An approved filtering mask should be worn when working on the brakes. DO NOT use petroleum-* *based solvents to clean brake parts - use brake cleaner or methylated spirit only.*

Inspection

1   Remove the brake drum as described in Section 12.

2   Working carefully, remove all traces of brake dust from the brake drum, backplate and shoes.

3   Measure the thickness of each brake shoe (friction material and shoe) at several points; if either shoe is worn at any point to the specified minimum thickness or less, all four shoes must be renewed as a set. Also, the shoes should be renewed if any are fouled with oil or grease; there is no satisfactory way of degreasing friction material once contaminated.

4   If any of the brake shoes are worn unevenly, or fouled with oil or grease, trace and rectify the cause before reassembly.

Renewal

5   The procedure now varies according to which make of brake is fitted.

Bendix brake shoes

6   Using a pair of pliers, remove the shoe retainer spring cups by depressing and turning them through 90° (see illustration). With the cups removed, lift off the springs and withdraw the retainer pins.

7   Ease the shoes out one at a time from the lower pivot point, to release the tension of the return spring, then disconnect the lower return spring from both shoes (see illustration).

9

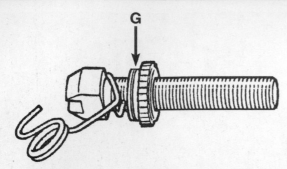

13.11 Bendix rear brake left-hand adjuster strut bolt can be identified by groove (G) on adjuster wheel collar

13.12 Correct fitted position of Bendix adjuster strut spring components

8   Ease the upper end of both shoes out from their wheel cylinder locations, taking care not to damage the wheel cylinder seals, and disconnect the handbrake cable from the trailing shoe. The brake shoe and adjuster strut assembly can then be manoeuvred out of position and away from the backplate. Do not depress the brake pedal until the brakes are reassembled; wrap a strong elastic band around the wheel cylinder pistons to retain them.

9   With the shoe and adjuster strut assembly on the bench, make a note of the correct fitted positions of the springs and adjuster strut, to use as a guide on reassembly. Release the handbrake lever stop-peg (if not already done), then detach the adjuster strut bolt retaining spring from the leading shoe. Disconnect the upper return spring, then detach the leading shoe and return spring from the trailing shoe and strut assembly. Unhook the spring securing the adjuster strut to the trailing shoe, and separate the two.

10   If genuine Renault brake shoes are being installed, it will be necessary to remove the handbrake lever from the original trailing shoe and fit it to the new shoe. Secure the lever in position with the new retaining clip which is supplied with the brake shoes. All return springs should be renewed, regardless of their apparent condition; spring kits are also available from Renault dealers.

11   Withdraw the adjuster bolt from the strut, and carefully examine the assembly for signs of wear or damage, paying particular attention to the threads of the adjuster bolt and the knurled adjuster wheel, and renew if necessary. Note that left-hand and right-hand struts are not interchangeable - they are marked "G" (gauche/left) and "D" (droit/right) respectively. Also note that the strut adjuster bolts are not interchangeable; the left-hand strut bolt has a left-hand thread, and the right-hand bolt a right-hand thread. The left-hand bolt can be identified by the groove on its adjuster wheel collar **(see illustration)**. The right-hand bolt does not have a groove on the adjuster wheel collar, but the bolt itself is painted.

12   Ensure the components on the end of the strut are correctly positioned **(see illustration)**, then apply a little high melting-point grease to the threads of the adjuster bolt. Screw the adjuster wheel onto the bolt until only a small gap exists between the wheel and the head of the bolt, then install the bolt in the strut.

13   Fit the adjuster strut retaining spring to the trailing shoe, ensuring that the shorter hook of the spring is engaged with the shoe. Attach the adjuster strut to the spring end, then ease the strut into position in its slot in the trailing shoe.

14   Engage the upper return spring with the trailing shoe. Hook the leading shoe onto the other end of the spring, and lever the leading shoe down until the adjuster bolt head is correctly located in its groove. Once the bolt is correctly located, hook its retaining spring into the slot on the leading shoe.

15   Remove the elastic band fitted to the wheel cylinder. Peel back the rubber protective caps, and check the wheel cylinder for fluid leaks or other damage. Also check that both cylinder pistons are free to move easily. Refer to Section 14, if necessary, for information on wheel cylinder renewal.

16   Prior to installation, clean the backplate and apply a thin smear of high-temperature brake grease or anti-seize compound to all those surfaces of the backplate which bear on the shoes, particularly the

wheel cylinder pistons and lower pivot point **(see illustration)**. Do not use too much, and don't allow the lubricant to foul the friction material.

17   Ensure that the handbrake lever stop-peg is correctly located against the edge of the trailing shoe.

18   Manoeuvre the shoe and strut assembly into position on the vehicle. Engage the upper ends of both shoes with the wheel cylinder pistons. Attach the handbrake cable to the trailing shoe lever. Fit the lower return spring to both shoes, and ease the shoes into position on the lower pivot point.

19   Centralise the shoes relative to the backplate by tapping them. Refit the shoe retainer pins and springs, and secure them in position with the spring cups **(see illustration)**.

20   Using a screwdriver, turn the strut adjuster wheel until the diameter of the shoes is between 179.2 and 179.5 mm. This should allow the brake drum to just pass over the shoes.

21   Slide the drum into position over the linings, but do not refit the hub nut yet.

22   Repeat the above procedure on the remaining rear brake.

23   Once both sets of rear shoes have been renewed, adjust the lining-to-drum clearance by repeatedly depressing the brake pedal. Whilst depressing the pedal, have an assistant listen to the rear drums, to check that the adjuster strut is functioning correctly; if this is so, a clicking sound will be emitted by the strut as the pedal is depressed.

24   Remove both the rear drums, and check that the handbrake lever stop-pegs are still correctly located against the edges of the trailing shoes, and that each lever operates smoothly. If all is well, with the aid of an assistant, adjust the handbrake cable so that the handbrake lever on each rear brake assembly starts to move as the handbrake is moved between the first and second notch (click) of its ratchet mechanism, ie so that the stop-pegs are still in contact with the shoes when the handbrake is on the first notch of the ratchet, but no longer contact the shoes when the handbrake is on the second notch. Once the handbrake adjustment is correct, hold the adjuster nut and securely tighten the locknut. Where necessary, refit the exhaust system heat shield to the vehicle underbody.

25   Refit the brake drums as described in Section 12.

26   On completion, check the hydraulic fluid level as described in Chapter 1.

Girling brake shoes

27   Make a note of the correct fitted positions of the springs and adjuster strut, to use as a guide on reassembly.

28   Carefully unhook both the upper and lower return springs, and remove them from the brake shoes.

29   Using a pair of pliers, remove the leading shoe retainer spring cup by depressing it and turning through 90°. With the cup removed, lift off the spring, then withdraw the retainer pin and remove the shoe from the backplate. Unhook the adjusting lever spring, and remove it from the leading shoe.

13.16 Apply a little high-melting point grease to shoe contact points on the backplate

13.38 On Girling rear brakes, adjuster strut fork cut-out (A) must engage with leading shoe adjusting lever on refitting

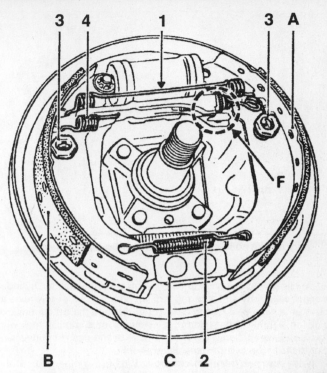

13.19 Correct fitted positions of Bendix rear brake components

A	Leading shoe	2	Lower return spring
B	Trailing shoe	3	Retaining pin, spring and
C	Lower pivot point		spring cup
F	Adjuster strut mechanism	4	Adjuster strut to trailing
1	Upper return spring		shoe spring

30   Detach the adjuster strut and remove it from the trailing shoe.

31   Remove the trailing shoe retainer spring cup, spring and pin as described above, then detach the handbrake cable and remove the shoe from the vehicle. Do not depress the brake pedal until the brakes are reassembled; wrap a strong elastic band around the wheel cylinder pistons to retain them.

32   If genuine Renault brake shoes are being installed, it will be necessary to remove the adjusting lever from the original leading shoe and install it on the new shoe. All return springs should be renewed, regardless of their apparent condition; spring kits are also available from Renault dealers.

33   Withdraw the forked end from the adjuster strut. Carefully examine the assembly for signs of wear or damage, paying particular attention to the threads and the knurled adjuster wheel, and renew if necessary. Note that left-hand and right-hand struts are not interchangeable; the left-hand fork has a right-hand thread, and the right-hand fork a left-hand thread. The forks can also be identified by their colour: the left-hand fork is silver, and the right-hand fork is gold.

34   Remove the elastic band fitted to the wheel cylinder. Peel back the rubber protective caps, and check the wheel cylinder for fluid leaks or other damage. Check that both cylinder pistons are free to move easily. Refer to Section 14, if necessary, for information on wheel cylinder renewal.

35   Prior to installation, clean the backplate and apply a thin smear of high-temperature brake grease or anti-seize compound to all those surfaces of the backplate which bear on the shoes, particularly the wheel cylinder pistons and lower pivot point. Do not allow the lubricant to foul the friction material.

36   Ensure that the handbrake lever stop-peg is correctly located against the edge of the trailing shoe.

37   Locate the upper end of the trailing shoe in the wheel cylinder piston, then refit the retainer pin and spring, and secure it in position with the spring cup. Connect the handbrake cable to the lever.

38   Screw in the adjuster wheel until the minimum strut length is obtained, then hook the strut into position on the trailing shoe. Rotate the adjuster strut forked end so that the cut-out of the fork will engage with the leading shoe adjusting lever **(see illustration)**.

39   Fit the spring to the leading shoe adjusting lever, so that the shorter hook of the spring engages with the lever.

40   Slide the leading shoe assembly into position, ensuring that it is correctly engaged with the adjuster strut fork, and that the fork cut-out is engaged with the adjusting lever. Engage the upper end of the shoe in the wheel cylinder piston, then secure the shoe in position with the retainer pin, spring and spring cup.

41   Install the upper and lower return springs, then tap the shoes to centralise them on the backplate.

42   Using a screwdriver, turn the strut adjuster wheel until the diameter of the shoes is between 178.7 and 179.2 mm. This should just allow the brake drum to pass over the shoes.

43   Slide the drum into position over the linings, but do not refit the hub nut yet.

44   Repeat the above procedure on the remaining rear brake.

45   Carry out the procedures described above in paragraphs 23 to 26.

All brake shoes

46   If new shoes have been fitted, full braking efficiency will not be obtained until the linings have bedded-in. Be prepared for longer stopping distances, and avoid harsh braking as far as possible for the first hundred miles or so after fitting new shoes.

14   Rear wheel cylinder - removal and refitting

Note: *Before starting work, refer to the warnings at the beginning of Section 6 concerning the dangers of hydraulic fluid, and at the beginning of Section 13 concerning the dangers of asbestos dust.*

Removal

1   Remove the brake drum as described in Section 12.

2   Using pliers, carefully unhook the brake shoe upper return spring and remove it from the brake shoes. Pull the upper ends of the shoes away from the wheel cylinder to disengage them from the pistons.

9

14.3 Brake hose clamp fitted to rear brake flexible hose

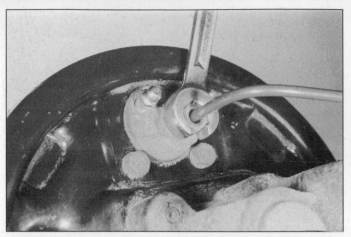

14.4 Unscrewing the union nut from the rear of the wheel cylinder

3   Minimise fluid loss, either by removing the master cylinder reservoir cap and then tightening it down onto a piece of polythene to obtain an airtight seal (taking care not to damage the sender unit), or by using a brake hose clamp, a G-clamp or a similar tool with protected jaws to clamp the flexible hose at the nearest convenient point to the wheel cylinder **(see illustration)**.

4   Wipe away all traces of dirt around the brake pipe union at the rear of the wheel cylinder, and unscrew the union nut **(see illustration)**. Carefully ease the pipe out of the wheel cylinder, and plug or tape over its end to prevent dirt entry. Wipe off any spilt fluid immediately.

5   Unscrew the two wheel cylinder retaining bolts from the rear of the backplate. Remove the cylinder, taking care not to allow hydraulic fluid to contaminate the brake shoe linings.

6   It is not possible to overhaul the cylinder, since no components are available separately. If faulty, the complete wheel cylinder assembly must be renewed.

Refitting

7   Ensure the backplate and wheel cylinder mating surfaces are clean, then spread the brake shoes and manoeuvre the wheel cylinder into position.

8   Engage the brake pipe, and screw in the union nut two or three turns to ensure that the thread has started.

9   Insert the two wheel cylinder retaining bolts, and tighten them securely. Now fully tighten the brake pipe union nut.

10   Remove the clamp from the brake hose, or the polythene from the master cylinder reservoir (as applicable).

11   Ensure that the brake shoes are correctly located in the cylinder pistons. Carefully refit the brake shoe upper return spring, using a screwdriver to stretch the spring into position.

12   Refit the brake drum as described in Section 12.

13   Bleed the brake hydraulic system as described in Section 6. Providing suitable precautions were taken to minimise loss of fluid, it should only be necessary to bleed the relevant rear brake.

15   Handbrake lever - removal and refitting

Removal

1   Chock the front wheels, engage reverse gear and release the handbrake. Jack up the rear of the vehicle and support it on axle stands.

2   Working from underneath the vehicle, undo the nuts securing the exhaust system heat shield to the vehicle underbody. Manoeuvre the heat shield out from under the vehicle.

3   Unscrew the handbrake cable adjuster locknut and the adjuster nut from the end of the handbrake lever linkage rod. Disengage the cable equalizer plate from the end of the linkage rod, then free the rod from its support guide.

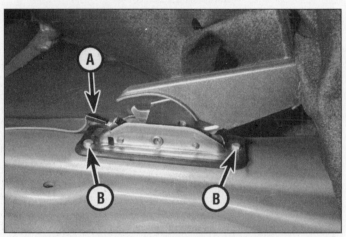

15.5 Handbrake lever warning switch wire (A) and mounting bolts (B) (carpet lifted)

4   Working from inside the vehicle, prise off the trim covers and unbolt the seat belt stalk anchorages from both front seats. Make a slit in the carpet, just to the rear of the lever assembly, to provide access to the lever mountings. Alternatively, the seats can be removed and the carpet lifted to gain access to the lever (see Chapter 11).

5   Disconnect the handbrake warning light switch wires from the rear of the lever **(see illustration)**.

6   Unscrew the bolts securing the lever to the floor, and remove the assembly from inside the vehicle.

Refitting

7   Refitting is a reversal of removal. Adjust the handbrake as described in Chapter 1.

16   Handbrake cables - removal and refitting

Removal

1   The handbrake cable consists of two sections, a right- and left-hand section, which are linked to the lever assembly by an equalizer plate. Each section can be removed individually as follows.

2   Chock the front wheels, engage reverse gear and release the handbrake. Jack up the rear of the vehicle and support it on axle stands.

3   Working from underneath the vehicle, undo the nut(s) securing the exhaust system heat shield to the vehicle underbody. Lower the rear of the heat shield to gain access to the handbrake cable adjuster nuts.

4   Slacken the cable locknut and adjuster nut until there is sufficient

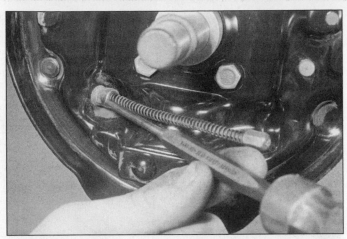

16.5 Drive the handbrake outer cable from the brake backplate

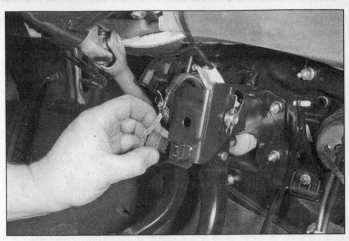

17.2a Disconnect the wiring connector . . .

17.2b . . . and unscrew the stop-light switch (facia panel removed for clarity)

18.2 Unscrew the vacuum pipe union nut (later models)

slack in the inner cable to allow it to be disconnected from the equalizer plate.

5   Remove the rear brake shoes from the appropriate side as described in Section 13. Using a hammer and pin punch, carefully tap the outer cable from the brake backplate **(see illustration)**.

6   Working along the length of the cable, remove any retaining bolts and screws, and free the cable from the retaining clips and ties. Remove the cable from under the vehicle.

Refitting

7   Refitting is a reversal of removal. Adjust the handbrake as described in Chapter 1. Note that the cable is adjusted before the brake drum is refitted.

17 Stop-light switch - removal, refitting and adjustment

Removal

1   The stop-light switch is located on the pedal bracket beneath the facia.

2   To remove the switch, reach up behind the facia, disconnect the wiring connector and unscrew the switch from the bracket **(see illustrations)**.

Refitting and adjustment

3   Screw the switch back into position in the mounting bracket.

4   Connect a continuity tester (ohmmeter or self-powered test light)

across the switch terminals. Screw the switch in until an open-circuit is present between the switch terminals (infinite resistance, or light goes out). Gently depress the pedal and check that continuity exists between the switch terminals (zero resistance, or light comes on) after the pedal has travelled approximately 5 mm. If necessary, reposition the switch until it operates as specified.

5   In the absence of a continuity tester, the same adjustment can be made by reconnecting the switch and having an assistant observe the stop-lights (ignition on).

6   Once the stop-light switch is correctly adjusted, remake the original wiring connections, and recheck the operation of the stop-lights.

18 Vacuum pump - removal and refitting

Note: *There are two types of vacuum pump fitted - the early type is in two sections, the pump itself is sealed to an adapter bracket by means of an O-ring and the bracket is sealed to the end of the cylinder head by means of a gasket - the later type has only one section which is sealed to the cylinder head by means of a gasket. A new gasket and/or O-ring will be required on refitting.*

Removal

1   The vacuum pump is driven directly from the camshaft at the flywheel end of the engine.

2   Unscrew the union nut (where applicable), and disconnect the vacuum pipe from the pump **(see illustration)**.

9

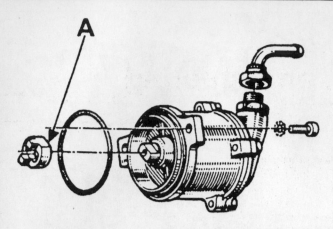

18.3 Vacuum pump and adapter bracket (early models)

A   Drive dog

18.4 Withdrawing the brake vacuum pump

3   If it is required to remove the pump only on early models, unscrew the two mounting bolts and separate the pump from the adapter bracket **(see illustration)**. Recover the O-ring. Also recover the drive dog from the end of the camshaft if necessary. **Note:** *Renault recommend that the drive dog is renewed whenever the vacuum pump is renewed.*

4   Unscrew the two upper mounting nuts and the two lower mounting bolts, and withdraw the adapter bracket (early models) or pump (later models) from the studs on the cylinder head **(see illustration)**. Note the location of any brackets secured by the nuts and bolts. If the pump is stuck, tap it gently with a soft-faced mallet. Recover the gasket.

Refitting

5   Refitting is a reversal of removal, but ensure that the drive lugs engage correctly with the slots in the camshaft, and use a new O-ring and/or gasket **(see illustration)**.

19   Vacuum pump - testing and overhaul

Testing

1   The operation of the braking system vacuum pump can be checked using a vacuum gauge.

2   Disconnect the vacuum pipe from the pump and connect the gauge to the pump union using a suitable length of hose.

3   Start the engine and allow it to idle until it reaches normal operating temperature.

4   When warm, accelerate the engine to 4000 rpm, and note the reading on the vacuum gauge. Do not allow the engine to run at this speed for more than a few seconds. The minimum vacuum obtained

18.5 Ensure that the pump drive lugs engage with the slots (arrowed) in the camshaft

within 3 seconds should be approximately 525 mm Hg (700 mbar).

5   If the vacuum registered is significantly less than specified, it is likely that the pump is faulty. However, seek the advice of a Renault dealer before condemning the pump.

Overhaul

6   Overhaul of the pump is not possible since no components are available separately for it. If faulty the complete pump unit must be renewed.

Chapter 10 Suspension and steering

Contents

Specifications

Front suspension

Type	Independent by MacPherson struts, with inclined coil springs and integral shock absorbers. Anti-roll bar on all models
Hub bearing endfloat	0 to 0.05 mm
Front underbody height (H1 minus H2)	87.0 ± 7.5 mm

Rear suspension

Type	Trailing arms, with transverse torsion bars (enclosed type) and telescopic shock absorbers, rear anti-roll bar on all models
Hub bearing endfloat	0 to 0.03 mm
Rear underbody height checking dimension (H4 minus H5 - see text)	4.0 ± 7.5 mm

Steering

Type	Rack-and-pinion, power-assisted on some models

Wheel alignment and steering angles

Front wheel camber angle at underbody height (H1 minus H2) stated:

75 mm	-0° 10' ± 30'
85 mm	-0° 20' ± 30'
95 mm	-0° 30' ± 30'
115 mm	-0° 30' ± 30'
165 mm	-0° 10' ± 30'

Castor angle at underbody height (H5 minus H2) stated:

41 mm	2° 55' ± 30'
60 mm	2° 25' ± 30'
79 mm	1° 55' ± 30'
98 mm	1° 25' ± 30'
117 mm	0° 55' ± 30'

Steering axis inclination/kingpin inclination at underbody height (H1 minus H2) stated:

75 mm	9° 50' ± 30'
85 mm	10° 00' ± 30'
95 mm	10° 20' ± 30'
115 mm	10° 40' ± 30'
165 mm	11° 10' ± 30'
Front wheel toe setting (vehicle unladen)	0° 10' ± 10' (1 ± 1 mm) toe-out
Rear wheel camber setting (vehicle unladen)	-0° 50' ± 30'
Rear wheel toe setting (vehicle unladen)	0° 15' ± 10' (1.5 ± 1 mm) toe-in

Roadwheels

Type	Pressed-steel or aluminium alloy (depending on model)
Size	5B x 13
Maximum run-out at rim	1.2 mm
Maximum eccentricity on tyre bead locating surface...........................	0.8 mm

Tyres

Tyre size..	155/70 R 13S or 165/65 R 13T (depending on model)
Pressures - (tyres cold):	
Front...	2.4 bars (35 lbf/in2)
Rear...	2.4 bars (35 lbf/in2)

Note: *Pressures apply only to original equipment tyres, and may vary if any other make or type is fitted; check with the tyre manufacturer or supplier for correct pressures if necessary.*

Torque wrench settings

	Nm	lbf ft
Front suspension		
Strut-to-swivel hub bolts	110	81
Strut upper mounting nut	60	44
Anti-roll bar mounting clamp bolts	35	26
Anti-roll bar-to-lower arm bolt..	20	15
Lower arm balljoint clamp bolt	55	41
Lower arm balljoint retaining nuts	75	55
Lower arm pivot bolts..	110	81
Rear suspension		
Shock absorber upper mounting bolt...............................	80	59
Shock absorber lower mounting bolt	60	44
Anti-roll bar mounting bolts	50	37
Bearing bracket mounting bolts	85	63
Hub nut*...	160	118

* Renew this nut every time

	Nm	lbf ft
Steering		
Track rod end balljoint-to-swivel hub retaining nut	35	26
Track rod end balljoint locknut	35	26
Track rod to steering rack	50	37
Steering gear mounting bolts	50	37
Steering wheel nut/bolt..	40	30
Intermediate shaft universal joint clamp bolt..	30	22
Roadwheels		
Wheel bolts	90	66

---

1   General information

The independent front suspension is of the MacPherson strut type, incorporating coil springs and integral telescopic shock absorbers **(see illustration)**. The MacPherson struts are located by transverse lower suspension arms, which utilize rubber inner mounting bushes and incorporate a balljoint at the outer ends. The front swivel hubs, which carry the wheel bearings, brake calipers and the hub/disc assemblies, are bolted to the MacPherson struts and connected to the lower arms via the balljoints. A front anti-roll bar is fitted to all models. The anti-roll bar is rubber-mounted onto the subframe, and connects both the lower suspension arms.

The rear suspension incorporates an enclosed-bar type rear axle, which consists of two torsion bars within a tubular crossmember which connects both the rear trailing arms **(see illustration)**. An anti-roll bar is situated just to the rear of the crossmember, and is also connected to both trailing arms.

The steering column is connected by a universal joint to an intermediate shaft, which has a second universal joint at its lower end. The lower universal joint is attached to the steering gear pinion by means of a clamp bolt.

The steering gear is mounted onto the front subframe. It is connected by two track rods and balljoints to steering arms projecting rearwards from the swivel hubs. The track rod ends are threaded to enable wheel alignment adjustment.

Power-assisted steering is available on all models. An electrically-powered pump is used to power the steering hydraulic system; this is due to lack of space in the engine compartment to house a belt-driven pump.

---

2   Front swivel hub assembly - removal and refitting

Removal

1   Chock the rear wheels, firmly apply the handbrake, then jack up the front of the vehicle and support it on axle stands. Remove the appropriate front roadwheel.

2   Refit at least two roadwheel bolts to the front hub, and tighten them securely. Remove the driveshaft nut (see Chapter 8, Section 2, for full details). Discard the driveshaft nut; a new one should be used on refitting.

3   If the hub bearings are to be disturbed, remove the brake disc as described in Chapter 9. If not, unscrew the two bolts securing the brake caliper assembly to the swivel hub, and slide the caliper assembly off the disc. Using a piece of wire or string, tie the caliper to the front suspension coil spring, to avoid straining the brake hose.

4   Remove the nut securing the track rod end balljoint to the swivel hub. Release the balljoint tapered shank using a universal balljoint separator.

5   Remove the nut and clamp bolt securing the lower suspension arm

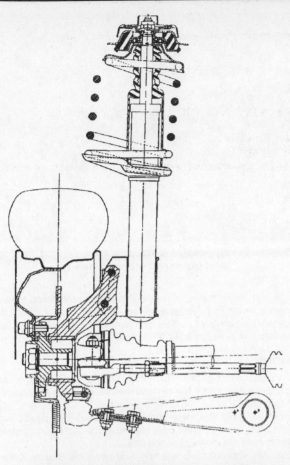

1.1 Cross-section of the front suspension

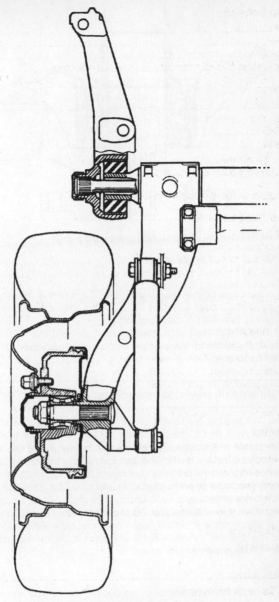

1.2 Cross-section of the rear suspension

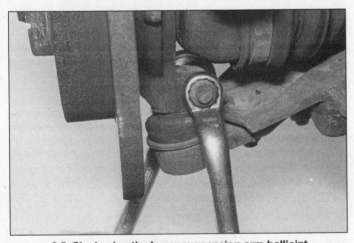

**2.5 Slackening the lower suspension arm balljoint
clamp bolt and nut**

to the swivel hub **(see illustration)**. Carefully lever the balljoint out of the swivel hub, taking care not to damage the balljoint or driveshaft gaiters. Note the plastic protector plate which is fitted to the balljoint shank.

6   Remove the two nuts and washers from the bolts securing the swivel hub to the suspension strut, noting that the nuts are positioned on the rear side of the strut. Withdraw the bolts and support the swivel hub assembly.

7   Release the driveshaft joint from the hub, and remove the swivel hub assembly from the vehicle. Note that locking fluid is applied to the joint splines during assembly, so it is likely that they will be a tight fit in the hub. Use a hammer and soft metal drift to tap the joint out of the hub, or use a puller to draw the swivel hub assembly off the joint splines.

Refitting

8   Ensure that the driveshaft joint and hub splines are clean and dry, then apply a coat of locking fluid to the joint splines.

9   Engage the joint splines with the hub, and slide the hub fully onto the driveshaft. Insert the two swivel hub-to-suspension strut mounting bolts from the front side of the strut, then refit the washers and nuts to the rear of the bolts and tighten them to the specified torque.

10   Slide on the washer and fit the new driveshaft nut, tightening it by hand only at this stage.

11   Ensure that the plastic protector is still fitted to the lower arm balljoint, then locate the balljoint shank in the swivel hub. Refit the balljoint clamp bolt, and tighten its retaining nut to the specified torque.

12   Reconnect the track rod end balljoint to the swivel hub, and tighten its retaining nut to the specified torque.

13   Refit the brake disc (if removed), aligning the marks made on removal, and securely tighten its retaining screws. Slide the brake caliper assembly into position over the brake disc. Apply a few drops of locking fluid to the caliper bolt threads. Refit the bolts and tighten them to the specified torque (Chapter 9).

10

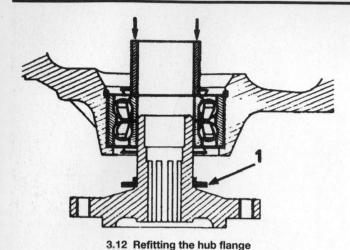

3.12 Refitting the hub flange

1 Thrustwasher

4.3 Slacken the suspension strut upper mounting nut, holding the strut piston rod with an Allen key

14   Insert and tighten two wheel bolts. Tighten the driveshaft nut to the specified torque (Chapter 8), using the method employed during removal to prevent the hub from rotating.

15   Check that the hub rotates freely, then refit the roadwheel and lower the vehicle to the ground. Tighten the roadwheel bolts to the specified torque.

3 Front hub bearings - checking, removal and refitting

Note: *The bearing is a sealed, pre-adjusted and pre-lubricated, double-row roller type, and is intended to last the car's entire service life without maintenance or attention. Do not attempt to remove the bearing unless absolutely necessary, as it will be damaged during the removal operation. Never overtighten the driveshaft nut in an attempt to "adjust" the bearing. A press will be required to dismantle and rebuild the assembly; if such a tool is not available, a large bench vice and spacers (such as large sockets) will serve as an adequate substitute. The bearing's inner races are an interference fit on the hub; if the inner race remains on the hub when it is pressed out of the hub carrier, a suitable knife-edged bearing puller will be required to remove it.*

Checking

1   Wear in the front hub bearings can be checked by measuring the amount of side play present. To do this, a dial gauge should be fixed so that its probe is in contact with the disc face of the hub. The play should be between 0 and 0.05 mm. If it is greater than this, the bearings are worn excessively, and should be renewed.

Removal

2   Remove the swivel hub assembly as described in Section 2, then undo the brake disc shield retaining screws and remove the shield from the hub.

3   Support the swivel hub securely on blocks or in a vice. Using a tubular spacer which bears only on the inner end of the hub flange, press the hub flange out of the bearing. If the bearing outboard inner race remains on the hub, remove it using a suitable bearing puller (see note above), then slide the thrustwasher off the hub flange, noting which way round it is fitted.

4   Extract the bearing retaining circlip from the inner end of the swivel hub assembly.

5   Where necessary, refit the inner race in position over the ball cage, and securely support the inner face of the swivel hub. Using a tubular spacer which bears only on the inner race, press the complete bearing assembly out of the swivel hub.

6   Thoroughly clean the hub and swivel hub, removing all traces of dirt and grease. Polish away any burrs or raised edges which might hinder reassembly. Check for cracks or any other signs of wear or

damage, and renew the components if necessary. As noted above, the bearing and its circlip must be renewed whenever they are disturbed. A replacement bearing kit, which consists of the bearing, circlip and thrustwasher, is available from Renault dealers.

Refitting

7   On reassembly, check (if possible) that the new bearing is packed with grease. Apply a light film of oil to the bearing outer race and to the hub flange shaft.

8   Before fitting the new bearing, remove the plastic covers protecting the seals at each end, but leave the inner plastic sleeve in position to hold the inner races together.

9   Securely support the swivel hub, and locate the bearing in the hub. Press the bearing into position, ensuring that it enters the hub squarely, using a suitable tubular spacer which bears only on the outer race.

10   Once the bearing is correctly seated, secure it with the new circlip and remove the plastic sleeve. Apply a smear of grease to the oil seal lips.

11   Slide the thrustwasher onto the hub flange, ensuring that its flat surface is facing the flange. Securely support the outer face of the hub flange.

12   Locate the bearing inner race over the end of the hub flange. Press the bearing onto the hub, using a tubular spacer which bears only on the inner race, until it seats against the thrustwasher **(see illustration)**. Check that the hub flange rotates freely. Wipe off any excess oil or grease.

13   Refit the brake disc shield to the swivel hub, and tighten its retaining screws.

14   Refit the swivel hub assembly as described in Section 2.

4 Front strut - removal and refitting

Removal

1   Chock the rear wheels, firmly apply the handbrake, then jack up the front of the vehicle and support it on axle stands. Remove the appropriate roadwheel.

2   Remove the two nuts and washers from the bolts securing the swivel hub to the suspension strut, noting that the nuts are positioned on the rear side of the strut. Withdraw the bolts, and support the swivel hub assembly.

3   From within the engine compartment, remove the strut cover (where fitted). Slacken the suspension strut upper mounting nut, holding the strut piston rod with an Allen key **(see illustration)**. Remove the nut.

4   Release the strut from the swivel hub, and withdraw it from under the wheel arch, taking care to prevent damage to the driveshaft gaiter **(see illustration)**.

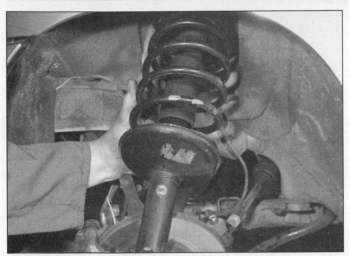

4.4 Removing the front suspension strut

4.6 Tightening a swivel hub-to-strut nut and bolt. Note that the bolt heads face forwards

Refitting

5   Manoeuvre the strut assembly into position, taking care not damage the driveshaft gaiter.

6   Insert the two swivel hub-to-suspension strut mounting bolts from the front side of the strut. Refit the washers and nuts to the rear of the bolts, and tighten them to the specified torque **(see illustration)**.

7   Refit the upper mounting nut **(see illustration)** and tighten it to the specified torque. When applicable, refit the cover.

8   Refit the roadwheel, lower the vehicle to the ground and tighten the roadwheel bolts to the specified torque.

5   Front strut - dismantling, inspection and reassembly

Warning: *Before attempting to dismantle the front suspension strut, a suitable tool to hold the coil spring in compression must be obtained. Adjustable coil spring compressors are readily available, and are recommended for this operation. Any attempt to dismantle the strut without such a tool is likely to result in damage or personal injury.*

Dismantling

1   With the strut removed from the vehicle as described in Section 4, clean away all external dirt. Mount the strut upright in a vice.

2   Remove the upper mounting rubber. Fit the spring compressor, and compress the coil spring until all tension is relieved from the upper mounting plate **(see illustration)**.

4.7 Refit the upper mounting nut

3   Carefully prise the retaining clip out of its groove in the top of the strut piston, then slide off the retaining collar, noting which way around it is fitted **(see illustrations)**. Discard the retaining clip; this must be renewed whenever it is disturbed.

4   Lift off the upper mounting plate, the bearing and the upper spring seat. Remove the coil spring, and slide the rubber dust cover off the strut piston.

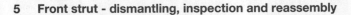

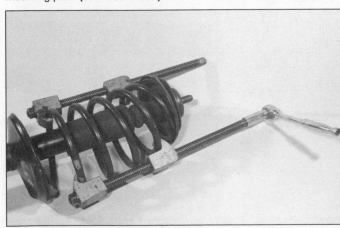

5.2 Using spring compressors, compress the suspension strut coil spring . . .

5.3a . . . then prise out the retaining clip . . .

10

Inspection

5   With the strut assembly now completely dismantled, examine all the components for wear, damage or deformation, and check the bearing for smoothness of operation. Renew any of the components as necessary.

6   Examine the strut for signs of fluid leakage. Check the strut piston for signs of pitting along its entire length, and check the strut body for signs of damage. Test the operation of the strut, while holding it in an upright position, by moving the piston through a full stroke and then through short strokes of 50 to 100 mm. In both cases, the resistance felt should be smooth and continuous. If the resistance is jerky or uneven, or if there is any visible sign of wear or damage, renewal is necessary.

7   If any doubt exists about the condition of the coil spring, gradually release the spring compressor, and check the spring for distortion and signs of cracking. Since no minimum free length is specified by Renault, the only way to check the tension of the spring is to compare it to a new component. Renew the spring if it is damaged or distorted, or if there is any doubt as to its condition.

8   Inspect all other components for signs of damage or deterioration, and renew any that are suspect.

Reassembly

9   Ensure that all components are clean and dry. Slide the dust cover into position over the strut piston **(see illustration)**.

10   Refit the coil spring, followed by the upper spring seat. Ensure that both ends of the spring are correctly located in the spring seats **(see illustrations)**.

11   Fit the strut bearing, with its flat surface at the bottom, then refit the upper mounting plate **(see illustrations)**.

5.3b . . . and remove the retaining collar

12   Slide the retaining collar onto the strut piston, and secure it in position with the new retaining clip **(see illustration)**. Ensure that the clip is correctly seated in the strut piston groove. Slowly and carefully release the spring compressor, watching to make sure that both ends of the spring remain correctly located in the spring seats.

13   Fit the upper mounting rubber on the mounting plate **(see illustration)**.

14   Refit the strut to the vehicle as described in Section 4.

5.9 Refit the rubber dust cover to the strut piston

5.10a Coil spring lower end correctly located in spring seat

5.10b Fitting the upper spring seat

5.11a Fit the strut bearing with its flat surface at the bottom . . .

5.11b . . . then refit the upper mounting plate

5.12 Refit the retaining collar, and secure it in position with a new retaining clip

5.13 Remove the spring compressors, and refit the mounting rubber to the upper mounting plate

6.4 Removing a front anti-roll bar mounting bolt

6 Front anti-roll bar - removal and refitting

Removal

1   Chock the rear wheels, apply the handbrake, then jack up the front of the vehicle and support it on axle stands. Remove both front roadwheels.
2   Remove the exhaust downpipe as described in Chapter 4.
3   Disconnect the gearchange mechanism from the gearbox. Refer to Chapter 7.
4   Remove the nuts and bolts securing each end of the anti-roll bar to the lower suspension arms, noting the positions of the rubber mounting spacers **(see illustration)**.
5   Unbolt the anti-roll bar mounting clamps **(see illustration)**.
6   Manoeuvre the anti-roll bar out from underneath the vehicle, and remove the rubber mounting bushes.
7   Carefully examine the anti-roll bar components for signs of wear, damage or deterioration, paying particular attention to the mounting bushes. Renew worn components as necessary.

Refitting

8   Lubricate the rubber mounting bushes with a suitable grease (Elf Multi MOS2 or equivalent). Fit the bushes onto the anti-roll bar.
9   Manoeuvre the anti-roll bar into position underneath the vehicle. Position the bushes so that their splits are against the subframe, then refit the mounting clamps. Do not tighten the mounting clamp nuts or bolts fully yet.
10   Secure the ends of the anti-roll bar to the lower suspension arms, ensuring that the rubber mounting spacers are correctly positioned. Fit the nuts and bolts, but do not tighten them fully yet.
11   Reconnect the selector mechanism as described in Chapter 7.
12   Refit the exhaust downpipe as described in Chapter 4.
13   Refit the roadwheels, lower the vehicle to the ground and tighten the wheel bolts to the specified torque.
14   Tighten the anti-roll bar fastenings to the specified torque, starting with the mounting clamps.

7 Front lower arm - removal, overhaul and refitting

Removal

1   Chock the rear wheels, apply the handbrake, jack up the front of the vehicle and support it on axle stands. Remove the appropriate front roadwheel.
2   Disconnect the end of the anti-roll bar from the lower suspension arm, as described in the previous Section.
3   When applicable, remove the bolt securing the support bar to the front wing valance, and the nut securing it to the front pivot bolt. Remove the support bar from the vehicle **(see illustrations)**.
4   Remove the nut and clamp bolt securing the lower suspension

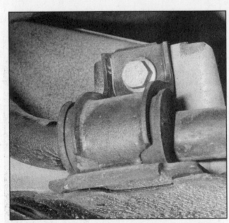

6.5 Front anti-roll bar mounting clamp

7.3a Where fitted, undo the support bar upper mounting bolt . . .

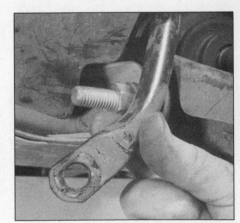

7.3b . . . and remove the bar from the suspension arm pivot bolt

10

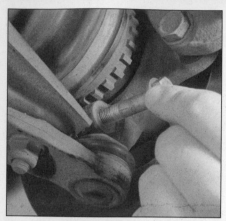

7.4a Remove the balljoint clamp bolt . . .

7.4b . . . then free the balljoint from the swivel hub, and remove the plastic protector plate

7.5 Undo the nuts and withdraw the lower suspension arm pivot bolts

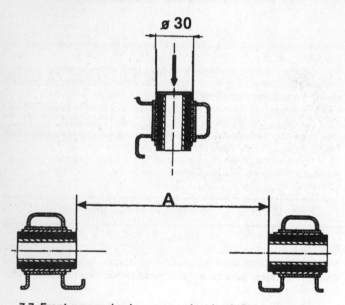

7.7 Front suspension lower arm pivot bush fitting dimension

A = 147 ± 0.5 mm

7.9 Tightening the balljoint clamp bolt

arm balljoint to the swivel hub. Carefully lever the balljoint out of the swivel hub, taking care not to damage the balljoint or driveshaft gaiters. Remove the plastic protector plate which is fitted to the balljoint shank **(see illustrations)**.

5   Remove the two pivot nuts and bolts, and remove the lower suspension arm from the vehicle **(see illustration)**.

Overhaul

6   Clean the lower arm and the area around the arm mountings, then check for cracks, distortion or any other signs of damage. On some models, a brake disc cooling shield is clipped to the arm; this should also be removed. Check that the lower arm balljoint moves freely, without any sign of roughness, and that the balljoint gaiter is free from cracks and splits. Examine the shank of the pivot bolts for signs of wear or scoring. Renew worn components as necessary.

7   Inspect the lower arm pivot bushes. If they are worn, cracked, split or perished, they must be renewed. To renew the bushes, support the lower arm, and press the first bush out using a tubular spacer, such as a socket, which bears only on the hard, outer edge of the bush. **Note:** *Remove only one bush at a time from the arm, to ensure that each new bush is correctly positioned on installation.* Thoroughly clean the lower arm bore, removing all traces of dirt and grease, and polish

away any burrs or raised edges which might hinder reassembly. Apply a smear of a suitable grease to the outer edge of the new bush. Press the bush into position until the distance "A" between the inner edges of the lower arm bushes is as shown **(see illustration)**. Wipe away surplus grease and repeat the procedure on the remaining bush.

Refitting

8   Offer up the lower suspension arm, and insert the two pivot bolts from the rear of the suspension arm. Refit the nuts, but tighten them by hand only at this stage.

9   Refit the plastic protector to the lower arm balljoint, then locate the balljoint shank in the swivel hub. Refit the balljoint clamp bolt, and tighten its retaining nut to the specified torque **(see illustration)**.

10   When applicable, refit the support bar on the front pivot bolt shank. Fit the retaining bolt and nut, tightening both by hand only at this stage.

11   Reconnect the end of the anti-roll bar to the lower suspension arm, ensuring that the rubber mounting spacers are correctly positioned. Do not fully tighten the fastenings yet.

12   Refit the roadwheel, lower the vehicle and tighten the roadwheel bolts to the specified torque.

13   With the vehicle standing on its wheels, rock the vehicle to settle the lower arm bushes in position. Tighten the lower arm pivot bolts and the anti-roll bar fixing to the specified torque. When the pivot bolts have been tightened, secure the support bar in position (if applicable) by securely tightening its retaining nut and bolt.

8.5 Front lower suspension arm balljoint retaining nuts

9.4 Extract the circlip . . .

8 Front lower arm balljoint - removal and refitting

Removal

1   Chock the rear wheels, apply the handbrake, jack up the front of the vehicle and support it on axle stands. Remove the appropriate front roadwheel.

2   Disconnect the end of the anti-roll bar from the lower suspension arm, as described in Section 6.

3   Slacken the nut securing the support bar (where fitted) to the lower arm front pivot bolt, then slacken both the lower suspension arm pivot bolts.

4   Remove the nut and clamp bolt securing the lower suspension arm to the swivel hub. Carefully lever the balljoint out of the swivel hub, taking care not to damage the balljoint or driveshaft gaiters. Remove the plastic protector plate which is fitted to the balljoint shank.

5   Remove the two nuts and bolts securing the balljoint to the lower suspension arm **(see illustration)**. Remove the balljoint.

6   Check that the balljoint moves freely, without any sign of roughness or free play. Examine the balljoint gaiter for signs of damage and deterioration such as cracks or splits. Renew the complete balljoint assembly if damaged; it is not possible to renew the balljoint gaiter separately. The balljoint renewal kit obtainable from Renault dealers contains the balljoint, the plastic protector plate and all fixings.

Refitting

7   Fit the balljoint to the suspension arm. Insert the bolts and washers, and tighten the retaining nuts to the specified torque.

8   Fit the plastic protector to the balljoint shank, then locate the shank in the swivel hub. Refit the balljoint clamp bolt, and tighten its retaining nut to the specified torque.

9   Reconnect the end of the anti-roll bar to the lower suspension arm, ensuring that the rubber mounting spacers are correctly positioned. Do not fully tighten the fastenings yet.

10   Refit the roadwheel, lower the vehicle and tighten the roadwheel bolts to the specified torque.

11   With the vehicle standing on its wheels, rock the vehicle to settle the lower arm bushes in position. Tighten the lower arm pivot bolts and the anti-roll bar fixing to the specified torque. When the pivot bolts have been tightened, secure the support bar in position (if applicable) by securely tightening its retaining nut and bolt.

9 Rear hub bearings - checking, removal and refitting

Note: *The bearing is a sealed, pre-adjusted and pre-lubricated, double-row tapered-roller type, and is intended to last the car's entire*

9.5 . . . then drive the bearing out of the hub using a tubular drift

service life without maintenance or attention. Never overtighten the hub nut in an attempt to "adjust" the bearings.

Checking

1   Chock the front wheels and engage reverse gear. Jack up the rear of the vehicle and support it on axle stands. Remove the appropriate rear roadwheel, and fully release the handbrake.

2   Wear in the rear hub bearings can be checked by measuring the amount of side play present. To do this, a dial test indicator should be fixed so that its probe is in contact with the hub outer face. The play should be between 0 and 0.03 mm. If it is greater than this, the bearings are worn excessively and should be renewed.

Removal

3   Remove the rear brake drum, as described in Chapter 9.

4   Using circlip pliers, extract the bearing retaining circlip from the centre of the brake drum **(see illustration)**.

5   Securely support the drum hub. Press or drive the bearing out of the hub, using a tubular drift of 49 mm diameter **(see illustration)**.

6   Thoroughly clean the hub, removing all traces of dirt and grease. Polish away any burrs or raised edges which might hinder reassembly. Check the hub for cracks or any other signs of damage, and renew if necessary. The bearing and its circlip must be renewed whenever they are disturbed. A replacement bearing kit is available from Renault dealers, consisting of the bearing, circlip, spacer, thrustwasher, hub nut and grease cap.

10

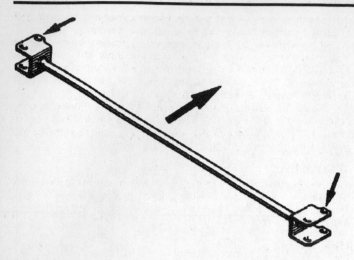

11.4 Cutaway ends of rear anti-roll bar brackets (small arrows) must face the front of the vehicle

Refitting

7   On reassembly, check (if possible) that the new bearing is packed with grease. Apply a light film of gear oil to the bearing outer race and stub axle.

8   Securely support the hub. Press the bearing into position, ensuring that it enters the hub squarely, using a tube (diameter 51 mm) which presses only on the bearing outer race.

9   Ensure that the bearing is correctly seated against the hub shoulder, and secure it in position with the new circlip. Ensure that the circlip is correctly seated in its groove.

10   Refit the brake drum as described in Chapter 9.

10   Rear shock absorber - removal, testing and refitting

Removal

1   Chock the front wheels and engage reverse gear. Jack up the rear of the vehicle and support it on axle stands. Remove the appropriate rear roadwheel.

2   Using a jack, raise the trailing arm slightly until the shock absorber is slightly compressed. Remove the lower mounting bolt.

3   Slacken and remove the upper mounting nut and bolt, and remove the shock absorber from the vehicle.

Testing

4   Mount the shock absorber in a vice, and test as described in Section 5 for the front suspension strut. Also check the rubber mounting bushes for damage and deterioration. Renew the complete shock absorber if any damage or wear is evident; the mounting bushes are not available separately. Inspect the mounting bolts for signs of wear or damage, and renew as necessary.

Refitting

5   Prior to refitting the shock absorber, mount it upright in the vice, and operate it fully through several strokes in order to prime it. (This is necessary even if a new unit is being fitted, as it may have been stored horizontally, and so need priming). Apply a smear of multi-purpose grease to the shock absorber mounting bolts.

6   Offer up the shock absorber, then install its upper mounting bolt and nut, tightening it by hand only at this stage.

7   Refit the lower shock absorber mounting bolt, again tightening it by hand only. Remove the jack from under the trailing arm.

8   Refit the roadwheel, lower the vehicle to the ground and tighten the roadwheel bolts to the specified torque.

9   Rock the vehicle to settle the shock absorber mounting bushes in position, then tighten both the mounting bolts to the specified torque.

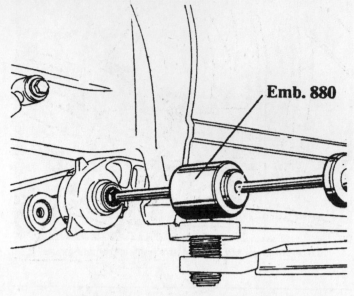

12.5 Using a slide hammer (Renault tool Emb.880 shown) to remove a torsion bar

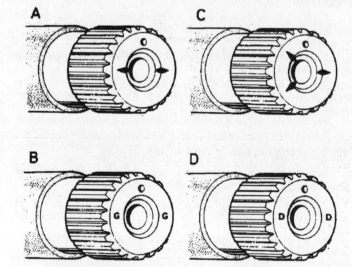

12.7 Rear suspension torsion bar identification markings

A & B - Left-hand   *C & D - Right-hand*

11   Rear anti-roll bar - removal and refitting

Removal

1   Chock the front wheels and engage reverse gear. Jack up the rear of the vehicle and support it on axle stands.

2   Remove the bolts securing the ends of the anti-roll bar to the rear suspension trailing arms, noting the fitted positions of the handbrake cable retaining clips. Recover the anti-roll bar retaining nut plates from the top of the trailing arms.

3   Withdraw the anti-roll bar from under the vehicle.

Refitting

4   Refit the anti-roll bar to the vehicle, noting that the cutaway ends of the anti-roll bar retaining bolt brackets must face towards the front of the vehicle **(see illustration)**.

5   Position the retaining nut plates on the top of the trailing arms. Refit the retaining bolts, ensuring that the handbrake cable retaining

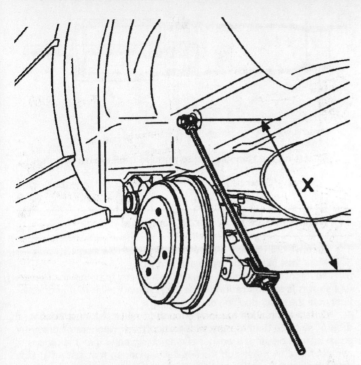

12.11 A tool made from a length of threaded bar can be fitted to the shock absorber mounting holes and used to set dimension 'X' - see text

clips are correctly positioned. Tighten the anti-roll bar retaining bolts to the specified torque.
6   Lower the vehicle to the ground.

12 Rear torsion bar - removal and refitting

Removal

1   Chock the front wheels and engage reverse gear. Jack up the rear of the vehicle and support it on axle stands. Remove the appropriate roadwheel.
2   Remove the rear shock absorber, as described in Section 10.
3   Prise off the cap from the trailing arm bearing bracket, to gain access to the torsion bar end.
4   Mark the position of the torsion bar in relation to the bearing bracket. With the trailing arm unsupported, measure the distance between the centres of the shock absorber upper and lower mounting bolt holes. Note the distance; if the original bar is to be refitted, this will be needed on refitting.
5   The torsion bar can now be withdrawn outwards, using a slide hammer such as Renault tool Emb.880 or a suitable alternative **(see illustration)**. It is possible to improvise by screwing a long bolt with a flat washer into the torsion bar, and placing the jaws of a spanner against the washer. Striking the spanner sharply with a hammer should free the torsion bar.
6   Once the splines of the torsion bar are free, the bar can be withdrawn completely from its location.
7   Note that the left-hand and right-hand bars are not interchangeable; they can be identified by the markings on their ends **(see illustration)**.

Refitting

8   Ensure that the bearing bracket and torsion bar splines are clean and dry. Lubricate the splines with molybdenum disulphide grease, and insert the bar into the bracket.
9   If the original bar is being refitted, position the trailing arm so that

the distance between the centres of the upper and lower shock absorber mounting bolt holes is as noted prior to removal.
10   If a new torsion bar is being fitted, the trailing arm must be raised until the distance between the centres of the upper and lower shock absorber mounting bolt holes is 400 mm. This measurement is known as dimension "X". With dimension "X" correctly set, all the torsional forces will be removed from the bar.
11   Raise the trailing arm to the required position using a jack. Alternatively, a tool similar to that shown **(see illustration)** can be fabricated from a length of threaded bar, and used to position the trailing arm.

Original bar

12   Rotate the torsion bar to align the marks made on removal, then engage the bar with the bearing bracket and bearing/centre link splines. Tap the bar fully into position using a hammer and a soft metal drift.

New bar

13   Rotate the torsion bar until the position is found where the bar can be freely engaged with the splines on the bearing bracket and bearing. Having found this, tap the bar fully home using a hammer and a soft metal drift.

Both types

14   Refit the torsion bar cap(s) to the bearing bracket.
15   Refit the rear shock absorber, as described in Section 10.
16   Check the rear underbody height, as described in Section 16.

13 Rear trailing arm - removal and refitting

Removal

1   Chock the front wheels and engage reverse gear. Jack up the rear of the vehicle and support it on axle stands. Remove the appropriate rear roadwheel.
2   Remove the rear anti-roll bar, as described in Section 11.
3   Remove the appropriate torsion bar, as described in Section 12.
4   Remove the brake shoes from the side in question, as described in Chapter 9.
5   Using a hammer and pin punch, tap the handbrake outer cable out of the backplate. Work back along the length of the cable, and release it from any clips or ties securing it to the trailing arm.
6   Minimise brake fluid loss by removing the master cylinder reservoir cap, and then tightening it down onto a piece of polythene to obtain an airtight seal (taking care not to damage the sender unit). Alternatively, use a brake hose clamp, a G-clamp or a similar tool with protected jaws, to clamp the flexible hose at the nearest convenient point to the wheel cylinder.
7   Wipe away all traces of dirt around the brake pipe union at the rear of the wheel cylinder, and unscrew the union nut. Carefully ease the pipe out of the wheel cylinder, and plug or tape over its end to prevent dirt entry. Wash off any spilt fluid immediately.
8   Support the weight of the trailing arm on a jack.
9   Lift the rear seat cushion to gain access to the trailing arm bearing bracket mounting bolt heads.
10   From underneath the vehicle, unscrew the trailing arm bearing bracket mounting nuts on the side to be removed. Tap the bolts through the bearing bracket with a suitable drift. Loosen the mounting nuts on the opposite bearing bracket.
11   Lower the jack until the trailing arm assembly is clear of the sill, then pull the trailing arm out of the opposite arm, and remove it from the vehicle.
12   Inspect the trailing arm bearings and tracks for signs of wear or damage. Renew them if necessary as described in Section 14. If a new trailing arm is being fitted, undo the four retaining bolts and remove the brake backplate. Fit the backplate to the new trailing arm, apply thread-locking compound to the retaining bolts, and tighten them securely.

10

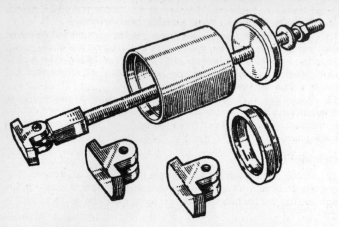

14.3 Renault tool for removing the rear suspension trailing arm bearings

Refitting

13   Ensure that the trailing arm bearings are sufficiently greased, then engage the removed trailing arm with the opposite arm. Temporarily position the anti-roll bar over its mounting bolt holes, ensuring that the cutaway ends of the retaining bolt brackets face towards the front of the vehicle. Push the trailing arm into position until the anti-roll bar bracket holes are correctly aligned with the bolt holes in the trailing arms.

14   Once the trailing arms are correctly interlocked, remove the anti-roll bar. Raise the trolley jack, and insert the bearing bracket mounting bolts from inside the vehicle, ensuring that the bolt retaining plate is correctly fitted. Refit the mounting nuts and tighten them to the specified torque. Lower the seat cushion.

15   Refit the brake pipe to the wheel cylinder, and securely tighten its union nut. Remove the clamp from the brake hose or the polythene from the master cylinder reservoir (as applicable).

16   Tap the handbrake cable back into position in the brake backplate, and secure it in position with the ties or clips. Refit the brake shoes as described in Chapter 9.

17   Refit the torsion bar as described in Section 12.

18   Refit the anti-roll bar as described in Section 11.

19   Bleed the brake hydraulic system as described in Chapter 9. Providing the precautions described were taken to minimise brake fluid loss, it should only be necessary to bleed the relevant rear brake.

20   Refit the roadwheel, lower the vehicle to the ground and tighten the wheel bolts to the specified torque.

21   Check the rear underbody height as described in Section 16.

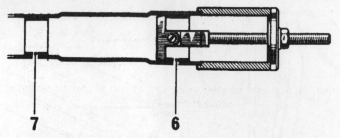

14.4 Using the Renault tool to remove trailing arm bearings

6   *Outer bearing*   7   *Inner bearing*

14 Rear trailing arm bearings - renewal

1   Remove both trailing arms with reference to Section 13.

2   Mount the left-hand trailing arm in a vice.

3   To remove the bearings, it will be necessary to obtain the Renault tool shown **(see illustration)**, or to fabricate a similar tool as follows. First note the exact position of the bearings.

4   Obtain a threaded rod long enough to reach the inner bearing, a tube of suitable diameter as shown, two thick washers of diameter equal to each bearing, a washer of diameter greater than the tube, and two nuts. Cut two sides off the smaller washer so that just a flat strip with a hole in the centre remains. This will form the swivelling end part shown on the Renault tool. Pass the threaded rod through the hole in the strip, and screw on a nut. Feed the strip and rod through the bearing so that the strip locates behind the bearing. Place the tube over the rod and in contact with the edge of the arm. Place the large washer over the end of the tube, and then screw on the remaining nut. Hold the rod with grips, and tighten the nut to draw out the bearing, then repeat this operation to remove the remaining bearing **(see illustration)**.

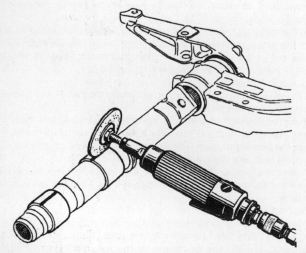

14.7 Removing the rear axle bearing inner tracks using a grinder

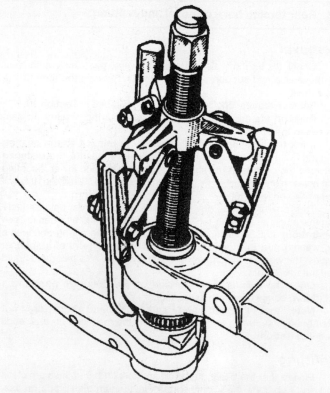

15.4 Using a puller to remove the rear suspension bearing bracket from the trailing arm

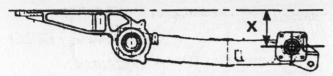

15.7 Vertical assembly dimension of the rear suspension bearing bracket and trailing arm

X = 80 mm

5 Thoroughly clean the bore, removing all traces of dirt and grease. Polish away any burrs or raised edges which might hinder reassembly. Apply a smear of multi-purpose grease to the outer edge of the new bearings, then carefully press them squarely into position, using a tubular spacer which presses only on the hard outer edge of the bearing.
6 Mount the right-hand trailing arm in the vice.
7 Mark the exact position of the bearing inner tracks on the trailing arm. Cut or grind almost through both bearing inner tracks, taking care not to damage the tube **(see illustration)**. Using a cold chisel, split the tracks and remove them from the tube. Also cut and remove the seal from the tube.
8 Clean the arm and fit the new seal.
9 Press on the new inner tracks, making sure that the lead chamfer goes on first. When doing this, if the load is being taken on the axle support assemblies, make sure that the torsion bars are correctly located in the anchor points.
10 It is not necessary to grease the bearing needle races, as they are supplied already greased.
11 Reassemble and refit the trailing arms with reference to Section 13.

15 Rear bearing bracket bushes - renewal

Note: *If either bearing bracket bush requires renewal, it will be necessary to renew the complete bearing bracket assembly, since it is not possible to obtain the bush separately.*
1 Remove the trailing arm as described in Section 13.
2 Soak the bearing bracket bush in brake fluid for some time, to soften the bush rubber.
3 Wipe off all traces of brake fluid, then mark the position of the bush inner edge on the trailing arm shaft.
4 Using a two- or three-legged puller, draw the bearing bracket off the trailing arm; the rubber of the bush will tear during this process, leaving the inner part of the bush on the arm **(see illustration)**.
5 Remove the remaining inner part of the bush by cutting with a hacksaw, taking care not to damage the trailing arm shaft.
6 Thoroughly clean the trailing arm shaft, removing all traces of rubber and grease. Polish away any burrs or raised edges which might hinder reassembly. Apply a smear of suitable grease to the inner edges of the new bush to aid installation.
7 Securely support the trailing arm, then position the new bearing bracket in relation to the trailing arm as shown **(see illustration)**. Press the bracket onto the trailing arm shaft until the bush reaches the alignment mark made prior to removal.
8 Temporarily refit the trailing arm into position as described in Section 13, paragraph 13. Check that the dimension between the inner bolt hole centres of the left and right-hand bearing brackets is as shown **(see illustration)**. If this is not the case, remove the arm and adjust the position of the bearing bracket as necessary.
9 Once the bearing bracket is correctly positioned, refit the trailing arm as described in Section 13.

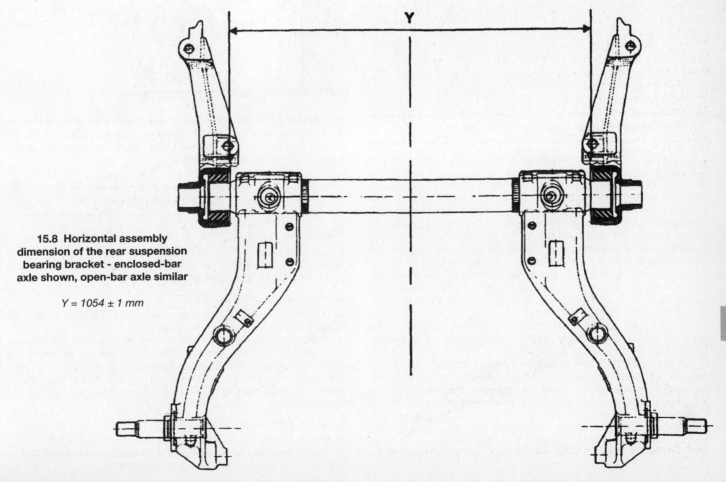

15.8 Horizontal assembly dimension of the rear suspension bearing bracket - enclosed-bar axle shown, open-bar axle similar

Y = 1054 ± 1 mm

10

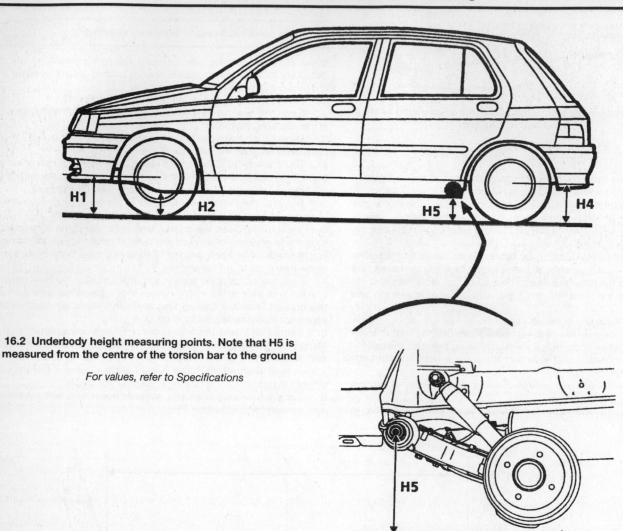

16.2 Underbody height measuring points. Note that H5 is measured from the centre of the torsion bar to the ground

For values, refer to Specifications

16 Underbody height - checking and adjustment

1   Position the unladen vehicle on a level surface, with the tyres correctly inflated and the fuel tank full.

2   It is only possible to adjust the rear suspension height in steps of 3 mm. First measure and record the dimensions H4 and H5 on both sides of the vehicle as shown **(see illustration)**, noting that dimension H5 is measured from the centre of the torsion bar to the ground. Subtract H5 from H4 to find the underbody height checking dimension. Check that this dimension is within the range given in the Specifications at the start of this Chapter. If adjustment is necessary, proceed as follows.

3   Determine by how many splines the torsion bar must be moved, noting that one spline is equal to a 3 mm change of height. For example, if the height needs adjusting by 10 mm, the torsion bar should be moved by three splines.

4   Chock the front wheels and engage reverse gear. Jack up the rear of the vehicle and support it on axle stands. Remove the appropriate rear roadwheel.

5   Position a trolley jack beneath the end of the trailing arm, then remove the torsion bar with reference to Section 12. With the bar removed, raise or lower the trailing arm by the required amount, so that it rotates by the required number of splines in relation to the bearing bracket. Once correctly positioned, adjust the trailing arm position slightly until the torsion bar can be slid freely back into position. Use a hammer and a soft metal drift to tap the bar fully home.

6   Refit the roadwheel, lower the vehicle to the ground and tighten the wheel bolts to the specified torque.

7   Recheck that the underbody height is within the specified range. If not, repeat the adjustment procedure. Note that after making the adjustment, it may be necessary to adjust the headlight beam alignment with reference to Chapter 1.

17 Steering wheel - removal and refitting

Removal

1   Set the front wheels in the straight-ahead position. Release the steering lock by inserting the ignition key then proceed as described under the relevant sub-heading.

Models without an air bag

2   Carefully ease off the steering wheel centre pad, then remove the steering wheel retaining nut **(see illustration)**.

3   Mark the steering wheel and steering column shaft in relation to each other, then lift the steering wheel off the column splines. If it is tight, screw the nut back on a few turns. Tap the steering wheel near the centre, using the palm of the hand, or rock it from side to side whilst pulling upwards to release it from the shaft splines. Remove the nut again and lift off the steering wheel.

Models with an air bag

Note: *Refer to the warnings given in Section 36 of Chapter 12.*

4   Slacken and remove the two screws securing the air bag unit to the rear of the steering wheel then carefully remove the unit from the

17.2 Removing the steering wheel retaining nut

18.9 Fold back the protective cover for access to the universal joint clamp bolt (arrowed) - shown with engine removed for clarity

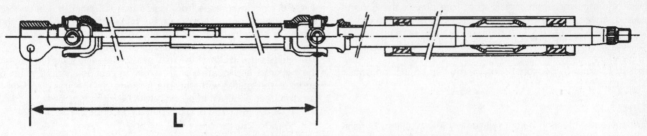

18.13 Steering column intermediate shaft checking dimension (L)

Right-hand drive models with manual steering - 446.0 ± 1 mm   *Right-hand drive models with power steering - 396.0 ± 1 mm*

centre of the steering wheel and disconnect its wiring connector. **Note:** *Do not disturb the inertia switch assembly.*

5   Unscrew the steering wheel retaining bolt then mark the steering wheel and steering column shaft in relation to each other. Lift the steering wheel off the column splines. If it is tight, rock it from side to side whilst pulling upwards to release it from the shaft splines.

Refitting

6   Refitting is a reversal of removal. Align the marks made on removal, and tighten the retaining nut/bolt to the specified torque.

---

18   Steering column - removal, checking and refitting

Removal

1   Disconnect the battery negative lead.
2   Remove the steering wheel as described in Section 17.
3   Pull the bonnet release lever down to expose the release lever assembly securing bolt, then unscrew the bolt. Remove the two retaining screws from the upper edge of the panel, then carefully lower the panel away from the facia to gain the clearance necessary for column removal.
4   On models fitted with a radio/cassette player remote control switch, slide back the cover from the front of the switch assembly, and loosen the switch clamp screw.
5   Working underneath the steering column, undo the three retaining screws, then pull the lower shroud down to release its retaining clips. Withdraw the lower shroud, then remove the two retaining screws from the front of the upper shroud. Remove the upper shroud from the steering column.
6   Slacken the combination switch assembly clamp bolt. Slide the switch assembly off the steering column, disconnecting the wiring

connectors as they become accessible. Disconnect the wiring from the ignition switch, and free it from any retaining clips.
7   Remove the two bolts securing the facia to the top of the steering column.
8   Apply the handbrake, jack up the front of the vehicle and support it on axle stands.
9   On models with manual steering, working from underneath the vehicle, cut the retaining clip, then fold the rubber protective cover back from the steering gear to gain access to the intermediate shaft universal joint **(see illustration)**.
10   On all models, mark the exact relationship between the intermediate shaft universal joint and the steering gear drive pinion, using paint marks, or a hammer and punch. Remove the nut and clamp bolt securing the joint to the pinion.
11   From inside the vehicle, slacken and remove the four steering column mounting nuts and bolts. Release the steering column from its mountings and the facia panel. On models equipped with power steering, also release the steering column lower gaiter from the bulkhead.
12   Disengage the universal joint from the steering gear pinion, and remove the steering column assembly from the vehicle.

Checking

13   The intermediate shaft attached to the bottom of the steering column incorporates a telescopic safety feature. In the event of a front-end crash, the shaft collapses and prevents the steering wheel injuring the driver. Before refitting the steering column, the length of the intermediate shaft must be checked. Refer to the accompanying illustration for the checking dimension **(see illustration)**. If the length is shorter than specified, the complete steering column must be renewed. Damage to the intermediate shaft is also implied if it is found that the clamp bolt at its base cannot be inserted freely when refitting the column.

10

20.5a Manual steering gear mounting nut (arrowed) . . .

20.5b . . . and bolt (arrowed) - viewed from underneath

14   Check the steering shaft for signs of free play in the column bushes, and check the universal joints for signs of damage or roughness in the joint bearings. If damage or wear is found on the steering shaft universal joints or shaft bushes, the column must be renewed as an assembly.
15   Refer to Chapter 5, Section 12 for information on ignition switch renewal.

Refitting

16   Manoeuvre the steering column assembly into position. Engage the universal joint with the steering gear pinion splines, aligning the marks made prior to removal.
17   Refit and tighten the steering column mounting nuts and bolts. On models equipped with power steering, refit the column gaiter to the bulkhead.
18   From underneath the vehicle, refit the universal joint clamp bolt and nut, and tighten it to the specified torque. On models equipped with manual steering, relocate the protective cover on the steering gear, and secure it in position with a new cable tie. Lower the vehicle to the ground.
19   Refit the two bolts securing the facia to the top of the steering column, and tighten them securely.
20   Ensuring that the wiring is correctly routed, reconnect the wiring connectors to the combination switch assembly. Locate the switch assembly on the top of the steering column, and securely tighten its clamp bolt. Reconnect the wiring to the ignition switch.
21   Refit the upper shroud, tightening its retaining screws securely. Clip the lower shroud onto the steering column, and tighten its retaining screws. Where applicable, refit the radio/cassette remote control switch.
22   Clip the lower facia panel back into position, and secure it in position with its retaining screws, not forgetting the bonnet release lever securing bolt.
23   Refit the steering wheel as described in Section 17, and reconnect the battery negative terminal.

19   Steering gear rubber gaiter - renewal

1   Remove the track rod end balljoint as described in Section 24.
2   Mark the correct fitted position of the gaiter on the track rod. Release the retaining clips, and slide the gaiter off the steering gear housing and track rod end.
3   Thoroughly clean the track rod and the steering gear housing, using fine abrasive paper to polish off any corrosion, burrs or sharp edges which might damage the sealing lips of the new gaiter on installation.

4   Recover the grease from inside the old gaiter. If it is uncontam-inated with dirt or grit, apply it to the track rod inner balljoint. If the old grease is contaminated, or it is suspected that some has been lost, apply some new molybdenum disulphide grease.
5   Grease the inside of the new gaiter. Carefully slide the gaiter onto the track rod, and locate it on the steering gear housing. Align the outer edge of the gaiter with the mark made on the track rod prior to removal, then secure it in position with new retaining clips.
6   Refit the track rod end balljoint as described in Section 24.

20   Manual steering gear - removal, overhaul and refitting

Removal

1   Chock the rear wheels, apply the handbrake, jack up the front of the vehicle and support it on axle stands. Remove both front roadwheels.
2   Remove the nuts securing the track rod balljoints to the swivel hubs. Release the balljoint tapered shanks using a universal balljoint separator.
3   Working from underneath the vehicle, cut the retaining clip, then fold the protective cover back from the steering gear to gain access to the intermediate shaft universal joint clamp bolt.
4   Mark the relationship between the intermediate shaft universal joint and the steering gear drive pinion, using a hammer and punch, white paint or similar. Remove the nut and clamp bolt securing the joint to the pinion.
5   Remove the two nuts and bolts securing the steering gear assembly to the rear of the front subframe. Release the steering gear pinion from the universal joint, and manoeuvre the assembly sideways out of position **(see illustrations)**.

Overhaul

General

6   Renewal procedures for the gaiters, the track rod end balljoints and the track rods (with inner balljoints) are given in Sections 19, 24 and 25 respectively.
7   Examine the steering gear assembly for signs of wear or damage. Check that the rack moves freely over the full length of its travel, with no signs of roughness or excessive free play between the steering gear pinion and rack. Internal wear or damage can only be cured by renewing the steering gear assembly, but note the points in the following paragraphs.

Thrust plunger adjustment

8   If there is excessive free play of the rack in the steering gear

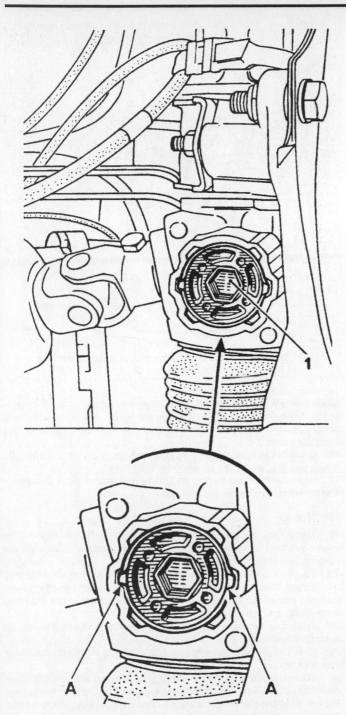

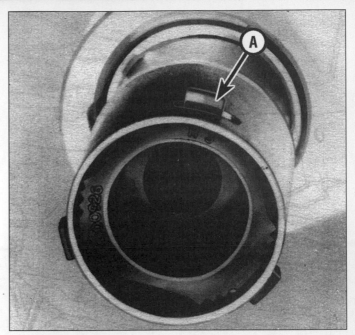

20.10 Steering rack anti-noise bush. Lugs (A) must engage in slots

retaining clip, from your Renault dealer. Cut the clip securing the gaiter to the opposite end of the steering gear from the pinion housing (ie the left-hand end on right-hand drive models, right-hand end on left-hand drive models). Peel the gaiter back from the housing. Move the steering rack so that its exposed end is fully extended, then smear the grease over the steering rack surface. Refit the gaiter to the housing, and secure it in position with the new retaining clip.

10   The anti-noise bush can be renewed if necessary. After removing the track rod on the side concerned, prise the old bush out using a screwdriver. Fit the new bush, making sure that its lugs engage in the slots in the rack housing **(see illustration)**. Lubricate the bush as just described.

Refitting

11   Manoeuvre the steering gear assembly into position. Engage the universal joint with the steering gear pinion splines, aligning the marks made prior to removal.

12   Insert the steering gear mounting bolts from the rear of the subframe. Refit the nuts and tighten them to the specified torque.

13   Refit the universal joint clamp bolt and nut, and tighten it to the specified torque. Relocate the protective cover on the steering gear, and secure it in position with a new cable tie.

14   Reconnect the track rod balljoints to the swivel hubs, and tighten their retaining nuts to the specified torque.

15   Refit the roadwheels, lower the vehicle to the ground and tighten the wheel bolts to the specified torque.

16   Check the front wheel toe setting as described in Section 26.

20.8 Steering rack thrust plunger adjustment

1   Adjusting nut   *A   Staking points*

housing, accompanied by a knocking noise, it may be possible to correct this by adjusting the rack thrust plunger. Relieve the staking on the plunger adjusting nut. Using a 10 mm Allen key, tighten the adjusting nut until the free play disappears (but by no more than three flats). Check that the rack still moves freely over its full travel, then secure the adjusting nut by staking it **(see illustration)**.

Anti-noise bush

9   If a grating noise has been noticed from the steering assembly whilst the steering wheel is being turned, this is probably due to the anti-noise bush being dry. To lubricate this bush, first obtain a sachet of the specified grease (Molykote 33 medium) and a steering gaiter

---

21   Power steering gear - removal, overhaul and refitting   **10**

Removal

1   Remove the battery as described in Chapter 5.

2   Chock the rear wheels, firmly apply the handbrake, jack up the front of the vehicle and support on axle stands.

3   Remove the front roadwheels.

4   Remove the nuts securing the track rod balljoints to the swivel hubs. Release the balljoint tapered shanks using a universal balljoint separator.

5   Using a hammer and punch, white paint or similar, mark the

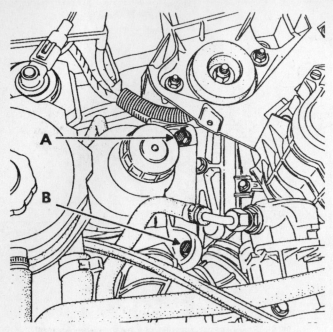

21.6a Electric power steering pump upper mounting bolts (A and B)

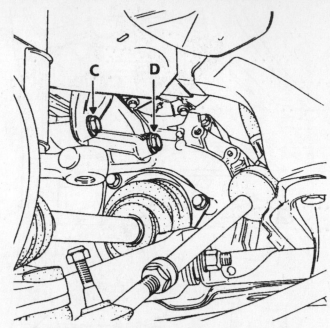

21.6b Electric power steering pump lower mounting bolts (C and D)

relationship between the intermediate shaft universal joint and the steering gear drive pinion. Slacken and remove the nut and clamp bolt securing the joint to the pinion.

6   Unscrew the two upper and two lower mounting bolts securing the electric power steering pump to its mounting bracket **(see illustrations)**. Note that the lower bolts also secure the bracket to the gearbox. Remove the mounting bracket.

7   Mark the fitted position of the hose retaining blocks to ensure correct refitting, then remove them.

8   Position a suitable container beneath the electric power steering pump, then unscrew the union nuts and disconnect the high and low pressure lines from the pump.

9   Unscrew the two terminal nuts and disconnect the wiring from the pump.

10   Withdraw the electric pump from the engine compartment taking care not to spill any fluid on the vehicle paintwork.

11   Remove the nut securing the feed pipe support bracket to the steering gear housing. Mark the pipe unions to ensure they are correctly positioned on reassembly, then unscrew the feed and return pipe union nuts; be prepared for fluid spillage by placing a suitable container beneath the pipes whilst unscrewing the union nuts. The spilt fluid must be disposed of, and new fluid of the specified type (see Chapter 1) used when refilling. Disconnect both pipes. Plug the pipe ends and steering gear/electric pump orifices, to prevent fluid leakage and the entry of dirt into the hydraulic system.

12   Disconnect the exhaust downpipe from the intermediate section with reference to Chapter 4, then carefully push the downpipe towards the front of the vehicle.

13   Remove the four mounting nuts and bolts securing the steering gear to the rear of the front subframe. Remove the mounting clamps and brackets from both ends of the steering gear **(see illustration)**.

14   Release the steering gear pinion from the universal joint, and manoeuvre the assembly sideways out of position.

Overhaul

15   Examine the steering gear for signs of wear or damage. Check that the rack moves freely over the full length of its travel, with no signs of roughness or excessive free play between the pinion and rack. The steering gear must be renewed as an assembly if internal wear or damage is present. Track rod, track rod balljoint and steering gear

gaiter renewal procedures are given in Sections 25, 24 and 19 respectively. Note that it is also possible to renew the pinion housing assembly, but it is recommended that this task be entrusted to a Renault dealer.

16   Inspect the steering gear fluid unions for signs of leakage, and check that the union nuts are securely tightened.

17   Examine the steering gear mounting rubbers for signs of damage and deterioration; renew as necessary.

Refitting

18   Manoeuvre the steering gear assembly into position. Aligning the marks made prior to removal, engage the universal joint with the steering gear pinion splines.

19   Locate the mounting brackets and clamps on the steering gear mounting rubbers, then insert the four steering gear mounting bolts from the rear of the subframe. Refit the nuts and tighten the mounting bolts to the specified torque.

20   Refit the exhaust downpipe to the intermediate section as described in Chapter 4.

21   Refit the universal joint clamp bolt and nut, and tighten it to the specified torque.

22   Wipe clean the feed and return pipe unions, then refit them to their respective positions on the steering gear. Tighten the union nuts. Refit and tighten the nut securing the feed pipe support bracket to the steering gear housing.

23   Locate the electric power steering pump in the engine compartment and reconnect the wiring to the terminals. Tighten the two terminal nuts.

24   Reconnect the high and low pressure lines to the pump and tighten the union nuts.

25   Refit the hose retaining blocks, and the electric pump together with its mounting bracket. Tighten all mounting bolts.

26   Reconnect the track rod balljoints to the swivel hubs. Tighten their retaining nuts to the specified torque.

27   Refit the roadwheels, lower the vehicle to the ground and tighten the wheel bolts to the specified torque.

28   Refit the battery with reference to Chapter 5.

29   On completion top-up and bleed the power steering hydraulic system as described in Section 23, then check the front wheel toe setting as described in Section 26.

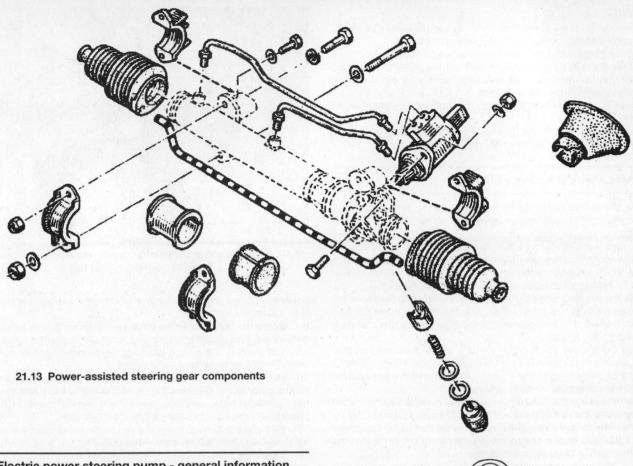

21.13 Power-assisted steering gear components

22 Electric power steering pump - general information, removal and refitting

General information

1   An electrically-powered steering pump is used on all models covered by this manual. This is because there is insufficient space in the engine compartment to mount a conventional belt-driven pump.

2   The operation of the pump is controlled by an oil pressure switch on the engine, and by either three or four relays, depending on model. The pump is prevented from running during starting and when the ignition is switched on with the engine stationary. The two power steering pump relays are situated in the engine compartment, mounted on the side of the left-hand suspension turret. On three-relay versions, the system control relay is fixed on the lid of the relay/junction box, which is mounted on the front of the left-hand suspension turret. On four-relay versions, there are two system control relays, both of which are also situated in the relay/junction box; one of them is fixed on the lid of the box, and the other is inside the bottom of the box.

3   Operation of the system is complex. If any fault develops, the vehicle should be taken to a Renault dealer for the fault to be diagnosed. The pump itself can be removed and refitted as follows.

Removal

4   Remove the battery as described in Chapter 5.

5   Apply the handbrake, jack up the front of the vehicle and support it on axle stands. Remove the left-hand roadwheel.

6   Clamp the feed and return hoses as near to the power steering pump as possible, using brake hose clamps. This will minimise fluid loss during subsequent operations.

7   Mark the pipe unions to ensure they are correctly positioned on reassembly, then unscrew the feed and return pipe union nuts; be prepared for fluid spillage by positioning a container beneath the pipes. The spilt fluid must be disposed of, and new fluid of the

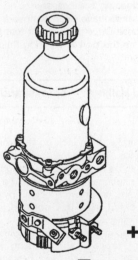

22.9 Electric power steering pump and terminal connections

specified type (see Chapter 1) used when refilling. Disconnect both pipes, and plug the pipe ends and pump unions (working quickly to minimise fluid loss), to prevent the entry of dirt into the hydraulic system.

8   Remove the two pump upper mounting bracket bolts. From underneath the vehicle, remove the two lower mounting bracket bolts.

9   Lift up the pump until its wiring connectors are accessible, then disconnect them from the base of the pump. Make a note of the locations of the wires, to ensure they are correctly reconnected on refitting **(see illustration)**. Remove the pump and reservoir assembly from the engine compartment.

10

Refitting

10   Manoeuvre the pump/reservoir assembly into position. Reconnect the wiring, using the notes made on removal.
11   Refit and tighten the four mounting bracket retaining bolts.
12   Renew the fluid pipe union O-rings. Refit the pipes to the pump, using the marks made on removal to ensure they are correctly reconnected, and tighten the union nuts.
13   Remove the hose clamps. Refit the battery as described in Chapter 5.
14   Lower the vehicle to the ground. Top-up and bleed the power steering hydraulic system as described in Section 23.

23 Power steering system - bleeding

1   This procedure will only be necessary when any part of the hydraulic system has been disconnected, or if air has entered because of leakage.
2   Remove the fluid reservoir filler cap, and top-up the fluid level to the maximum mark, using only the specified fluid. Refer to Chapter 1 *"Lubricants, fluids and capacities"* for fluid specifications, and to Chapter 1, Section 8 for details of the fluid reservoir markings.
3   With the engine stopped, slowly move the steering from lock-to-lock several times to expel trapped air, then top-up the level in the fluid reservoir. Repeat this procedure until the fluid level in the reservoir does not drop any further.
4   Start the engine so that the electric power steering pump is running. Slowly move the steering from lock-to-lock several times to expel any air remaining in the system. Repeat this procedure until bubbles cease to appear in the fluid reservoir.
5   If, when turning the steering, an abnormal noise is heard from the fluid pipes, it indicates that there is still air in the system. Check this by turning the wheels to the straight-ahead position and switching off the engine. If the fluid level in the reservoir rises, air is still present in the system, and further bleeding is necessary.
6   Once all traces of air have been removed, stop the engine and allow the system to cool. Once cool, check that the fluid level is up to the maximum mark on the power steering fluid reservoir; top-up if necessary.

24 Track rod end balljoint - removal and refitting

Removal

1   Apply the handbrake, then jack up the front of the vehicle and support it on axle stands. Remove the appropriate front roadwheel.
2   If the balljoint is to be re-used, use a straight-edge and a scriber, or similar, to mark its relationship to the track rod.
3   Holding the balljoint, unscrew its locknut by one quarter of a turn. Do not move the locknut from this position, as it will serve as a reference mark on refitting.
4   Remove the nut securing the track rod balljoint to the swivel hub. Release the balljoint tapered shank using a universal balljoint separator. If the balljoint is to be re-used, protect the threaded end of the shank by screwing the nut back on a few turns before using the separator **(see illustration)**.
5   Counting the **exact** number of turns necessary to do so, unscrew the balljoint from the track rod end.
6   Count the number of exposed threads between the end of the balljoint and the locknut, and record this figure. If a new balljoint is to be fitted, unscrew the locknut from the old balljoint.
7   Carefully clean the balljoint and the threads. Renew the balljoint if its movement is sloppy or if it is too stiff, if it is excessively worn, or if it is damaged in any way. Carefully check the shank taper and threads. If the balljoint gaiter is damaged, the complete balljoint must be renewed; it is not possible to obtain the gaiter separately.

Refitting

8   If applicable, screw the locknut onto the new balljoint, and

24.4 Using a universal balljoint separator to release the track rod balljoint from the swivel hub

position it so that the same number of exposed threads are visible as was noted prior to removal.
9   Screw the balljoint into the track rod by the number of turns noted on removal. This should bring the balljoint locknut to within a quarter of a turn of the end of the track rod, with the alignment marks that were made (if applicable) on removal lined up.
10   Refit the balljoint shank to the swivel hub, and tighten the retaining nut to the specified torque. If difficulty is experienced due to the balljoint shank rotating, jam it by exerting pressure on the underside of the balljoint, using a tyre lever or a jack.
11   Refit the roadwheel, lower the vehicle to the ground and tighten the roadwheel bolts to the specified torque.
12   Check the front wheel toe setting as described in Section 26, then tighten the balljoint locknut to the specified torque.

25 Track rod and inner balljoint - removal and refitting

Removal

1   Remove the track rod end balljoint as described in Section 24.
2   Cut the retaining clips, and slide the steering gear gaiter off the track rod.
3   Using a suitable pair of grips, unscrew the track rod inner balljoint from the steering rack end. Prevent the steering rack from turning by holding the balljoint lockwasher with a second pair of grips. Take care not to mark the surfaces of the rack and balljoint.
4   Remove the track rod/inner balljoint assembly and discard the lockwasher; a new one must be used on refitting.
5   Examine the inner balljoint for signs of slackness or tight spots. Check that the track rod itself is straight and free from damage. If necessary, renew the track rod/inner balljoint; the new one will be supplied complete with a new lockwasher and a new end balljoint. It is also recommended that the steering gear gaiter be renewed.

Refitting

6   If a new track rod is being installed, remove the outer balljoint from the track rod end.
7   Locate the new lockwasher assembly on the end of the steering rack, ensuring that its locating tabs are correctly located with the flats on the rack end.
8   Apply a few drops of locking fluid to the inner balljoint threads. Screw the balljoint into the steering rack and tighten it securely. Again, take care not to damage or mark the balljoint or steering rack.
9   Slide the new gaiter onto the track rod end, and locate it on the steering gear housing. Turn the steering from lock-to-lock to check that the gaiter is correctly positioned, then secure it with new retaining clips.
10   Refit the track rod end balljoint as described in Section 24.

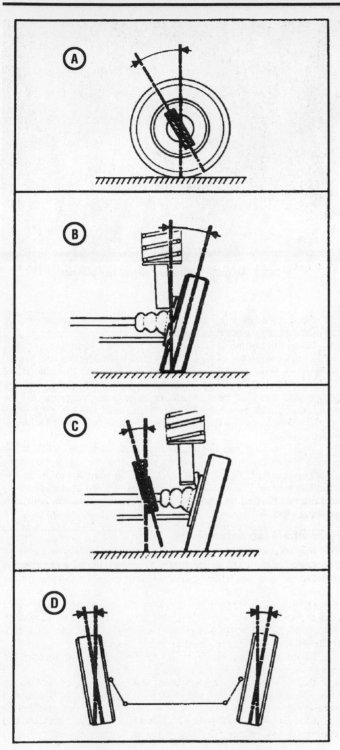

26.1 Wheel alignment and steering angles

A Castor
B Camber
C Steering axis inclination
D Toe

26 Wheel alignment and steering angles

General information

1 A car's steering and suspension geometry is defined in four basic settings. For this purpose, all angles are expressed in degrees (toe settings are also expressed as a measurement of length) **(see illustration)**. The steering axis is defined as an imaginary line drawn through the axis of the suspension strut, extended where necessary to contact the ground.

2 **Camber** is the angle between each roadwheel and a vertical line drawn through its centre and tyre contact patch, when viewed from the front or rear of the car. Positive camber is when the roadwheels are tilted outwards from the vertical at the top; negative camber is when they are tilted inwards.

3 Camber is not adjustable. Values are given for reference only. Checking is possible using a camber checking gauge, but if the figure obtained is significantly different from that specified, the vehicle must be taken for careful checking by a professional. Wrong camber settings can only be caused by wear or damage to the body or suspension components.

4 **Castor** is the angle between the steering axis and a vertical line drawn through each roadwheel's centre and tyre contact patch, when viewed from the side of the car. Positive castor is when the steering axis is tilted so that it contacts the ground ahead of the vertical; negative castor is when it contacts the ground behind the vertical.

5 Castor is not adjustable. As with camber, values are given for reference only; deviation can only be due to wear or damage.

6 **Steering axis inclination/SAI** - also known as **kingpin inclination/KPI** - is the angle between the steering axis and a vertical line drawn through each roadwheel's centre and tyre contact patch, when viewed from the front or rear of the car.

7 SAI/KPI is not adjustable, and is given for reference only.

8 **Toe** is the amount by which the roadwheels point outwards or inwards, viewed from above. "Toe-in" is when the roadwheels point inwards, towards each other at the front, while "toe-out" is when they splay outwards from each other at the front. The value for toe can be expressed as an angle (taking the centre-line of the car as zero), or as a measurement of length (taking measurements between the inside rims of the wheels at hub height).

9 The front wheel toe setting is adjusted by screwing the balljoints in or out of their track rods to alter the effective length of the track rod assemblies.

10 Rear wheel toe setting is not adjustable, and is given for reference only. While it can be checked, if the figure obtained is significantly different from that specified, the vehicle must be taken for careful checking by a professional, as the fault can only be caused by wear or damage to the body or suspension components.

Checking - general

11 Due to the special measuring equipment necessary to check the wheel alignment, and the skill required to use it properly, the checking and adjustment of these settings is best left to a Renault dealer or similar expert. Most tyre-fitting shops now possess sophisticated checking equipment.

12 For accurate checking, the vehicle must be at the kerb weight specified in *"General dimensions and weights"*.

13 Before starting work, check first that the tyre sizes and types are as specified, then check tyre pressures and tread wear. Also check roadwheel run-out, the condition of the hub bearings, the steering wheel free play and the condition of the front suspension components (Chapter 1). Correct any faults found.

14 Park the vehicle on level ground, with the front roadwheels in the straight-ahead position. Rock the rear and front ends to settle the suspension. Release the handbrake and roll the vehicle backwards 1 metre, then forwards again, to relieve any stresses in the steering and suspension components.

10

Toe setting - checking and adjusting

Front wheels - checking

15 Two methods are available to the home mechanic for checking the front wheel toe setting. One method is to use a gauge to measure the distance between the front and rear inside edges of the roadwheels. The other method is to use a scuff plate, in which each front wheel is rolled across a movable plate which records any deviation, or scuff, of the tyre from the straight-ahead position as it moves across the plate. Such gauges are available in relatively-

inexpensive form from accessory outlets. It is up to the owner to decide whether the expense is justified, in view of the small amount of use such equipment would normally receive.

16   Prepare the vehicle as described in paragraphs 12 to 14 above.

17   If the measurement procedure is being used, carefully measure the distance between the front edges of the roadwheel rims and the rear edges of the rims. Subtract the rear measurement from the front measurement, and check that the result is within the specified range. If not, adjust the toe setting as described in paragraph 19.

18   If scuff plates are to be used, roll the vehicle backwards, check that the roadwheels are in the straight-ahead position, then roll it across the scuff plates so that each front roadwheel passes squarely over the centre of its respective plate. Note the angle recorded by the scuff plates. To ensure accuracy, repeat the check three times, and take the average of the three readings. If the roadwheels are running parallel, there will of course be no angle recorded; if a deviation value is shown on the scuff plates, compare the reading obtained for each wheel with that specified. If the value recorded is outside the specified tolerance, the toe setting is incorrect, and must be adjusted as follows.

Front wheels - adjusting

19   Apply the handbrake, jack up the front of the vehicle and support it securely on axle stands. Turn the steering wheel onto full-left lock, and record the number of exposed threads on the right-hand track rod end. Now turn the steering onto full-right lock, and record the number of threads on the left-hand side. If there are the same number of threads visible on both sides, then subsequent adjustment should be made equally on both sides. If there are more threads visible on one side than the other, it will be necessary to compensate for this during adjustment. **Note:** *It is important that, after adjustment, the same number of threads be visible on each track rod end.*

20   First clean the track rod threads; if they are corroded, apply penetrating fluid before starting adjustment. Release the rubber gaiter outboard clips, then peel back the gaiters and apply a smear of grease, so that both gaiters are free and will not be twisted or strained as their respective track rods are rotated.

21   Use a straight-edge and a scriber or similar to mark the relationship of each track rod to its balljoint. Holding each track rod in turn, unscrew its locknut fully.

22   Alter the length of the track rods, bearing in mind the note in paragraph 19, by screwing them into or out of the balljoints. Rotate the track rod using an open-ended spanner fitted to the flats provided. Shortening the track rods (screwing them onto their balljoints) will reduce toe-in and increase toe-out. Each complete turn of the track

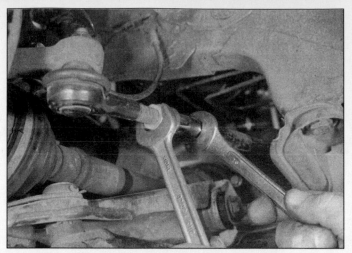

26.22 Adjusting the front wheel toe setting

rod effectively adjusts the toe setting by 30' or 3 mm (depending on the method being used) **(see illustration)**.

23   When the setting is correct, hold the track rods and securely tighten the balljoint locknuts. Check that the balljoints are seated correctly in their sockets, and count the exposed threads. If the number of threads exposed is not the same on both sides, then the adjustment has not been made equally, and problems will be encountered with tyre scrubbing in turns; also, the steering wheel spokes will no longer be horizontal when the wheels are in the straight-ahead position.

24   When the track rod lengths are the same, lower the vehicle to the ground and re-check the toe setting; readjust if necessary. When the setting is correct, tighten the track rod balljoint locknuts to the specified torque. Ensure that the rubber gaiters are seated correctly and are not twisted or strained; secure them in position with new retaining clips.

Rear wheel toe setting

25   The procedure for checking the rear toe setting is same as described for the front in paragraph 17. However, no adjustment is possible.

Chapter 11   Bodywork and fittings

Contents

11

Specifications

Torque wrench setting	Nm	lbf ft
Seat belt and seat belt height adjuster mountings*	20	15

* No figure specified by Renault - suggested value only

1   General information and maintenance

General information

The bodyshell and floorpan are manufactured from pressed-steel, and form an integral part of the vehicle's structure (monocoque), without the need for a separate chassis. The Clio is available in 3- and 5-door Hatchback body styles, with a Van version also available in some markets.

Various areas of the structure are strengthened to provide for suspension, steering and engine mounting points, and load distribution.

Corrosion protection is applied to all new vehicles. Various anti-corrosion preparations are used, including galvanising, zinc phosphate, and PVC underseal. An "anti-gravel" undercoat is applied to the front section of the bonnet, to prevent corrosion and paint chipping caused by stones and other road debris hitting the front of the vehicle. Protective wax is injected into the box sections and other hollow cavities.

Extensive use is made of plastic for peripheral components, such as the radiator grille, bumpers and wheel trims, and for much of the interior trim. Plastic wheel arch liners are fitted, to protect the metal body panels against corrosion due to a build-up of road dirt.

Interior fittings are to a high standard on all models, and a wide range of optional equipment is available throughout the range.

Maintenance - bodywork and underframe

Cleaning the vehicle's exterior

The general condition of a vehicle's bodywork is the one thing that significantly affects its value. Maintenance is easy, but needs to be regular. Neglect, particularly after minor damage, can lead quickly to further deterioration and costly repair bills. It is important also to keep watch on those parts of the vehicle not immediately visible, for instance the underbody, inside all the wheel arches and the lower part of the engine compartment.

The basic maintenance routine for the bodywork is washing - preferably with a lot of water, from a hose. This will remove all the loose solids which may have stuck to the vehicle. It is important to flush these off in such a way as to prevent grit from scratching the finish. The wheel arches and underbody need washing in the same way to remove any accumulated mud, which will retain moisture and tend to encourage rust, particularly in Winter, when it is essential that any salt (from that put down on the roads) is washed off. Paradoxically enough, the best time to clean the underbody and wheel arches is in wet weather, when the mud is thoroughly wet and soft. In very wet weather, the underbody is usually cleaned automatically of large accumulations; this is therefore a good time for inspection.

If the vehicle is very dirty, especially underneath or in the engine compartment, it is tempting to use one of the pressure-washers or steam-cleaners available on garage forecourts; while these are quick and effective, especially for the removal of the accumulation of oily grime which sometimes is allowed to become thick in certain areas, their usage does have some disadvantages. If caked-on dirt is simply blasted off the paintwork, its finish soon becomes scratched and dull, and the pressure can allow water to penetrate door and window seals and the lock mechanisms; if the full force of such a jet is directed at the vehicle's underbody, the wax-based protective coating can easily be damaged, and water (with whatever cleaning solvent is used) could be forced into crevices or components that it would not normally reach. Similarly, if such equipment is used to clean the engine compartment, water can be forced into the components of the fuel and electrical systems, and the protective coating can be removed that is applied to many small components during manufacture; this may therefore actually *promote* corrosion (especially inside electrical connectors) and initiate engine problems or other electrical faults. Also, if the jet is pointed directly at any of the oil seals, water can be forced past the seal lips and into the engine or transmission. Great care is required, therefore, if such equipment is used and, in general, regular cleaning by such methods should be avoided.

A much better solution in the long term is just to flush away as much loose dirt as possible using a hose alone, even if this leaves the engine compartment looking "dirty". If an oil leak has developed, or if any other accumulation of oil or grease is to be removed, there are one or two excellent grease solvents available, which can be brush-applied. The dirt can then be simply hosed off. Take care to replace the wax-based protective coat, if this was affected by the solvent.

Normal washing of the vehicle's bodywork is best carried out using cold or warm water, with a proprietary vehicle shampoo. Remove dead insects with a proprietary remover; tar spots can be removed either by using white spirit, followed by soapy water to remove all traces of spirit. Try to keep water out of the bonnet air intakes, and check afterwards that the heater air inlet box drain tube is clear, so that any water has drained out of the box.

After washing the paintwork, wipe off with a chamois leather to give an unspotted clear finish. A coat of clear protective wax polish will give added protection against chemical pollutants in the air. If the paintwork sheen has dulled or oxidised, use a cleaner/polisher combination to restore the brilliance of the shine. This requires a little effort, but such dulling is usually caused because regular washing has been neglected. Care needs to be taken with metallic paintwork, as special non-abrasive cleaner/polisher is required to avoid damage to the finish.

Brightwork should be treated in the same way as paintwork.

Windscreens and windows can be kept clear of the smeary film which often appears, by the use of proprietary glass cleaner. Never use any form of wax or other body or chromium polish on glass.

Exterior paintwork and body panels check

Once the vehicle has been washed, and all tar spots and other surface blemishes have been cleaned off, check carefully all paintwork, looking closely for chips or scratches; check with particular care vulnerable areas such as the front (bonnet and spoiler) and around the wheel arches. Any damage to the paintwork must be rectified as soon as possible, to comply with the terms of the manufacturer's cosmetic and anti-corrosion warranties; check with a Renault dealer for details.

If a chip or (light) scratch is found that is recent and still free from rust, it can be touched-up using the appropriate touch-up pencil; these can be obtained from Renault dealers. Any more serious damage, or rusted stone chips, can be repaired as described in Section 2, but if damage or corrosion is so severe that a panel must be renewed, seek professional advice as soon as possible.

Always check that any door and ventilator opening drain holes and pipes are completely clear, so that water can drain out.

Underbody sealer check

The wax-based underbody protective coating should be inspected annually, preferably just prior to Winter, when the underbody should be washed down as thoroughly but gently as possible (see the above concerning steam cleaners, etc) and any damage to the coating repaired; if any of the body panels are disturbed for repair or renewed, do not forget to replace the coating and to inject wax into door panels, sills, box sections etc, to maintain the level of protection provided by the vehicle manufacturer.

Maintenance - upholstery and carpets

Mats and carpets should be brushed or vacuum-cleaned regularly, to keep them free of grit. If they are badly stained, remove them from the vehicle for scrubbing or sponging, and make quite sure they are dry before refitting.

Fabric-trimmed seats and interior trim panels can be kept clean by wiping with a damp cloth. If they do become stained (which can be more apparent on light-coloured upholstery) use a little liquid detergent and a soft nail brush to scour the grime out of the grain of the material. Do not forget to keep the headlining clean in the same way as the (fabric) upholstery.

When using liquid cleaners of any sort inside the vehicle, do not over-wet the surfaces being cleaned. Excessive damp could get into the seams and padded interior, causing stains, offensive odours or even rot. If the inside of the vehicle gets wet accidentally, it is worthwhile taking some trouble to dry it out properly, particularly where carpets are involved. *Do not leave oil/paraffin-burning or electric heaters inside the vehicle for this purpose.*

2 Minor body damage - repair

Repair of minor scratches in bodywork

If the scratch is very superficial and does not penetrate to the metal of the bodywork, repair is very simple. Lightly rub the area of the scratch with a paintwork renovator, or a very fine cutting paste, to remove loose paint from the scratch and to clear the surrounding bodywork of wax polish. Rinse the area with clean water.

Apply touch-up paint, or a paint film to the scratch using a fine paint brush; continue to apply fine layers of paint until the surface of the paint in the scratch is level with the surrounding paintwork. Allow the new paint at least two weeks to harden, then blend it into the surrounding paintwork by rubbing the scratched area with a paintwork renovator, or a very fine cutting paste. Finally apply wax polish.

Where the scratch has penetrated right through to the metal of the bodywork, causing the metal to rust, a different repair technique is required. Remove any loose rust from the bottom of the scratch with a penknife, then apply rust-inhibiting paint to prevent the formation of rust in the future. Using a rubber or nylon applicator, fill the scratch with bodystopper paste. If required, this paste can be mixed with cellulose thinners to provide a very thin paste which is ideal for filling narrow scratches. Before the stopper-paste in the scratch hardens, wrap a piece of smooth cotton rag around the top of a finger. Dip the finger in cellulose thinners and quickly sweep it across the surface of the stopper-paste in the scratch; this will ensure that the surface of the stopper-paste is slightly hollowed. The scratch can now be painted over as described earlier in this Section.

Repair of dents in bodywork

When deep denting of the vehicle's bodywork has taken place, the first task is to pull the dent out, until the affected bodywork almost attains its original shape. There is little point in trying to restore the original shape completely, as the metal in the damaged area will have stretched on impact and cannot be reshaped fully to its original contour. It is better to bring the level of the dent up to a point which is about 3 mm below the level of the surrounding bodywork. In cases where the dent is very shallow anyway, it is not worth trying to pull it out at all. If the underside of the dent is accessible, it can be hammered out gently from behind, using a mallet with a wooden or plastic head. Whilst doing this, hold a suitable block of wood firmly against the outside of the panel, to absorb the impact from the hammer blows and thus prevent a large area of the bodywork from being "belled-out".

Should the dent be in a section of the bodywork which has a double skin or some other factor making it inaccessible from behind, a different technique is called for. Drill several small holes through the metal inside the area - particularly in the deeper section. Then screw long self-tapping screws into the holes just sufficiently for them to gain a good purchase in the metal. Now the dent can be pulled out by pulling on the protruding heads of the screws with a pair of pliers.

The next stage of the repair is the removal of the paint from the damaged area, and from an inch or so of the surrounding "sound" bodywork. This is accomplished most easily by using a wire brush or abrasive pad on a power drill, although it can be done just as effectively by hand, using sheets of abrasive paper. To complete the preparation for filling, score the surface of the bare metal with a screwdriver or the tang of a file, or alternatively, drill small holes in the affected area. This will provide a really good "key" for the filler paste.

To complete the repair, see the Section on filling and respraying.

Repair of rust holes or gashes in bodywork

Remove all paint from the affected area, and from an inch or so of the surrounding "sound" bodywork, using an abrasive pad or a wire brush on a power drill. If these are not available, a few sheets of abrasive paper will do the job most effectively. With the paint removed, you will be able to judge the severity of the corrosion, and therefore decide whether to renew the whole panel (if this is possible) or to repair the affected area. New body panels are not as expensive as most people think, and it is often quicker and more satisfactory to fit a new panel than to attempt to repair large areas of corrosion.

Remove all fittings from the affected area except those which will act as a guide to the original shape of the damaged bodywork (eg headlight shells etc). Then, using tin snips or a hacksaw blade, remove all loose metal and any other metal badly affected by corrosion. Hammer the edges of the hole inwards in order to create a slight depression for the filler paste.

Wire brush the affected area to remove the powdery rust from the surface of the remaining metal. Paint the affected area with rust-inhibiting paint; if the back of the rusted area is accessible, treat this also.

Before filling can take place, it will be necessary to block the hole in some way. This can be achieved by the use of aluminium or plastic mesh, or aluminium tape.

Aluminium or plastic mesh or glass-fibre matting is probably the best material to use for a large hole. Cut a piece to the approximate size and shape of the hole to be filled, then position it in the hole so that its edges are below the level of the surrounding bodywork. It can be retained in position by several blobs of filler paste around its periphery.

Aluminium tape should be used for small or very narrow holes. Pull a piece off the roll, and trim it to the approximate size and shape required, then pull off the backing paper (if used) and stick the tape over the hole; it can be overlapped if the thickness of one piece is insufficient. Burnish down the edges of the tape with the handle of a screwdriver or similar, to ensure that the tape is securely attached to the metal underneath.

Bodywork repairs - filling and respraying

Before using this Section, see the Sections on repairing dents, deep scratches, rust holes and gashes.

Many types of bodyfiller are available, but generally speaking, those proprietary kits which contain a tin of filler paste and a tube of resin hardener are best for this type of repair. A wide, flexible plastic or nylon applicator will be found invaluable for imparting a smooth and well-contoured finish to the surface of the filler.

Mix up a little filler on a clean piece of card or board - measure the hardener carefully (follow the maker's instructions on the pack), otherwise the filler will set too rapidly or too slowly. Using the applicator, apply the filler paste to the prepared area; draw the applicator across the surface of the filler to achieve the correct contour and to level the surface. As soon as a contour that approximates to the correct one is achieved, stop working the paste - if you carry on too long, the paste will become sticky and begin to "pick-up" on the applicator. Continue to add thin layers of filler paste at twenty-minute intervals until the level of the filler is just proud of the surrounding bodywork.

Once the filler has hardened, excess can be removed using a metal plane or file. From then on, progressively finer grades of abrasive paper should be used, starting with a 40-grade production paper, and finishing with a 400-grade wet-and-dry paper. Always wrap the abrasive paper around a flat rubber, cork, or wooden block - otherwise the surface of the filler will not be completely flat. During the smoothing of the filler surface, the wet-and-dry paper should be periodically rinsed in water. This will ensure that a very smooth finish is imparted to the filler at the final stage.

At this stage, the "dent" should be surrounded by a ring of bare metal, which in turn should be encircled by the finely "feathered" edge of the good paintwork. Rinse the repair area with clean water, until all of the dust produced by the rubbing-down operation has gone.

Spray the whole area with a light coat of primer - this will show up any imperfections in the surface of the filler. Repair these imperfections with fresh filler paste or bodystopper, and once more smooth the surface with abrasive paper. If bodystopper is used, it can be mixed with cellulose thinners to form a really thin paste which is ideal for filling small holes. Repeat this spray-and-repair procedure until you are satisfied that the surface of the filler and the feathered edge of the paintwork are perfect. Clean the repair area with clean water, and allow to dry fully.

11

4.4 Unscrewing a front bumper front securing nut

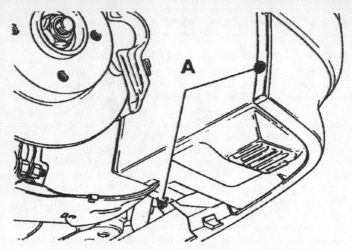

4.6 Front wheel arch splash shield lower fixings (A)

The repair area is now ready for final spraying. Paint spraying must be carried out in a warm, dry, windless and dust-free atmosphere. This condition can be created artificially if you have access to a large indoor working area, but if you are forced to work in the open, you will have to pick your day very carefully. If you are working indoors, dousing the floor in the work area with water will help to settle the dust which would otherwise be in the atmosphere. If the repair area is confined to one body panel, mask off the surrounding panels; this will help to minimise the effects of a slight mis-match in paint colours. Bodywork fittings (eg chrome strips, door handles etc) will also need to be masked off. Use genuine masking tape and several thicknesses of newspaper for the masking operations.

Before starting to spray, agitate the aerosol can thoroughly, then spray a test area (an old tin, or similar) until the technique is mastered. Cover the repair area with a thick coat of primer; the thickness should be built up using several thin layers of paint rather than one thick one. Using 400-grade wet-and-dry paper, rub down the surface of the primer until it is really smooth. While doing this, the work area should be thoroughly doused with water, and the wet-and-dry paper periodically rinsed in water. Allow to dry before spraying on more paint.

Spray on the top coat, again building up the thickness by using several thin layers of paint. Start spraying in the centre of the repair area, and then, with a side-to-side motion, work outwards until the whole repair area and about 50 mm of the surrounding original paintwork is covered. Remove all masking material 10 to 15 minutes after spraying on the final coat of paint.

Allow the new paint at least two weeks to harden, then, using a paintwork renovator or a very fine cutting paste, blend the edges of the paint into the existing paintwork. Finally, apply wax polish.

Plastic components

With the use of more and more plastic body components by the vehicle manufacturers (eg bumpers, spoilers and in some cases major body panels), rectification of more serious damage to such items has become a matter of either entrusting repair work to a specialist in this field, or of renewing complete components. Repair of such damage by the DIY owner is not really feasible, owing to the cost of the equipment and materials required for effecting such repairs. The basic technique involves making a groove along the line of the crack in the plastic, using a rotary burr in a power drill. The damaged part is then welded back together by using a hot air gun to heat up and fuse a plastic filler rod into the groove. Any excess plastic is then removed, and the area rubbed down to a smooth finish. It is important that a filler rod of the correct plastic is used, as body components can be made of a variety of different types (eg polycarbonate, ABS, polypropylene).

Damage of a less serious nature (abrasions, minor cracks etc) can be repaired by the DIY owner using a two-part epoxy filler repair material, which can be used directly from the tube. Once mixed in equal proportions this is used in similar fashion to the bodywork filler used on metal panels. The filler is usually cured in twenty to thirty minutes, ready for sanding and painting.

If the owner is renewing a complete component himself, or if he has repaired it with epoxy filler, he will be left with the problem of finding a suitable paint for finishing which is compatible with the type of plastic used. At one time, the use of a universal paint was not possible, owing to the complex range of plastics encountered in body component applications. Standard paints, generally speaking, will not bond satisfactorily to plastic or rubber, but paints to match any plastic or rubber finish can be obtained from dealers. However, it is now possible to obtain a plastic body parts finishing kit which consists of a pre-primer treatment, a primer and coloured top coat. Full instructions are normally supplied with a kit, but basically the method of use is to first apply the pre-primer to the component concerned, and allow it to dry for up to 30 minutes. Then the primer is applied and left to dry for about an hour before finally applying the special-coloured top coat. The result is a correctly-coloured component where the paint will flex with the plastic or rubber, a property that standard paint does not normally possess.

3   Major body damage - repair

Where serious damage has occurred, or large areas need renewal due to neglect, it means that complete new panels will need welding-in; this is best left to professionals. If the damage is due to impact, it will also be necessary to check completely the alignment of the bodyshell; this can only be carried out accurately by a Renault dealer using special jigs. If the body is misaligned, it is dangerous, as the car will not handle properly. In addition, uneven stresses will be imposed on the steering, suspension and possibly transmission, causing abnormal wear or complete failure, particularly of items such as the tyres.

4   Bumpers - removal and refitting

Front bumper

Removal

1   On models fitted with front foglights, disconnect the battery negative lead.
2   Remove the radiator grille panel, as described in Section 5.
3   Remove the front number plate. If the number plate is secured by self-tapping screws, take care not to strip the threads in the bumper.
4   Remove the now-exposed bumper securing nut, and recover the washer **(see illustration)**.
5   To improve access, jack up the front of the car and support it securely on axle stands.

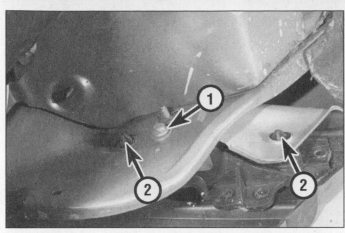

4.8 Front bumper side securing screw (1) and bumper locating clips (2) - wheel arch splash shield removed for clarity

6   Working under the right-hand side of the car, remove the securing screw and nut, and detach the wheel arch splash shield from the bumper **(see illustration)**.

7   Carefully pull the splash shield back from the bumper for access to the bumper side and lower fixings.

8   Unscrew the bumper side securing screw, and recover the washer **(see illustration)**.

9   Loosen the bumper lower securing nut (there is no need to remove it) **(see illustration)**.

10   Reach up behind the splash shield, and locate the front foglight wiring connector **(see illustration)**. Separate the two halves of the connector.

11   Repeat the procedure given in paragraphs 6 to 9 on the left-hand side of the car.

12   Have an assistant support the bumper, then pull the sides of the bumper out from the front wings to release the securing clips.

13   Carefully withdraw the bumper from the car.

Refitting

14   Refitting is a reversal of removal.

Rear bumper

Removal

15   Disconnect the battery negative lead.

16   To improve access, chock the front wheels, then jack up the rear of the car and support it securely on axle stands.

17   Working on the right-hand side of the car, remove the securing screw and nut, and remove the wheel arch splash shield.

18   Remove the now-exposed bumper side securing screw and washer.

19   Working on the left-hand side of the car, remove the two securing screws and the securing nut, and remove the wheel arch splash shield **(see illustrations)**.

20   Remove the now-exposed bumper side securing screw and washer.

21   Working under the car, remove the seven nuts (four upper and three lower) securing the bumper to the body **(see illustration)**.

4.9 Front bumper lower securing nut (arrowed)

4.10 Front foglight wiring connector (arrowed) - wheel arch splash shield removed for clarity

4.19a Left-hand rear wheel arch splash shield securing screws (arrowed)

4.19b Removing the rear wheel arch liner

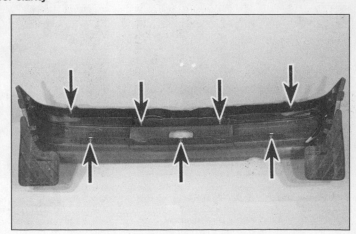

4.21 Rear bumper removed, showing securing nut locations (arrowed)

11

1

This photographic sequence shows the steps taken to repair the dent and paintwork damage shown above. In general, the procedure for repairing a hole will be similar; where there are substantial differences, the procedure is clearly described and shown in a separate photograph.

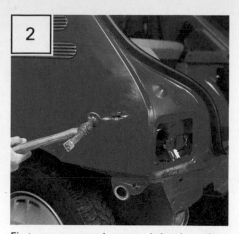

2

First remove any trim around the dent, then hammer out the dent where access is possible. This will minimise filling. Here, after the large dent has been hammered out, the damaged area is being made slightly concave.

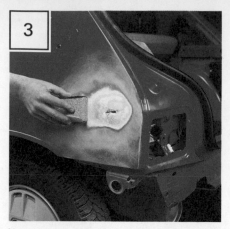

3

Next, remove all paint from the damaged area by rubbing with coarse abrasive paper or using a power drill fitted with a wire brush or abrasive pad. 'Feather' the edge of the boundary with good paintwork using a finer grade of abrasive paper.

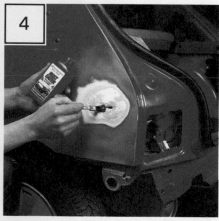

4

Where there are holes or other damage, the sheet metal should be cut away before proceeding further. The damaged area and any signs of rust should be treated with Turtle Wax Hi-Tech Rust Eater, which will also inhibit further rust formation.

5

For a large dent or hole mix Holts Body Plus Resin and Hardener according to the manufacturer's instructions and apply around the edge of the repair. Press Glass Fibre Matting over the repair area and leave for 20-30 minutes to harden. Then ...

5A

... brush more Holts Body Plus Resin and Hardener onto the matting and leave to harden. Repeat the sequence with two or three layers of matting, checking that the final layer is lower than the surrounding area. Apply Holts Body Plus Filler Paste as shown in Step 5B.

5B

For a medium dent, mix Holts Body Plus Filler Paste and Hardener according to the manufacturer's instructions and apply it with a flexible applicator. Apply thin layers of filler at 20-minute intervals, until the filler surface is slightly proud of the surrounding bodywork.

5C

For small dents and scratches use Holts No Mix Filler Paste straight from the tube. Apply it according to the instructions in thin layers, using the spatula provided. It will harden in minutes if applied outdoors and may then be used as its own knifing putty.

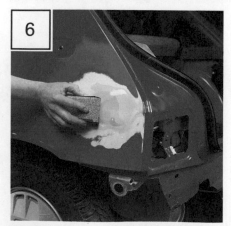

6

Use a plane or file for initial shaping. Then, using progressively finer grades of wet-and-dry paper, wrapped round a sanding block, and copious amounts of clean water, rub down the filler until glass smooth. 'Feather' the edges of adjoining paintwork.

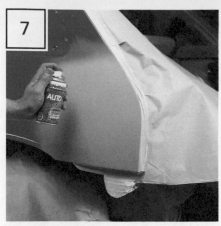

7

Protect adjoining areas before spraying the whole repair area and at least one inch of the surrounding sound paintwork with Holts Dupli-Color primer.

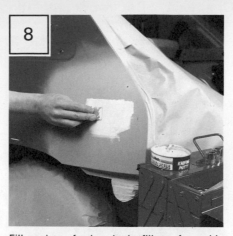

8

Fill any imperfections in the filler surface with a small amount of Holts Body Plus Knifing Putty. Using plenty of clean water, rub down the surface with a fine grade wet-and-dry paper – 400 grade is recommended – until it is really smooth.

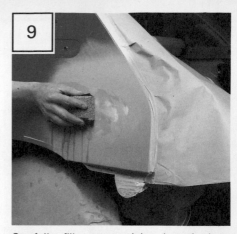

9

Carefully fill any remaining imperfections with knifing putty before applying the last coat of primer. Then rub down the surface with Holts Body Plus Rubbing Compound to ensure a really smooth surface.

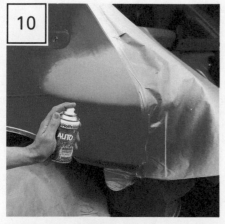

10

Protect surrounding areas from overspray before applying the topcoat in several thin layers. Agitate Holts Dupli-Color aerosol thoroughly. Start at the repair centre, spraying outwards with a side-to-side motion.

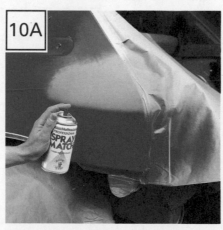

10A

If the exact colour is not available off the shelf, local Holts Professional Spraymatch Centres will custom fill an aerosol to match perfectly.

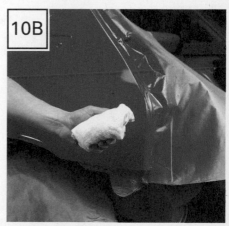

10B

To identify whether a lacquer finish is required, rub a painted unrepaired part of the body with wax and a clean cloth.

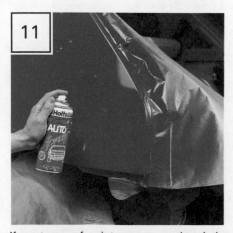

11

If *no* traces of paint appear on the cloth, spray Holts Dupli-Color clear lacquer over the repaired area to achieve the correct gloss level.

12

13

The paint will take about two weeks to harden fully. After this time it can be 'cut' with a mild cutting compound such as Turtle Wax Minute Cut prior to polishing with a final coating of Turtle Wax Extra.

14

When carrying out bodywork repairs, remember that the quality of the finished job is proportional to the time and effort expended.

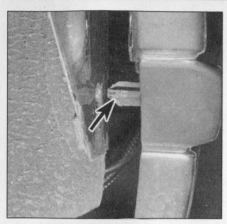

4.22 Rear bumper locating clip (arrowed) released from wing

4.23 Separating the two halves of the rear number plate light wiring connector

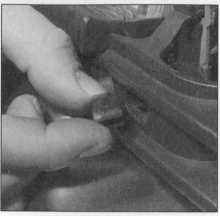

5.2a Prise out the covers . . .

22   Have an assistant support the bumper, then pull the sides of the bumper out from the rear wings to release the locating clips **(see illustration)**.

23   Carefully lower the bumper from the car. Locate the rear number plate light wiring connector, which is clipped to the body panel below the left-hand rear light cluster, and separate the two halves of the connector **(see illustration)**.

24   Withdraw the bumper from the car.

Refitting

25   Refitting is a reversal of removal.

---

5   Radiator grille panel - removal and refitting

Removal

1   Open the bonnet.

2   On early models, carefully prise the covers from the grille panel securing screws, then remove the screws. Using a suitable screwdriver, carefully release the plastic securing clips (two at each end, and one in the centre), and pull the grille panel from the body **(see illustrations)**.

3   On later (1994-on) models, undo the two retaining screws (one at each end of the grille) then release the centre retaining peg from the bumper and remove the grille.

Refitting

4   Refitting is a reversal of removal.

6   Windscreen cowl panels - removal and refitting

Note: *There are two windscreen cowl panels (one each side). Even if only one panel is to be removed, it is preferable to remove the two panels as an assembly, and then separate the two parts.*

Removal

1   Open the bonnet.

2   Remove the windscreen wiper arms, as described in Chapter 12.

3   Remove the five cowl panel securing screws **(see illustration)**.

4   Carefully release the cowl panel securing clips (located at the base of the windscreen) by pulling the panels upwards **(see illustration)**.

5   Release the weatherseal from the front edge of the panels, noting how it is located **(see illustration)**, then withdraw the assembly. Disconnect the washer fluid hose connector as the assembly is withdrawn.

6   If desired, the two halves of the assembly can be unclipped from each other after removal.

Refitting

7   Refitting is a reversal of removal, bearing in mind the following points.

8   If the two halves of the assembly have been separated, ensure that they are securely clipped together before refitting.

9   Ensure that the weatherseal is correctly located over the front of the panels, and that the panel securing clips are correctly engaged.

10   Refit the windscreen wiper arms with reference to Chapter 12.

5.2b . . . and remove the front grille panel securing screws

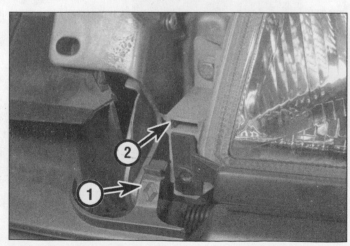

5.2c Front grille panel securing clip (1) released from headlight (2)

7 Bonnet and hinges - removal and refitting

Bonnet

Removal

1   Have an assistant support the bonnet in the open position.
2   If the original bonnet is to be refitted, mark the position of the hinges on the front edge of the bonnet, to aid alignment on refitting.
3   Remove the nuts securing the bonnet to the hinges (two nuts at each side), then carefully withdraw the bonnet from the car.

Refitting

4   Refitting is a reversal of removal, bearing in mind the following points.
5   Where applicable, align the hinges with the marks made on the bonnet before removal.
6   Close the bonnet (carefully, in case it fouls the surrounding bodywork), and check the alignment with the surrounding body panels.
7   If necessary, the alignment of the front and sides of the bonnet can be adjusted by altering the position of the front edge of the bonnet on the hinges, using the elongated holes provided. The alignment of the rear of the bonnet can be adjusted by altering the position of the bonnet lock assembly on the bulkhead, using the elongated bolt holes provided.

Hinges

8   The bonnet hinges are welded to the body, and cannot easily be removed.

8 Bonnet lock components - removal and refitting

Bonnet lock assembly

Removal

1   Open the bonnet.
2   Mark the position of the lock on the bulkhead, to aid correct alignment when refitting.
3   Unscrew the two securing bolts and recover the washers, then lift the lock assembly from the bulkhead (see illustration).
4   Remove the securing clip, and release the cable sheath from the lock.
5   Disconnect the end of the bonnet release cable from the lock operating lever, then withdraw the lock assembly.

Refitting

6   Refitting is a reversal of removal, but align the assembly with the marks made on the bulkhead before removal.
7   On completion, if necessary adjust the alignment of the rear of the

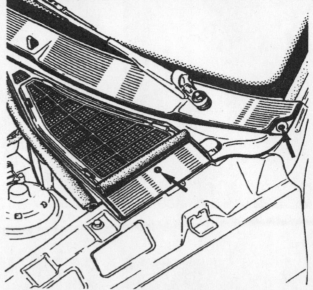

6.3 Two of the windscreen cowl panel securing screws (arrowed)

bonnet with the surrounding body panels by altering the position of the lock assembly, using the elongated bolt holes provided.

Bonnet lock striker

8   The bonnet lock striker is fixed to the bonnet, and cannot be removed or adjusted.

Bonnet lock release cable/lever assembly

Removal

9   Remove the driver's side lower facia panel, as described in Section 26. Note that, where applicable, there is no need to remove the headlight aim adjustment switch from the panel.
10   Working in the engine compartment, remove the securing clip, and release the cable sheath from the lock.
11   Disconnect the end of the bonnet release cable from the lock operating lever.
12   Working inside the car, carefully pull the cable through the bulkhead grommet into the car, noting the cable routing.

Refitting

13   Refitting is a reversal of removal, but ensure that the bulkhead grommet is securely located in the bulkhead, and route the cable as noted during removal.

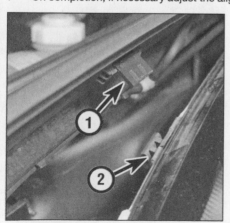

6.4 Windscreen cowl panel securing clip (1) released from body (2)

6.5 Releasing the weatherseal from the windscreen cowl panels

8.3 Bonnet lock assembly securing bolts (arrowed)

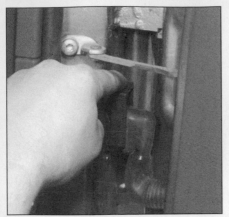

9.2a Slide the securing clip up . . .

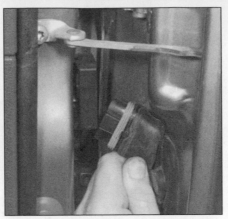

9.2b . . . and disconnect the door wiring connector

9.3 Door check strap securing screw (arrowed)

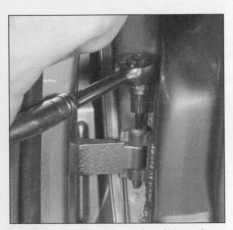

9.4 Loosening a front door hinge pin

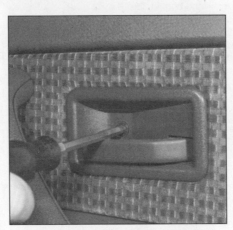

10.1a Remove the interior handle securing screw . . .

10.1b . . . then disconnect the operating rod

9   Doors and check straps - removal, refitting and adjustment

Doors

Removal

1   To remove a door, open it fully, and support it under its lower edge on blocks covered with pads of rag.

2   Where applicable, disconnect the battery negative lead, then disconnect the door wiring connector from the door pillar. To disconnect the connector, slide the securing clip up, then pull the connector from its socket **(see illustrations)**.

3   Using a suitable Torx bit, unscrew the door check strap from the body **(see illustration)**.

4   Again using a suitable Torx bit, loosen the two hinge pins from the hinges, but do not remove the pins at this stage **(see illustration)**.

5   Have an assistant support the door, then remove the hinge pins and withdraw the door from the car.

Refitting

6   Refitting is a reversal of removal.

Adjustment

7   The door hinges are welded onto the door frame and the body pillar, so that there is no provision for adjustment or alignment.

8   Door closure may be adjusted by altering the position of the lock striker on the body pillar, using a suitable Torx bit.

Door check straps

Removal

9   Open the door fully.

10   Using a suitable Torx bit, unscrew the door check strap from the body.

11   Remove the door inner trim panel, as described in Section 24.

12   Working at the outer front edge of the door, unscrew the two nuts securing the check strap to the door.

13   Withdraw the check strap through the inside of the door.

Refitting

14   Refitting is a reversal of removal.

10   Door handle and lock components - removal and refitting

Door interior handle

Removal

1   Remove the single screw securing the door interior handle to the door, then withdraw the handle and disconnect the operating rod from the rear of the handle by releasing the securing clip **(see illustrations)**.

2   Withdraw the handle from the door.

Refitting

3   Refitting is a reversal of removal.

10.6 Front door exterior handle securing nuts (arrowed)

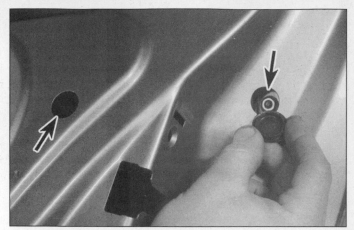

10.10 Rear door exterior handle securing nut locations (arrowed)

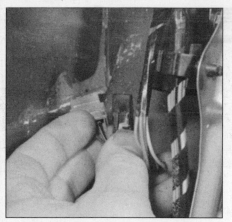

10.16 Disconnecting the wiring plugs from the driver's door lock operating motor

10.18 Removing a front door lock

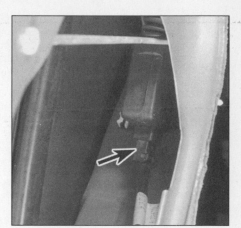

10.22 Disconnect the wiring plug (arrowed) from the lock operating motor

Front door exterior handle

Removal
4 Remove the door inner trim panel as described in Section 24.
5 Working inside the door, release the securing clips, and disconnect the exterior handle operating rod from the lock and the handle.
6 Unscrew the two exterior handle securing nuts from inside the door (see illustration), then tilt the handle and remove it from outside the door.

Refitting
7 Refitting is a reversal of removal, but refit the door inner trim panel as described in Section 24.

Rear door exterior handle

Removal
8 Remove the door inner trim panel as described in Section 24.
9 Remove the door lock as described later in this Section.
10 Carefully prise the two plastic covers from the door skin for access to the exterior handle securing nuts (see illustration).
11 Working inside the door, release the securing clip and disconnect the exterior handle operating rod from the handle.
12 Unscrew the two exterior handle securing nuts from inside the door, then tilt the handle and remove it from outside the door.

Refitting
13 Refitting is a reversal of removal, refitting the door lock as described later in this Section, and the door inner trim panel as described in Section 24.

Front door lock

Removal
14 Remove the door inner trim panel as described in Section 24.
15 Working inside the door, release the securing clips and disconnect the exterior handle, lock cylinder and lock button operating rods from the lock. Lift the lock button and operating rod from the door.
16 On models fitted with central locking, disconnect the battery negative lead, if not already done, and disconnect the wiring plug(s) from the lock operating motor (see illustration).
17 Unscrew the three lock securing screws from the rear edge of the door, and recover the washers.
18 Working inside the door, withdraw the lock assembly, complete with the interior handle operating rod, through the door aperture (see illustration).

Refitting
19 Refitting is a reversal of removal, refitting the door inner trim panel as described in Section 24.

Rear door lock

Removal
20 Remove the door inner trim panel, as described in Section 24.
21 Working inside the door, release the securing clips, and disconnect the exterior handle and lock button operating rods from the lock.
22 On models fitted with central locking, disconnect the battery negative lead, and disconnect the wiring plug from the lock operating motor (see illustration).

11

10.23 Unscrewing a rear door lock securing screw

10.24 Withdrawing a rear door lock from the door

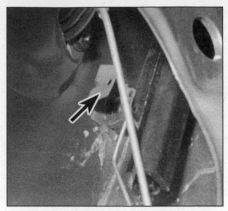

10.28a Remove the metal securing clip (arrowed) . . .

23   Unscrew the three lock securing screws from the rear edge of the door, and recover the washers **(see illustration)**.
24   Working inside the door, withdraw the lock assembly, complete with the interior handle operating rod, through the door aperture **(see illustration)**.

Refitting

25   Refitting is a reversal of removal, refitting the door inner trim panel as described in Section 24.

Front door lock cylinder

Removal

26   Remove the door inner trim panel, as described in Section 24.
27   Working inside the door, disconnect the operating rod from the lock cylinder.
28   Slide the metal securing clip from the lock cylinder, then withdraw the lock cylinder from outside the door **(see illustrations)**.

Refitting

29   Refitting is a reversal of removal, bearing in mind the following points.
30   When refitting the lock cylinder, ensure that the lugs on the assembly engage with the corresponding cut-outs in the door panel.
31   Refit the door inner trim panel as described in Section 24.

Lock striker

Removal

32   The lock striker is screwed into the door pillar on the body.
33   Before removing the striker, mark its position, so that it can be

refitted in exactly the same position.
34   To remove the striker, simply unscrew the securing screw using a suitable Torx bit.

Refitting

35   Refitting is a reversal of removal, but if necessary, adjust the position of the striker to achieve satisfactory closing of the door.

Central locking components

36   Refer to Section 14.

---

11 Door window glass and regulators - removal and refitting

Front door window glass

Removal

1   Remove the door inner trim panel, as described in Section 24.
2   Fully lower the window. On models with electric windows, temporarily reconnect the battery negative lead, and reconnect the wiring plug to the electric window operating switch, to enable the window to be lowered.
3   Carefully prise the weatherseal from the inner lower edge of the window aperture.
4   Working at the rear of the window glass, release the securing lugs and remove the plastic clip securing the window glass to the guide block **(see illustration)**.
5   Carefully pull the guide block back to disengage the lug from the hole in the glass, then support the glass.

10.28b . . . and withdraw the lock cylinder

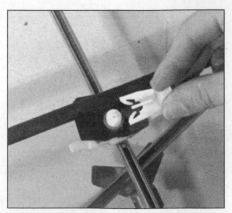

11.4 Removing the plastic clip securing the window glass to the guide block - assembly removed for clarity

11.6 Guide plate (arrowed) on front door window glass

6   Working inside the rear edge of the door, carefully disengage the guide plate (riveted to the rear upper edge of the glass) from the lower end of the weatherseal/guide channel inside the door **(see illustration)**.

7   Carefully push the glass upwards, tilt the rear edge forwards, and manipulate the glass out through the inside of the window aperture **(see illustration)**.

Refitting

8   Refitting is a reversal of removal, bearing in mind the following points.

9   Ensure that the guide plate at the rear upper edge of the glass is correctly engaged with the weatherseal/guide channel inside the door.

10   When refitting the weatherseal to the lower edge of the window aperture, ensure that the seal is correctly orientated, with the cut-out for the lock operating button at the rear **(see illustration)**.

11   Before refitting the door inner trim panel, check the operation of the window mechanism, reconnecting the battery and the electric windows operating switch, or refitting the window winder handle, as applicable.

12   Refit the door inner trim panel as described in Section 24.

Rear door fixed window glass

Removal

13   Remove the door inner trim panel, as described in Section 24.

14   Fully lower the sliding window glass.

15   Carefully prise the inner and outer weatherseals from the lower edge of the window aperture.

16   Temporarily refit the window winder handle. Raise the window until the screws securing the window glass to the regulator bracket are accessible.

11.7 Removing the front door window glass

17   If the original sliding glass is to be refitted, mark the positions of the screws securing the window glass to the regulator bracket, then remove the screws and carefully lower the window glass into the door **(see illustration)**.

18   Remove the upper Torx screw, middle bolt and lower nut securing the window rear guide rail to the door. Support the fixed window glass, and carefully withdraw the guide rail through the window aperture **(see illustrations)**.

19   Carefully slide the fixed window glass from its location **(see illustration)**.

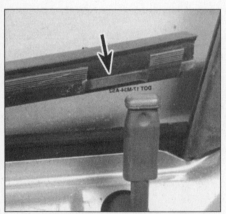

11.10 The cut-out for the lock operating button (arrowed) should be positioned at the rear of the weatherseal

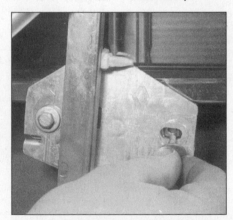

11.17 Removing a rear door window glass-to-regulator bracket securing screw

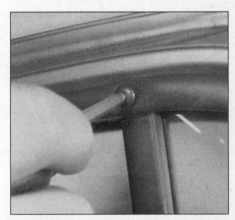

11.18a Remove the upper Torx screw, . . .

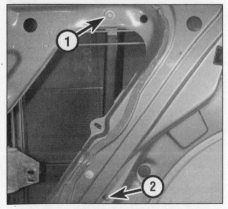

11.18b . . . the middle bolt (1) and the lower nut (2), . . .

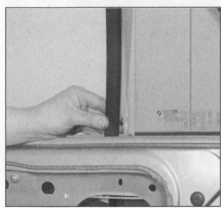

11.18c . . . then withdraw the window guide rail

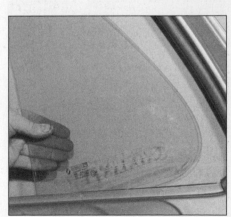

11.19 Removing the fixed rear window glass

11

11.23a Ensure that the inner . . .

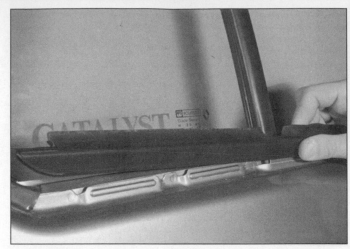

11.23b . . . and outer weatherseals are correctly located

Refitting

20   Refitting is a reversal of removal, bearing in mind the following points.

21   When refitting the window fixed glass, ensure that the glass engages correctly with the seals around the edges of the window aperture.

22   Where applicable, refit the screws securing the sliding window glass to the regulator bracket in the positions marked before removal.

23   Make sure that the weatherseals are correctly located on the lower edge of the window aperture **(see illustrations)**.

24   Before refitting the door inner trim panel, temporarily refit the window winder handle, and check the operation of the regulator mechanism. If necessary, the alignment of the glass can be adjusted by altering the position of the screws securing the window glass to the regulator bracket, using the elongated holes provided.

25   Refit the door inner trim panel, as described in Section 24.

Rear door sliding window glass

Removal

26   Remove the fixed window glass as described earlier in this Section.

27   Carefully lift the sliding window glass out through the inside of the window aperture **(see illustration)**.

Refitting

28   Lower the window glass into the door, then refit the fixed window glass as described earlier in this Section.

Front door window regulator

Removal

29   Remove the door inner trim panel, as described in Section 24.

30   Lower the interior handle operating rod clear of the regulator assembly.

31   Fully lower the window. On models with electric windows, temporarily reconnect the battery negative lead, and reconnect the wiring plug to the electric window operating switch, to enable the window to be lowered.

32   Proceed as described in paragraphs 4 and 5.

33   Lift the window glass clear of the regulator assembly, and support it securely (for instance, by using strong adhesive tape to secure the glass to the top edge of the window aperture).

34   On models fitted with electric windows, disconnect the wiring plug from the electric window motor.

35   Remove the five screws securing the regulator assembly to the door (three screws securing the regulator, and the upper and lower screws securing the window guide rail) **(see illustration)**.

36   Carefully manipulate the regulator assembly out through the rear aperture in the door **(see illustration)**.

Refitting

37   Refitting is a reversal of removal, bearing in mind the following points.

38   Before refitting the door inner trim panel, check the operation of the window mechanism, reconnecting the battery and the electric

11.27 Lifting the rear door sliding window glass from the door

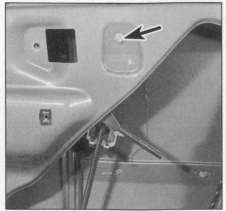

11.35 Removing the lower window guide rail screw from the front door - upper guide rail securing screw arrowed

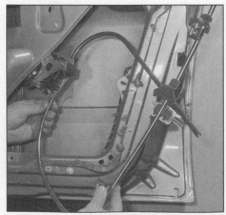

11.36 Removing the front door window regulator assembly

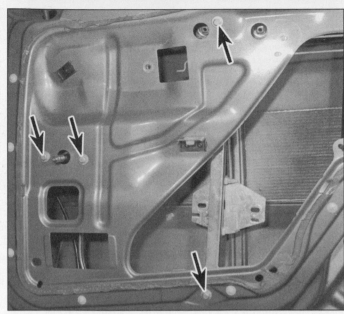

11.44a Rear door window regulator assembly securing screws (arrowed)

windows operating switch, or refitting the window winder handle, as applicable.

39 Refit the door inner trim panel as described in Section 24.

Rear door window regulator

Removal

40 Remove the door inner trim panel, as described in Section 24.

41 Temporarily refit the window winder handle. Lower the window glass until the screws securing the window glass to the regulator bracket are accessible.

42 Mark the positions of the screws securing the window glass to the regulator bracket, then remove the screws and raise the window glass. Support the window glass securely in the fully-raised position (for instance, by using strong adhesive tape to secure the glass to the top edge of the window aperture).

43 Reach up inside the door, and disconnect the lock operating rod from the lock button bellcrank at the front of the door. Note how the operating rod is routed through the regulator mechanism.

44 Remove the four securing screws (two screws securing the regulator, and the upper and lower screws securing the window guide rail), then carefully manipulate the regulator assembly out through the door aperture **(see illustrations)**.

Refitting

45 Refitting is a reversal of removal, bearing in mind the following points.

46 When reconnecting the lock operating rod to the bellcrank, ensure that the rod is correctly routed around the regulator assembly, as noted before removal.

47 Ensure that the screws securing the sliding window glass to the regulator bracket are refitted in their original positions marked before removal.

48 Before refitting the door inner trim panel, temporarily refit the window winder handle, and check the operation of the regulator mechanism. If necessary, the alignment of the glass can be adjusted by altering the position of the screws securing the window glass to the regulator bracket, using the elongated holes provided.

49 Refit the door inner trim panel as described in Section 24.

Electric window components

50 Refer to Section 15.

---

12 Tailgate, hinges and support struts - removal and refitting

Tailgate

Removal

1 Disconnect the battery negative lead.

2 Open the tailgate.

3 Carefully pull the inner trim panel from the tailgate **(see illustration)**. If necessary, release the trim clips using a suitable forked tool.

4 Disconnect the wiring from the heated rear window, tailgate wiper motor, and central locking motor, as applicable. Disconnect the washer fluid hose, where applicable; be prepared for fluid spillage.

5 Release the wiring loom and hose grommets from the edge of the tailgate. Tie string to the wiring loom and hose, and pull them through the edge of the tailgate. Leave the string in position in the tailgate, to aid refitting.

6 Have an assistant support the tailgate. Disconnect the support struts from the tailgate by prising out the retaining clips using a screwdriver.

7 Prise the plastic covers from the headlining for access to the tailgate securing nuts **(see illustration)**.

8 If the original tailgate is to be refitted, mark the positions of the securing nuts on the hinges.

9 Unscrew the nuts, and carefully withdraw the tailgate from the vehicle.

Refitting

10 Refitting is a reversal of removal, but where applicable, fit the tailgate securing nuts in their original positions, as noted before

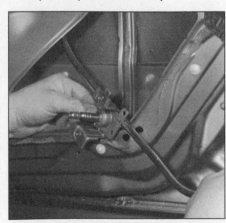

11.44b Removing the rear door window regulator mechanism

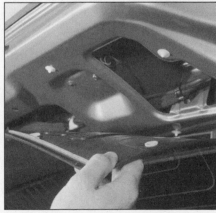

12.3 Removing the tailgate inner trim panel

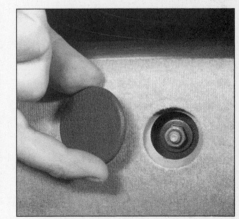

12.7 Removing a tailgate securing nut cover

11

removal. Do not fully tighten the tailgate securing nuts until the top of the tailgate is aligned correctly with the roof panel and the rear body pillars.

11   On completion, if adjustment of the tailgate lower edge alignment is required, remove the securing clip and unclip the plastic cover for access to the lock striker on the lower body panel.

12   Alter the position of the lock striker on the body using screws "A" **(see illustration)** in their elongated holes to give correct alignment of the lower edge of the tailgate with the surrounding body panels.

13   Once the tailgate is correctly aligned, if necessary adjust the closure using the adjustment screw "B" **(see illustration 12.12).**

Hinges

14   The tailgate hinges are welded to the tailgate, and the hinge pins are an interference fit in the hinges. The hinges cannot therefore easily be removed.

Support struts

Removal

15   Open the tailgate, and have an assistant support it in the fully-open position.

16   Disconnect the support strut from the tailgate by prising out the securing clip using a suitable screwdriver **(see illustration).**

17   Repeat the procedure for the clip securing the strut to the body, and withdraw the strut from the vehicle.

Refitting

18   Refitting is a reversal of removal.

---

13   Tailgate lock components - removal and refitting

Lock

Removal

1   Open the tailgate, then carefully pull the inner trim panel from the tailgate. If necessary, release the trim clips using a suitable forked tool.

2   Unscrew the two lock securing screws and recover the washers **(see illustration)**. Withdraw the lock from its location in the tailgate. Turn the lock as required to disconnect the operating rod.

Refitting

3   Refitting is a reversal of removal.

Lock barrel assembly

Removal

4   Remove the inner trim panel as described in paragraph 1.

5   Reach up through the tailgate aperture, and release the securing clip(s). Disconnect the lock operating rod, and where applicable the central locking motor operating rod, from the lock barrel assembly.

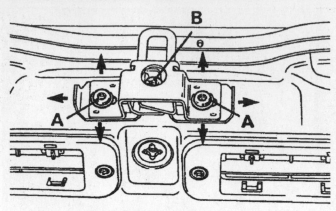

12.12 Tailgate lock striker assembly

A   Striker securing screws
B   Striker adjustment screw

6   Disconnect the water drain hose from the spout at the lower edge of the tailgate.

7   Remove the metal securing clip from the rear of the lock barrel, then withdraw the lock barrel assembly from outside the tailgate **(see illustrations).**

Refitting

8   Refitting is a reversal of removal. Ensure that the water drain hose is securely reconnected at both ends.

Lock striker

Removal

9   The lock striker is attached to the lower body panel.

10   Remove the securing clip (using a forked tool if necessary), and withdraw the plastic cover from the lock striker assembly **(see illustrations).**

11   Remove the two securing screws now exposed, recover the washers, and withdraw the lock striker assembly.

Refitting

12   Refitting is a reversal of removal, but if necessary adjust the position of the striker (by means of the elongated screw holes) to achieve satisfactory alignment of the bottom of the tailgate with the surrounding body panels.

13   On completion, if necessary adjust screw "B" **(see illustration 12.12)** to achieve satisfactory closing of the tailgate.

Central locking motor

14   Refer to Section 14.

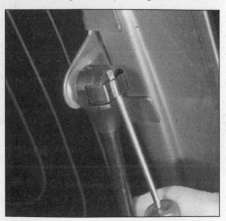

12.16 Prising out a tailgate support strut securing clip

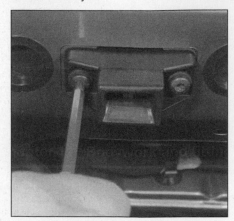

13.2 Unscrewing a tailgate lock securing screw

13.7a Remove the securing clip (arrowed) from the rear of the lock barrel . . .

13.7b . . . then withdraw the assembly

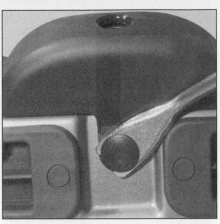

13.10a Remove the securing clip (note the use of a forked tool) . . .

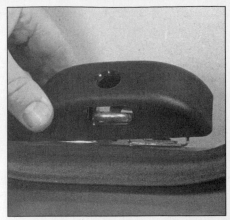

13.10b . . . and withdraw the cover from the tailgate lock striker

14.2 Withdrawing the central locking remote control receiver

14.6 Removing the ashtray and housing from the centre console

14.7 Removing the central locking switch from the centre console

14 Central locking components - removal and refitting

Remote control receiver

Removal

1 Disconnect the battery negative lead.
2 Carefully grip the front of the receiver unit, and pull it from its location in the roof console **(see illustration)**.
3 Disconnect the wiring plug and remove the unit.

Refitting

4 Refitting is a reversal of removal.

Driver's door operating switch

5 The switch is integral with the motor assembly, and cannot be removed independently.

Centre console-mounted switch

Removal

6 Pull the ashtray and housing from the centre console **(see illustration)**. Working through the aperture, push the cigarette lighter/switch mounting panel from the centre console.
7 Disconnect the wiring plugs from the switch, then push the switch out through the top of the panel **(see illustration)**.

Refitting

8 Refit by reversing the removal operations.

Front door lock operating motor

Removal

9 Remove the door lock, as described in Section 10. Remove the clip securing the lock operating rod to the motor operating rod and the lock lever **(see illustration)**.
10 Remove the single screw securing the motor to the lock assembly, then withdraw the motor.

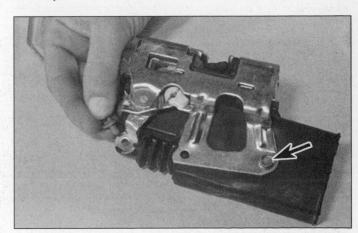

14.9 Removing the clip securing the lock operating rod to the central locking motor operating rod and lock lever. Motor securing screw arrowed

11

14.13 Driving out the roll pin securing the rear door central locking motor to the lock assembly

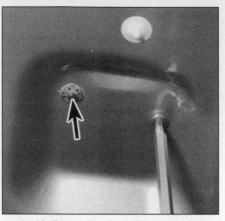

14.19 Removing the tailgate central locking operating motor securing screw - star-clip arrowed

14.20 Removing the tailgate central locking operating motor

15.2 Withdrawing the door pocket from the door

15.3 Disconnecting an electric window switch wiring plug

Refitting

11   Refitting is a reversal of removal. Refit the door lock as described in Section 10.

Rear door lock operating motor

Removal

12   Remove the door lock as described in Section 10.
13   Using a suitable pin punch, drive out the roll pin securing the motor to the lock assembly **(see illustration)**.
14   Disconnect the motor operating arm from the lock, then carefully slide the motor from the locating rail on the lock assembly.

Refitting

15   Refitting is a reversal of removal. Refit the door lock as described in Section 10.

Tailgate lock operating motor

Removal

16   Disconnect the battery negative lead.
17   Open the tailgate. Release the securing clips (using a suitable forked tool) and remove the tailgate interior trim panel.
18   Reach up through the tailgate aperture, and disconnect the motor operating rod from the lock.
19   Remove the single screw securing the motor to the tailgate. Prise off the securing star-clip, taking care not to damage the motor or the

tailgate **(see illustration)**.
20   Withdraw the motor from the tailgate, and disconnect the wiring plug **(see illustration)**.

Refitting

21   Refitting is a reversal of removal.

---

15   Electric window components - removal and refitting

Operating switches

Removal

1   Disconnect the battery negative lead.
2   Unscrew the four securing screws, and withdraw the door pocket from the door **(see illustration)**.
3   Reach behind the door pocket, release the securing clips, and push the switch assembly out through the top of the door pocket **(see illustration)**.
4   Disconnect the wiring plug(s) and withdraw the switch assembly.

Refitting

5   Refitting is a reversal of removal.

Operating motors

6   The motors are an integral part of the window regulator

16.2 Removing the mirror trim panel

16.3a Unscrewing an adjuster housing securing screw - manually-adjustable mirror

16.3b Unscrewing the adjuster lever clamp screw - manually-adjustable mirror

16.4a Mirror cover panel securing screws - electrically-operated mirror

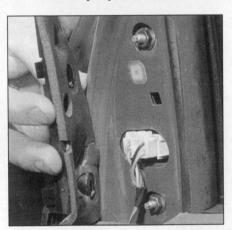

16.4b Removing the mirror cover panel to expose the wiring plug - electrically-operated mirror

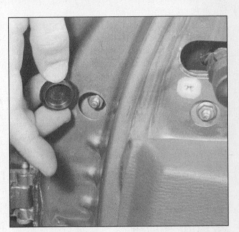

16.5 Removing the cover from the mirror lower securing nut

assemblies, and cannot be renewed independently.

7   Removal and refitting of the regulator assemblies is described in Section 11.

16 Mirrors - removal, refitting and glass renewal

Door mirror

Removal

1   On models fitted with electric mirrors, disconnect the battery negative lead.

2   Carefully prise the mirror trim panel from the front edge of the door **(see illustration)**.

3   On models fitted with manually-adjustable mirrors, unscrew the three adjuster housing securing screws now exposed. Unscrew the clamp screw securing the adjuster lever to the housing, and remove the housing from the door **(see illustrations)**.

4   On models fitted with electrically-operated mirrors, unscrew the two screws securing the mirror cover panel to the door, then unplug the wiring plug(s) from the mirror **(see illustrations)**.

5   Prise the plastic cover from the front edge of the door to expose the mirror front lower securing nut **(see illustration)**.

6   Unscrew the three mirror securing nuts, and withdraw the mirror from the door. On models with manually-adjustable mirrors, feed the adjuster cable and lever through the aperture in the door as the mirror is removed **(see illustration)**.

Refitting

7   Refitting is a reversal of removal, but on models fitted with manually-operated mirrors, when refitting the adjuster lever to the housing, proceed as follows.

8   Push the adjuster into the housing until the rear lug on the adjuster engages with the slot in the housing, and the front of the

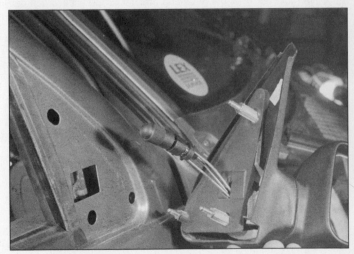

16.6 Withdrawing a manually-adjustable mirror

11

adjuster is flush with the end of the housing (see illustration). Refit and tighten the clamp screw.

Glass renewal - mirror with glass retained by wire clip

9   Using a thin-bladed screwdriver, carefully probe under the edge of the mirror glass, and locate the ends of the wire clip retaining the glass.
10   Support the glass.
11   Push one of the ends of the clip towards the centre of the mirror, then back into the mirror body, to release the glass (see illustrations). Take care not to drop the mirror glass as the clip is released.
12   To refit the glass, re-engage the metal clip with the lugs on the rear of the glass, then push the glass into position in the mirror until the clip engages securely.

Glass renewal - mirror with glass retained by locking ring

13   Using a thin-bladed screwdriver, probe through the hole provided in the bottom of the mirror body, and locate the serrated portion of the locking ring securing the glass.
14   Carefully turn the locking ring, using the screwdriver, until the glass is released.
15   To refit the glass, locate the glass in the mirror using the four guides (C) shown (see illustration).
16   Insert the screwdriver through the hole in the mirror body, and turn the locking ring in the opposite direction to that used for removal, to lock the glass in position.

Electric mirror operating switch removal and refitting

17   The switch is located in the driver's door armrest, with the electric window switches.
18   The procedure is as described for the electric window switches in Section 15.

Electric mirror motor removal and refitting

19   The motor is not available separately from the mirror. If it is faulty, the complete mirror assembly must be renewed.

Interior mirror

Removal

20   The mirror can be removed by carefully pulling it from the balljoint on the mounting bracket attached to the windscreen.
21   The mounting bracket is fixed to the windscreen using a special adhesive, and should not be disturbed unless absolutely necessary. Note that there is a risk of cracking the windscreen glass if an attempt is made to remove a securely-bonded mounting bracket.

Refitting

22   Refitting is a reversal of removal. If necessary, the special adhesive required to fix the mounting bracket to the windscreen can be obtained from a Renault dealer.

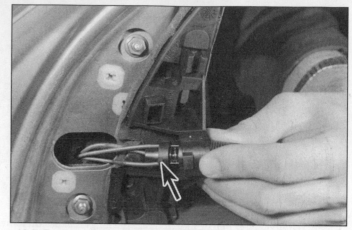
16.8 Ensure that the rear lug (arrowed) on the adjuster engages with the slot in the housing

17   Windscreen and tailgate window glass - general information

Windscreen

1   The windscreen is bonded in position using a special adhesive.
2   Special tools, adhesives and expertise are required for successful removal and refitting of glass fixed by this method. Such work must therefore be entrusted to a Renault dealer, a windscreen specialist, or other competent professional.

Tailgate window glass

Removal

3   The tailgate window glass is secured by the clamping action of the weatherseal.
4   To remove the glass, first remove the tailgate trim panel; pull the panel down to release the securing clips, or use a forked tool.
5   Disconnect the battery negative lead, then disconnect the wiring plugs from the heated rear window element.
6   Have an assistant support the window glass from outside the car.
7   Using a blunt flat-bladed screwdriver, carefully prise the weatherseal back from the flange on the tailgate. Withdraw the glass from outside the car.

Refitting

8   Fit the weatherseal to the edge of the glass.
9   Engage a cord in the groove in the weatherseal (see illustration), so that the ends of the cord emerge from the groove at the centre of

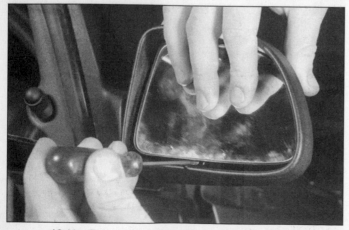
16.11a Release the mirror glass retaining clip . . .

16.11b . . . and withdraw the glass

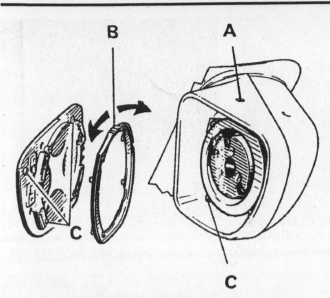

16.15 Door mirror glass components - mirror with glass retained by locking ring

A   *Access hole (underside of mirror)*
B   *Locking ring serrated portion*
C   *Glass locating guides*

the bottom edge of the glass. Overlap the ends of the cord by approximately 200 mm.
10   Offer the glass up to the tailgate, passing the ends of the cord through inside the tailgate.
11   Slowly pull one of the ends of the cords to seat the weatherseal over the flange on the tailgate.
12   Have an assistant apply gentle pressure to the glass from outside the car, to aid withdrawal of the cord.
13   When the cord reaches the centre of the upper edge of the glass, repeat the operation with the remaining end of the cord.
14   Check that the glass is secure and that the weatherseal is correctly seated, then reconnect the heated rear window wiring, and refit the tailgate trim panel.

18   Rear quarter window components - removal and refitting

Fixed rear quarter window

Removal

1   The window glass is secured by the clamping action of the weatherseal.
2   Remove the B-pillar trim panel, the roof side trim panel, and the rear side trim panel, as described in Section 24.
3   Have an assistant support the window glass from outside the car.
4   Using a blunt flat-bladed screwdriver, carefully prise the window weatherseal back from the flange on the body, then withdraw the glass from outside the car.

Refitting

5   The procedure is as described for the tailgate window glass in Section 17, paragraphs 8 to 13 inclusive.
6   Check that the glass is secure and that the weatherseal is correctly seated, then refit the interior trim panels.

Opening rear quarter windows

Removal

7   Open the window, then remove the screw securing the window glass to the catch.

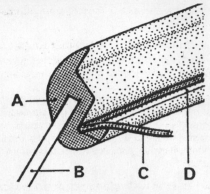

17.9 Cross-section of the tailgate window weatherseal, with cord inserted for refitting

A   *Weatherseal*   C   *Refitting cord*
B   *Glass*   D   *Groove*

19.2 Removing the cover from a sunroof glass panel-to-hinge securing screw

8   Have an assistant support the glass. Carefully unscrew the two screws securing the glass to the hinges, and lift the glass from the car.

Refitting

9   Refitting is a reversal of removal.

Opening rear quarter window catch

Removal

10   Open the window, and remove the screw securing the catch to the glass.
11   Remove the two screws securing the catch to the body, then withdraw the catch.

Refitting

12   Refitting is a reversal of removal.

19   Sunroof components - removal and refitting

Glass panel - models with tilting glass panel

Removal

1   Open the sunroof, and remove the screw(s) securing the handle assembly to the glass panel.
2   Hold the panel in the open position, then remove the plastic covers from the screws securing the panel to the hinges **(see illustration)**.
3   Remove the hinge screws, and lift the panel from the roof.

Refitting

4   Refitting is a reversal of removal.

11

19.6 Removing a sunroof handle trim panel securing screw

19.7 Sunroof handle-to-roof securing screws (arrowed)

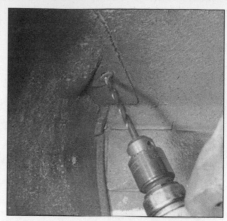

20.2 Drilling out a front wheel arch splash shield upper securing rivet

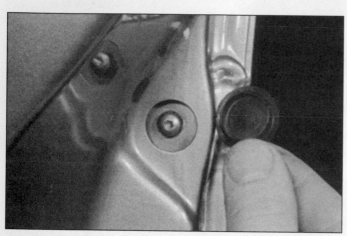

20.3 Removing the cover from a door rubbing strip securing screw

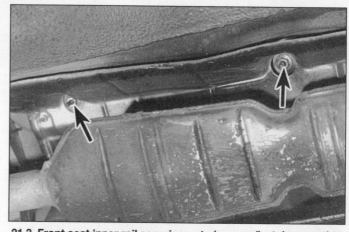

21.3 Front seat inner rail securing nuts (arrowed) - take care that the exhaust system is not hot

Sunroof handle - models with tilting glass panel

Removal

5   Open the sunroof, and remove the screw(s) securing the handle assembly to the glass panel.

6   Remove the two securing screws, and withdraw the handle trim panel from the roof (see illustration).

7   Remove the three screws securing the handle assembly to the roof, then withdraw the assembly (see illustration).

Refitting

8   Refitting is a reversal of removal.

Tilt/slide sunroof components

9   No information was available for the tilt/slide sunroof components at the time of writing. This type of sunroof is a complex piece of equipment, consisting of a large number of components. It is strongly recommended that the sunroof mechanism is not disturbed unless absolutely necessary. If the sunroof mechanism is faulty, or requires overhaul, consult a Renault dealer for advice.

20 Body exterior fittings - removal and refitting

Engine and wheel arch splash shields

1   Various plastic shields may be fitted to the wheel arches and various engine components to protect against road dirt and moisture.

2   The shields are secured by a combination of plastic clips, screws, nuts and pop-rivets (see illustration). Removal and refitting should be self-evident. Take particular care not to break plastic clips when removing them. Renew any pop-rivets on refitting where necessary.

Door rubbing strips

Removal

3   Open the door, and remove the plastic cover from the rear edge of the door to expose the rubbing strip securing screw (see illustration). Remove the screw.

4   Working outside the door, unclip the rubbing strip by pushing it towards the rear of the door.

5   If desired, the rubbing strip securing clips can be removed from the door by turning them one quarter of a turn anti-clockwise with pliers.

Refitting

6   To refit a rubbing strip, align the holes in the strip with the corresponding clips in the door. Push the strip towards the front of the door to engage the clips.

7   On completion, refit the securing screw and its plastic cover.

Badges

Removal

8   The various badges are secured with adhesives. To remove them, either soften the adhesive using a hot air gun or hairdryer (taking care to avoid damage to the paintwork), or separate the badge from the body by "sawing" through the adhesive using a length of nylon cord.

Refitting

9   Clean off all traces of adhesive using white spirit, then wash the area with warm soapy water to remove all traces of spirit, and allow to

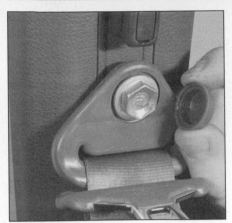

22.2a Prise off the cover . . .

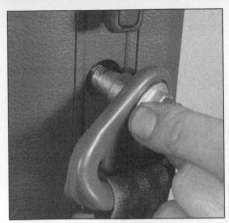

22.2b . . . and remove the upper seat belt mounting bolt

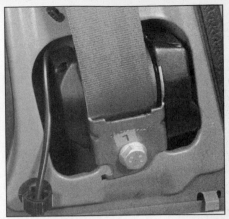

22.3 Footwell side/sill trim panel removed to expose front seat belt inertia reel assembly

dry. Ensure that the surface to which the new badge is to be fastened is completely clean, and free from grease and dirt.

10   Use the hot air gun to soften the adhesive on the new badge, then press it firmly into position.

21   Seats - removal and refitting

Front seat

Removal

1   If desired, remove the seat side trim panels for improved access.

2   Working inside the car, remove the two bolts securing the seat outer rail to the floor.

3   Working underneath the car, unscrew the two nuts securing the seat inner rail to the floor (see illustration). Depending on which seat is being removed, take care not to burn yourself if the exhaust is still hot.

4   Carefully lift the seat from the vehicle. On later (1994-on) models it will be necessary to disconnect the seat belt tensioner wiring connector as the seat is removed.

Refitting

5   Refitting is a reversal of removal.

Rear seat cushion

Removal

6   Tilt the seat cushion forwards, then lift it to disengage the securing lugs from the holes in the floor.

Refitting

7   Refitting is a reversal of removal.

Rear seat back

Removal

8   Release the securing catches at the top of the seat backs. Fold the seat backs forwards.

9   Working at the lower edges of the seat backs, release the catches securing the seat backs to the body, then withdraw the assembly from the car.

Refitting

10   Refitting is a reversal of removal.

22   Seat belt components - removal and refitting

Warning: *If the vehicle has been in an accident in which structural damage was sustained, all the seat belt components must be renewed.*

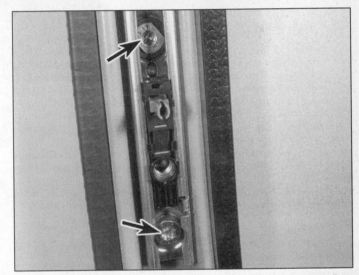

22.6 Front seat belt height adjuster securing bolts (arrowed)

Front seat belt

Removal

1   Remove the front footwell side/sill trim panel, as described in Section 24.

2   Prise off the cover and unscrew the seat belt upper mounting bolt (see illustrations).

3   Unscrew the mounting bolt, and withdraw the inertia reel assembly from the door pillar (see illustration). Remove the seat belt assembly from the car.

Refitting

4   Refitting is a reversal of removal. Tighten the seat belt mounting bolts to the specified torque.

Front seat belt height adjuster

Removal

5   Remove the B-pillar trim panel, as described in Section 24.

6   Unscrew the two securing bolts, and withdraw the adjuster from the pillar (see illustration).

Refitting

7   Refitting is a reversal of removal. Ensure that the B-pillar trim panel locates correctly over the door aperture weatherseals. Tighten the seat belt mountings to the specified torque.

11

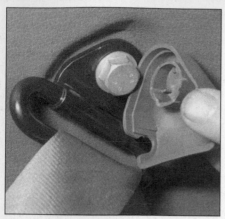

22.8a Prise off the cover . . .

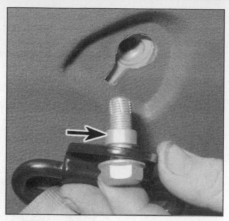

**22.8b . . . then unscrew the seat belt
upper mounting bolt. Spacer ring arrowed**

**22.11 Luggage compartment side trim
pulled back to expose seat belt inertia
reel mounting bolt (arrowed)**

Rear inertia reel seat belt

Removal

8   Prise off the cover, and unscrew the seat belt upper mounting bolt. Note the location of the spacer ring on the bolt **(see illustrations)**.
9   Remove the rear seat cushion, with reference to Section 21, for access to the seat belt lower mounting bolt. Unscrew the bolt.
10   Unclip the seat belt surround from the rear quarter trim panel.
11   Working in the luggage compartment, pull back the side trim to expose the inertia reel mounting bolt **(see illustration)**.
12   Unscrew the securing bolt and withdraw the inertia reel from its location. Feed the seat belt through the hole in the rear quarter trim panel.
13   The seat belt buckle can be unbolted from the floor, after removing the rear seat cushion for access.

Refitting

14   Refitting is a reversal of removal. Tighten the seat belt mountings to the specified torque.

Rear lap seat belt

Removal

15   The seat belt components can be removed, after removing the rear seat cushion for access to the securing bolts.

Refitting

16   Refitting is a reversal of removal. Tighten the securing bolts to the specified torque.

---

23   Interior trim - general information

Interior trim panels

1   The interior trim panels are all secured using either screws or various types of plastic fasteners.
2   Before removing a panel, study it carefully, noting how it is secured. Often, other panels or ancillary components (such as seat belt mountings, grab handles, etc) must be removed before a particular panel can be withdrawn.
3   Once any such components have been removed, check that there are no other panels overlapping the one to be removed. Usually, the sequence to be followed will become obvious on close inspection.
4   Remove all obvious fasteners, such as screws, many of which may have plastic covers fitted. If the panel cannot be freed, it is probably secured by hidden clips or fasteners on the rear of the panel. Such fasteners are usually situated around the edge of the panel, and can be prised up to release them. Note that plastic clips can break

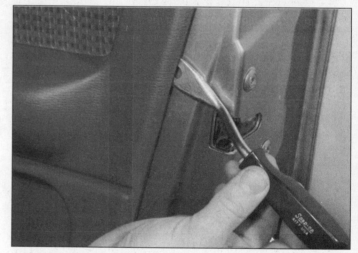

23.4 Forked tool for releasing plastic trim panel securing clips

quite easily, so it is advisable to have a few replacement clips of the correct type available for refitting. Generally, the best way of releasing such clips is to use a forked tool **(see illustration)**. If this is not available, an old, broad-bladed screwdriver with the edges rounded-off and wrapped in insulating tape will serve as a good substitute.
5   The following Section and the accompanying illustrations and photographs describe removal and refitting of all the major trim panels. Note that the type and number of fasteners used often varies during the production run of a particular model, so differences may be noted to the procedures provided for certain vehicles.
6   When removing a panel, **never** use excessive force, or the panel may be damaged. Always check carefully that all fasteners have been removed or released before attempting to withdraw a panel.
7   When refitting, secure the fasteners by pressing them firmly into place. Ensure that all disturbed components are correctly secured, to prevent rattles. If adhesives were found at any point during removal, use white spirit to remove the old adhesive, then wash off the white spirit using soapy water. Use a suitable trim adhesive (a Renault dealer should be able to recommend a proprietary product) on reassembly.

Carpets

8   The passenger compartment floor carpet rests on the floor, and is held in position by the sill trim panels and other surrounding panels and components.
9   Carpet removal and refitting is reasonably straightforward, but very time-consuming, due to the fact that many of the adjoining trim

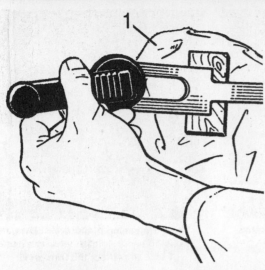

24.2 Using a forked tool to release the window regulator handle

1   *Protective cloth*

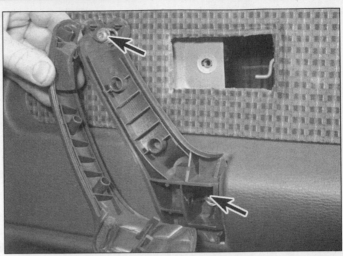

24.5 Prise the cover from the door grab handle to expose the securing screws (arrowed)

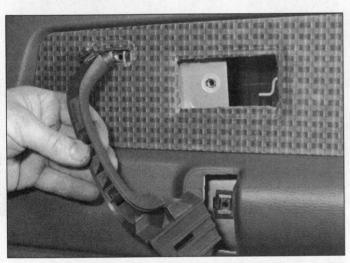

24.6 Withdrawing the front door grab handle

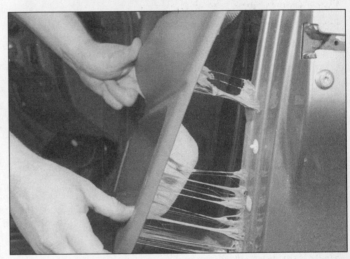

24.9 Pulling the trim panel from the front door

panels must be removed first. It will also be necessary to remove components such as the seats and their mountings, the centre console, etc.

Headlining

10   The headlining is clipped to the roof, and can be withdrawn after all fittings such as the grab handles, sun visors, sunroof trim, door pillar trim panels, rear quarter trim panels, weatherseals, etc, have been removed or prised clear.

11   Note that headlining removal requires considerable skill and patience if it is to be carried out without damage, and is therefore best entrusted to an expert.

24   Interior trim panels - removal and refitting

Front door inner trim panel

Removal

1   On models fitted with central locking, disconnect the battery negative lead.

2   On models fitted with manually-operated windows, note the position of the window winder handle with the window fully open, then release the securing clip and remove the handle. To release the securing clip, make up a forked tool similar to that shown **(see illustration)**; alternatively, insert a length of wire with a hooked end between the handle and the trim panel, and manipulate it to free the securing clip from the handle. Take care not to damage the trim panel.

3   Remove the single screw securing the door interior handle to the door. Withdraw the handle and disconnect the operating rod from the rear of the handle by releasing the securing clip.

4   Withdraw the handle from the door.

5   Prise the cover from the door grab handle to expose the two securing screws **(see illustration)**.

6   Remove the securing screws and withdraw the grab handle from the door **(see illustration)**.

7   Remove the securing screws and withdraw the door pocket from the door. On models fitted with electric windows, reach up behind the door pocket, and disconnect the wiring plugs from the electric window switches. Also disconnect the wiring plug from the electric mirror switch, where applicable.

8   Where applicable, remove the four securing screws and withdraw the loudspeaker cover, loudspeaker and loudspeaker housing from the door.

9   Carefully release the securing clips around the edge of the trim panel, preferably using a forked tool. Pull the trim panel from the door, noting that it is secured with sealing compound around its edge **(see illustration)**.

11

24.13 Removing the rear door window winder handle

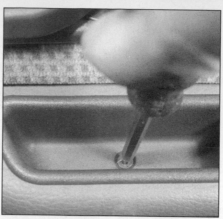

24.14 Removing the tray securing screw from the rear door armrest

24.16 Releasing a rear door ashtray housing securing clip - note the use of tape to protect the trim panel

24.19 Cover removed to expose seat belt mounting rail bolt - 3-door model

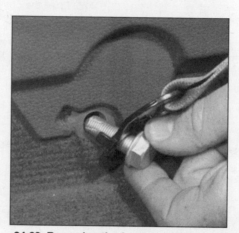

24.20 Removing the front seat belt lower mounting bolt - 5-door model

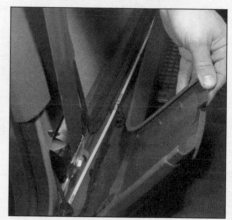

24.21a Removing a front footwell/side trim panel - front seat removed for clarity

Refitting

10 Refitting is a reversal of removal, bearing in mind the following points.

11 When refitting the panel to the door, ensure that the sealing compound provides a good seal between the door and the panel. If necessary, apply new sealing compound of a suitable type (available from a Renault dealer).

12 Where applicable, refit the window winder handle in the position noted before removal.

Rear door inner trim panel

Removal

13 Proceed as described in paragraphs 1 to 4 **(see illustration)**.

14 Remove the securing screw, then withdraw the tray from the armrest **(see illustration)**.

15 On models fitted with a door bin, unscrew the three securing screws and remove the door bin.

16 On models fitted with an ashtray, pull the ashtray from the housing, then release the housing securing clips (located at the bottom of the housing) using a screwdriver **(see illustration)**. Pull the ashtray housing from the door.

17 Carefully release the securing clips around the edge of the trim panel, preferably using a forked tool. Pull the trim panel from the door, noting that it is secured with sealing compound around its edge.

Refitting

18 Proceed as described in paragraphs 10 to 12.

Front footwell side/sill trim panel

Removal

19 On 3-door models, prise off the plastic cover and unscrew the bolt securing the seat belt mounting rail **(see illustration)**. Note the position of any washers and/or spacers. Carefully manipulate the rail to release the rear end from the trim panel.

20 On 5-door models, unbolt the front seat belt lower mounting **(see illustration)**.

21 Carefully pull the panel from the body to release the securing clips, and withdraw the panel from the sill **(see illustrations)**.

Refitting

22 Refitting is a reversal of removal. Ensure that the securing clips are correctly engaged, and tighten the seat belt mounting bolt to the specified torque.

Rear footwell side/sill trim panel - 5-door models

Removal

23 Remove the rear seat cushion, with reference to Section 21.

24 Unclip the rear of the front footwell side/sill trim panel to expose the rear footwell side/sill trim panel securing screw. Remove the screw.

25 Unbolt the rear seat belt lower mounting.

26 Carefully pull the panel from the body to release the securing clips, and withdraw the panel **(see illustration)**.

Refitting

27 Refitting is a reversal of removal.

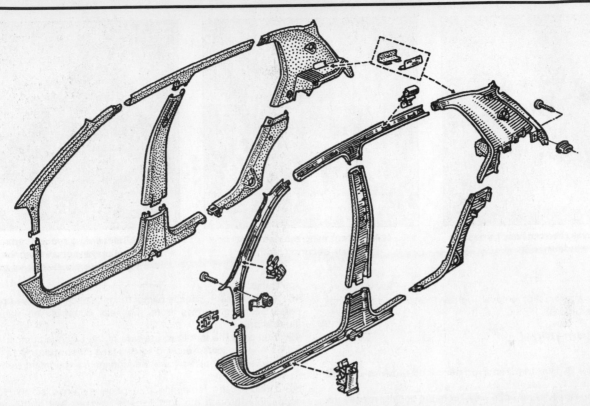

24.21b Body interior trim panels - 5-door models

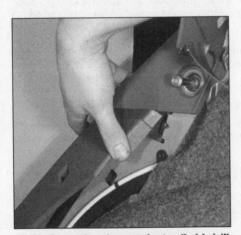

24.26 Removing the rear footwell side/sill trim panel - 5-door model

24.32a Prise the clip from the seat belt height adjustment knob, . . .

24.32b . . . then pull the knob from the adjuster

A-pillar trim panel

Removal

28   Remove the securing screw from the lower edge of the panel, then carefully pull the panel from the pillar to release the securing clips, and withdraw the panel.

Refitting

29   Refitting is a reversal of removal.

B-pillar trim panel - 5-door models

Removal

30   Remove the footwell side/sill trim panels as described earlier in this Section.
31   Prise off the cover, and unbolt the upper seat belt mounting.
32   Where applicable, prise the centre clip from the seat belt height adjustment knob, then pull the knob from the adjuster (see

illustrations).
33   Carefully pull the panel from the body to release the securing clips, and withdraw the panel.

Refitting

34   Refitting is a reversal of removal. Ensure that the panel locates correctly over the door aperture weatherseals, and tighten the seat belt mountings to the specified torque.

Rear side trim/B-pillar trim panel (3-door models)

Removal

35   Proceed as described in paragraphs 30 to 32.
36   Remove the rear seat cushion, with reference to Section 21.
37   Unbolt the rear seat belt lower mounting.
38   Carefully release the securing clips around the edge of the trim panel, preferably using a forked tool, then withdraw the panel.

11

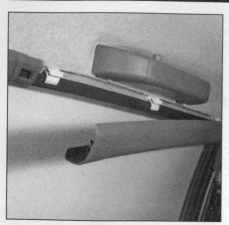

24.41 Removing the roof side trim panel

24.45 Removing the rear seat
back securing lug

24.48 Unscrewing a rear quarter trim
panel upper securing screw

Refitting

39   Refitting is a reversal of removal. Tighten the seat belt mountings to the specified torque.

Roof side trim panel

Removal

40   Remove the B-pillar trim panel, as described previously in this Section.

41   Carefully pull the roof side trim panel from the body to release the securing clips, and withdraw the panel (see illustration).

Refitting

42   Refitting is a reversal of removal. Refit the B-pillar trim panel as described previously in this Section.

Rear quarter trim panel

Removal

43   Prise off the plastic cover and unbolt the rear seat belt upper mounting. Note the position of the spacer on the bolt.

44   Lower the rear seat back.

45   Using a suitable Torx bit, unscrew the rear seat back securing lug (see illustration).

46   Unclip the seat belt surround from the rear quarter trim panel, then feed the seat belt through the hole in the panel into the luggage compartment.

47   Disconnect the battery negative lead, then disconnect the wiring from the loudspeaker, luggage compartment light and light switch, as

applicable.

48   Working in the luggage compartment, unscrew the two upper trim panel securing screws from the rear edge of the panel (see illustration).

49   Pull back the trim from the side of the luggage compartment to expose the two lower securing screws (see illustration). Note that one of the screws may also secure the luggage compartment light switch. Remove the screws.

50   Unscrew the remaining trim panel securing screw, which is accessible through the hole exposed by removal of the seat belt surround (see illustration).

51   Carefully pull the panel from the body to release the upper securing clip, and withdraw the panel from the car (see illustration).

Refitting

52   Refitting is a reversal of removal. Tighten the seat belt mounting bolt to the specified torque.

Roof console panel

Removal

53   Remove the interior light assembly as described in Chapter 12.

54   Remove the two securing screws, then lower the panel from the roof (see illustration).

55   Where applicable, disconnect the wiring from the remote control central locking receiver, then withdraw the panel (see illustration).

Refitting

56   Refitting is a reversal of removal.

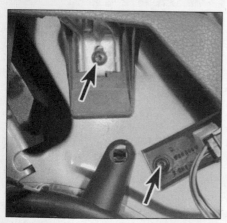

24.49 Rear quarter trim panel lower
securing screws (arrowed)

24.50 Rear quarter trim panel securing
screw (arrowed) accessible through
seat belt aperture

24.51 Removing the rear quarter
trim panel

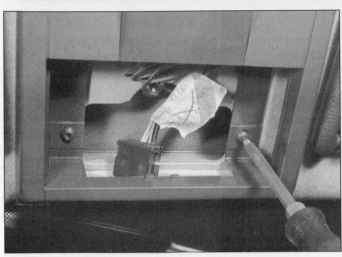

24.54 Removing a roof console panel securing screw

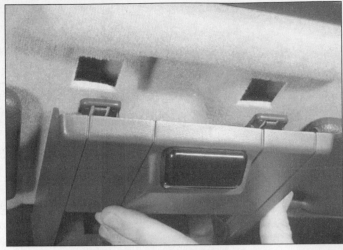

24.55 Withdrawing the roof console panel

Luggage compartment trim panels

57   The luggage compartment trim panels are clipped and glued in place. The edges of the panels can be unclipped for access to most components.

Tailgate trim panel

58   The panel is secured by plastic clips. Carefully pull the panel from the tailgate to release the clips (see illustration), or release the clips using a forked tool.

Front seat trim panels

59   The seat trim panels are clipped in place, except for the rear outer trim panel, which is also secured by a single screw through its rear. Removal and refitting are self-evident.

25 Centre console - removal and refitting

Removal

1   Disconnect the battery negative lead.
2   Where applicable, unscrew the two securing screws and remove the footrest from the floor next to the centre console (see illustration).
3   Ensure that the handbrake is fully applied.
4   Unclip the gear lever gaiter from the centre console (see illustration).

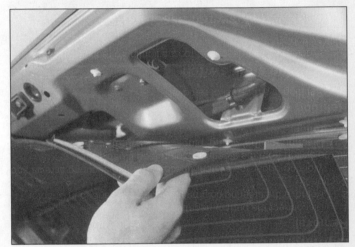

24.58 Removing the tailgate trim panel

5   Remove the four securing screws (two at the rear, and one each side at the front), and detach the centre console from the floor (see illustrations). Take care not to strain any wiring.
6   Reach up under the centre console, and disconnect the wiring from the cigarette lighter, cigarette lighter illumination bulb, and any

25.2 Unscrewing a footrest securing screw

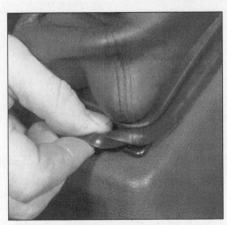

25.4 Unclipping the gear lever gaiter from the centre console

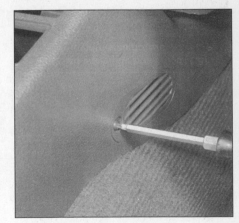

25.5a Remove the front . . .

11

25.5b ...and rear centre console
securing screws

25.7 Centre console partially withdrawn

26.1 Loosening the radio/cassette player
remote control switch clamp screw

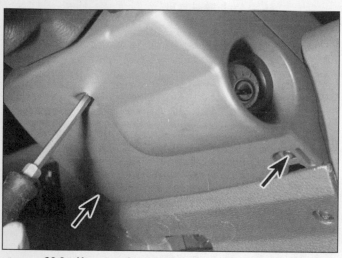

26.2a Unscrew the securing screws (arrowed) ...

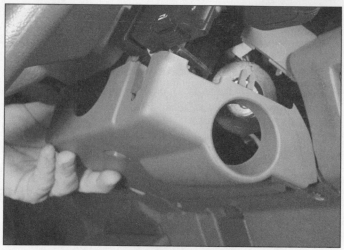

26.2b ... and withdraw the lower shroud

switches mounted in the centre console.

7   Lift the centre console over the gear lever and gaiter, and withdraw it from the car **(see illustration)**.

Refitting

8   Refitting is a reversal of removal.

26 Facia panels and components - removal and refitting

Steering column shrouds

Removal

1   On models fitted with a radio/cassette player remote control switch, turn the steering wheel as necessary to gain access to the switch assembly. Slide back the cover from the front of the switch assembly, and loosen the switch clamp screw **(see illustration)**.

2   Working under the steering column, unscrew the three securing screws, then carefully pull the lower shroud down to release the securing clips. Withdraw the lower shroud **(see illustrations)**.

3   Turn the steering wheel as necessary for access, and remove the two upper shroud securing screws from the front of the shroud. Withdraw the upper shroud **(see illustrations)**.

Refitting

4   Refitting is a reversal of removal. Where applicable, tighten the radio/cassette player remote control switch clamp screw after refitting the shrouds.

26.3a Remove the securing screws ...

Upper facia trim panel

Removal

5   Remove the five securing screws (three along the top edge of the panel, and one at each end of the panel), then lift the panel from the facia **(see illustrations)**.

Refitting

6   Refitting is a reversal of removal.

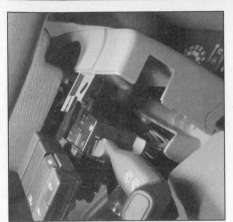

26.3b ... and withdraw the upper shroud

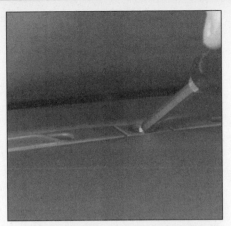

26.5a Unscrewing an upper facia trim panel top securing screw ...

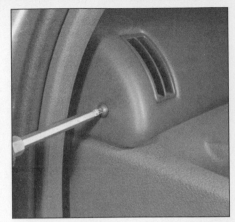

26.5b ... and side securing screw

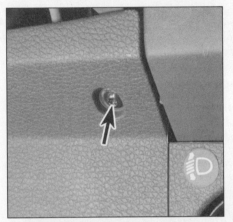

26.8 Driver's side lower facia panel securing screw (arrowed)

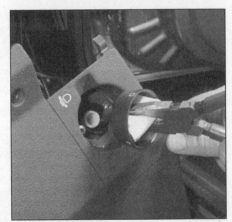

26.9a Pull the knob from the headlight aim adjustment control ...

26.9b ... and remove the two securing screws

26.10a Releasing the headlight aim adjustment control from the panel

26.10b Bonnet release lever securing clips (arrowed)

Driver's side lower facia panel

Removal

7   Pull the bonnet release lever down to expose the release lever assembly securing bolt, then unscrew the bolt.

8   Remove the two securing screws from the upper edge of the panel, then carefully lower the panel (see illustration).

9   On models fitted with a facia-mounted headlight aim adjustment control, carefully pull the knob from the control, using a pair of pliers and a piece of thick paper or card to protect the knob. Remove the two screws securing the control to the facia panel (see illustrations).

10   Take careful note of the routing of any cables and hoses, then unclip the bonnet release lever assembly and the headlight aim adjustment switch, as applicable, from the rear of the panel (see illustrations).

11   Withdraw the panel.

11

26.14a Remove the upper . . .

26.14b . . . and lower securing screws . . .

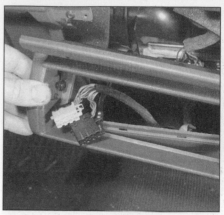

26.15 . . . and withdraw the radio/cassette
player housing from the facia

Refitting

12   Refitting is a reversal of removal, ensuring that any cables and hoses are routed as noted before removal.

Radio/cassette player housing

Removal

13   Remove the radio/cassette player as described in Chapter 12.
14   Remove the two upper and two lower securing screws **(see illustrations)**.
15   Withdraw the radio/cassette player housing from the facia, feeding the wiring plugs and aerial cable through the rear of the housing as it is withdrawn **(see illustration)**.

Refitting

16   Refitting is a reversal of removal. Refit the radio/cassette player with reference to Chapter 12.

Heater ducts and vents

17   Refer to Chapter 3, Section 12.

Glovebox lock

Removal

18   The lock striker mounted on the facia also incorporates the glovebox light switch (where applicable). To remove the striker assembly, remove the single securing screw. Withdraw the striker and, where applicable, disconnect the wiring plugs **(see illustration)**.
19   Two types of lock may be fitted to the glovebox lid. The first type is operated by pushing a button at the top of the lid. This type of lock can be removed after removing the single securing screw.

20   The second type of lock is operated by squeezing two buttons located on the front of the lid. This type of lock is secured by a metal clip on the rear of the lock. Remove the clip and pull the lock out from the front of the glovebox lid.

Refitting

21   Refitting is a reversal of removal.

Complete facia assembly

Note: *This is an involved procedure, which is likely to take some time. It is advisable to make careful notes as the procedure progresses, to ensure correct refitting of all components, and correct routing of all wiring, etc. Specific details of fixings and components may vary from model to model, but the following will serve as a guide. Provided plenty of time is allowed, removal of the facia assembly should not present any problems.*

Removal

22   Disconnect the battery negative lead.
23   Prise the centre cover from the steering wheel, then unscrew the securing nut and remove the steering wheel.
24   Remove the centre console as described in Section 25.
25   Remove both front footwell side/sill trim panels, as described in Section 24.
26   Remove the steering column shrouds, upper facia trim panel, driver's side lower facia panel, and radio/cassette player housing, as described earlier in this Section.
27   Working in the footwells, unscrew the securing bolts (one on each side), and disconnect the facia wiring harness earth leads **(see illustration)**.
28   Where applicable, disconnect the door wiring connectors from

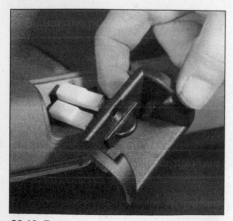

26.18 Removing the glovebox lock striker

26.27 Facia wiring harness earth lead
securing bolt (arrowed)

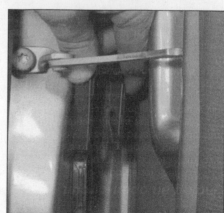

26.29a Pull the connector securing clip
from the wiring socket . . .

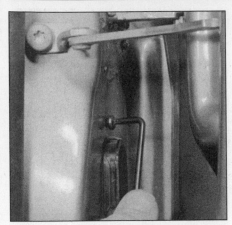

26.29b . . . then unscrew the socket securing screws

26.33 Remove the two screws securing the facia assembly to the steering column

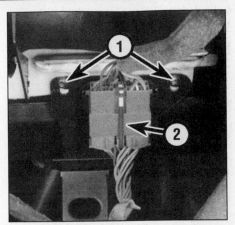

26.35 Remove the two screws (1) securing the facia to the mounting bracket. Note radio/cassette player wiring plug securing clip (2)

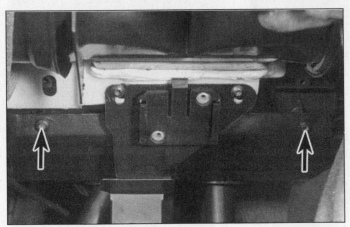

26.39 Heater ducting-to-facia securing screws (arrowed)

the door pillars. To release a connector, slide the securing clip up, then pull the connector from its socket.

29 Pull the connector securing clips from the wiring sockets, then unscrew the two securing screws in each case, and detach the door wiring sockets from the door pillars **(see illustrations)**.

30 On models fitted with a radio/cassette player remote control switch, slide the switch from its bracket on the steering column stalk switch assembly, then withdraw the switch, feeding the wiring through the facia. Note the routing of the wiring as it is withdrawn.

31 Remove the complete steering column stalk switch assembly, as described in Chapter 12, Section 15.

32 Working behind the facia, disconnect the ignition switch wiring connectors.

33 Remove the two screws securing the facia assembly to the steering column **(see illustration)**.

34 Remove the instrument panel as described in Chapter 12.

35 Working through the radio/cassette player housing aperture, remove the two screws securing the facia assembly to the metal mounting bracket **(see illustration)**.

36 Unclip the radio/cassette player wiring connector from the metal mounting bracket, and separate the two halves of the connector.

37 Remove the two securing screws from the lower edge of the heater control panel.

38 Withdraw the heater control panel from the facia, and disconnect the wiring plug.

39 Working through the radio/cassette player housing aperture, remove the two screws securing the heater ducting to the facia **(see illustration)**.

40 Locate the rivet securing the facia assembly to the metal bracket on the passenger's side of the heater control panel housing. Using a suitable diameter drill, carefully drill out the rivet.

41 The remaining facia panel wiring harness connectors must now be disconnected.

42 Note that most of the connectors are clipped to the bulkhead or the footwell panels. In certain cases, the two halves of the connector are fastened together by metal or plastic clips. Note the routing of all wiring as the connectors are disconnected **(see illustrations)**.

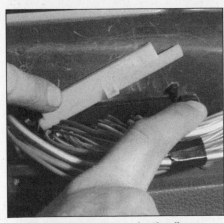

26.42a Removing a plastic clip . . .

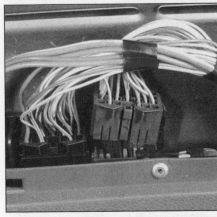

26.42b . . . and disconnecting bulkhead wiring connectors

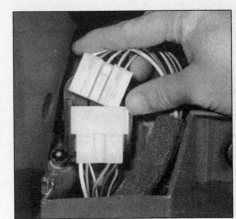

26.42c Disconnecting a bulkhead side wiring connector

11

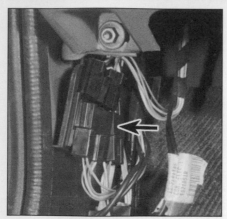

26.42d Facia footwell wiring connectors (arrowed)

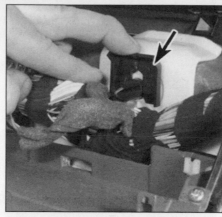

26.43 Removing the plastic securing clip (arrowed) from the top of the facia

26.44a Facia upper securing nut (arrowed)

26.44b Facia lower securing nut (arrowed)

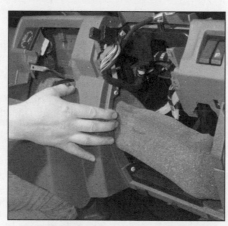

26.46 Withdrawing the facia assembly

26.50 If necessary, use a nut and a bolt (arrowed) in place of the original rivet

43   Remove the large plastic securing clip from the top centre of the facia assembly **(see illustration)**.

44   Working at each corner of the facia assembly, unscrew the four securing nuts (one nut at each corner) **(see illustrations)**.

45   Make a final check to ensure that all wires, cables and hoses are disconnected and moved clear of the facia.

46   With the aid of an assistant, carefully withdraw the facia assembly from the bulkhead, and withdraw it from the car through one of the front doors **(see illustration)**. If the facia is difficult to remove, do not use excessive force - check that all necessary wiring has been disconnected, and that the harnesses are not fouling surrounding components.

Refitting

47   Refitting is a reversal of removal, bearing in mind the following points.

48   As the facia assembly is offered to the bulkhead, ensure that none of the wiring harnesses, plugs, cables or hoses are trapped.

49   Ensure that all wiring connectors are securely reconnected, and that all connector securing clips are in place, where applicable.

50   Use a new pop rivet, or alternatively a suitable nut and bolt, to secure the facia assembly to the metal bracket on the passenger's side of the heater control panel housing **(see illustration)**.

51   Where applicable, do not fully tighten the radio/cassette player remote control switch clamp screw until the steering column shrouds

have been refitted.

52   On completion, check that all switches, lights and instruments function correctly.

27 Front seat belt tension mechanism (1994-on) - general information

On facelifted models (manufactured from early 1994 onwards), a front seat belt pre-tensioner system is fitted. The system is designed to instantaneously take up any slack in the seat belt in the case of a sudden frontal impact, therefore reducing the possibility of injury to the front seat occupants. Each front seat is fitted with its own system, the components of which are mounted in the seat frame.

The pre-tensioner is triggered by a heavy frontal impact. Lesser frontal impacts and impacts from behind, will not trigger the system.

When the system is triggered, a pre-tensioned spring draws back the seat belt via a cable which acts on the seat belt stalk. The cable pulls in the seat belt stalk, which reduces the slack in the seat belt around the shoulders and waist of the occupant.

There is a risk of injury if the system is triggered inadvertently when working on the vehicle, and it is therefore strongly recommended that any work involving the seat belt tensioner system is entrusted to a Renault dealer.

Chapter 12 Body electrical system

Contents

Specifications

Fuses in main fusebox

No	Rating (amps)*	Circuit(s) protected*
1	30	Front and rear right-hand electric windows
2	15	ABS (not applicable to models covered by this manual)
3	30	Front and rear left-hand electric windows
4	20	Heated seats
5	15	Courtesy light, radio, alarm
6	30	Accessories cut-off (master fuse)
7	10	Clock
8	15	Windscreen wash/wipe motors
9	15	Cigarette lighter
10	10	Stop-lights
11	10	Radio/cassette player
12	20	Central locking and electric mirror motors
13	20	Heated rear window and heated mirrors
14	10	Windscreen wash/wipe timer
15	-	Positive feed for caravan/trailer wiring
16	10	Direction indicators/hazard warning flashers
17	10	Rear foglight
18	10	Left-hand side and tail lights
19	10	Right-hand side and tail lights
20	-	Not used
21	20	Heater blower
22	10	Radio, alarm

12

Fuses in auxiliary fusebox

No	Rating (amps)*	Circuit(s) protected*
1	5	Reversing lights, alarm
2	25	Right-hand headlight dipped beam, and headlight wash/wipe
3	15	Left-hand headlight dipped beam
4	20	Front foglights
5	25	Engine cooling fan
6	30	Engine functions
7	25	Right-hand headlight dipped beam, and headlight wash/wipe (alternative to fuse No 2)
8	20	Horn
9	15	Left-hand headlight dipped beam (alternative to fuse No 4)
10	25	Engine functions
11	5	Automatic transmission (not applicable to models covered by this manual)
12	15	Right-hand headlight main beam
13	15	Left-hand headlight main beam
14	20	Fuel pump
15	30	Air conditioning (not applicable to models covered by this manual)

* Details given are typical. Fuse ratings and circuits protected may vary with territory, model and year. Refer to owner's handbook for further information.

1 General information and precautions

General information

The body electrical system consists of all lights, wash/wipe equipment, interior electrical equipment, and associated switches and wiring.

The electrical system is of the 12-volt negative earth type. Power to the body electrical system is provided by a 12-volt battery which is charged by the alternator (see Chapter 5).

The engine electrical system (battery, alternator, starter motor, pre-heating system, etc) is covered separately in Chapter 5.

Precautions

Refer to the precautions given in Chapter 5, Section 1 before carrying out any work on the body electrical system. In particular take note of the precautions to be observed before disconnecting the battery on a vehicle equipped with a security-coded radio/cassette unit.

2 Electrical fault-finding - general information

Note: *Refer to the precautions given in "Safety first!" and in Section 1 of Chapter 5 before starting work. The following tests relate to testing of the main electrical circuits, and should not be used to test delicate electronic circuits, particularly where an electronic control module is used.*

General

1   A typical electrical circuit consists of an electrical component, any switches, relays, motors, fuses, fusible links or circuit breakers related to that component, and the wiring and connectors which link the component to both the battery and the chassis. To help to pinpoint a problem in an electrical circuit, wiring diagrams are included at the end of this manual.

2   Before attempting to diagnose an electrical fault, first study the appropriate wiring diagram, to obtain a complete understanding of the components included in the particular circuit concerned. The possible sources of a fault can be narrowed down by noting if other components related to the circuit are operating properly. If several components or circuits fail at one time, the problem is likely to be related to a shared fuse or earth connection.

3   Electrical problems usually stem from simple causes, such as loose or corroded connections, a faulty earth connection, a blown fuse, a melted fusible link, or a faulty relay (refer to Section 13 for details of testing relays). Visually inspect the condition of all fuses, wires and connections in a problem circuit before testing the components. Use the wiring diagrams to determine which terminal connections will need to be checked in order to pinpoint the trouble-spot.

4   The basic tools required for electrical fault-finding include a circuit tester or voltmeter (a 12-volt bulb with a set of test leads can also be used for certain tests); a self-powered test light (sometimes known as a continuity tester); an ohmmeter (to measure resistance); a battery and set of test leads; and a jumper wire, preferably with a circuit breaker or fuse incorporated, which can be used to bypass suspect wires or electrical components. Before attempting to locate a problem with test instruments, use the wiring diagram to determine where to make the connections.

5   To find the source of an intermittent wiring fault (usually due to a poor or dirty connection, or damaged wiring insulation), a "wiggle" test can be performed on the wiring. This involves wiggling the wiring by hand to see if the fault occurs as the wiring is moved. It should be possible to narrow down the source of the fault to a particular section of wiring. This method of testing can be used in conjunction with any of the tests described in the following sub-Sections.

6   Apart from problems due to poor connections, two basic types of fault can occur in an electrical circuit - open-circuit, or short-circuit.

7   Open-circuit faults are caused by a break somewhere in the circuit, which prevents current from flowing. An open-circuit fault will prevent a component from working, but will not cause the relevant circuit fuse to blow.

8   Short-circuit faults are caused by a "short" somewhere in the circuit, which allows the current flowing in the circuit to "escape" along an alternative route, usually to earth. Short-circuit faults are normally caused by a breakdown in wiring insulation, which allows a feed wire to touch either another wire, or an earthed component such as the bodyshell. A short-circuit fault will normally cause the relevant circuit fuse to blow.

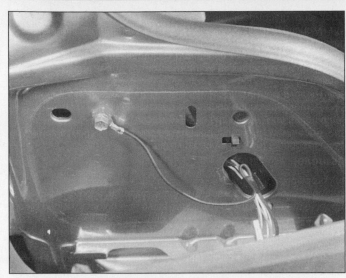

2.20 Rear light cluster earth connection (viewed with light cluster removed)

such as the engine/gearbox and the body, usually where there is no metal-to-metal contact between components due to flexible rubber mountings, etc **(see illustration)**.
21   To check whether a component is properly earthed, disconnect the battery, and connect one lead of an ohmmeter to a known good earth point. Connect the other lead to the wire or earth connection being tested. The resistance reading should be zero; if not, check the connection as follows.
22   If an earth connection is thought to be faulty, dismantle the connection, and clean back to bare metal both the bodyshell and the wire terminal or the component earth connection mating surface. Be careful to remove all traces of dirt and corrosion, then use a knife to trim away any paint, so that a clean metal-to-metal joint is made. On reassembly, tighten the joint fasteners securely; if a wire terminal is being refitted, use serrated washers between the terminal and the bodyshell to ensure a clean and secure connection. When the connection is remade, prevent the onset of corrosion in the future by applying a coat of petroleum jelly or silicone-based grease, or by spraying on (at regular intervals) a proprietary ignition sealer.

Finding an open-circuit

9   To check for an open-circuit, connect one lead of a circuit tester or voltmeter to the battery negative terminal, or to a known good earth.
10   Connect the other lead to a connector in the circuit being tested, preferably nearest to the battery or fuse.
11   Switch on the circuit, bearing in mind that some circuits are live only when the ignition switch is moved to a particular position.
12   If voltage is present (indicated either by the tester bulb lighting or a voltmeter reading, as applicable), this means that the section of the circuit between the relevant connector and the battery is problem-free.
13   Continue to check the remainder of the circuit in the same fashion.
14   When a point is reached at which no voltage is present, the problem must lie between that point and the previous test point with voltage. Most problems can be traced to a broken, corroded or loose connection.

Finding a short-circuit

15   To check for a short-circuit, first disconnect the load(s) from the circuit (loads are the components which draw current from a circuit, such as bulbs, motors, heating elements, etc).
16   Remove the relevant fuse from the circuit, and connect a circuit tester or voltmeter to the fuse connections.
17   Switch on the circuit, bearing in mind that some circuits are live only when the ignition switch is moved to a particular position.
18   If voltage is present (indicated either by the tester bulb lighting or a voltmeter reading, as applicable), this means that there is a short-circuit.
19   If no voltage is present, but the fuse still blows with the load(s) connected, this indicates an internal fault in the load(s).

Finding an earth fault

20   The battery negative terminal is connected to "earth" - the metal of the engine/gearbox unit and the car body. Most electrical systems are wired so that they only receive a positive feed, the current returning via the metal of the car body. This means that the component mounting and the body form part of that circuit. Loose or corroded mountings can therefore cause a range of electrical faults, ranging from total failure of a circuit, to a puzzling partial fault. In particular, lights may shine dimly (especially when another circuit sharing the same earth point is in operation), motors (eg wiper motors or the radiator cooling fan motor) may run slowly, and the operation of one circuit may have an apparently-unrelated effect on another. Note that on many vehicles, earth straps are used between certain components,

3   Battery - testing and charging

Refer to Chapter 5, Section 3.

4   Battery - removal and refitting

Refer to Chapter 5, Section 4.

5   Charging system - testing

Refer to Chapter 5, Section 5.

6   Auxiliary drivebelt - removal, refitting and tensioning

Refer to Chapter 1, Section 10.

7   Alternator - removal and refitting

Refer to Chapter 5, Section 7.

8   Alternator brushes and regulator - inspection and renewal

Refer to Chapter 5, Section 8.

9   Starting system - testing

Refer to Chapter 5, Section 9.

10   Starter motor - removal and refitting

Refer to Chapter 5, Section 10.

11   Starter motor - brush renewal

Refer to Chapter 5, Section 11.

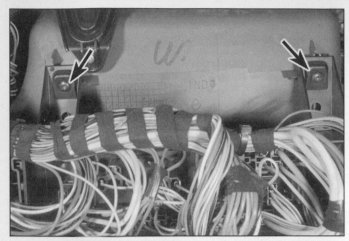

12.2 Fusebox upper securing screws (arrowed) viewed with facia removed

13.2 Fuse locations in main fusebox

For circuits protected, refer to Specifications

13.4a Auxiliary fusebox location in engine compartment

12 Fusebox - removal and refitting

Removal

1   Disconnect the battery negative lead.
2   Reach up under the facia, and unscrew the two securing screws from the rear of the fusebox **(see illustration)**.
3   Working at the bottom of the fusebox, unscrew the remaining two securing screws.
4   Carefully lower the fusebox from the facia. Disconnect all relevant wiring plugs to enable the fusebox to be withdrawn, noting their locations if necessary.

Refitting

5   Refitting is a reversal of removal.

13 Fuses and relays - testing and renewal

Fuses

1   Fuses are designed to break a circuit when a predetermined current is reached, in order to protect components and wiring which could be damaged by excessive current flow. Any excessive current flow will be due to a fault in the circuit, usually a short-circuit

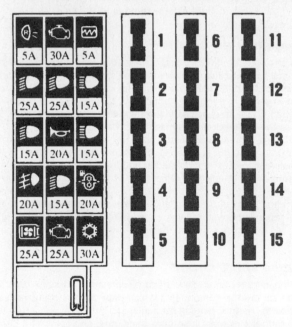

13.4b Fuse locations in auxiliary fusebox

For circuits protected, refer to Specifications

(see Section 2).
2   The main fuses are located in the fusebox, under the facia on the passenger's side **(see illustration)**.
3   For access to the fuses, press the two plastic securing tabs, then lower the fusebox panel from the facia. The circuits protected by the fuses are marked on a sticker at the bottom of the fusebox panel.
4   Additional fuses are located in an auxiliary fusebox under the bonnet, beneath the hinged flap in the windscreen cowl panel on the left-hand side. For access to these fuses, lift the cowl panel flap, then unclip the cover from the fusebox. The circuits protected by the fuses are marked on the inside of the panel cover. The fuse for the radio/cassette player is mounted on the rear of the unit **(see illustrations)**.
5   A blown fuse can be recognised from its melted or broken wire.
6   To remove a fuse, first ensure that the relevant circuit is switched off.
7   Using the plastic tool provided in the fusebox, pull the fuse from its location.
8   Spare fuses are provided at the lower left-hand side of the main fusebox, and at the left-hand side of the auxiliary fusebox.

13.4c Removing the fuse from the rear of the radio/cassette player

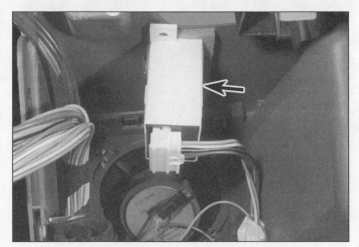

13.12b Tailgate wash/wipe relay (arrowed) viewed with facia removed

9   Before renewing a blown fuse, trace and rectify the cause, and always use a fuse of the correct rating. Never substitute a fuse of a higher rating, or make temporary repairs using wire or metal foil; more serious damage, or even fire, could result.

10   Note that the fuses are colour-coded as follows. Refer to the Specifications for details of the fuse ratings and the circuits protected.

Colour	Rating
Orange	5A
Red	10A
Blue	15A
Yellow	20A
Clear or white	25A
Green	30A

Relays

11   A relay is an electrically-operated switch, which is used for the following reasons.

a) *A relay can switch a heavy current remotely from the circuit in which the current is flowing, therefore allowing the use of lighter gauge wiring and switch contacts.*

b) *A relay can receive more than one control input, unlike a mechanical switch.*

c) *A relay can have a "timer" function - for example, the intermittent wiper relay.*

12   Most of the relays are located in the fusebox. Note that on some models, the tailgate wash/wipe relay is located behind the facia, to the

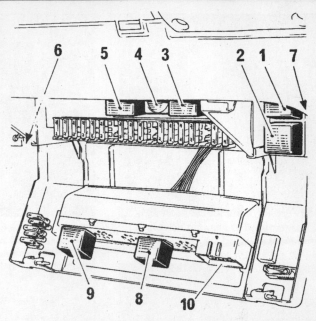

13.12a Identification of relays in the main fusebox

1   Rear foglight relay
2   Heated rear window relay
3   "Lights on" warning buzzer
4   Direction indicator/hazard flasher relay
5   Central locking timer relay
6   Windscreen wash/wipe delay relay
7   Tailgate wash/wipe delay relay
8   Front foglight relay
9   External temperature display relay
10   Diagnostic socket

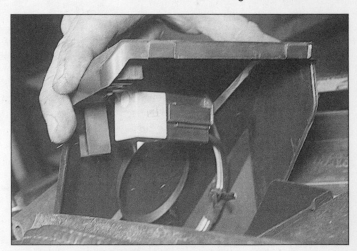

13.13 Removing the relay box cover

left of the fusebox **(see illustrations)**.

13   Certain models have a relay box located in the engine compartment, on the left-hand side, in front of the suspension turret **(see illustration)**. The box contains the relay for the power steering pump when fitted. Further details can be found in Chapter 10.

14   If a circuit controlled by a relay develops a fault, and the relay is suspect, operate the circuit. If the relay is functioning, it should be possible to hear the relay click as it is energised. If this is the case, the fault lies with the components or wiring in the system. If the relay is not being energised, then either the relay is not receiving a switching voltage, or the relay itself is faulty (do not overlook the relay socket terminals when tracing faults). Testing is by the substitution of a known good unit, but be careful; while some relays are identical in appearance and in operation, others look similar, but perform different functions.

12

15.3 Unscrew the securing screws . . .

15.4 . . . then disconnect the wiring plugs
and withdraw the stalk switch

15.11a Loosen the clamp screw . . .

15.11b . . . and withdraw the stalk
switch assembly

15.14 Disconnecting the remote control
switch wiring from the rear of the
radio/cassette player

15.16 Removing the radio/cassette player
remote control switch

14   "Lights on" warning buzzer - removal and refitting

The "lights on" warning buzzer is located in the fusebox, along with the relays. See illustration 13.12a.

15   Switches - removal and refitting

Lighting/direction indicator/horn stalk switch

Removal

1   Disconnect the battery negative lead.
2   Remove the steering column shrouds as described in Chapter 11, Section 26.
3   Working under the switch, unscrew the two securing screws and lift the switch from the steering column **(see illustration)**.
4   Disconnect the wiring plugs, and withdraw the switch **(see illustration)**.

Refitting

5   Refitting is a reversal of removal.

Wash/wipe stalk switch

6   Proceed as just described for the lighting/direction indicator/horn stalk switch.

Complete stalk switch assembly

Removal

7   Remove the steering wheel as described in Chapter 10.

8   Proceed as described in paragraphs 1 and 2.
9   Disconnect the wiring plugs from the switches.
10   Where applicable, slide the radio/cassette player remote control switch from the bracket on the stalk switch assembly.
11   Working at the top of the switch assembly, loosen the clamp screw, then withdraw the assembly from the steering column **(see illustrations)**.

Refitting

12   Refitting is a reversal of removal. Refit the steering wheel as described in Chapter 10.

Radio/cassette player remote control switch

Removal

13   Disconnect the battery negative lead.
14   Remove the radio/cassette player as described in Section 32. Disconnect the remote control switch wiring plug from the rear of the unit **(see illustration)**.
15   Remove the steering column shrouds as described in Chapter 11, Section 26.
16   Slide the switch from the bracket on the stalk switch assembly **(see illustration)**.
17   Feed the wiring through from behind the facia, noting its routing, and remove the switch.

Refitting

18   Refitting is a reversal of removal, bearing in mind the following points.
19   Refit the radio/cassette player with reference to Section 32.
20   Ensure that the wiring is routed as noted during removal.

15.23 Removing a facia-mounted rocker switch

15.28 Prise the instrument panel illumination control from the facia . . .

15.29 . . . then pull the control free and disconnect the wiring plug

15.35 Pull the rubber cover from the courtesy light switch . . .

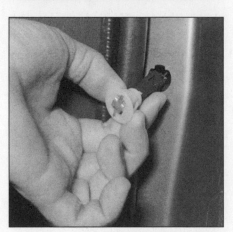

15.36 . . . then pull the switch from the door pillar

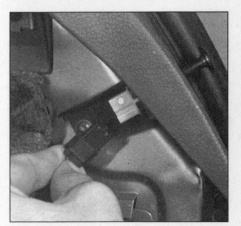

15.40 Disconnecting the wiring from the luggage compartment light switch

21 Do not fully tighten the switch clamp screw until the steering column shrouds have been refitted.

Facia-mounted rocker switches

Removal
22 Disconnect the battery negative lead.
23 Using two screwdrivers, carefully prise the switch to release it from the facia, taking care not to damage the facia trim **(see illustration)**.
24 Pull the switch from the facia and disconnect the wiring plug.

Refitting
25 Refitting is a reversal of removal.

Headlight aim adjustment control

26 The headlight aim adjustment control, hoses and actuators form a complete assembly; no parts are available separately. For further details, see Section 20.

Instrument panel illumination control

Removal
27 Disconnect the battery negative lead.
28 Using a screwdriver, carefully prise the control from the facia, taking care not to damage the facia trim **(see illustration)**.
29 Pull the control from the facia, and disconnect the wiring plug **(see illustration)**.

Refitting
30 Refitting is a reversal of removal.

Central locking operating switches

31 Refer to Chapter 11, Section 14.

Electric window operating switches

32 Refer to Chapter 11, Section 15.

Courtesy light switches

Removal
33 The switches are located in the front door pillars.
34 Disconnect the battery negative lead.
35 Pull the rubber cover from the switch **(see illustration)**.
36 Carefully prise the switch from the door pillar, and disconnect the wiring plug **(see illustration)**. Take care not to allow the wiring to drop down into the door pillar while the switch is removed - tape it to the door pillar if necessary.

Refitting
37 Refitting is a reversal of removal.

Luggage compartment light switch

Removal
38 Disconnect the battery negative lead.
39 Open the tailgate. Pull the luggage compartment right-hand side trim away from the body for access to the rear of the switch.
40 Disconnect the wiring plug from the switch **(see illustration)**.
41 Push the switch out through the rear quarter trim panel, and remove it **(see illustration)**.

12

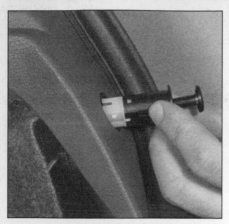

15.41 Removing the luggage compartment light switch

16.3 Pulling the wiring plug from the rear of the headlight

16.4 Withdrawing a headlight bulb

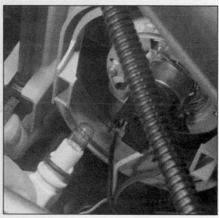

16.9 Removing the sidelight bulbholder

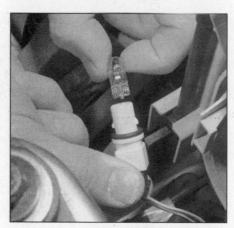

16.10 Removing the sidelight bulb from the bulbholder

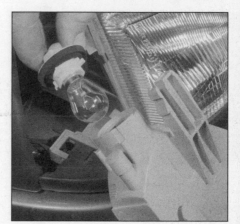

16.15 Removing a front direction indicator light bulb

Refitting

42 Refitting is a reversal of removal.

Glovebox light switch

43 The glovebox light switch is incorporated in the glovebox lock striker. For details see Chapter 11, Section 26.

Map reading light switch

44 The map reading light switch is integral with the roof console, and cannot be removed separately. Removal and refitting of the roof console panel is described in Chapter 11, Section 24.

16 Bulbs (exterior lights) - renewal

General

1 Whenever a bulb is renewed, note the following points.

a) *Disconnect the battery negative lead, or at least make sure that the lighting circuit is switched off, before starting work.*

b) *Remember that if the light has recently been in use, the bulb may be extremely hot.*

c) *Always check the bulb contacts and/or holder (as applicable). Ensure that there is clean metal-to-metal contact between the bulb contacts and the contacts in the holder, and/or the holder and the wiring plug. Clean off any corrosion or dirt before fitting a new bulb.*

d) *Ensure that the new bulb is of the correct rating and that it is completely clean before fitting; this applies particularly to headlight bulbs.*

Headlight

2 Working in the engine compartment, squeeze the retaining clip(s) and remove the plastic cover from the rear of the headlight.

3 Pull the wiring plug from the rear of the headlight bulb **(see illustration)**.

4 Release the bulb retaining spring clip. Grasp the bulb by its contacts and carefully withdraw it from the headlight unit **(see illustration)**.

5 When handling the new bulb, use a tissue or clean cloth to avoid touching the glass with the fingers; moisture and grease from the skin can cause blackening and rapid failure of this type of bulb. If the glass is accidentally touched, wipe it clean using methylated spirit.

6 Refitting is a reversal of removal. Note that the headlight cover is refitted with the cut-out for the wiring at the bottom.

Front sidelight

7 Working in the engine compartment, squeeze the retaining clip(s) and remove the plastic cover from the rear of the headlight.

8 Pull the wiring plug from the rear of the sidelight bulbholder.

9 Twist the bulbholder anti-clockwise, and remove it from the rear of the headlight assembly **(see illustration)**.

10 The bulb is a push-fit in the bulbholder **(see illustration)**.

11 Refitting is a reversal of removal, bearing in mind the following points.

12 Ensure that the rubber seal on the rear of the bulbholder is in good condition and is correctly fitted.

13 Refit the headlight cover with the cut-out for the wiring at the bottom.

16.18 Prise the direction indicator side repeater light from the trim plate . . .

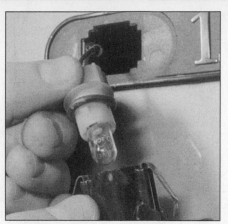

16.19 . . . remove the bulbholder . . .

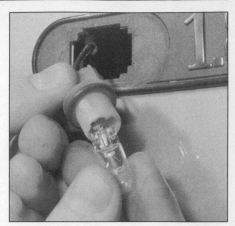

16.20 . . . and withdraw the bulb

16.22 Unscrewing a front foglight securing screw

Front direction indicator side repeater light

18   Carefully prise the light unit from the trim plate on the front wing **(see illustration)**.
19   Twist the bulbholder anti-clockwise, and withdraw it from the rear of the light unit **(see illustration)**.
20   The bulb is a push-fit in the bulbholder **(see illustration)**.
21   Refitting is a reversal of removal.

Front foglight

22   Unscrew the two securing screws, and remove the light from the front bumper **(see illustration)**.
23   Disconnect the wiring plug **(see illustration)**.
24   Twist the plastic cover anti-clockwise, and withdraw it from the rear of the light.
25   Disconnect the wiring from the rear of the bulb.
26   Release the bulb retaining spring clip, then grasp the bulb by its contacts and carefully withdraw it from the light unit **(see illustration)**.
27   When handling the new bulb, use a tissue or clean cloth to avoid touching the glass with the fingers; moisture and grease from the skin can cause blackening and rapid failure of this type of bulb. If the glass is accidentally touched, wipe it clean using methylated spirit.
28   Refitting is a reversal of removal.

Rear light cluster

29   Open the tailgate, and unscrew the rear light cluster securing nut **(see illustration)**.
30   Working outside the car, tilt the light cluster and lift it from the retaining lugs on the body. Disconnect the wiring plug.
31   Squeeze the securing clips towards the centre of the bulbholder,

Front direction indicator light

14   On models where the bulbholder is accessible from the engine compartment, twist the bulbholder anti-clockwise through a quarter of a turn, then withdraw the bulbholder.
15   On some models, access to the bulbholder is not possible from within the engine compartment. Remove the light unit as described in Section 18, then twist the bulbholder anti-clockwise to remove it **(see illustration)**.
16   The bulb is a bayonet fit in the bulbholder.
17   Refitting is a reversal of removal.

16.23 Disconnecting a front foglight wiring plug

16.26 Removing a front foglight bulb

16.29 Unscrewing a rear light cluster securing nut

12

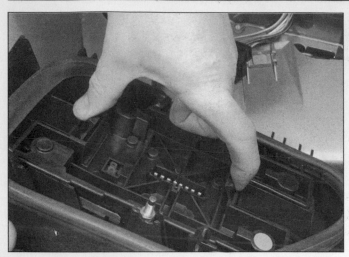

16.31a Squeeze the securing clips . . .

16.31b . . . and remove the rear light cluster bulbholder

and pull the bulbholder from the rear of the light cluster **(see illustrations)**.

32   The bulbs are a bayonet fit in their holders.

33   Refitting is a reversal of removal.

Rear number plate light

34   Using a screwdriver, carefully prise the number plate light assembly from its location in the bumper. Disconnect the wiring plug **(see illustration)**.

35   Release the securing tabs and unclip the lens from the light assembly **(see illustration)**.

36   Pull the bulb from its contacts.

37   Refitting is a reversal of removal. Ensure that the rubber seal is correctly located when refitting the lens.

---

17   Bulbs (interior lights) - renewal

General

1   Refer to Section 16, paragraph 1.

Courtesy light

2   Unclip the cover from the roof console for access to the bulb **(see illustration)**.

3   The bulb is a push-fit in its contacts **(see illustration)**.

4   Refitting is a reversal of removal.

Map reading light

5   Proceed as described previously for the courtesy light.

Glovebox light

6   Prise the light assembly from its location in the glovebox **(see illustration)**.

7   The bulb is a push-fit in its contacts.

8   Refitting is a reversal of removal.

Luggage compartment light

9   The procedure is as described previously for the glovebox light.

Instrument panel illumination and warning light bulbs

10   Refer to Section 22.

Cigarette lighter illumination bulb

11   Pull the ashtray and housing from the centre console.

12   Working through the aperture, push the cigarette lighter mounting panel from the centre console **(see illustration)**.

13   Disconnect the wiring from the cigarette lighter, and from any switches mounted in the panel **(see illustration)**.

14   Working at the rear of the cigarette lighter, pull the plastic cover from the bulb **(see illustration)**.

15   Using a small screwdriver inserted through the rear of the bulbholder, push the bulb from its contacts.

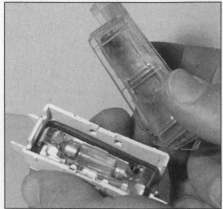

16.34 Removing the rear number plate light and wiring plug

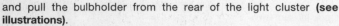

16.35 Unclip the lens to expose the bulb

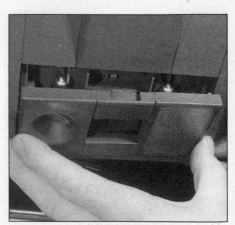

17.2 Remove the cover from the courtesy light . . .

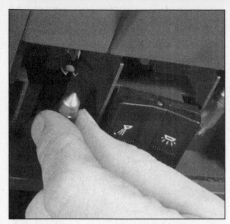

17.3 . . . for access to the bulb

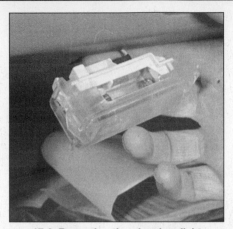

17.6 Removing the glovebox light

17.12 Push the cigarette lighter mounting panel from the centre console . . .

16   Push the new bulb into the bulbholder, then reassemble and refit the cigarette lighter using a reversal of the removal procedure.

Ashtray illumination bulb

17   The ashtray shares the same illumination bulb as the cigarette lighter. Refer to paragraphs 11 to 16 for details.

Clock illumination bulb

18   Remove the clock, as described in Section 23.
19   Twist the bulbholder anti-clockwise, and pull it from the rear of the clock.
20   The bulb is integral with the bulbholder.
21   Refitting is a reversal of removal.

18 Exterior light units - removal and refitting

Headlight unit

Removal

1   Remove the direction indicator light unit, as described later in this Section.
2   Remove the radiator grille panel, as described in Chapter 11.
3   Working at the rear of the headlight, squeeze the retaining clip(s) and remove the plastic cover from the rear of the headlight.
4   Disconnect the wiring plugs from the rear of the headlight and sidelight bulbs.
5   On models fitted with a remote headlight aim adjustment control,

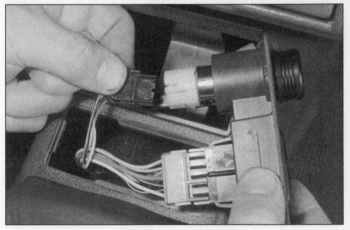

17.13 . . . and disconnect the wiring plugs

free the actuator from the rear of the headlight, by twisting the actuator anti-clockwise and pulling it sharply to release the balljoint.
6   Unscrew the three upper securing screws, and the single front securing screw, then withdraw the headlight **(see illustrations)**.

Refitting

7   Refitting is a reversal of removal, but where applicable, take care not to damage the headlight aim adjustment actuator balljoint when reconnecting it to the headlight.

17.14 Pull off the plastic cover to expose the cigarette lighter bulb

18.6a Unscrewing the headlight front securing screw. Upper securing screws arrowed

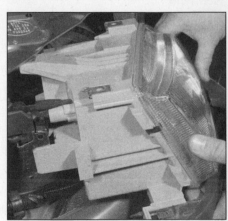

18.6b Withdrawing a headlight

12

18.8a Headlight beam vertical adjustment screw . . .

18.8b . . . and horizontal adjustment screw

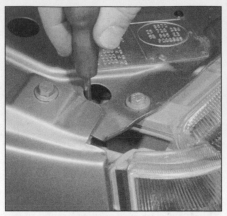

18.10 Depressing the direction indicator light unit retaining tab

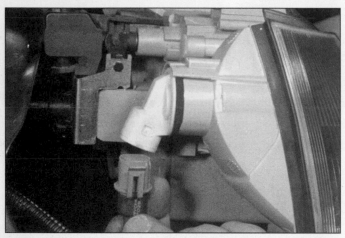

18.11 Disconnecting the direction indicator light unit wiring plug

18.14 Removing the front direction indicator side repeater light

Beam alignment

8   On completion, the headlight beam alignment should be checked, ideally using optical setting equipment. This check can be carried out by a Renault dealer or a suitably-equipped garage. The beam alignment is adjusted using the two screws provided on the light unit **(see illustrations)**.

Front direction indicator light unit

Removal

9   Open the bonnet and disconnect the battery negative lead.
10   Working through the hole in the top of the engine compartment front panel, depress the direction indicator light unit retaining tab with a screwdriver **(see illustration)**.
11   Pull the light unit forwards, and disconnect the wiring plug from the bulbholder **(see illustration)**.

Refitting

12   Refitting is a reversal of removal. Ensure that the weatherseal is correctly located between the light unit and the body.

Front direction indicator side repeater light

Removal

13   Disconnect the battery negative lead.
14   Carefully prise the light unit from the trim plate on the front wing **(see illustration)**. Disconnect the wiring plug from the rear of the bulbholder.

Refitting

15   Refitting is a reversal of removal.

Front foglight

Removal

16   Open the bonnet and disconnect the battery negative lead.
17   Unscrew the two securing screws from the front of the foglight, then pull the light from the bumper, and disconnect the wiring plug.

Refitting

18   Refitting is a reversal of removal. If necessary, the vertical alignment of the beam can be adjusted by turning screw "B" as shown **(see illustration)**.

Rear light cluster

Removal

19   Open the bonnet and disconnect the battery negative lead.
20   Open the tailgate and unscrew the plastic nut from the rear of the light cluster.
21   Withdraw the light cluster from outside the car, taking care not to damage the retaining lugs at the bottom of the light, then disconnect the wiring plugs **(see illustration)**.
22   Where applicable, feed the wiring through the grommet in the bottom of the light cluster. Withdraw the assembly from the car.

Refitting

23   Refitting is a reversal of removal, bearing in mind the following points.
24   Where applicable, make sure that the wiring grommet is correctly positioned in the bottom of the light cluster.
25   Ensure that the retaining lugs at the base of the light cluster are

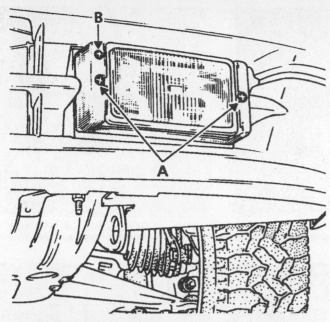

18.18 Front foglight securing screws (A), and beam adjustment screw (B)

18.21 Disconnecting a wiring plug from a rear light unit

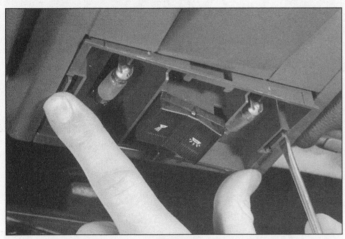

19.3a Releasing a courtesy light assembly securing lug

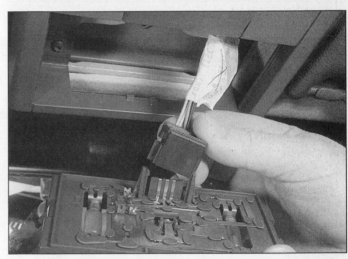

19.3b Disconnecting the courtesy light wiring plug

correctly engaged with the corresponding holes in the body.

26　Make sure that the weatherseal is correctly located between the light cluster and the body.

Rear number plate light

Removal

27　Using a screwdriver, carefully prise the light unit from its location in the bumper.

28　Disconnect the wiring and withdraw the unit from the car.

Refitting

29　Refitting is a reversal of removal.

19　Interior light units - removal and refitting

Courtesy light

Removal

1　Disconnect the battery negative lead.

2　On models with a separate courtesy light and no map reading

light, carefully prise the light assembly from its location in the roof panel, and disconnect the wiring plugs.

3　On models with a map reading light, carefully prise the cover from the light assembly. Using a screwdriver, release the securing lugs and pull the light assembly (complete with map reading light and switch) from the roof console panel. Disconnect the wiring plug and withdraw the light unit (see illustrations).

Refitting

4　Refitting is a reversal of removal.

Map reading light

5　The map reading light is integral with the courtesy light assembly. Removal and refitting are as described previously in this Section.

Glovebox light

Removal

6　Disconnect the battery negative lead.

7　Prise the light from its location, and disconnect the wiring plug.

Refitting

8　Refitting is a reversal of removal.

Luggage compartment light

9　Proceed as described previously for the glovebox light.

12

20.2 Headlight aim adjustment actuator (arrowed) removed from headlight

21.3a Unscrew the instrument panel upper . . .

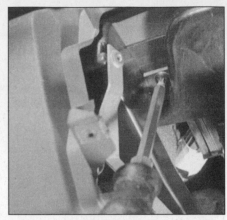

21.3b . . . and lower securing screws

20 Headlight aim adjustment components - removal and refitting

Note: *The headlight aim adjustment control, hoses and actuators form a complete assembly, and no parts are available separately.*

Removal

1   Remove the driver's side lower facia panel, as described in Chapter 11, Section 26.
2   Working in the engine compartment, release the actuator from each headlight in turn by twisting anti-clockwise and pulling sharply to release the balljoint **(see illustration)**.
3   Pull the adjuster hose grommet from the bulkhead into the car interior, then manipulate the actuators and the hoses through the hole in the bulkhead into the inside of the car. Take note of the routing of the hoses.
4   Withdraw the assembly from the car.

Refitting

5   Refitting is a reversal of removal, bearing in mind the following points.
6   Route the hoses as noted during removal.
7   Take care not to damage the actuator balljoints when reconnecting them to the headlights.
8   Make sure that the bulkhead grommet is securely located.
9   Refit the driver's side lower facia panel with reference to Chapter 11, Section 26.

21 Instrument panel - removal and refitting

Removal

1   Disconnect the battery negative lead.
2   Remove the steering column shrouds and the facia upper trim panel, as described in Chapter 11, Section 26.
3   Unscrew the four securing screws (two upper and two lower) **(see illustrations)**.
4   Pull the instrument panel forwards from the facia, at the same time disconnecting the wiring plugs and the speedometer cable from the rear of the assembly **(see illustrations)**. Where applicable, disconnect the wiring plug from the speed sensor on the end of the speedometer cable.
5   Withdraw the panel from the facia.

Refitting

6   Refitting is a reversal of removal, ensuring that all wiring plugs and the speedometer cable are securely reconnected.

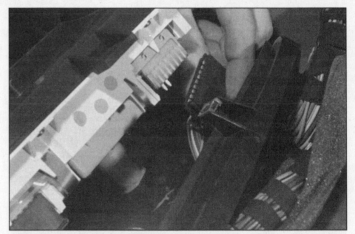

21.4a Disconnect the wiring plugs . . .

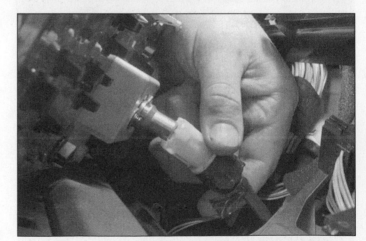

21.4b . . . and the speedometer cable from the rear of the instrument panel

7   Where applicable, do not fully tighten the radio/cassette player remote control switch clamp screw until the steering column shrouds have been refitted.

22 Instrument panel components - removal and refitting

1   With the instrument panel removed as described in Section 21, proceed as follows.

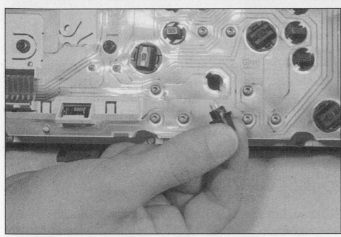

22.2 Withdrawing an instrument panel bulb

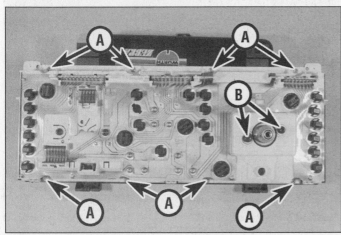

22.7 Instrument lens/cover assembly securing screws (A), and speedometer securing screws (B)

Panel illumination and warning light bulbs

Removal

2   Twist the appropriate bulbholder anti-clockwise, and withdraw it from the printed circuit board on the rear of the instrument panel **(see illustration)**.
3   The bulbs cannot be separated from the bulbholders.

Refitting

4   Refitting is a reversal of removal.

Instruments

Removal

5   Pull the trip meter reset button from the front of the instrument panel.
6   Working at the rear of the instrument panel, remove the securing screws, or release the securing clips, as applicable. Withdraw the lens/cover assembly from the front of the instrument panel.
7   Remove the appropriate securing screws from the rear of the panel, then withdraw the instrument from the front of the panel **(see illustration)**.

Refitting

8   Refitting is a reversal of removal.

Printed circuit board

Note: *No attempt should be made to remove the printed circuit board unless it is known to be faulty, and is to be renewed.*

Removal

9   Remove the illumination and warning light bulbs, and the instruments, as described previously in this Section.
10   The circuit board can now be unclipped from the rear of the instrument panel, noting how it is located.

Refitting

11   Refitting is a reversal of removal, remembering that the circuit board is fragile. Ensure that it is located as noted before removal, and that it fits correctly over the wiring connectors at the top of the panel.

23 Clock - removal and refitting

Lower facia-mounted clock

Removal

1   Disconnect the battery negative lead.
2   Remove the radio/cassette player, as described in Section 32.
3   Remove the radio/cassette player housing, as described in Chapter 11, Section 26.
4   Reach up behind the clock, and push it out through the front of the facia.
5   Disconnect the wiring plug and withdraw the clock.

Refitting

6   Refitting is a reversal of removal.

Upper facia-mounted clock

7   No information was available regarding the removal and refitting of the upper facia-mounted clock at the time of writing.

24 Outside air temperature display components - removal and refitting

Instrument panel-mounted display

1   Proceed as described in Section 22 for the instruments.

Upper facia-mounted display

2   No information was available regarding the removal and refitting of the upper facia-mounted display at the time of writing.

Sensor

Removal

3   The sensor is mounted in the bottom of the left-hand exterior mirror.
4   Disconnect the battery negative lead.
5   Open the door, and carefully prise the mirror trim panel from the front edge of the door.
6   Unscrew the two screws securing the mirror cover panel to the door, then disconnect the sensor wiring plug.
7   Remove the mirror glass, as described in Chapter 11, Section 16.
8   Remove the single securing screw, and withdraw the sensor from the mirror, feeding the wiring through the mirror body.

Refitting

9   Refitting is a reversal of removal.

25 Cigarette lighter - removal and refitting

Removal

1   Disconnect the battery negative lead.
2   Pull the ashtray and housing from the centre console. Working through the aperture, push the cigarette lighter mounting panel from the centre console.

12

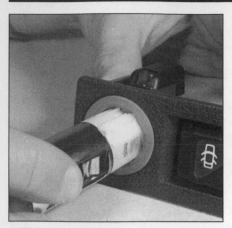

25.5 Withdrawing the cigarette lighter metal housing . . .

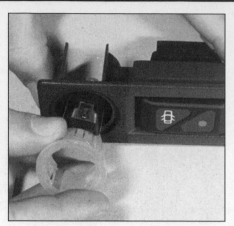

25.6 . . . and the plastic surround

26.1 Horn location (arrowed) viewed from underneath with front wheel arch splash shield removed

3   Disconnect the wiring plugs from the cigarette lighter, and from any switches mounted in the panel.
4   Remove the cigarette lighter from its housing.
5   Working through the cigarette lighter aperture, depress the retaining lugs, and prise the metal housing from the plastic surround. Push the housing out through the front of the assembly **(see illustration)**.
6   Release the securing lugs and push the plastic surround out through the front of the mounting panel **(see illustration)**.

Refitting

7   Refitting is a reversal of removal.

26 Horn - removal and refitting

Removal

1   The horn is located behind the right-hand side of the front bumper **(see illustration)**.
2   Disconnect the battery negative lead.
3   To gain access to the horn, remove the front wheel arch splash shield. Refer to Chapter 11, Section 20 if necessary.
4   Disconnect the wiring from the horn.
5   Unscrew the securing nut, and withdraw the horn from its mounting bracket.

Refitting

6   Refitting is a reversal of removal.

27 Speedometer cable - removal and refitting

Removal

1   Withdraw the instrument panel from the facia, and then disconnect the speedometer cable from the rear of the panel, as described in Section 21.
2   Working in the engine compartment, unclip or unscrew the end of the speedometer cable from the gearbox casing. Where applicable, note how the securing clip locates on the gearbox, as several different types of clip are used.
3   Working under the facia, locate the speedometer cable grommet in the bulkhead.
4   Pull the grommet and the cable through the bulkhead into the passenger compartment, noting the routing of the cable.
5   Take note of the routing of the cable behind the facia, then feed the cable through the facia and withdraw it from the car. Where

applicable, take care not to damage the speed sensor unit on the speedometer end of the cable.

Refitting

6   Refitting is a reversal of removal, bearing in mind the following points.
7   Make sure that the cable is routed as noted before removal, and be careful not to kink or twist it between the bulkhead and the rear of the instrument panel.
8   Ensure that the bulkhead grommet is correctly located.

28 Wiper arms - removal and refitting

Removal

1   The wiper motor should be in the parked position before removing the wiper arm. Mark the position of the blade on the glass with adhesive tape, as a guide to refitting.
2   If both windscreen wiper arms are to be removed, identify them so that they can be refitted in their original positions (the arms are of different lengths).
3   Lift the hinged cover, and remove the nut securing the arm to the spindle **(see illustration)**.
4   Pull or prise the arm from the spindle, using a screwdriver if necessary. Take care not to damage the trim or paintwork.

Refitting

5   Refitting is a reversal of removal. Position the arms so that the blades align with the tape applied to the glass before removal.

29 Windscreen wiper motor and linkage - removal and refitting

Removal

1   Make sure that the wipers are in the parked position.
2   Disconnect the battery negative lead.
3   Remove the windscreen wiper arms, as described in Section 28.
4   Remove the windscreen cowl panels, as described in Chapter 11.
5   Release the securing clip (pull upwards), and disconnect the wiring plug from the motor **(see illustration)**.
6   Unscrew the securing bolt, and remove the car jack from its location on the right-hand side of the scuttle.
7   To provide improved clearance for removal, carefully turn the motor and the spindles by hand to position the drive link (connecting the motor to the drive arms) approximately 110° from its parked

28.3 Unscrewing the tailgate wiper arm securing nut

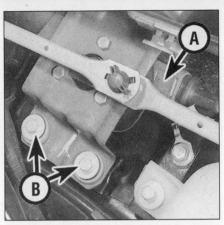

29.5 Windscreen wiper motor wiring plug (A) and mounting bolts (B)

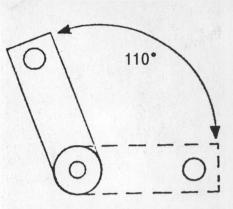

29.7 Drive link positioned for removal of windscreen wiper motor and linkage assembly

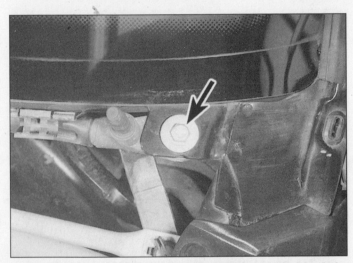

29.8 Unscrewing a windscreen wiper motor lower securing bolt

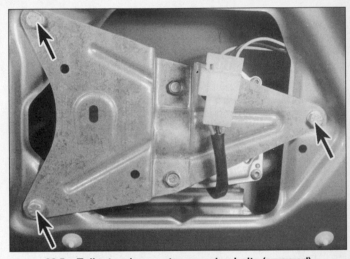

30.5a Tailgate wiper motor securing bolts (arrowed)

11   Manipulate the assembly out through the right-hand side of the scuttle, taking care not to damage surrounding components.

Refitting

12   Refitting is a reversal of removal, bearing in mind the following points.
13   Ensure that the assembly is mounted on the body brackets as noted before removal.
14   Before refitting the windscreen cowl panels, turn the drive link and the spindles by hand to the parked position.
15   Refit the windscreen wiper arms with reference to Section 28.

30   Tailgate wiper motor and linkage - removal and refitting

Removal

1   Disconnect the battery negative lead.
2   Remove the tailgate wiper arm, as described in Section 28.
3   Open the tailgate, then remove the tailgate interior trim panel.
4   Disconnect the motor wiring plug.
5   Unscrew the three bolts securing the motor mounting bracket to the tailgate. Withdraw the motor and bracket **(see illustrations)**.

Refitting

6   Refitting is a reversal of removal.

30.5b Withdrawing the tailgate wiper motor assembly

position **(see illustration)**.
8   Unscrew the motor/linkage assembly securing bolts (one at each end, and one or two lower bolts, depending on model), and recover the washers **(see illustration)**.
9   Note how the assembly is mounted on the body brackets.
10   If necessary, carefully remove the windscreen cowl panel securing clips from the body to provide additional clearance.

12

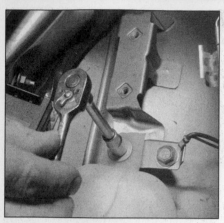

31.4 Unscrewing the washer fluid reservoir securing bolt

31.11a Removing a windscreen washer nozzle

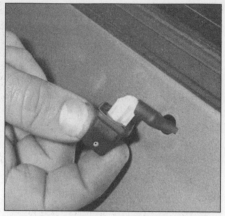

31.11b Removing the tailgate washer nozzle

31 Windscreen/tailgate/headlight washer system components - removal and refitting

Fluid reservoir

Removal

1   Disconnect the battery negative lead.
2   Remove the windscreen wiper arms as described in Section 28.
3   Remove the windscreen cowl panels as described in Chapter 11.
4   Unscrew the fluid reservoir securing bolt **(see illustration)**, then lift the reservoir sufficiently to disconnect the hoses and wiring from the pumps. Be prepared for fluid spillage.
5   Manipulate the reservoir out from the scuttle.

Refitting

6   Refitting is a reversal of removal. Refit the windscreen wiper arms with reference to Section 28.

Fluid pumps

Removal

7   Disconnect the battery negative lead.
8   Open the access hatch in the windscreen cowl panel.
9   Carefully pull the appropriate pump from the reservoir, then disconnect the wiring plug and the hose. Be prepared for fluid spillage.

Refitting

10   Refitting is a reversal of removal.

Washer nozzles

Removal

11   Carefully prise the nozzle from its mounting, then disconnect the fluid hose **(see illustrations)**.

Refitting

12   Refitting is a reversal of removal. The nozzle can be adjusted by inserting a pin into the jet, and swivelling it to the required position.

32 Radio/cassette player - removal and refitting

Removal

1   All the radio/cassette players fitted to the Clio range have DIN standard fixings. A pair of removal clips, obtainable from in-car entertainment specialists, will be required for removal.
2   Disconnect the battery negative lead.

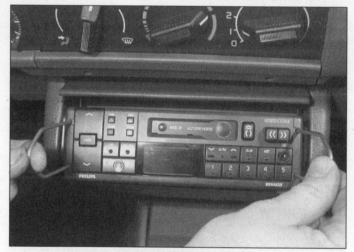

32.4 Using DIN standard removal clips to remove the radio/cassette player

3   Where applicable, prise the plastic covers from the sides of the radio/cassette player.
4   Insert the clips into the holes at the sides of the unit until they snap into place. Pull the clips rearwards (away from the facia) to release the unit **(see illustration)**.
5   Withdraw the radio/cassette unit from the facia. Disconnect the wiring plugs and the aerial cable from the rear of the unit **(see illustration)**.

Refitting

6   Reconnect the wiring plugs and the aerial cable to the rear of the unit.
7   Push the unit into its housing in the facia until the retaining lugs snap into place.
8   Where applicable, refit the covers to the sides of the unit, then reconnect the battery negative lead.

33 Loudspeakers - removal and refitting

Front door-mounted loudspeakers

Removal

1   Disconnect the battery negative lead.
2   Remove the four securing screws, then withdraw the loudspeaker

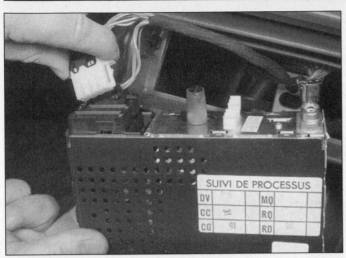

32.5 Disconnecting the radio/cassette player wiring plugs

33.2a Withdrawing a front door-mounted loudspeaker

33.2b Removing the front door-mounted loudspeaker housing

33.7 Unscrewing a facia-mounted loudspeaker securing screw

cover and the loudspeaker from the housing in the door. Note that the loudspeaker housing is also secured by the four screws **(see illustrations)**.

3 Disconnect the wiring and remove the loudspeaker.

Refitting

4 Refitting is a reversal of removal. Ensure that the plastic housing is correctly positioned in the door before refitting the loudspeaker.

Front facia-mounted loudspeakers

Removal

5 Disconnect the battery negative lead.

6 Remove the three securing screws (two lower screws, and one screw at the side nearest the door), and withdraw the facia side vent.

7 Unscrew the four loudspeaker securing screws **(see illustration)**.

8 Withdraw the loudspeaker from the facia, and disconnect the wiring plugs **(see illustration)**.

Refitting

9 Refitting is a reversal of removal.

Rear loudspeakers

Removal

10 Disconnect the battery negative lead.

11 Open the tailgate. Working under the rear quarter trim panel,

33.8 Removing a facia-mounted loudspeaker

unscrew the four loudspeaker securing screws. Lower the loudspeaker and its plastic shield, then disconnect the wiring plugs **(see illustrations)**.

12

33.11a Rear loudspeaker securing screws (arrowed)

33.11b Withdrawing the rear loudspeaker and its plastic shield

Refitting

12   Refitting is a reversal of removal.

34   Radio aerial - removal and refitting

Aerial assembly

Removal

1   Remove the courtesy light assembly, as described in Section 19, to expose the base of the aerial.
2   Unscrew the securing sleeve, and disconnect the aerial lead from the base of the aerial.
3   Unscrew the securing nut and recover the washers, then lift the aerial from the roof (see illustration).

Refitting

4   Refitting is a reversal of removal.

Aerial lead

Removal

5   With the lead disconnected from the aerial as described previously in this Section, tie a length of string to the end of the lead.
6   Observe the routing of the lead. Remove the A-pillar trim panel for access to the appropriate side, as described in Chapter 11, Section 24.
7   Remove the radio/cassette player and disconnect the aerial lead from the rear of the unit, as described in Section 32.
8   Pull the lower end of the lead. Feed the lead down the A-pillar, behind the facia, and out through the radio/cassette player aperture.
9   Untie the string from the lead, and leave it in position to aid refitting.

Refitting

10   Refitting is a reversal of removal, using the string to pull the lead into position. Take care not to damage the lead or surrounding components when feeding it through behind the facia.
11   Refit the radio/cassette player with reference to Section 32.

35   Anti-theft alarm system - general information

Certain models are fitted with an anti-theft alarm system, which uses various sensing systems and warning sirens, depending on model.

No information was available for the alarm systems at the time of writing. Any faults should be referred to a Renault dealer for diagnosis.

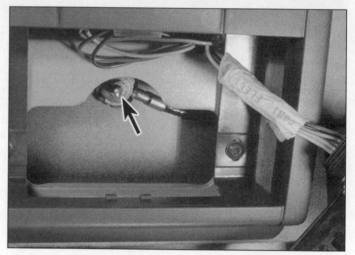

34.3 Radio aerial securing nut (arrowed)

36   Air bag system - general information and precautions

1   A driver's side air bag was introduced to the Clio range at the facelift in early 1994; the airbag is fitted as standard on higher-specification models and is offered as an option on other models. These models have the word AIRBAG stamped on the air bag unit, which is fitted to the centre of the steering wheel. The air bag system comprises of the air bag unit (complete with gas generator) which is fitted to the steering wheel, an impact sensor and battery. The whole unit is self contained within the steering wheel.
2   The air bag system is triggered by an inertia-type switch. The air bag is inflated within milliseconds and forms a safety cushion between the driver and steering wheel. This prevents contact between the driver's upper body and wheel and therefore greatly reduces the risk of injury. The air bag then deflates almost immediately. **Note:** *Any work involving the air bag system should be entrusted to a Renault dealer.*
Warning: *Note that the air bag must not be subjected to temperatures in excess of 90°C (194°F). When the air bag is removed, ensure that it is stored the correct way up to prevent possible inflation.*
Warning: *Do not allow any solvents or cleaning agents to contact the air bag assembly. The unit must be cleaned using only a damp cloth.*
Warning: *The air bag unit is sensitive to impact. If it is dropped, it must be renewed.*

NOTES

1 All diagrams are divided into numbered circuits depending on function e.g. Diagram 2 : Exterior lighting.
2 Items are arranged in relation to a plan view of the vehicle.
3 Wires may interconnect between diagrams and are located by using a grid reference e.g. 2/A1 denotes a position on diagram 2 grid location A1.
4 Complex items appear on the diagrams as blocks and are expanded on the internal connections page.
5 Brackets show how the circuit may be connected in more than one way.
6 Not all items are fitted to all models.

INTERNAL CONNECTION DETAILS

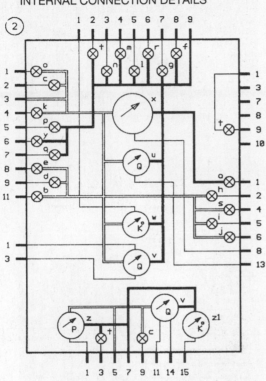

ENGINE FUSEBOX

FUSE	RATING	CIRCUIT
1	5A	Reversing lights and alarm
2	25A	RH dipped beam and headlight washer
3	15A	LH dipped beam
4	20A	Foglights front
5	25A	Cooling fan
6	30A	Engine functions
7		Spare
8	20A	Horn
9		Spare
10	25A	Engine functions
11	5A	Automatic transmission
12	15A	RH main beam
13	15A	LH main beam
14	20A	Fuel pump
15	30A	Air conditioning

PASSENGER FUSEBOX

FUSE	RATING	CIRCUIT
1	30A	RH electric window
2	15A	Anti-lock braking system
3	30A	LH electric window
4	20A	Heated seats
5	15A	Interior light, radio and alarm
6	30A	Accessories cut-off
7	10A	Clock
8	15A	Wash/wipe front
9	15A	Cigar lighter
10	10A	Stop lights
11	10A	Radio
12	20A	Central locking and electric mirrors
13	20A	Heated rear windows and mirrors
14	10A	Wiper timer front
15		+ve before ignition for caravan option
16	10A	Direction indicator flasher unit
17	10A	Foglight rear
18	10A	LH side/tail lights
19	10A	RH side/tail lights
20		Spare
21	20A	Heater blower
22	10A	Radio and alarm

KEY TO INSTRUMENT CLUSTER (ITEM 2)

a = Hazard warning light
b = No charge warning light
c = Oil pressure warning light
d = Brake system warning light
e = High temperature warning light
f = Rear foglight warning light
g = Heated rear window warning light
h = Brake pad wear warning light
i = Choke warning light
j = Auto. trans./injection warning light
k = Preheater warning light
l = Sidelight warning light
m = Dipped beam warning light
n = Main beam warning light
o = Low fuel warning light
p = Direction indicator LH
q = Direction indicator RH
r = Front foglight warning light
s = ABS warning light
t = Instrument illumination
u = Fuel gauge
v = Oil level gauge
w = Coolant temperature gauge
x = Tachometer
y = Direction indicator repeater
z = Oil pressure gauge
z1 = Oil temperature gauge

KEY TO SYMBOLS

PLUG-IN CONNECTOR

EARTH

BULB

DIODE

LINE CONNECTORS   B3   R107

FUSE/
FUSIBLE LINK

WIRE COLOURS

Ba   White
Be   Blue
Bj   Beige
Cy   Clear
Gr   Grey
Ja   Yellow
Ma   Brown
No   Black
Or   Orange
Rg   Red
Sa   Pink
Ve   Green
Vi   Mauve

12

Notes, internal connection details, key to symbols and wire colours

H24940

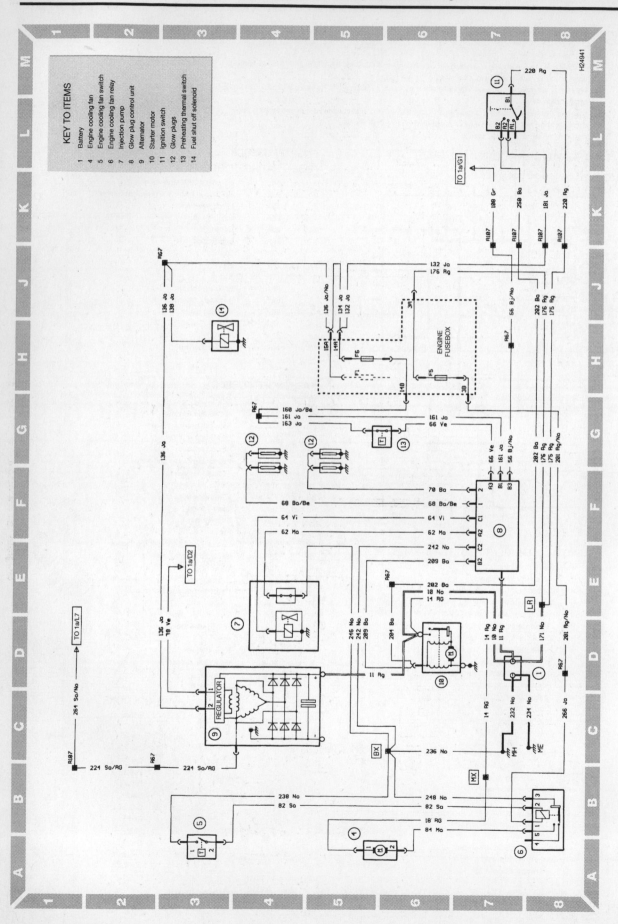

KEY TO ITEMS

1 Battery
4 Engine cooling fan
5 Engine cooling fan switch
6 Engine cooling fan relay
7 Injection pump
8 Glow plug control unit
9 Alternator
10 Starter motor
11 Ignition switch
12 Glow plugs
13 Preheating thermal switch
14 Fuel shut off solenoid

Diagram 1 : Starting, charging, cooling fan and glow plugs

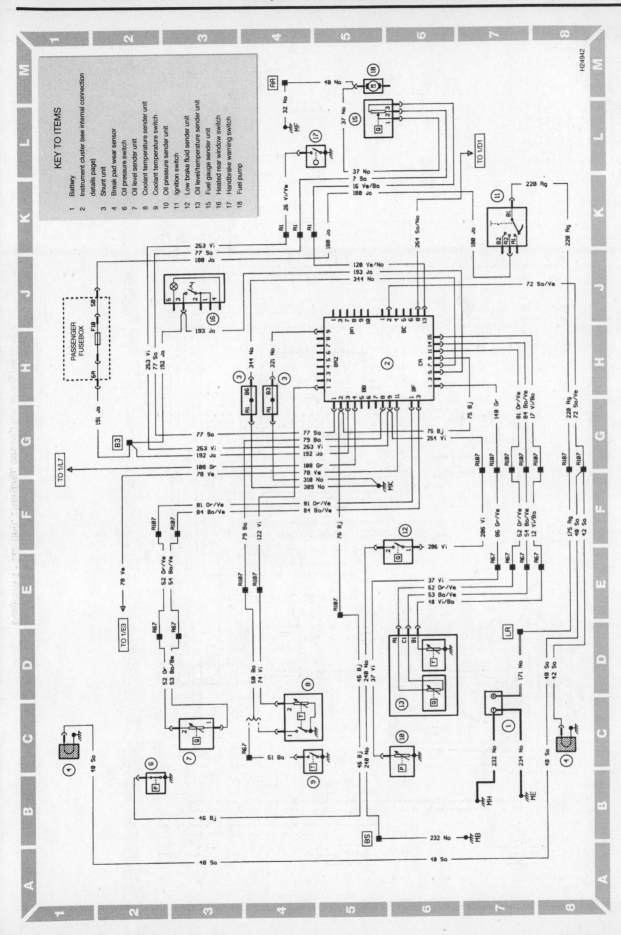

KEY TO ITEMS

1 Battery
2 Instrument cluster (see internal connection details page)
3 Shunt unit
4 Break pad wear sensor
5 Oil pressure switch
6 Oil level sender unit
7 Coolant temperature sender unit
8 Coolant temperature switch
9 Oil pressure sender unit
10 Oil level sender unit
11 Ignition switch
12 Low brake fluid sender unit
13 Oil level/temperature sender unit
14 Fuel gauge sender unit
15 Heated rear window switch
16 Handbrake warning switch
17 Fuel pump

Diagram 1a : Warning lights and instruments

12

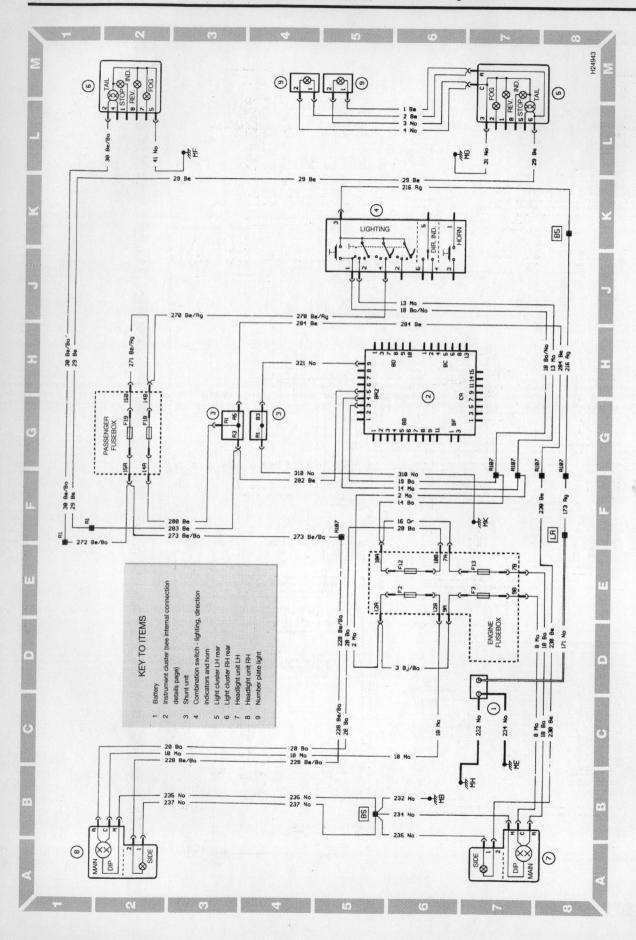

Diagram 2 : Exterior lighting - sidelights and headlights

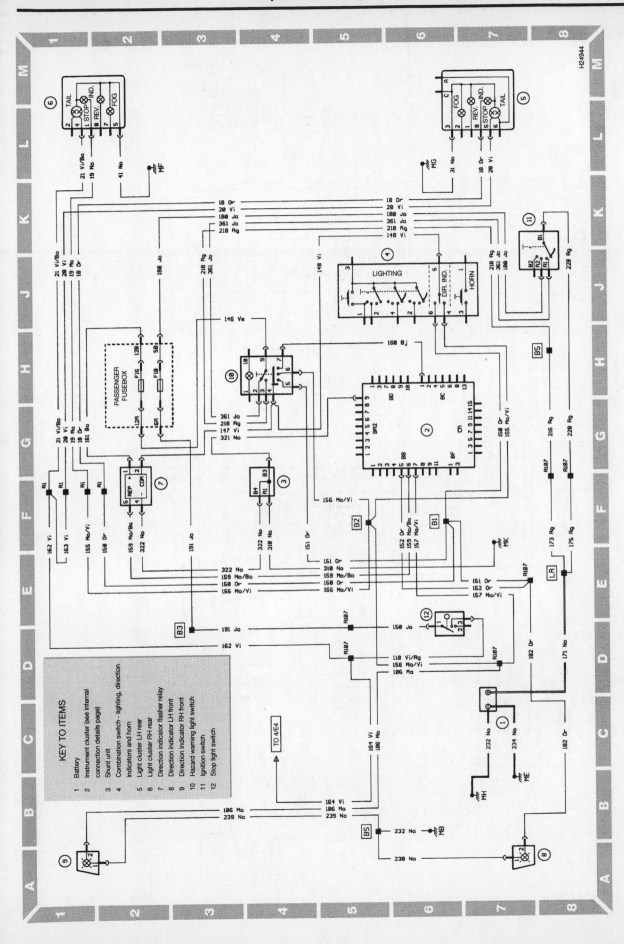

Diagram 2a : Exterior lighting - direction indicators and stop lights

KEY TO ITEMS

1 Battery
2 Instrument cluster (see internal connection details page)
3 Shunt unit
4 Combination switch - lighting, direction indicators and horn
5 Light cluster LH rear
6 Light cluster RH rear
7 Direction indicator flasher relay
8 Direction indicator LH front
9 Direction indicator RH front
10 Hazard warning light switch
11 Ignition switch
12 Stop light switch

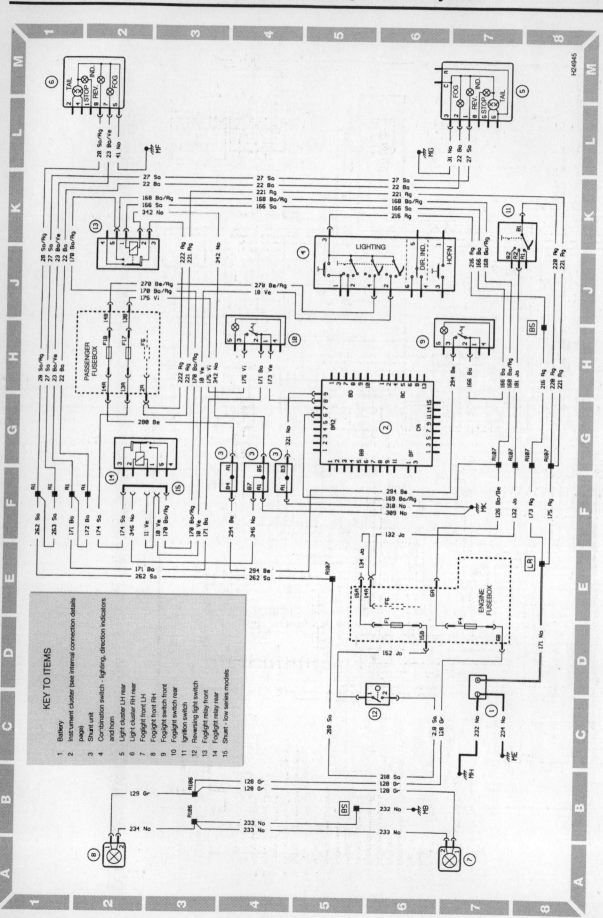

Diagram 2b : Exterior lighting - fog and reversing lights

KEY TO ITEMS

1   Battery
2   Instrument cluster (see internal connection details page)
3   Shunt unit
4   Combination switch - lighting, direction indicators and horn
5   Light cluster LH rear
6   Light cluster RH rear
7   Foglight front LH
8   Foglight front RH
9   Foglight switch front
10 Foglight switch rear
11 Ignition switch
12 Reversing light switch
13 Foglight relay front
14 Foglight relay rear
15 Shunt - low series models

LIGHTING   DIR. IND.   HORN

PASSENGER FUSEBOX

ENGINE FUSEBOX

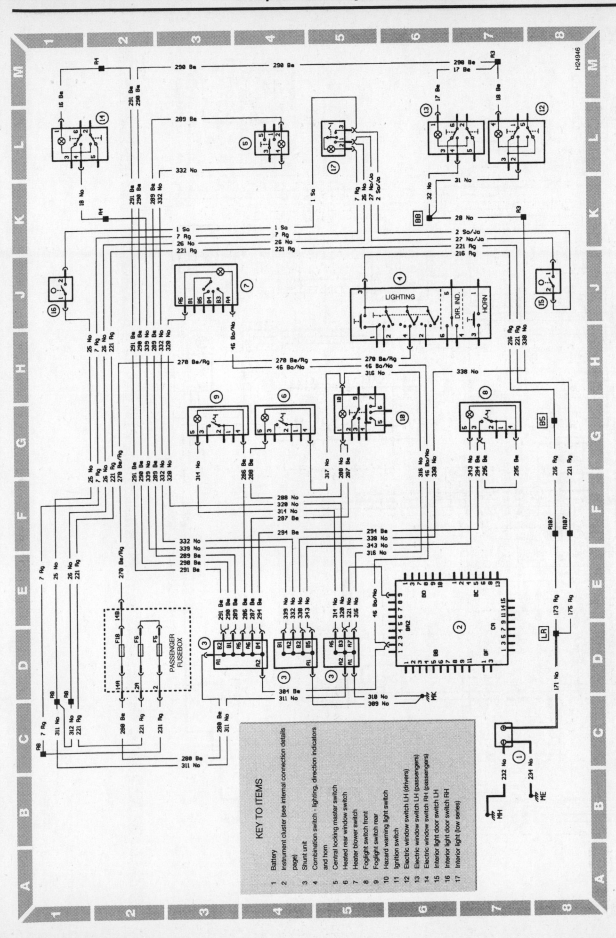

Diagram 2c : Interior lighting - switches and courtesy light (low-series)

H24946

KEY TO ITEMS

1 Battery
2 Instrument cluster (see internal connection details page)
3 Shunt unit
4 Combination switch - lighting, direction indicators and horn
5 Central locking master switch
6 Heated rear window switch
7 Heater blower switch
8 Foglight switch front
9 Foglight switch rear
10 Hazard warning light switch
11 Ignition switch
12 Electric window switch LH (drivers)
13 Electric window switch LH (passengers)
14 Electric window switch RH (passengers)
15 Interior light door switch LH
16 Interior light door switch RH
17 Interior light (low series)

12

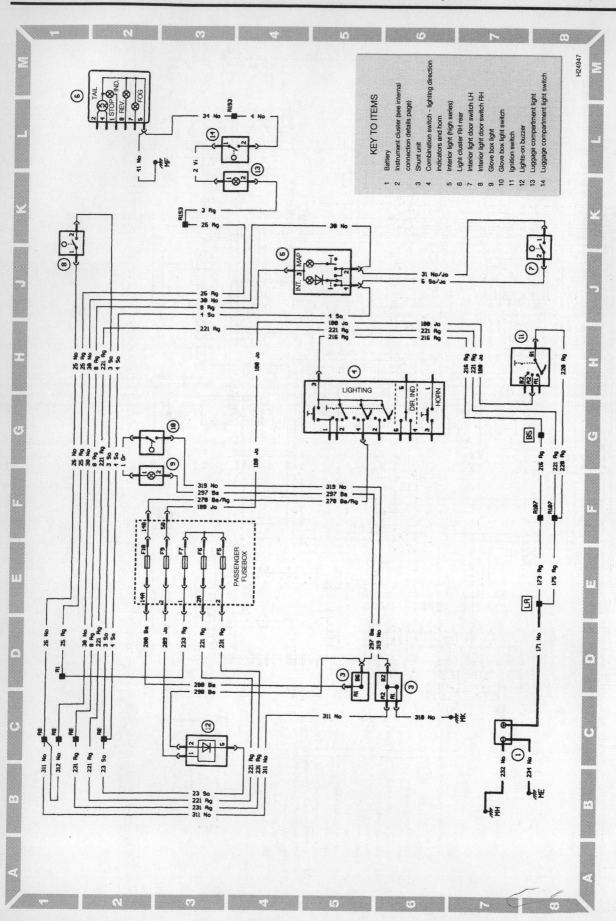

Diagram 2d : Interior lighting – "lights-on" buzzer, courtesy light (high-series), luggage and glove compartment lights

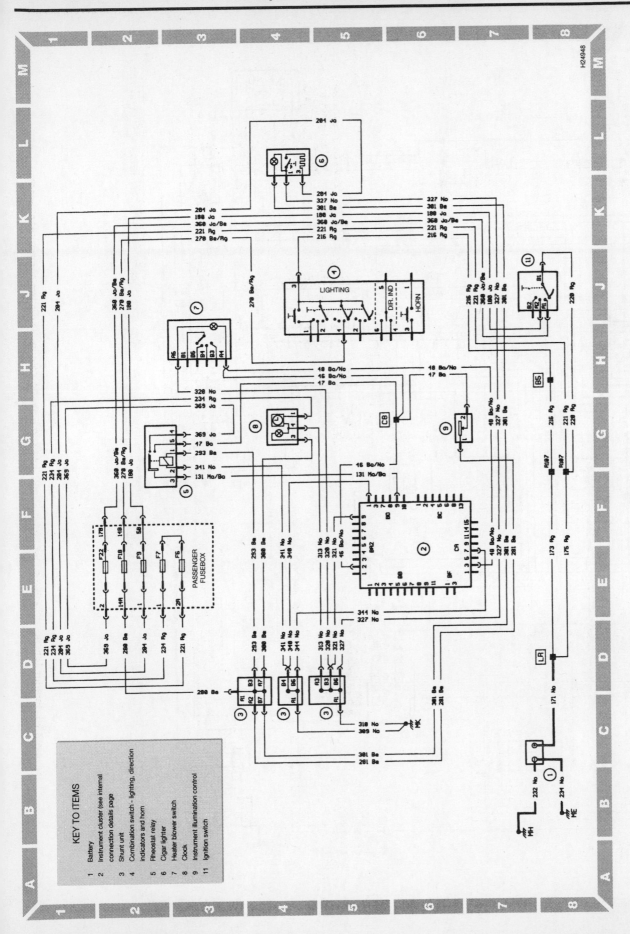

Diagram 2e : Interior lighting - instruments, instrument illumination, clock and cigarette lighter

KEY TO ITEMS

1   Battery
2   Instrument cluster (see internal connection details page)
3   Shunt unit
4   Combination switch - lighting, direction indicators and horn
5   Rheostat relay
6   Cigar lighter
7   Heater blower switch
8   Clock
9   Instrument illumination control
11 Ignition switch

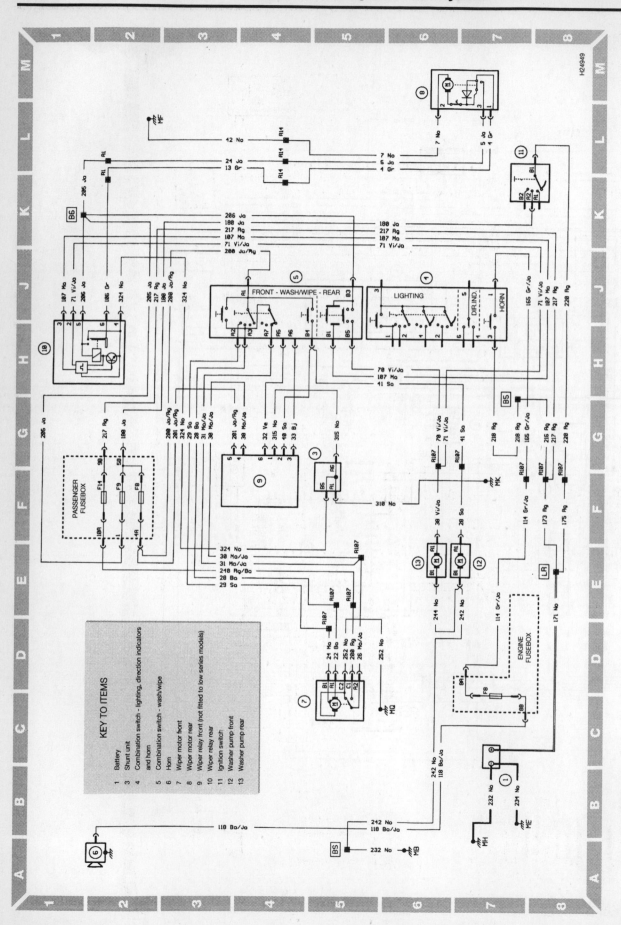

KEY TO ITEMS

1 Battery
3 Shunt unit
4 Combination switch - lighting, direction indicators and horn
5 Combination switch - wash/wipe
6 Horn
7 Wiper motor front
8 Wiper motor rear
9 Wiper relay front (not fitted to low series models)
10 Wiper relay rear
11 Ignition switch
12 Washer pump front
13 Washer pump rear

Diagram 3 : Ancillary circuits - wash/wipe (low-series) and horn

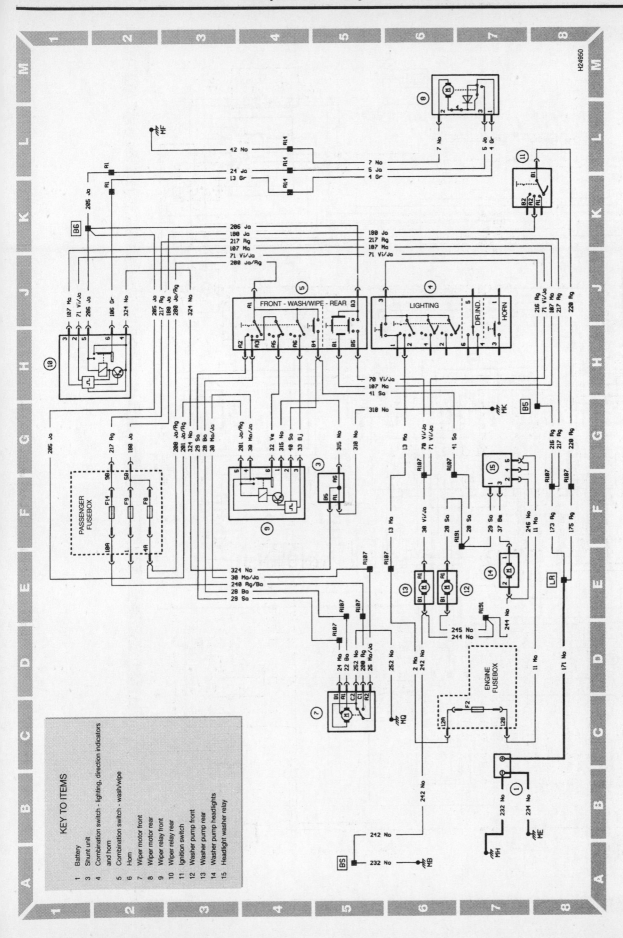

Diagram 3a : Ancillary circuits - headlight wash and wash/wipe (high-series)

KEY TO ITEMS

1 Battery
3 Shunt unit
4 Combination switch - lighting, direction indicators and horn
5 Combination switch - wash/wipe
6 Horn
7 Wiper motor front
8 Wiper motor rear
9 Wiper relay front
10 Wiper relay rear
11 Ignition switch
12 Washer pump front
13 Washer pump rear
14 Washer pump headlights
15 Headlight washer relay

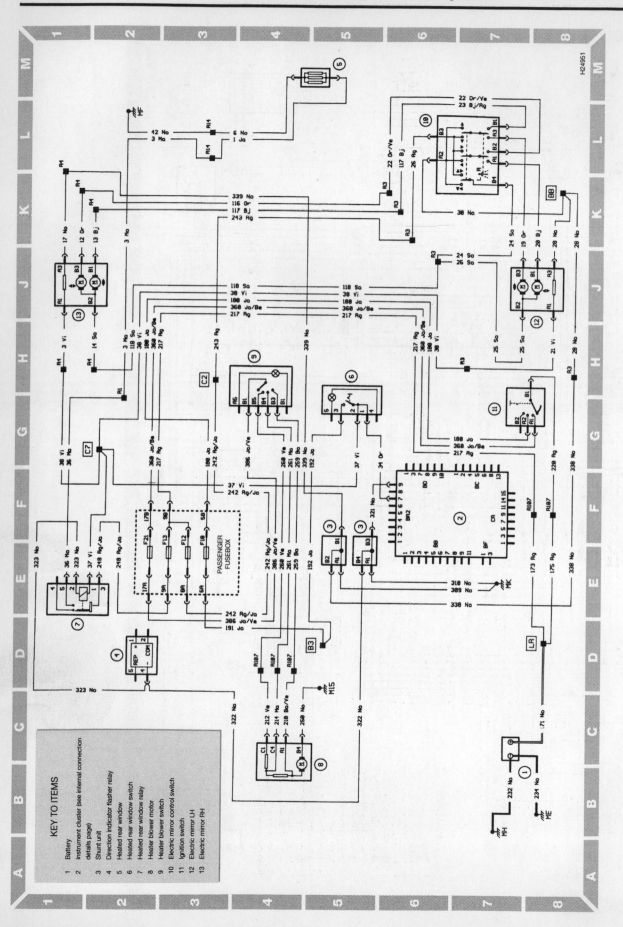

Diagram 3b : Ancillary circuits - heated rear window, heater blower and electric door mirrors

KEY TO ITEMS

1   Battery
2   Instrument cluster (see internal connection details page)
3   Shunt unit
4   Direction indicator flasher relay
5   Heated rear window
6   Heated rear window switch
7   Heated rear window relay
8   Heater blower motor
9   Heater blower switch
10   Electric mirror control switch
11   Ignition switch
12   Electric mirror LH
13   Electric mirror RH

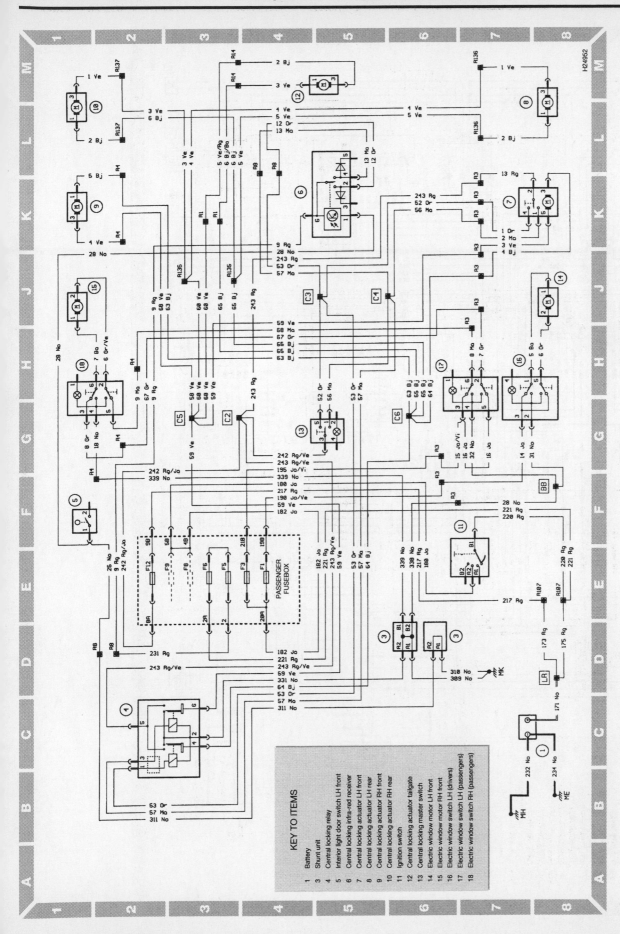

Diagram 3c : Electric windows and central door locking

KEY TO ITEMS

1   Battery
3   Shunt unit
4   Central locking relay
5   Interior light door switch LH front
6   Central locking infra-red receiver
7   Central locking actuator LH front
8   Central locking actuator LH rear
9   Central locking actuator RH front
10 Central locking actuator RH rear
11 Ignition switch
12 Central locking actuator tailgate
13 Central locking master switch
14 Electric window motor LH front
15 Electric window motor RH front
16 Electric window switch LH (drivers)
17 Electric window switch LH (passengers)
18 Electric window switch RH (passengers)

12

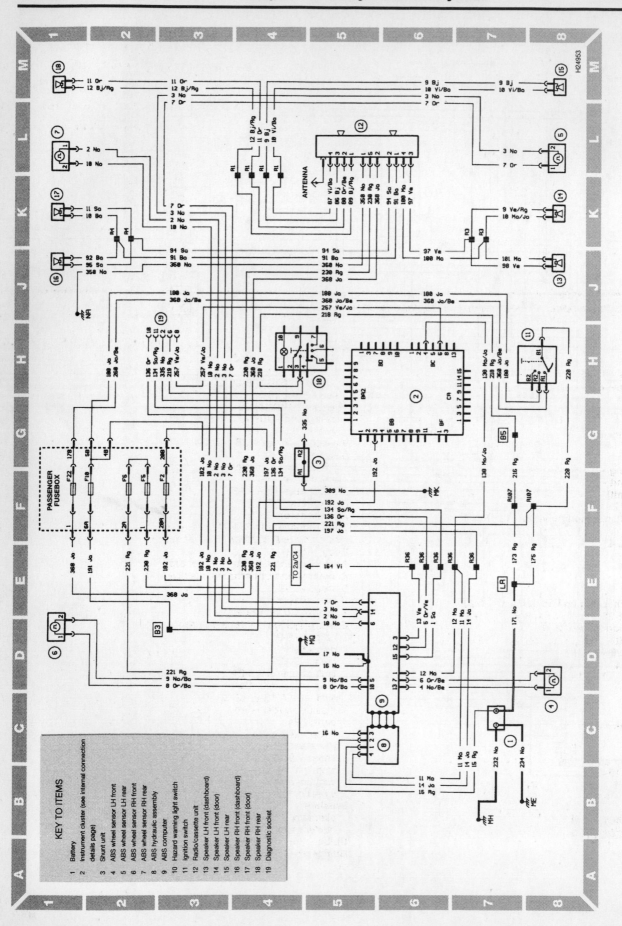

Diagram 4 : Anti-lock braking system (ABS) and radio/cassette

KEY TO ITEMS

1   Battery
2   Instrument cluster (see internal connection details page)
3   Shunt unit
4   ABS wheel sensor LH front
5   ABS wheel sensor LH rear
6   ABS wheel sensor RH front
7   ABS wheel sensor RH rear
8   ABS hydraulic assembly
9   ABS computer
10 Hazard warning light switch
11 Ignition switch
12 Radio/cassette unit
13 Speaker LH front (dashboard)
14 Speaker LH front (door)
15 Speaker LH rear
16 Speaker RH front (dashboard)
17 Speaker RH front (door)
18 Speaker RH rear
19 Diagnostic socket

H24953

Index

Note: *References throughout this index relate to Chapter and page numbers, separated by a hyphen.*